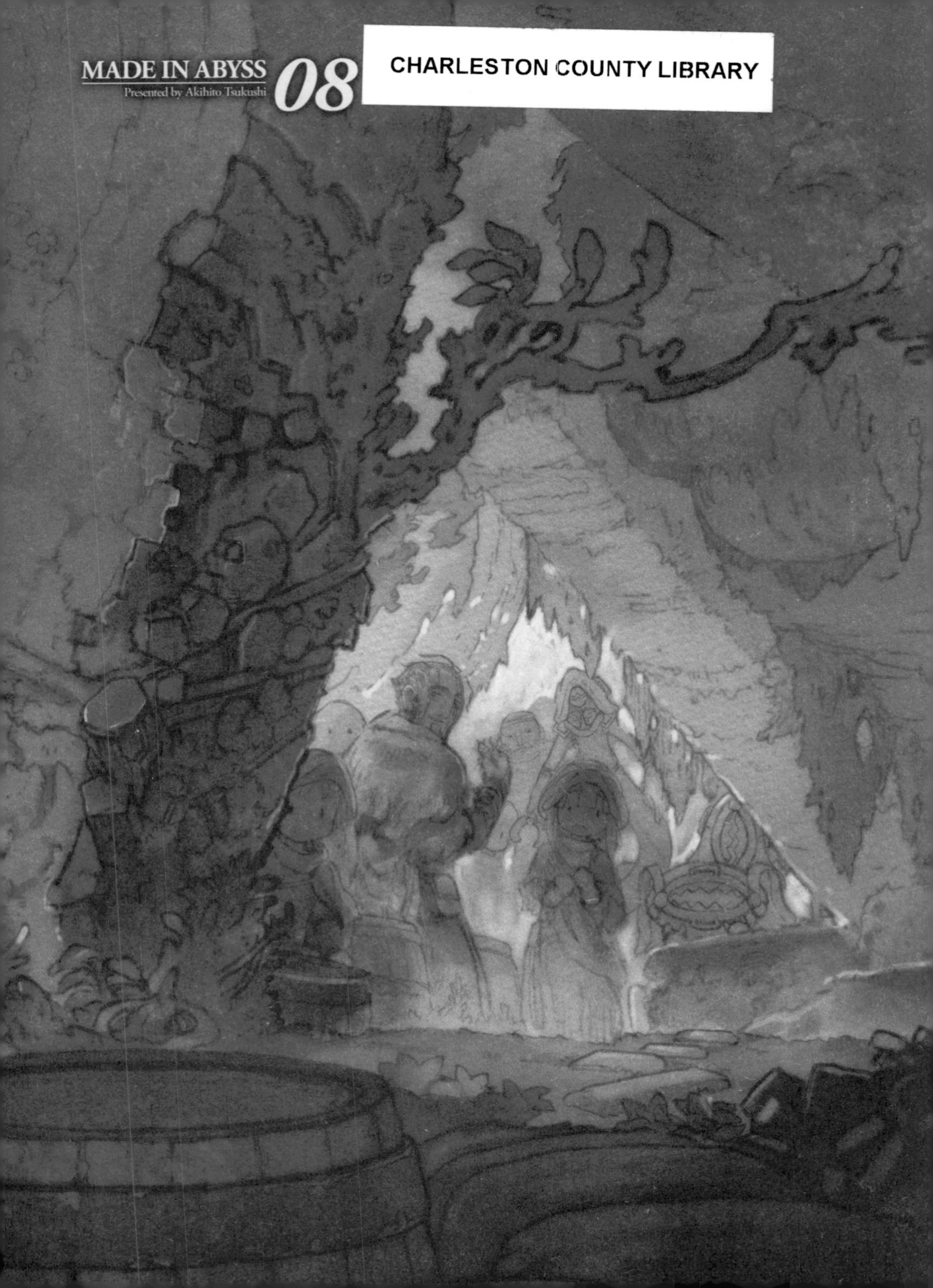
MADE IN ABYSS
Presented by Akihito Tsukushi
08

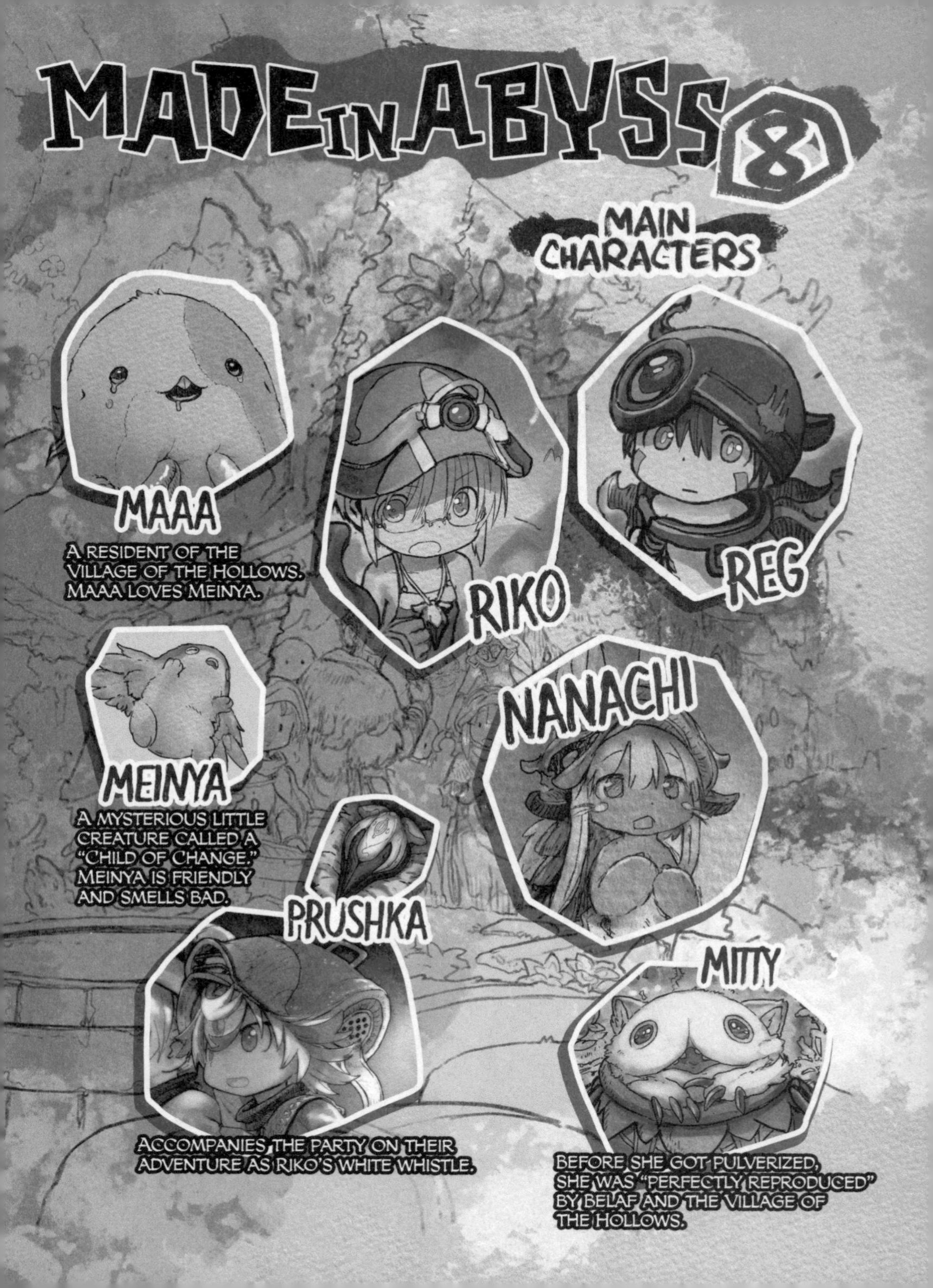
MADE IN ABYSS 8
MAIN CHARACTERS
MAAA
A RESIDENT OF THE VILLAGE OF THE HOLLOWS. MAAA LOVES MEINYA.
RIKO
REG
MEINYA
A MYSTERIOUS LITTLE CREATURE CALLED A "CHILD OF CHANGE." MEINYA IS FRIENDLY AND SMELLS BAD.
NANACHI
PRUSHKA
ACCOMPANIES THE PARTY ON THEIR ADVENTURE AS RIKO'S WHITE WHISTLE.
MITTY
BEFORE SHE GOT PULVERIZED, SHE WAS "PERFECTLY REPRODUCED" BY BELAF AND THE VILLAGE OF THE HOLLOWS.

THE THREE SAGES

THE EMINENT INDIVIDUALS CONSIDERED TO HAVE CREATED THE VILLAGE OF THE HOLLOWS. THE RESIDENTS CALL THE VILLAGE IRUBURU.

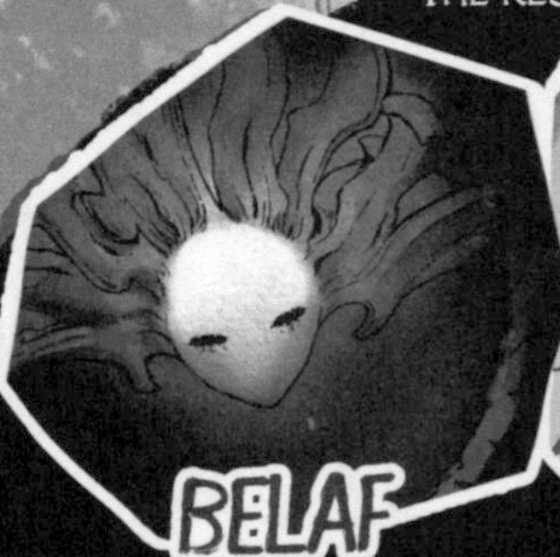

BELAF

HAS A REALLY LONG BODY. BELAF HAD BEEN ABSORBING THE REPRODUCED MITTY, BUT NANACHI WAS HORRIFIED BY THIS AND BOUGHT MITTY FROM BELAF. HOWEVER, BELAF WAS HAPPY TO RECEIVE NANACHI THEMSELF IN EXCHANGE.

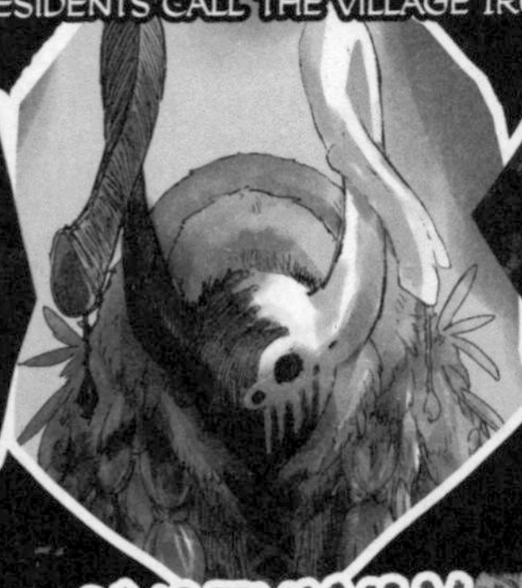

WAZUKYAN

ACTS LIKE A KNOW-IT-ALL BUT IS PRETTY LIGHTHEARTED. BE THEY ARMS OR BE THEY FINGERS, HE HAS LOTS OF THEM.

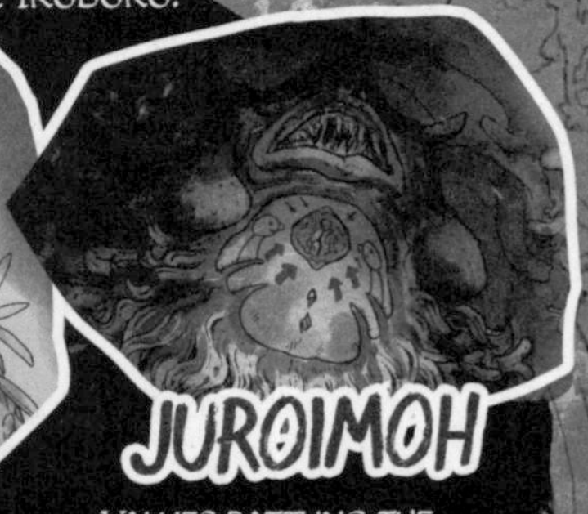

JUROIMOH

VALUES BATTLING THE STRONG. EXUDES A LONG SLIME-COVERED OBJECT CALLED THE "GREAT SWORD."

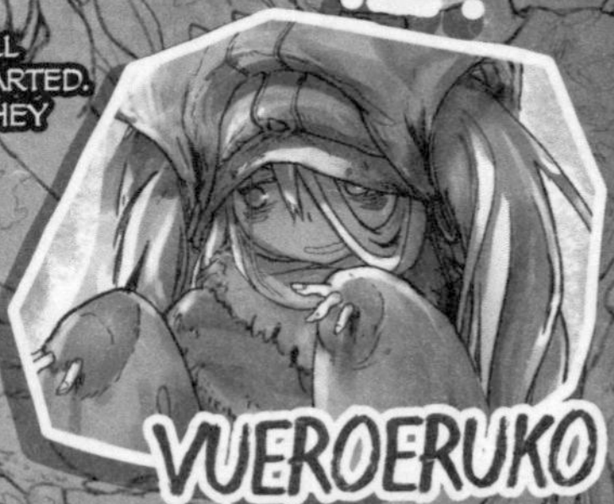

VUEROERUKO

COMMONLY KNOWN AS VUEKO. DUE TO CERTAIN CIRCUMSTANCES, SHE WAS CONCEALED IN THE DEPTHS OF THE EYE. SHE USED TO BE ONE OF THE THREE SAGES AND KNOWS THE ORIGINS OF THE VILLAGE.

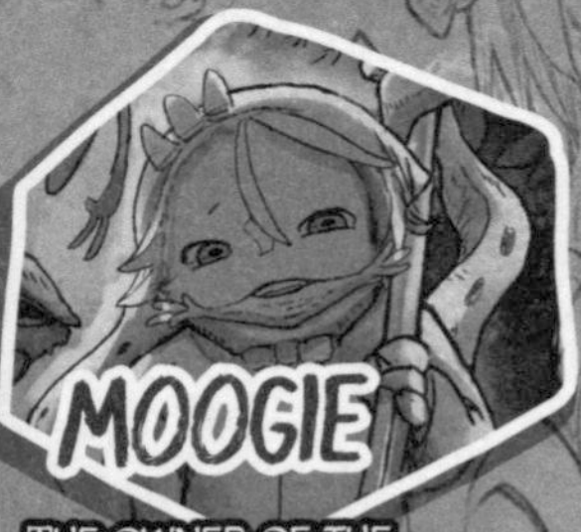

MOOGIE

THE OWNER OF THE RESTAURANT. GENDER UNKNOWN. DUE TO WORKING IN THE RESTAURANT, MOOGIE HAS LEARNED--TO SOME EXTENT--A VARIETY OF LANGUAGES.

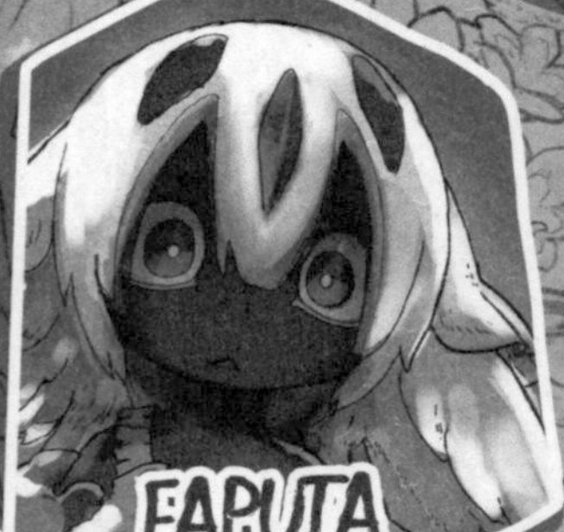

FAPUTA

IMMORTAL. SHE IS THE PRINCESS OF THE HOLLOWS AND IS CALLED THE "EMBODIMENT OF VALUE." SHE SAYS IT IS HER WISH TO ERADICATE THOSE WHO RESIDE IN THE VILLAGE. SHE SEEMS TO HAVE A DEEP CONNECTION WITH REG AND IS VERY ATTACHED TO HIM.

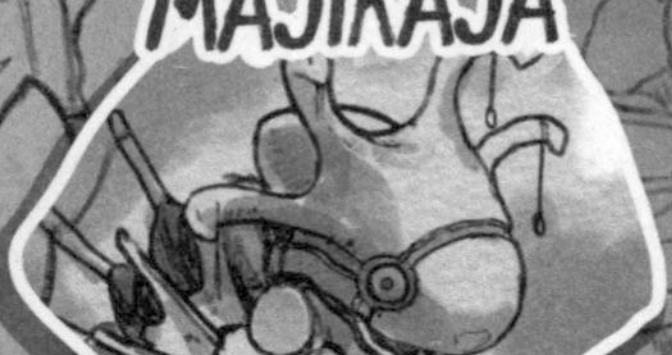

MAJIKAJA

WHAT LOOKS LIKE MAJIKAJA'S BODY IS REALLY JUST A VESSEL. MAJIKAJA SAYS THEIR BODY IS ACTUALLY GASEOUS. THEY ARE A BUSYBODY WHO LIKES TO SHOW NEW ARRIVALS AROUND THE VILLAGE.

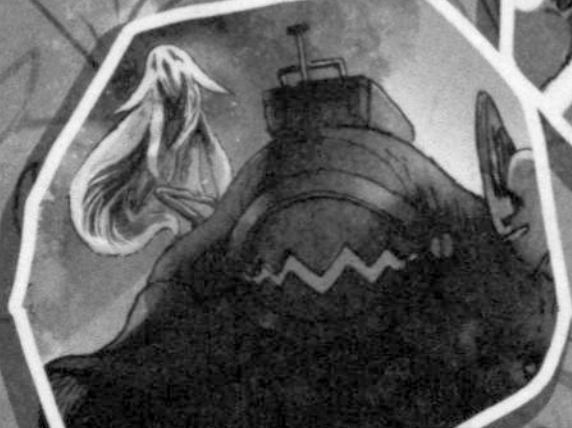

A SO-CALLED "INTERFERENCE UNIT," ONE OF THE MYSTERIOUS DOLLS THAT HAVE EXISTED IN THE ABYSS SINCE ANCIENT TIMES.

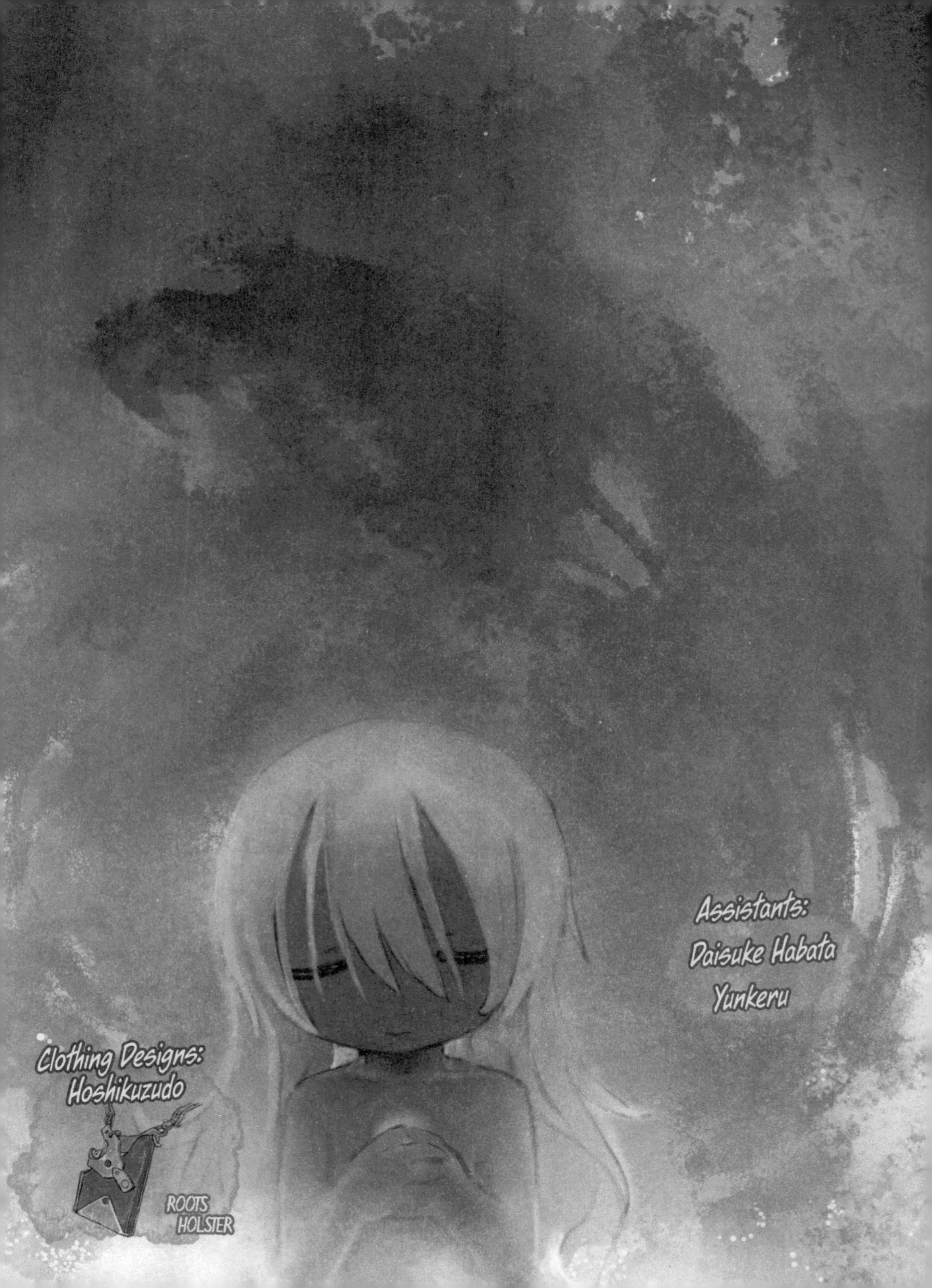
Assistants:
Daisuke Habata
Yunkeru
Clothing Designs:
Hoshikuzudo
ROOTS HOLSTER

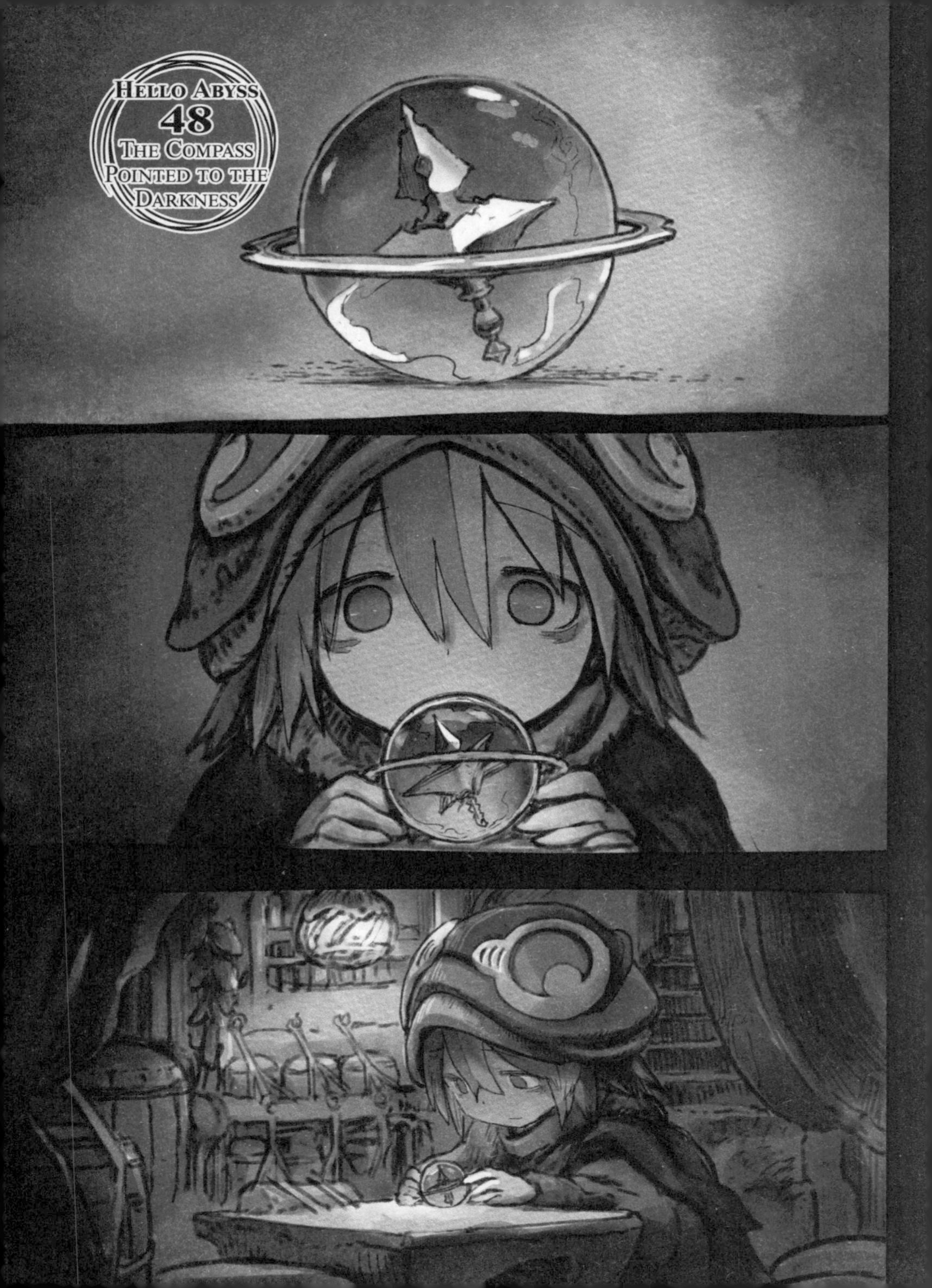
HELLO ABYSS
48
THE COMPASS
POINTED TO THE
DARKNESS

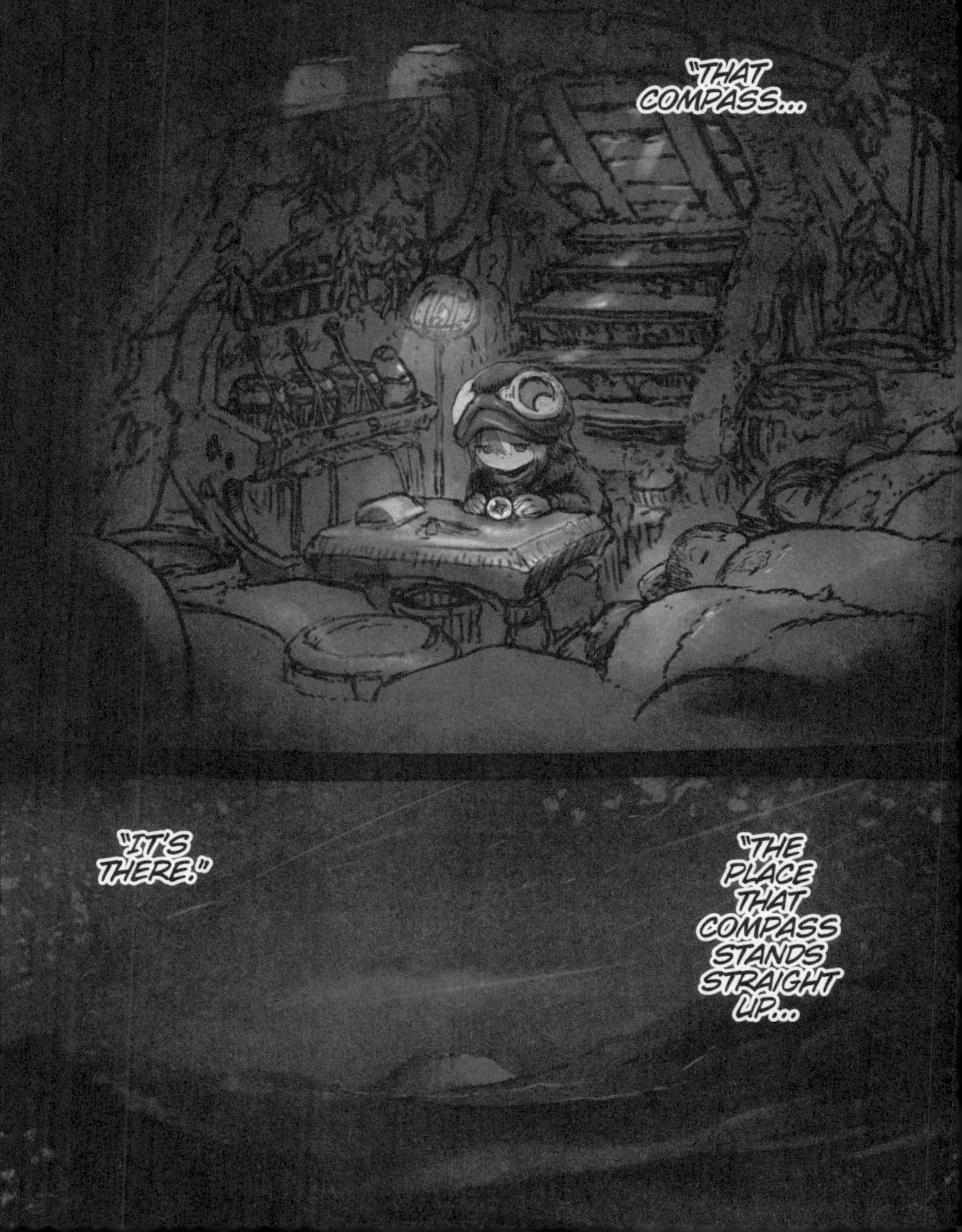
"THAT COMPASS...
"THE PLACE THAT COMPASS STANDS STRAIGHT UP...
"IT'S THERE."

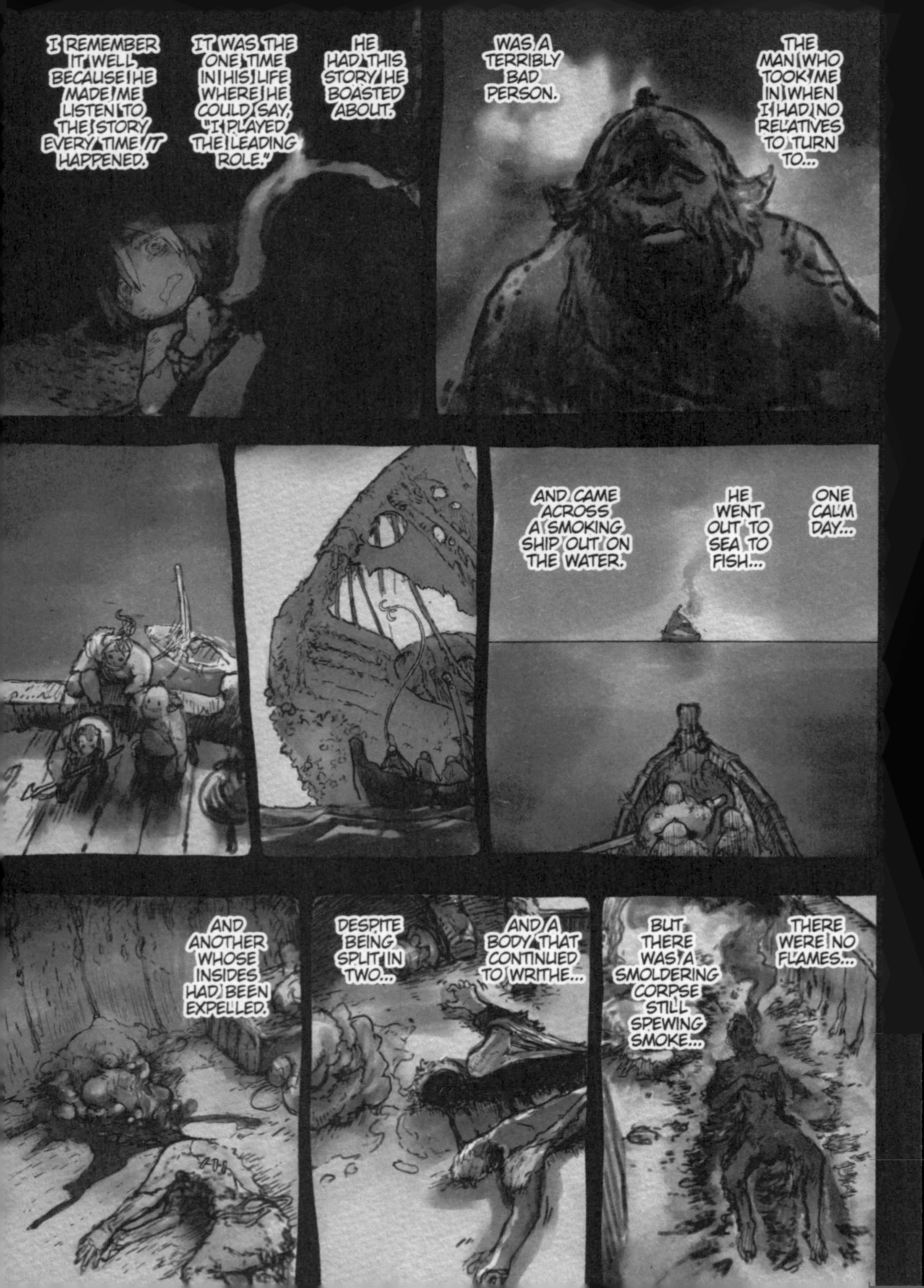
THE MAN WHO TOOK ME IN WHEN I HAD NO RELATIVES TO TURN TO...
WAS A TERRIBLY BAD PERSON.
HE HAD THIS STORY HE BOASTED ABOUT.
IT WAS THE ONE TIME IN HIS LIFE WHERE HE COULD SAY, "I PLAYED THE LEADING ROLE."
I REMEMBER IT WELL BECAUSE HE MADE ME LISTEN TO THE STORY EVERY TIME IT HAPPENED.
ONE CALM DAY...
HE WENT OUT TO SEA TO FISH...
AND CAME ACROSS A SMOKING SHIP OUT ON THE WATER.
THERE WERE NO FLAMES...
BUT THERE WAS A SMOLDERING CORPSE STILL SPEWING SMOKE...
AND A BODY THAT CONTINUED TO WRITHE...
DESPITE BEING SPLIT IN TWO...
AND ANOTHER WHOSE INSIDES HAD BEEN EXPELLED.

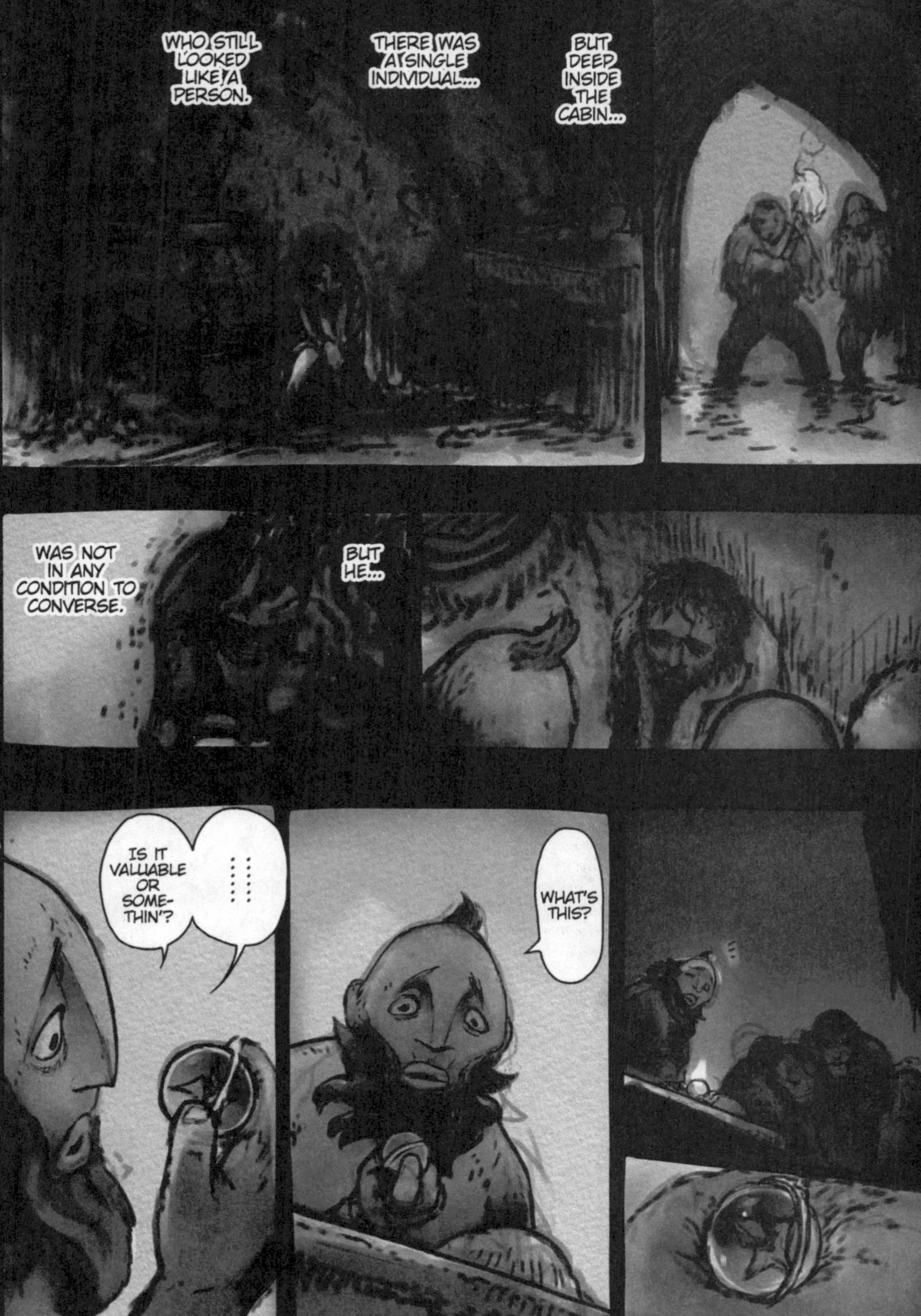
BUT DEEP INSIDE THE CABIN...
THERE WAS A SINGLE INDIVIDUAL...
WHO STILL LOOKED LIKE A PERSON.
BUT HE...
WAS NOT IN ANY CONDITION TO CONVERSE.
WHAT'S THIS?
......
IS IT VALUABLE OR SOME-THIN'?

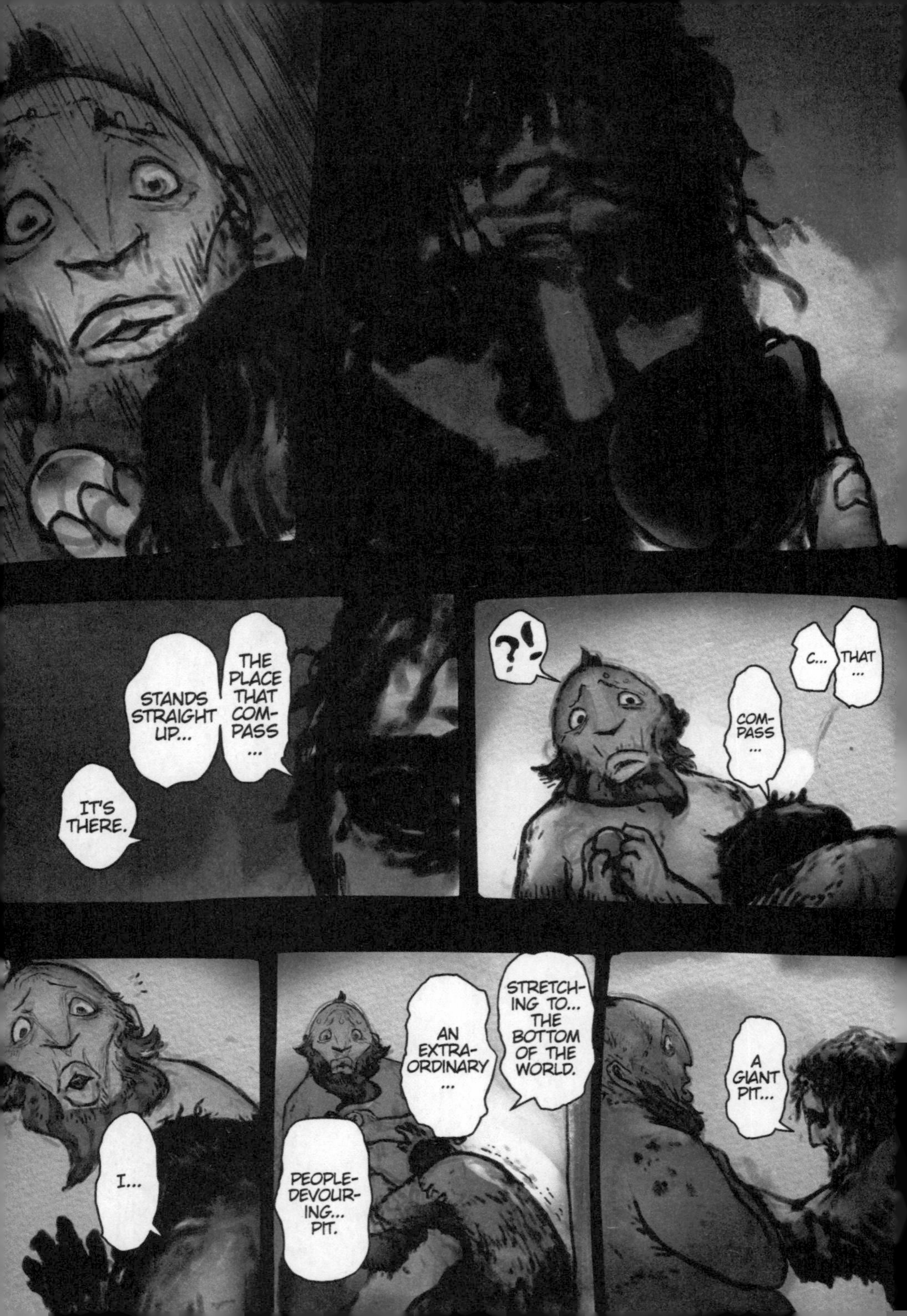
THAT ...
C...
?!
COMPASS ...
THE PLACE THAT COMPASS ...
STANDS STRAIGHT UP...
IT'S THERE.
A GIANT PIT...
STRETCHING TO... THE BOTTOM OF THE WORLD.
AN EXTRAORDINARY ...
PEOPLE-DEVOURING... PIT.
I...

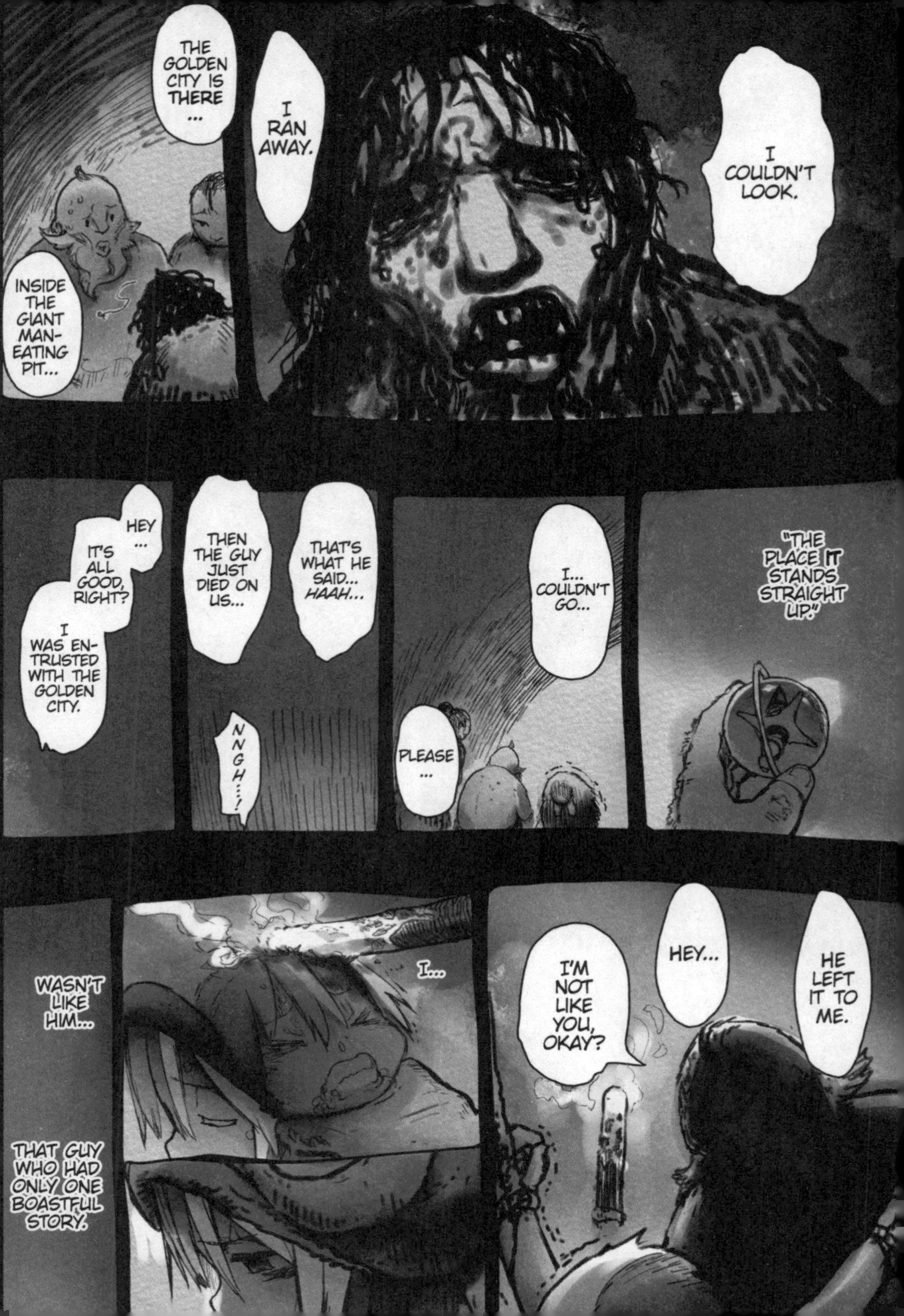
I COULDN'T LOOK.
I RAN AWAY.
THE GOLDEN CITY IS THERE...
INSIDE THE GIANT MAN-EATING PIT...
"THE PLACE IT STANDS STRAIGHT UP."
I... COULDN'T GO...
PLEASE...
THAT'S WHAT HE SAID... *HAAH*...
THEN THE GUY JUST DIED ON US...
NNGH...!
HEY...
IT'S ALL GOOD, RIGHT?
I WAS EN-TRUSTED WITH THE GOLDEN CITY.
HE LEFT IT TO ME.
HEY...
I'M NOT LIKE YOU, OKAY?
I...
WASN'T LIKE HIM...
THAT GUY WHO HAD ONLY ONE BOASTFUL STORY.

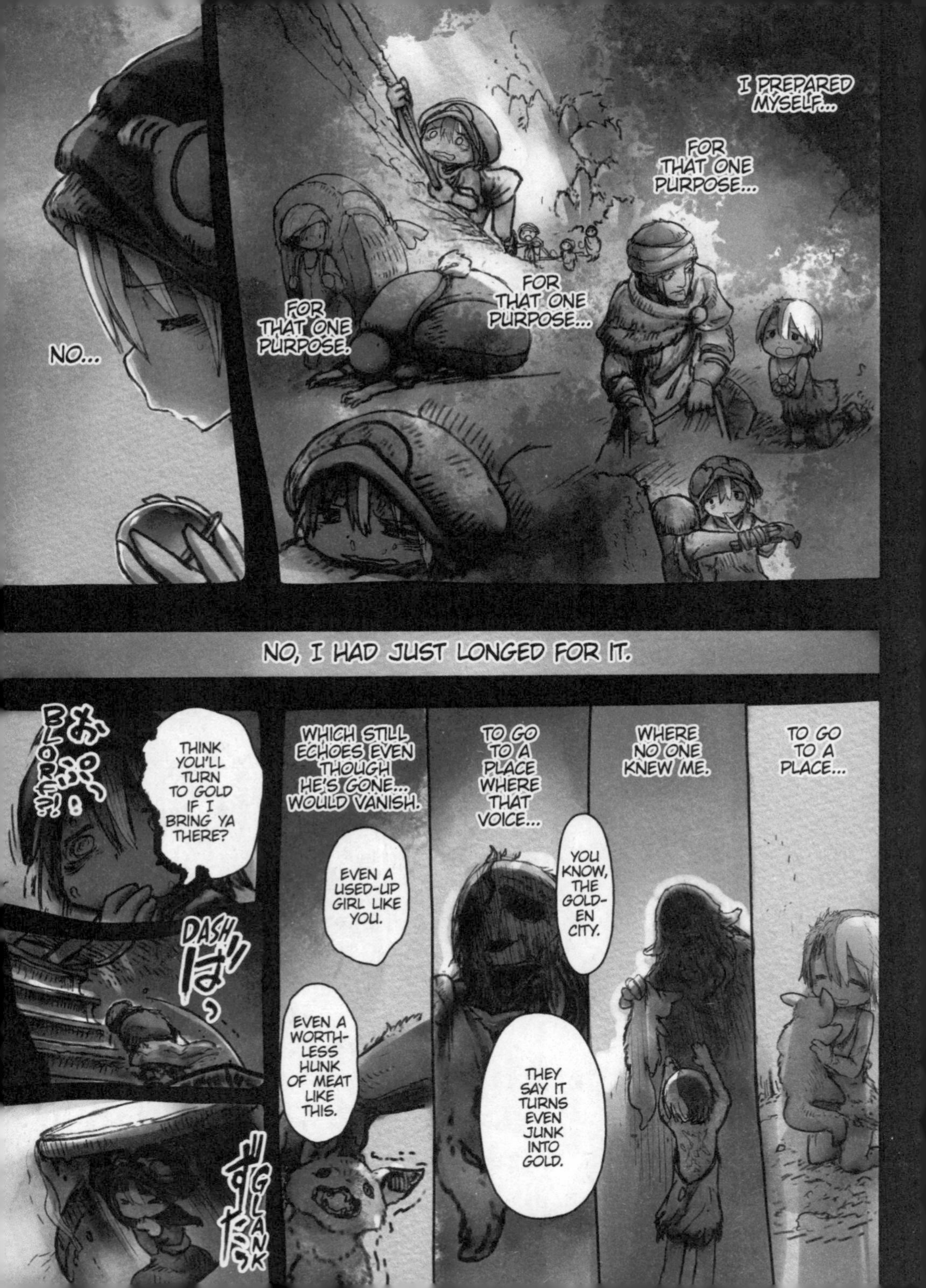
I PREPARED MYSELF...
FOR THAT ONE PURPOSE...
FOR THAT ONE PURPOSE...
FOR THAT ONE PURPOSE.
NO...
NO, I HAD JUST LONGED FOR IT.
TO GO TO A PLACE...
WHERE NO ONE KNEW ME.
YOU KNOW, THE GOLD-EN CITY.
THEY SAY IT TURNS EVEN JUNK INTO GOLD.
TO GO TO A PLACE WHERE THAT VOICE...
WHICH STILL ECHOES EVEN THOUGH HE'S GONE... WOULD VANISH.
EVEN A USED-UP GIRL LIKE YOU.
EVEN A WORTHLESS HUNK OF MEAT LIKE THIS.
THINK YOU'LL TURN TO GOLD IF I BRING YA THERE?
BLORF?!
DASH
GLANK

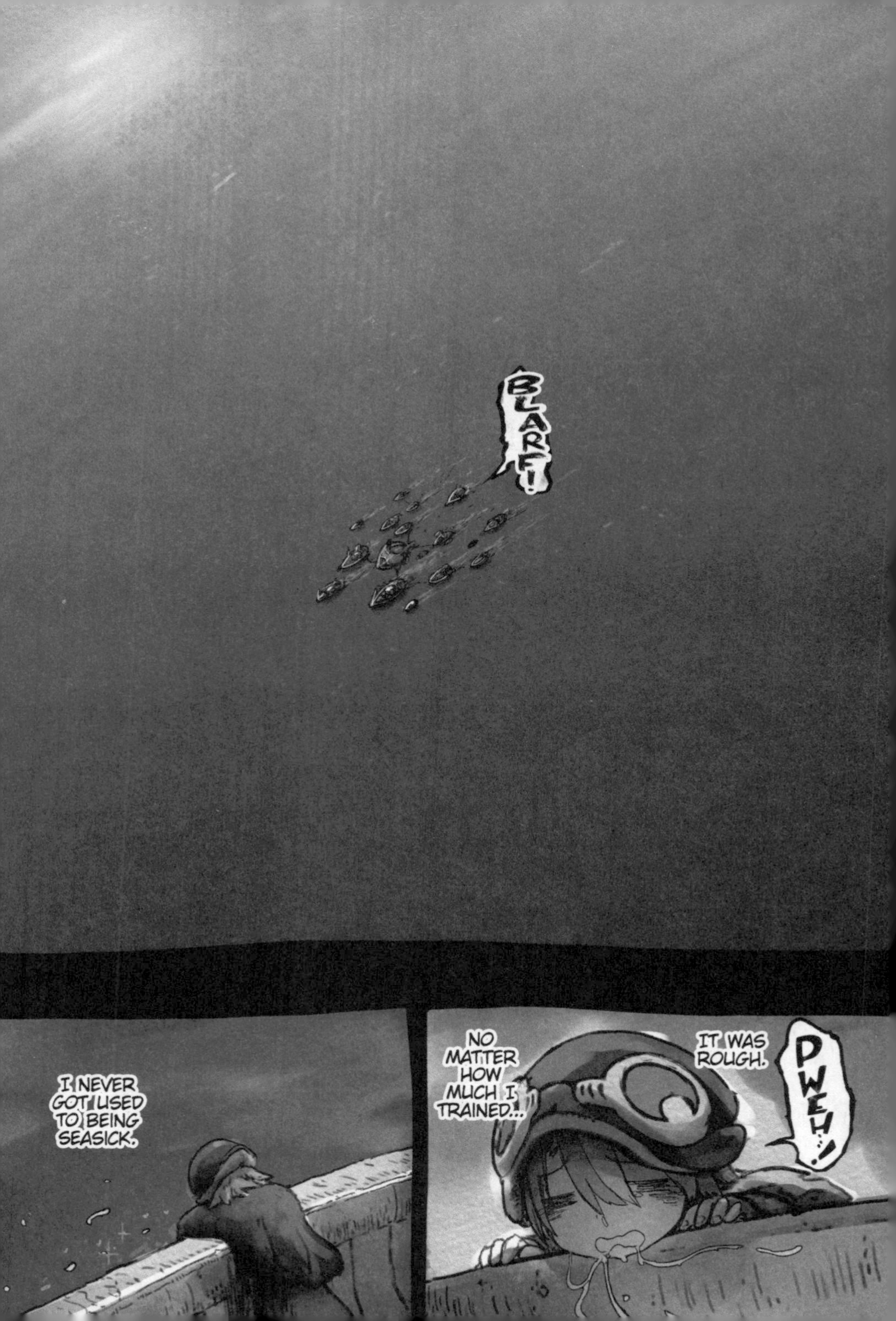
BLARF!
DWEH...!
IT WAS ROUGH.
NO MATTER HOW MUCH I TRAINED...
I NEVER GOT USED TO BEING SEASICK.

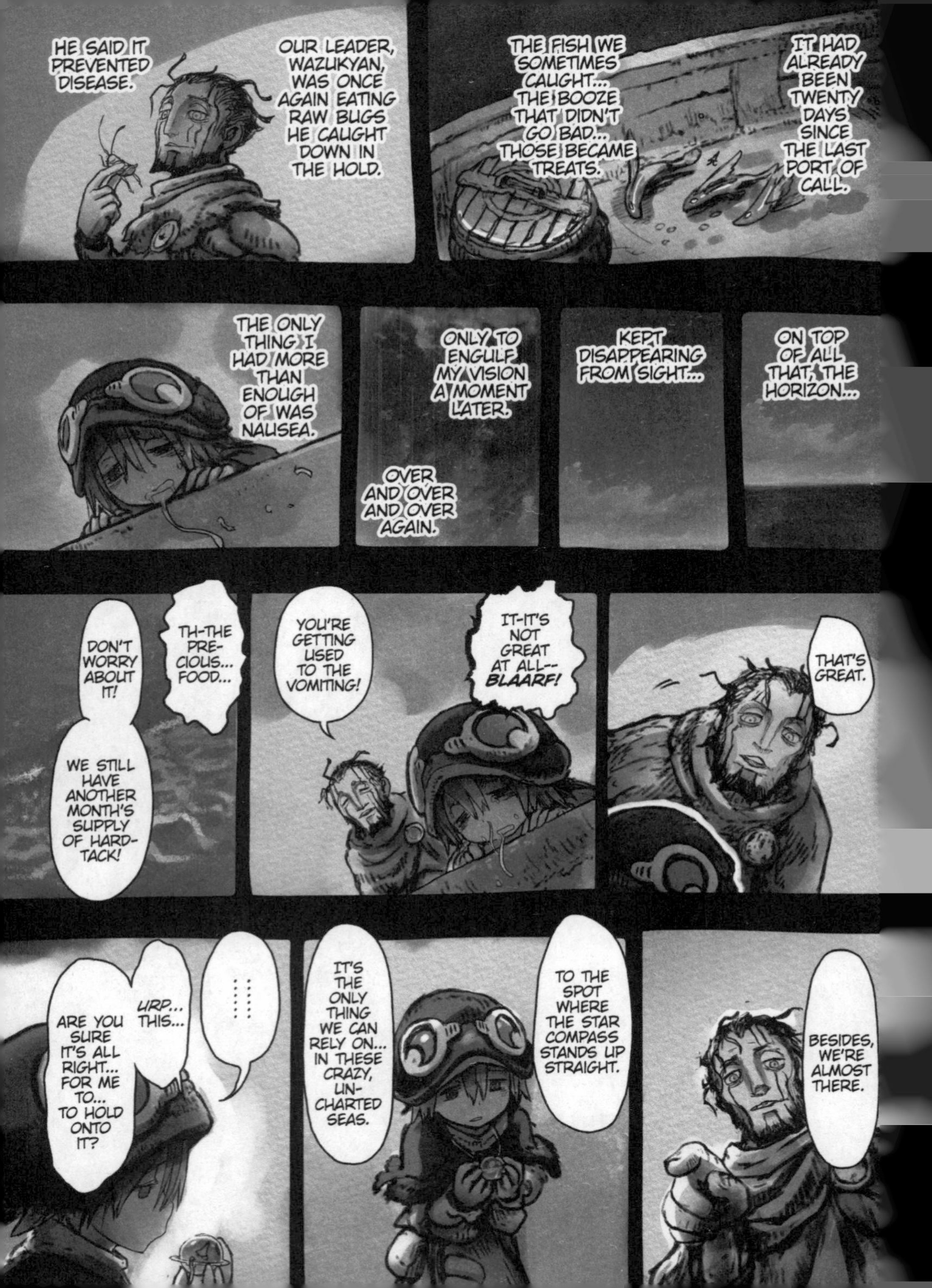
IT HAD ALREADY BEEN TWENTY DAYS SINCE THE LAST PORT OF CALL.
THE FISH WE SOMETIMES CAUGHT... THE BOOZE THAT DIDN'T GO BAD... THOSE BECAME TREATS.
OUR LEADER, WAZUKYAN, WAS ONCE AGAIN EATING RAW BUGS HE CAUGHT DOWN IN THE HOLD.
HE SAID IT PREVENTED DISEASE.
ON TOP OF ALL THAT, THE HORIZON...
KEPT DISAPPEARING FROM SIGHT...
ONLY TO ENGULF MY VISION A MOMENT LATER.
OVER AND OVER AND OVER AGAIN.
THE ONLY THING I HAD MORE THAN ENOUGH OF WAS NAUSEA.
THAT'S GREAT.
IT-IT'S NOT GREAT AT ALL-- *BLAARF!*
YOU'RE GETTING USED TO THE VOMITING!
TH-THE PRECIOUS... FOOD...
DON'T WORRY ABOUT IT!
WE STILL HAVE ANOTHER MONTH'S SUPPLY OF HARDTACK!
BESIDES, WE'RE ALMOST THERE.
TO THE SPOT WHERE THE STAR COMPASS STANDS UP STRAIGHT.
IT'S THE ONLY THING WE CAN RELY ON... IN THESE CRAZY, UNCHARTED SEAS.
......
URP... THIS...
ARE YOU SURE IT'S ALL RIGHT... FOR ME TO... TO HOLD ONTO IT?

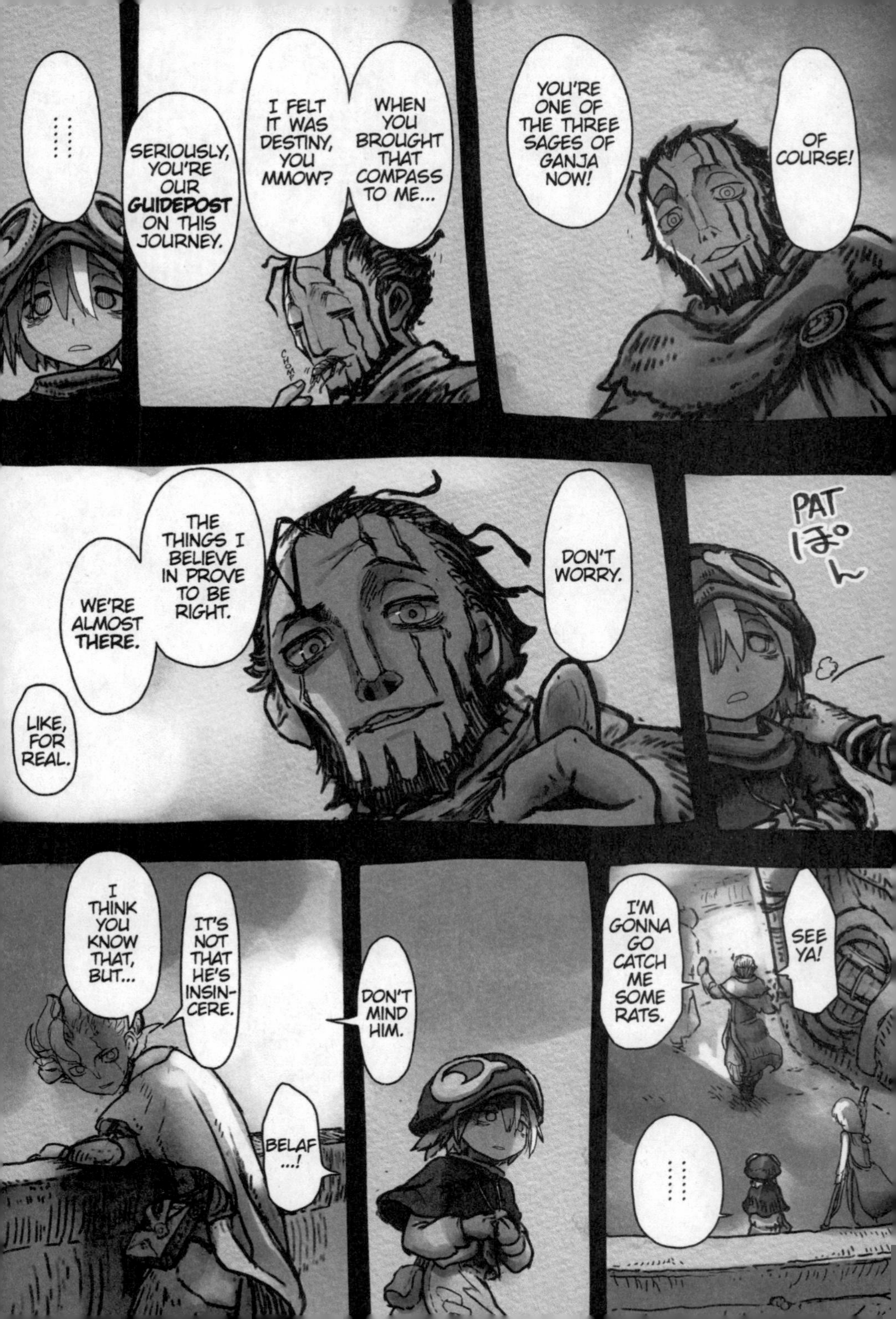
OF COURSE!
YOU'RE ONE OF THE THREE SAGES OF GANJA NOW!
WHEN YOU BROUGHT THAT COMPASS TO ME...
I FELT IT WAS DESTINY, YOU MMOW?
CHOMP
SERIOUSLY, YOU'RE OUR **GUIDEPOST** ON THIS JOURNEY.
……
PAT
ぽん
DON'T WORRY.
THE THINGS I BELIEVE IN PROVE TO BE RIGHT.
WE'RE ALMOST THERE.
LIKE, FOR REAL.
SEE YA!
I'M GONNA GO CATCH ME SOME RATS.
……
DON'T MIND HIM.
BELAF ...!
IT'S NOT THAT HE'S INSINCERE.
I THINK YOU KNOW THAT, BUT...

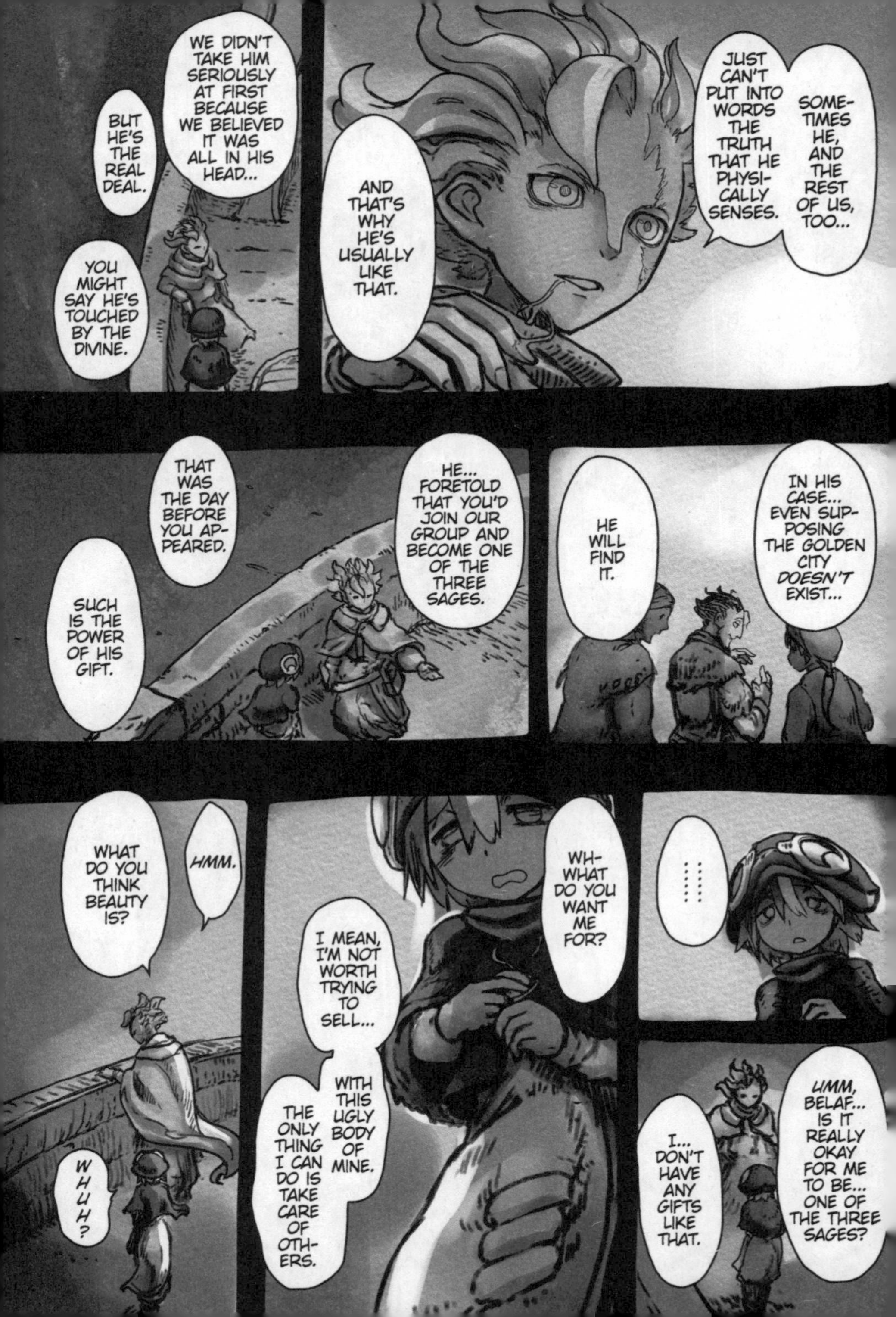
SOMETIMES HE, AND THE REST OF US, TOO...
JUST CAN'T PUT INTO WORDS THE TRUTH THAT HE PHYSICALLY SENSES.
AND THAT'S WHY HE'S USUALLY LIKE THAT.
WE DIDN'T TAKE HIM SERIOUSLY AT FIRST BECAUSE WE BELIEVED IT WAS ALL IN HIS HEAD...
BUT HE'S THE REAL DEAL.
YOU MIGHT SAY HE'S TOUCHED BY THE DIVINE.
IN HIS CASE... EVEN SUPPOSING THE GOLDEN CITY *DOESN'T* EXIST...
HE WILL FIND IT.
HE... FORETOLD THAT YOU'D JOIN OUR GROUP AND BECOME ONE OF THE THREE SAGES.
THAT WAS THE DAY BEFORE YOU APPEARED.
SUCH IS THE POWER OF HIS GIFT.
......
UMM, BELAF... IS IT REALLY OKAY FOR ME TO BE... ONE OF THE THREE SAGES?
I... DON'T HAVE ANY GIFTS LIKE THAT.
WH-WHAT DO YOU WANT ME FOR?
I MEAN, I'M NOT WORTH TRYING TO SELL...
WITH THIS UGLY BODY OF MINE.
THE ONLY THING I CAN DO IS TAKE CARE OF OTHERS.
HMM.
WHAT DO YOU THINK BEAUTY IS?
WHUH?

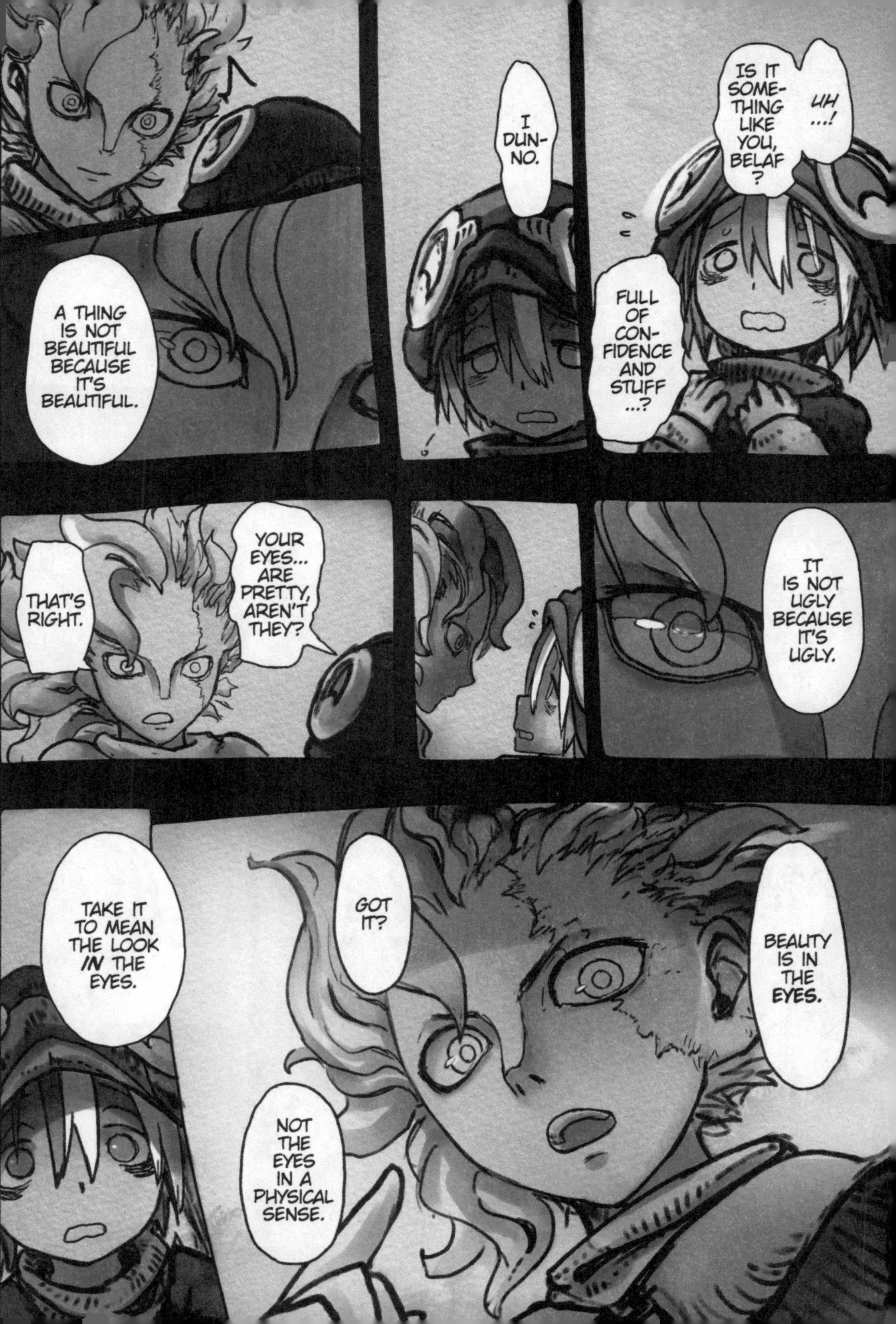
UH ...!
IS IT SOMETHING-THING LIKE YOU, BELAF?
FULL OF CONFIDENCE AND STUFF ...?
I DUN-NO.
A THING IS NOT BEAUTIFUL BECAUSE IT'S BEAUTIFUL.
IT IS NOT UGLY BECAUSE IT'S UGLY.
YOUR EYES... ARE PRETTY, AREN'T THEY?
THAT'S RIGHT.
BEAUTY IS IN THE EYES.
GOT IT?
TAKE IT TO MEAN THE LOOK *IN* THE EYES.
NOT THE EYES IN A PHYSICAL SENSE.

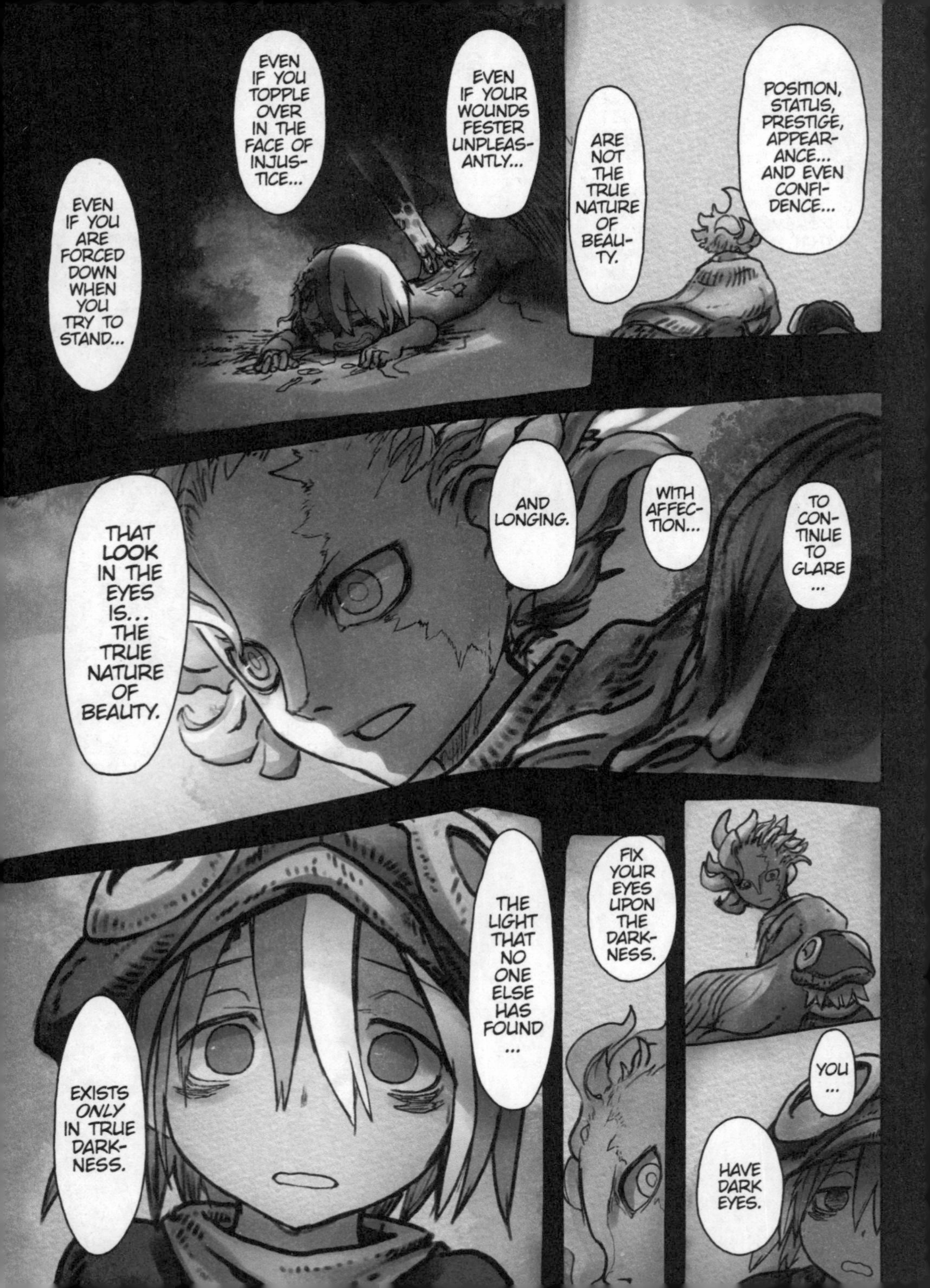
POSITION, STATUS, PRESTIGE, APPEARANCE... AND EVEN CONFIDENCE...
ARE NOT THE TRUE NATURE OF BEAUTY.
EVEN IF YOUR WOUNDS FESTER UNPLEASANTLY...
EVEN IF YOU TOPPLE OVER IN THE FACE OF INJUSTICE...
EVEN IF YOU ARE FORCED DOWN WHEN YOU TRY TO STAND...
TO CONTINUE TO GLARE...
WITH AFFECTION...
AND LONGING.
THAT LOOK IN THE EYES IS... THE TRUE NATURE OF BEAUTY.
YOU...
HAVE DARK EYES.
FIX YOUR EYES UPON THE DARKNESS.
THE LIGHT THAT NO ONE ELSE HAS FOUND...
EXISTS *ONLY* IN TRUE DARKNESS.

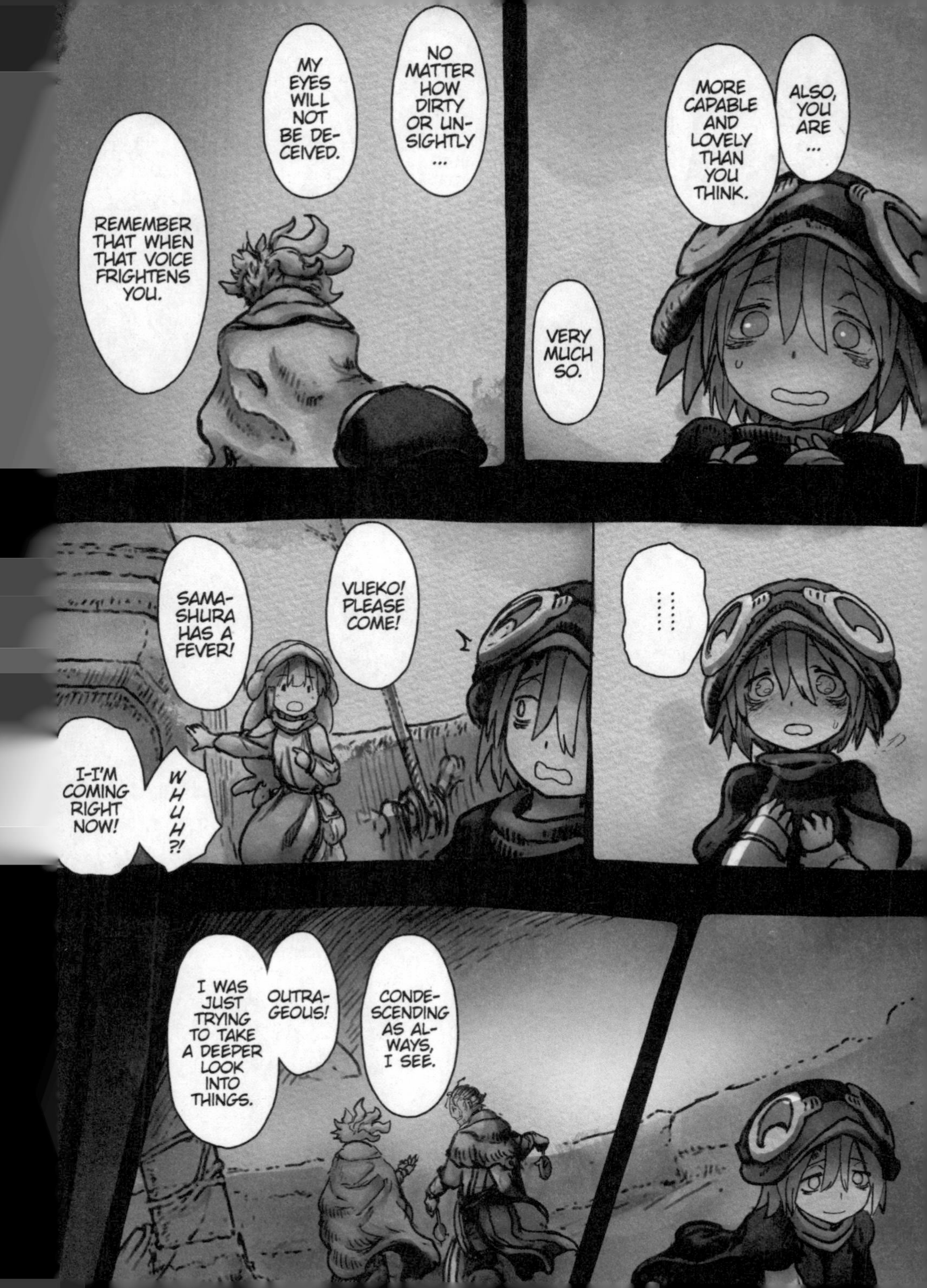

ALSO, YOU ARE ...
MORE CAPABLE AND LOVELY THAN YOU THINK.
VERY MUCH SO.
NO MATTER HOW DIRTY OR UN-SIGHTLY ...
MY EYES WILL NOT BE DE-CEIVED.
REMEMBER THAT WHEN THAT VOICE FRIGHTENS YOU.
......
VUEKO! PLEASE COME!
SAMA-SHURA HAS A FEVER!
WHUH?!
I-I'M COMING RIGHT NOW!
CONDE-SCENDING AS AL-WAYS, I SEE.
OUTRA-GEOUS!
I WAS JUST TRYING TO TAKE A DEEPER LOOK INTO THINGS.

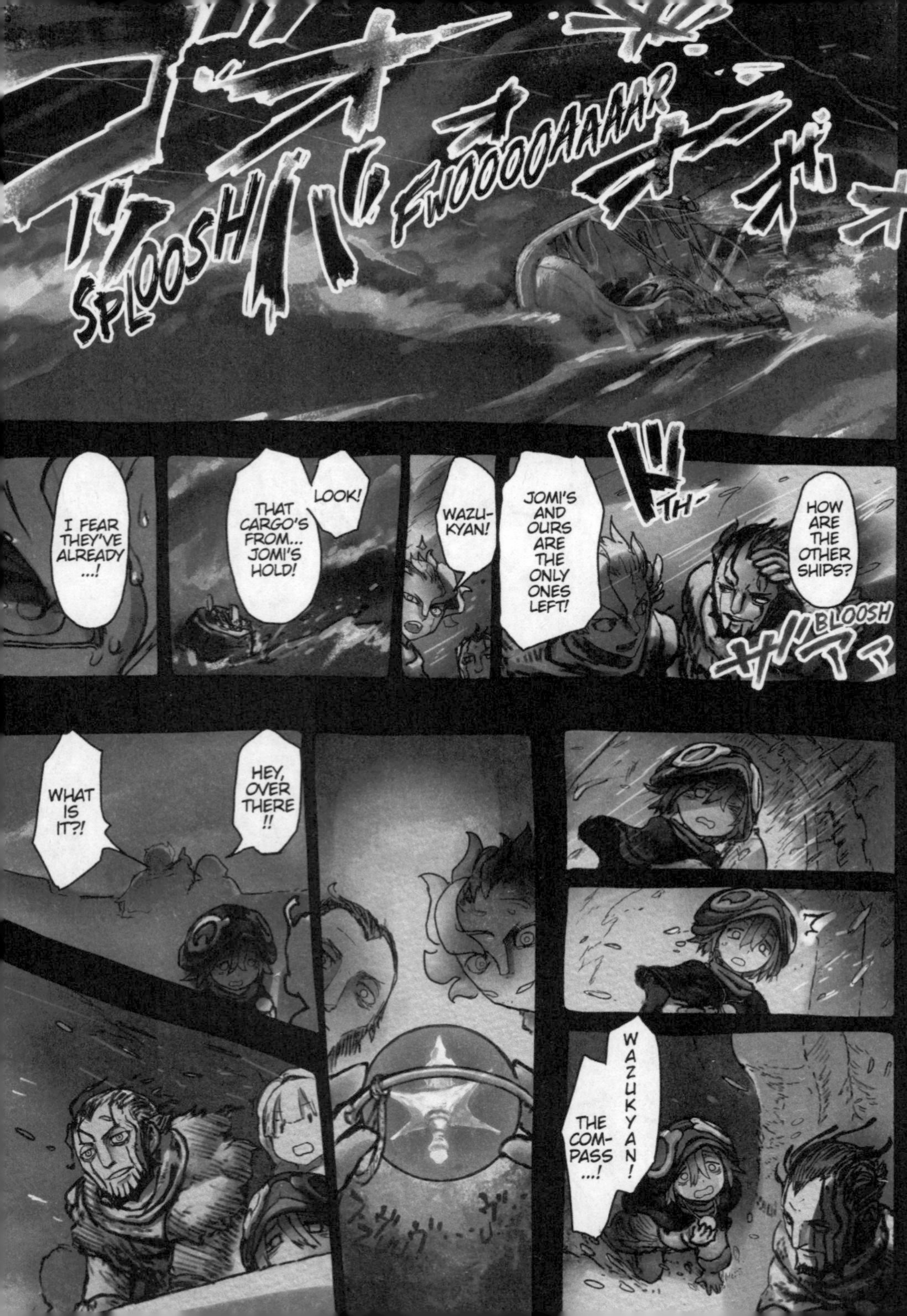
FWOOOOAAAAR
SPLOOSH
TH-
HOW ARE THE OTHER SHIPS?
BLOOSH
JOMI'S AND OURS ARE THE ONLY ONES LEFT!
WAZU-KYAN!
LOOK!
THAT CARGO'S FROM... JOMI'S HOLD!
I FEAR THEY'VE ALREADY ...!
WAZUKYAN!
THE COM-PASS ...!
HEY, OVER THERE !!
WHAT IS IT?!

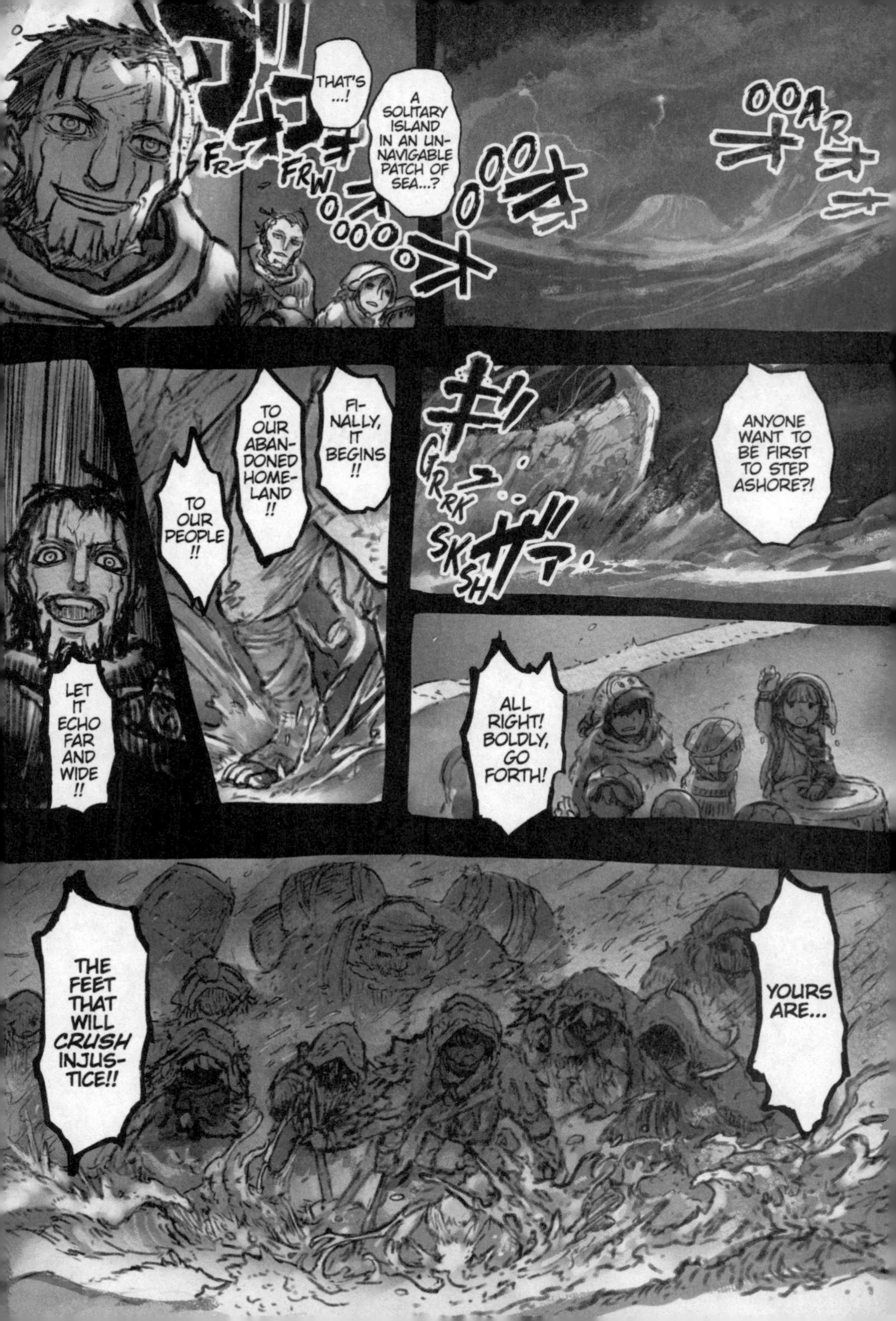
OOARRR
A SOLITARY ISLAND IN AN UN-NAVIGABLE PATCH OF SEA...?
THAT'S ...!
FR- FRWOOOOOOOOOO
ANYONE WANT TO BE FIRST TO STEP ASHORE?!
GRRK
SKSH
ALL RIGHT! BOLDLY, GO FORTH!
FI-NALLY, IT BEGINS!!
TO OUR ABAN-DONED HOME-LAND!!
TO OUR PEOPLE!!
LET IT ECHO FAR AND WIDE!!
YOURS ARE...
THE FEET THAT WILL *CRUSH* INJUS-TICE!!

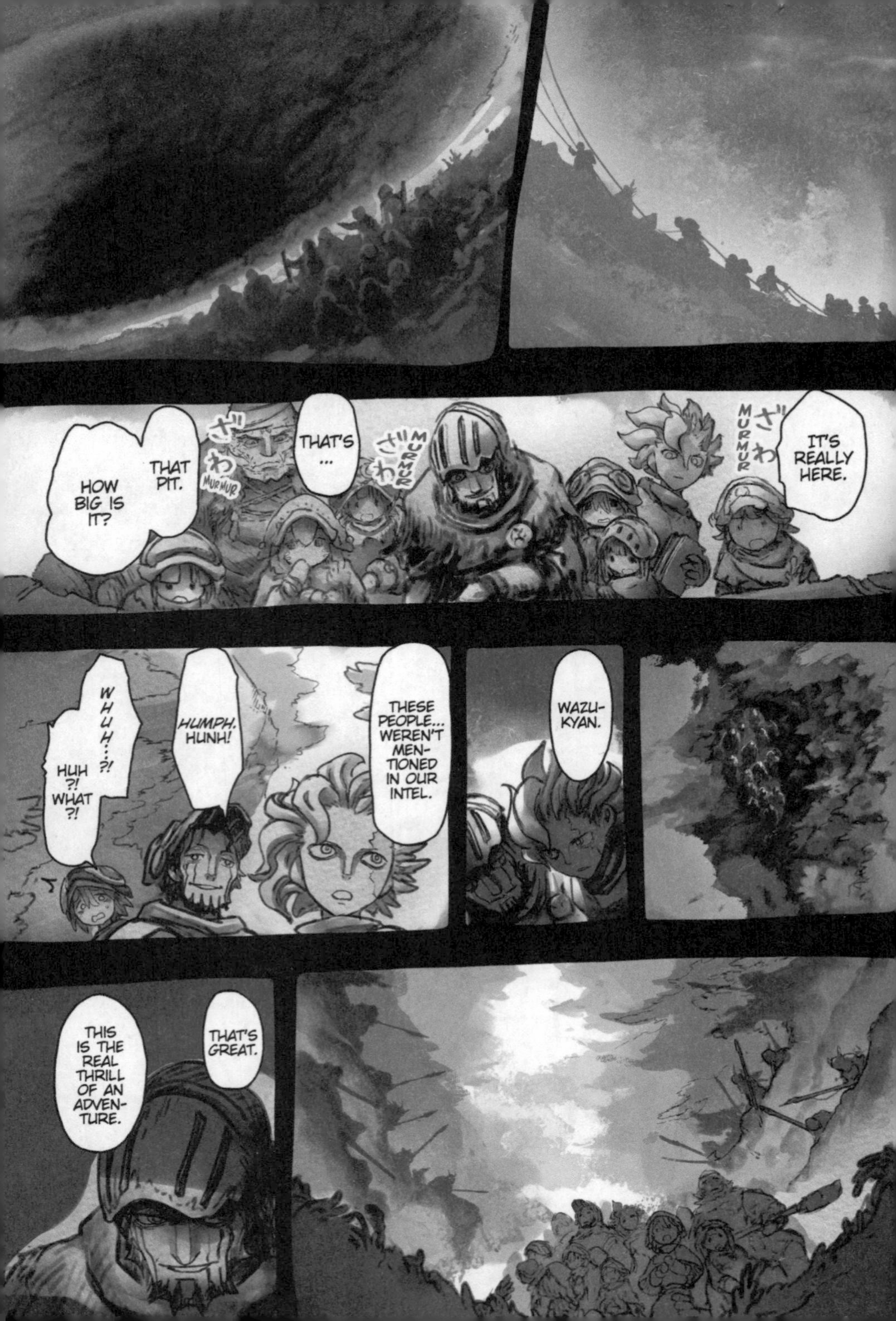
ざわ
MURMUR
IT'S REALLY HERE.
ざわ
MURMUR
THAT'S ...
ざわ
MURMUR
THAT PIT.
HOW BIG IS IT?
WAZU-KYAN.
THESE PEOPLE... WEREN'T MEN-TIONED IN OUR INTEL.
HUMPH. HUNH!
WHUH...?!
HUH?! WHAT?!
THAT'S GREAT.
THIS IS THE REAL THRILL OF AN ADVEN-TURE.

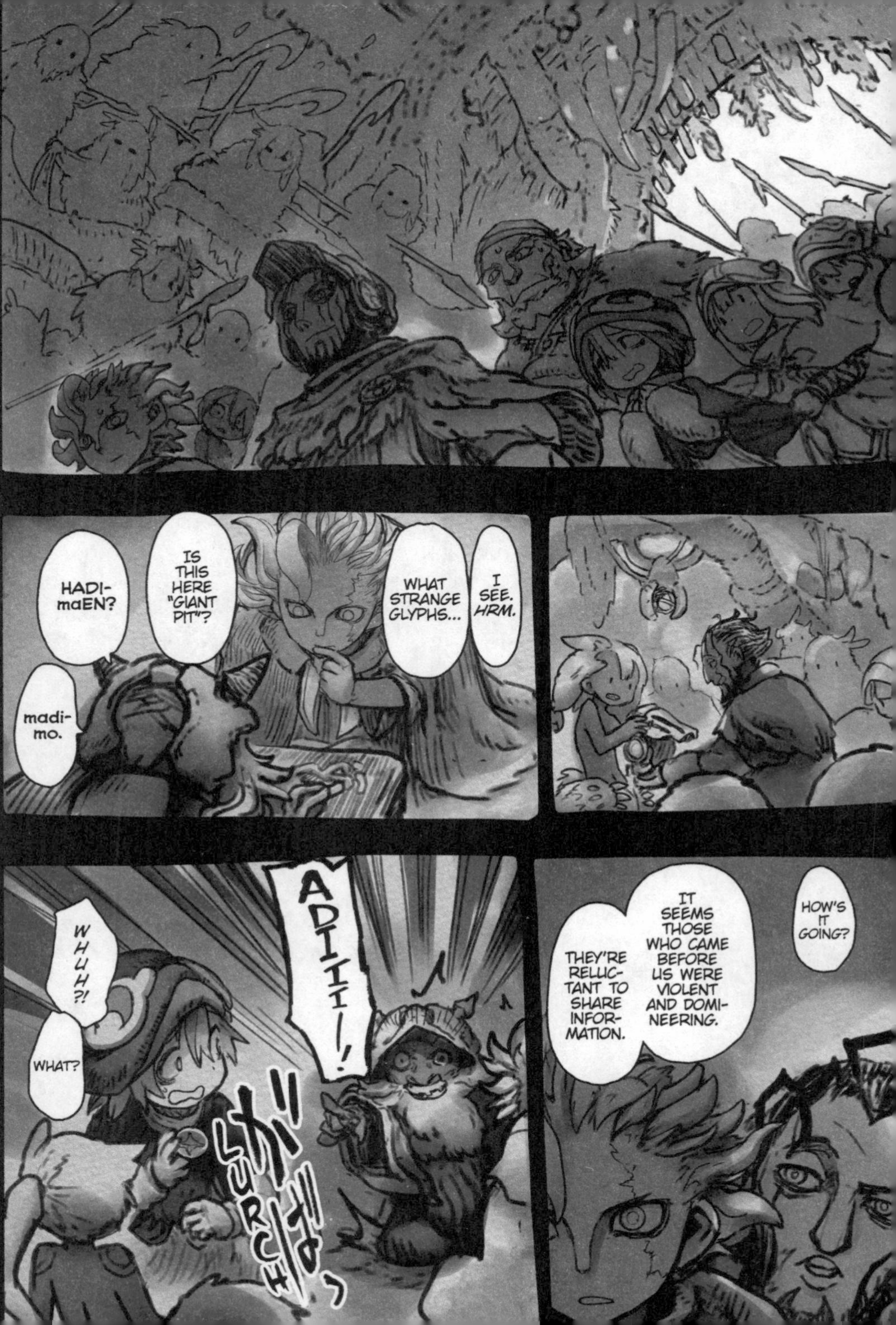
I SEE. HRM.
WHAT STRANGE GLYPHS...
IS THIS HERE "GIANT PIT"?
HADI-maEN?
madi-mo.
HOW'S IT GOING?
IT SEEMS THOSE WHO CAME BEFORE US WERE VIOLENT AND DOMINEERING.
THEY'RE RELUCTANT TO SHARE INFORMATION.
ADIIII!!
WHUH?!
WHAT?
LURCH

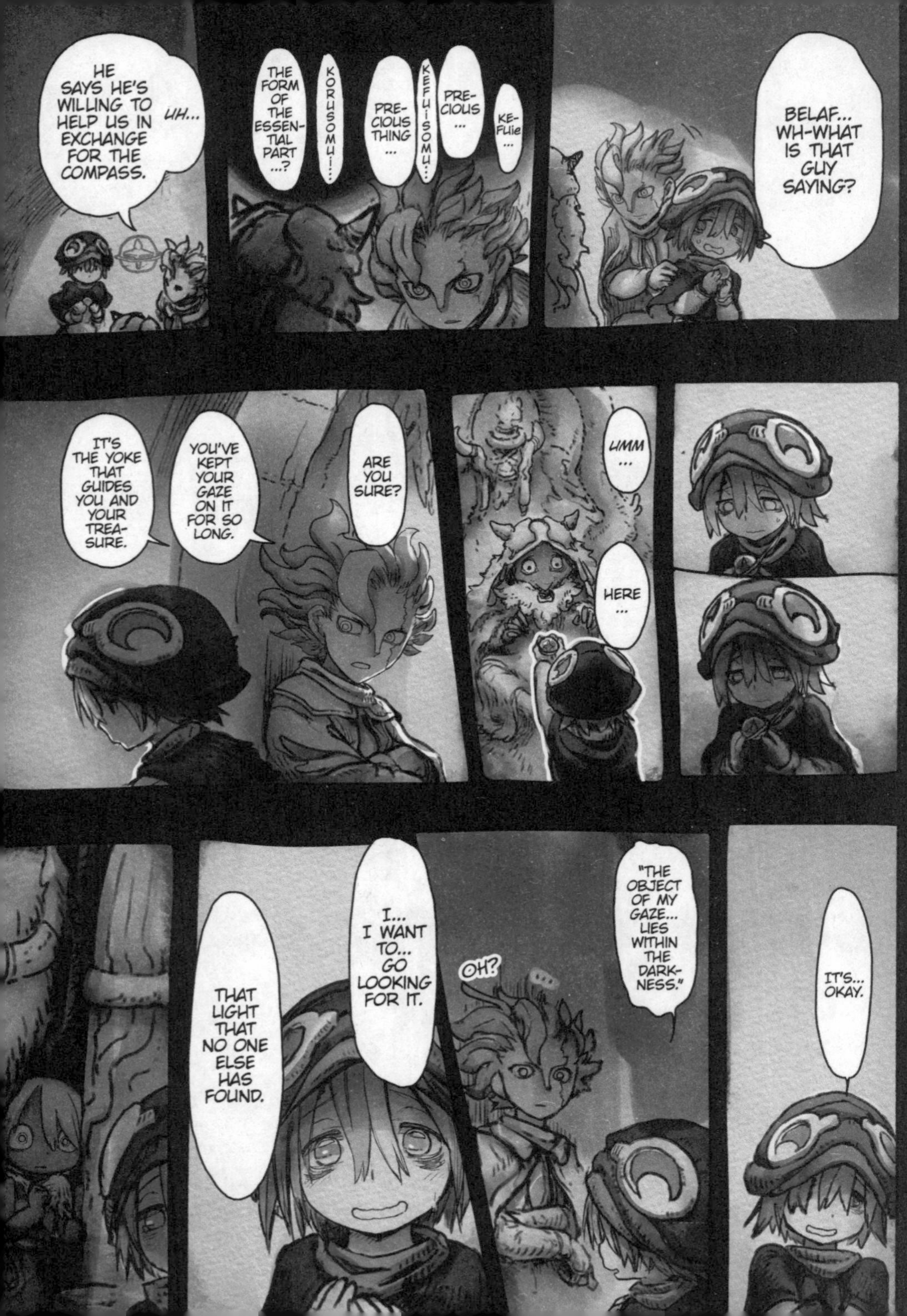
BELAF... WH-WHAT IS THAT GUY SAYING?
KE-Fuie ...
PRE-CIOUS ...
KEFUISOMU...
PRE-CIOUS THING ...
KORUSOMU!...
THE FORM OF THE ESSEN-TIAL PART ...?
UH...
HE SAYS HE'S WILLING TO HELP US IN EXCHANGE FOR THE COMPASS.
UMM ...
HERE ...
ARE YOU SURE?
YOU'VE KEPT YOUR GAZE ON IT FOR SO LONG.
IT'S THE YOKE THAT GUIDES YOU AND YOUR TREA-SURE.
IT'S... OKAY.
"THE OBJECT OF MY GAZE... LIES WITHIN THE DARK-NESS."
OH?
I... I WANT TO... GO LOOKING FOR IT.
THAT LIGHT THAT NO ONE ELSE HAS FOUND.

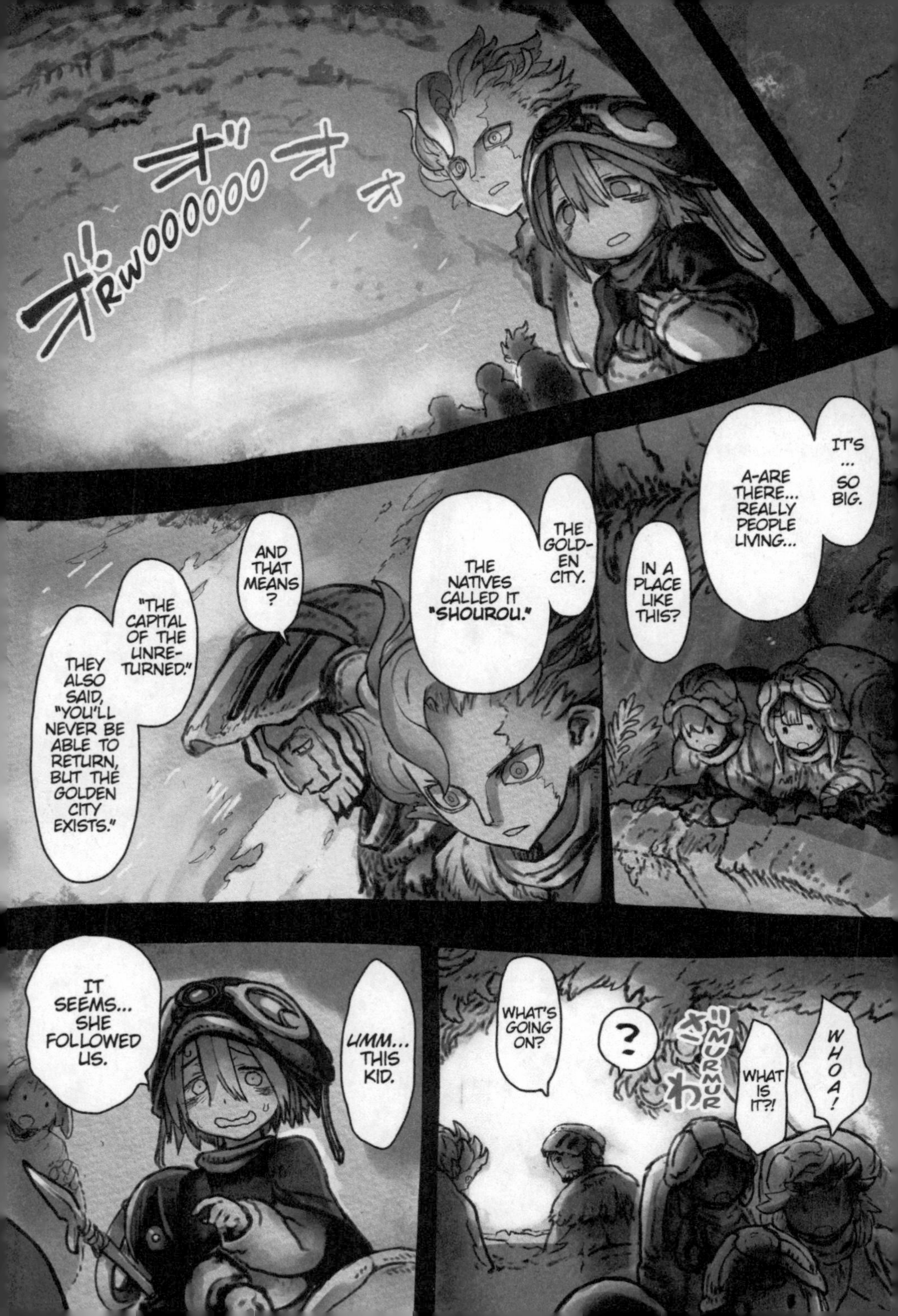
RWOOOOOO
IT'S... SO BIG.
A-ARE THERE... REALLY PEOPLE LIVING...
IN A PLACE LIKE THIS?
THE GOLDEN CITY.
THE NATIVES CALLED IT "SHOUROU."
AND THAT MEANS?
"THE CAPITAL OF THE UNRETURNED."
THEY ALSO SAID, "YOU'LL NEVER BE ABLE TO RETURN, BUT THE GOLDEN CITY EXISTS."
WHOA!
WHAT IS IT?!
ざわ MURMUR
?
WHAT'S GOING ON?
UMM... THIS KID.
IT SEEMS... SHE FOLLOWED US.

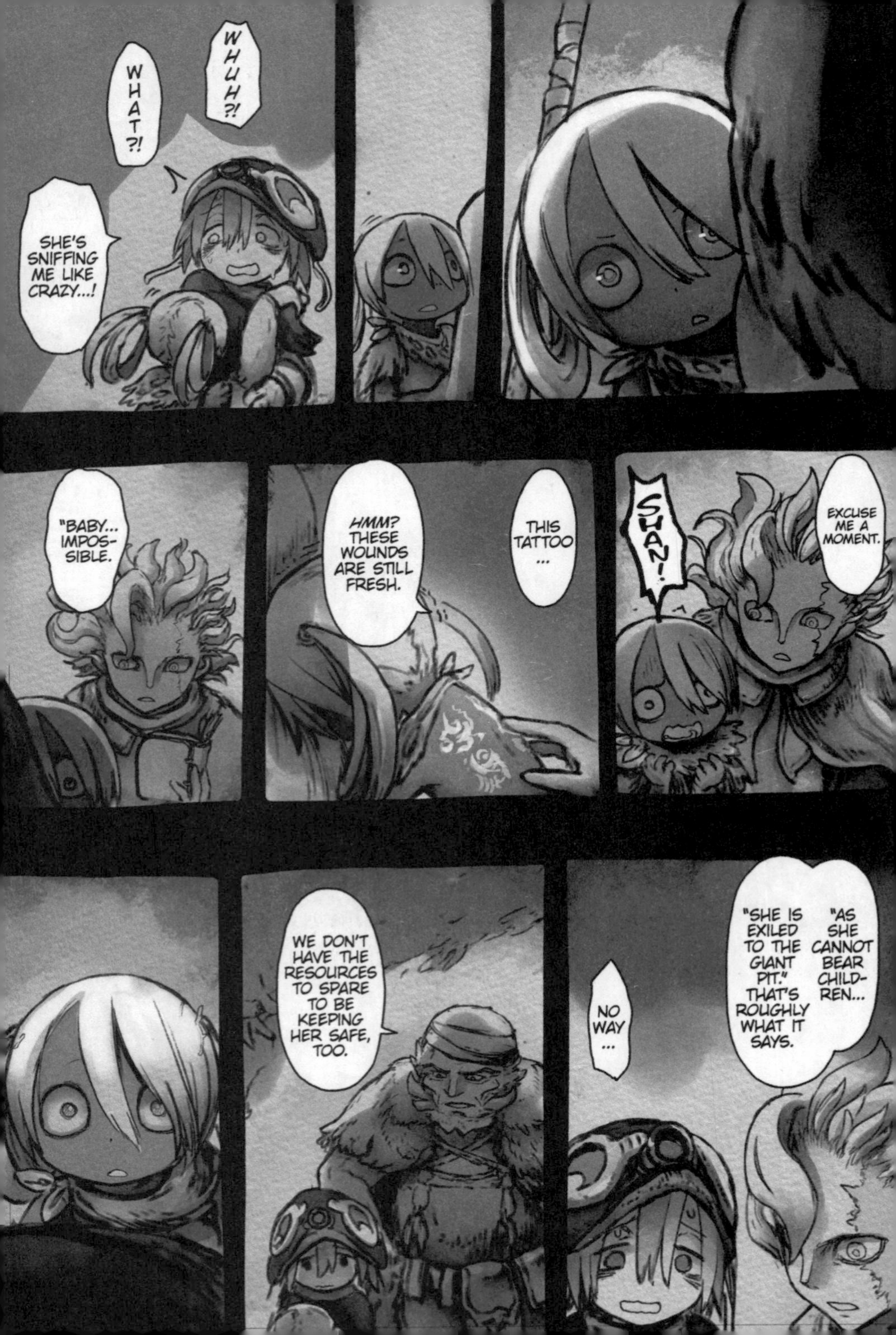
WHUH?!
WHAT?!
SHE'S SNIFFING ME LIKE CRAZY...!
EXCUSE ME A MOMENT.
SHAN!
THIS TATTOO ...
HMM? THESE WOUNDS ARE STILL FRESH.
"BABY... IMPOSSIBLE.
"AS SHE CANNOT BEAR CHILDREN...
"SHE IS EXILED TO THE GIANT PIT." THAT'S ROUGHLY WHAT IT SAYS.
NO WAY ...
WE DON'T HAVE THE RESOURCES TO SPARE TO BE KEEPING HER SAFE, TOO.

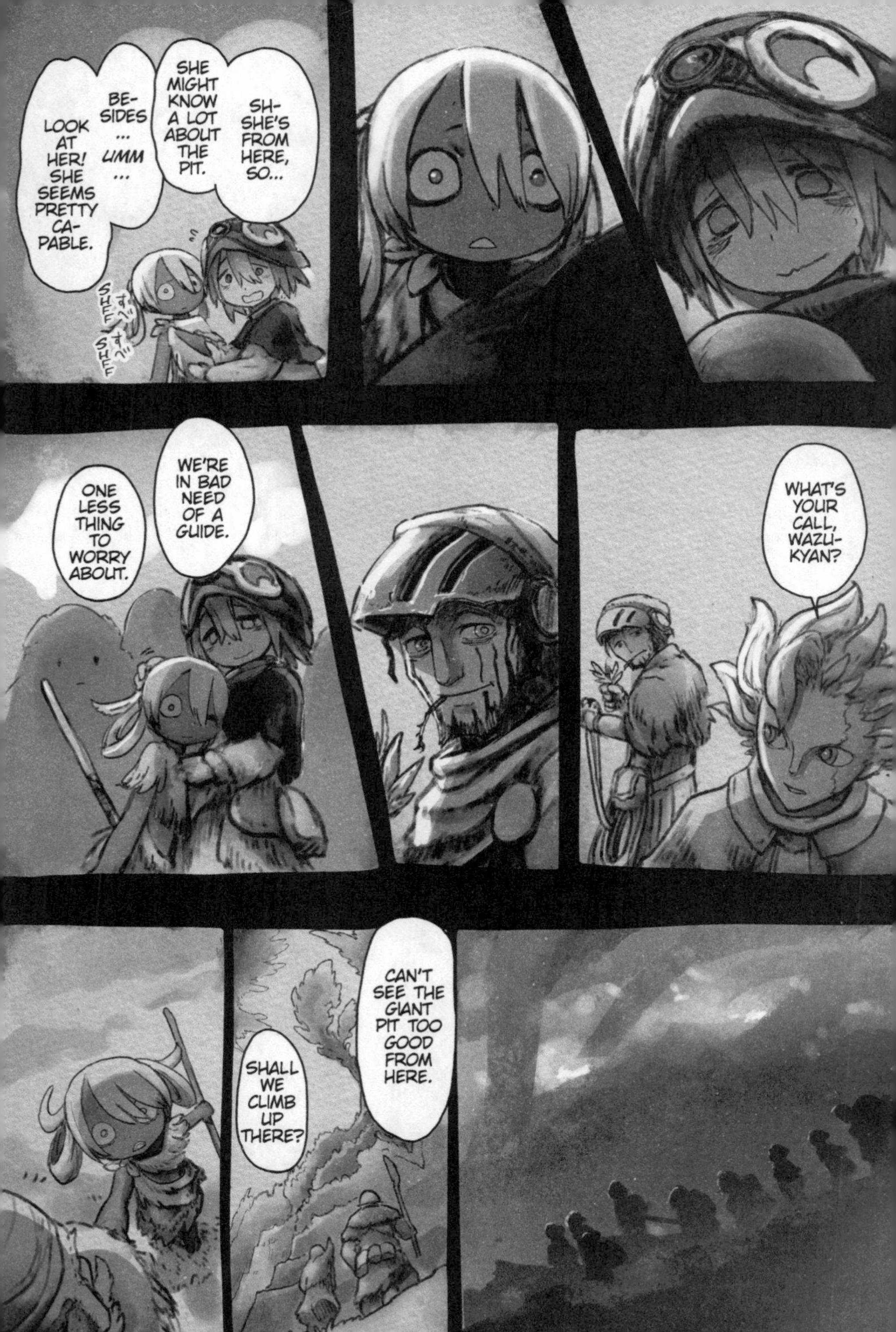
SH-SHE'S FROM HERE, SO...
SHE MIGHT KNOW A LOT ABOUT THE PIT.
BE-SIDES ... UMM ...
LOOK AT HER! SHE SEEMS PRETTY CA-PABLE.
すべ SHEFF
すべ SHEFF
WHAT'S YOUR CALL, WAZU-KYAN?
WE'RE IN BAD NEED OF A GUIDE.
ONE LESS THING TO WORRY ABOUT.
CAN'T SEE THE GIANT PIT TOO GOOD FROM HERE.
SHALL WE CLIMB UP THERE?

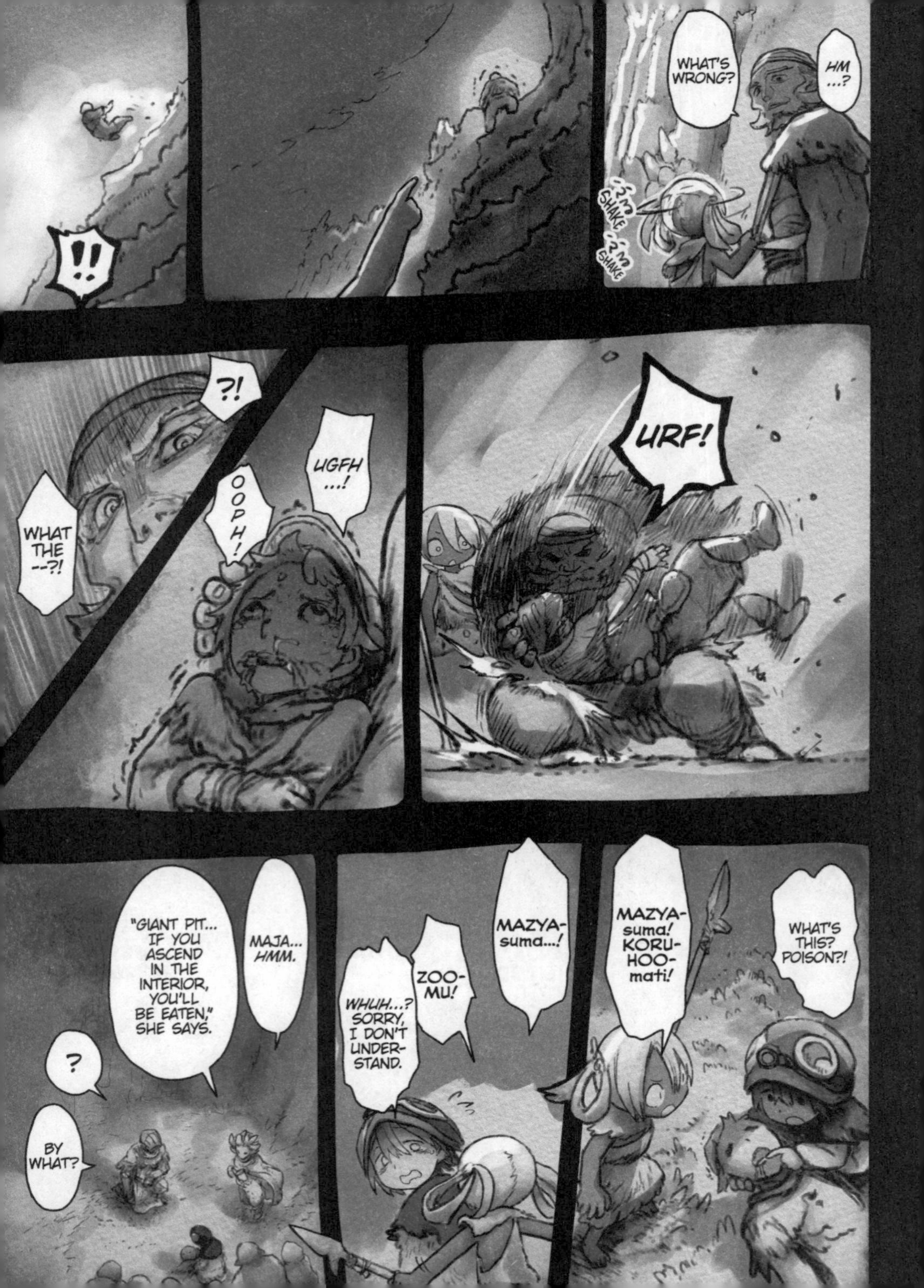
HM ...?
WHAT'S WRONG?
SHAKE
SHAKE
!!
URF!
UGFH ...!
OOPH!
?!
WHAT THE --?!
WHAT'S THIS? POISON?!
MAZYA-suma! KORU-HOO-mati!
MAZYA-suma...!
ZOO-MU!
WHUH...? SORRY, I DON'T UNDER-STAND.
MAJA... HMM.
"GIANT PIT... IF YOU ASCEND IN THE INTERIOR, YOU'LL BE EATEN," SHE SAYS.
?
BY WHAT?

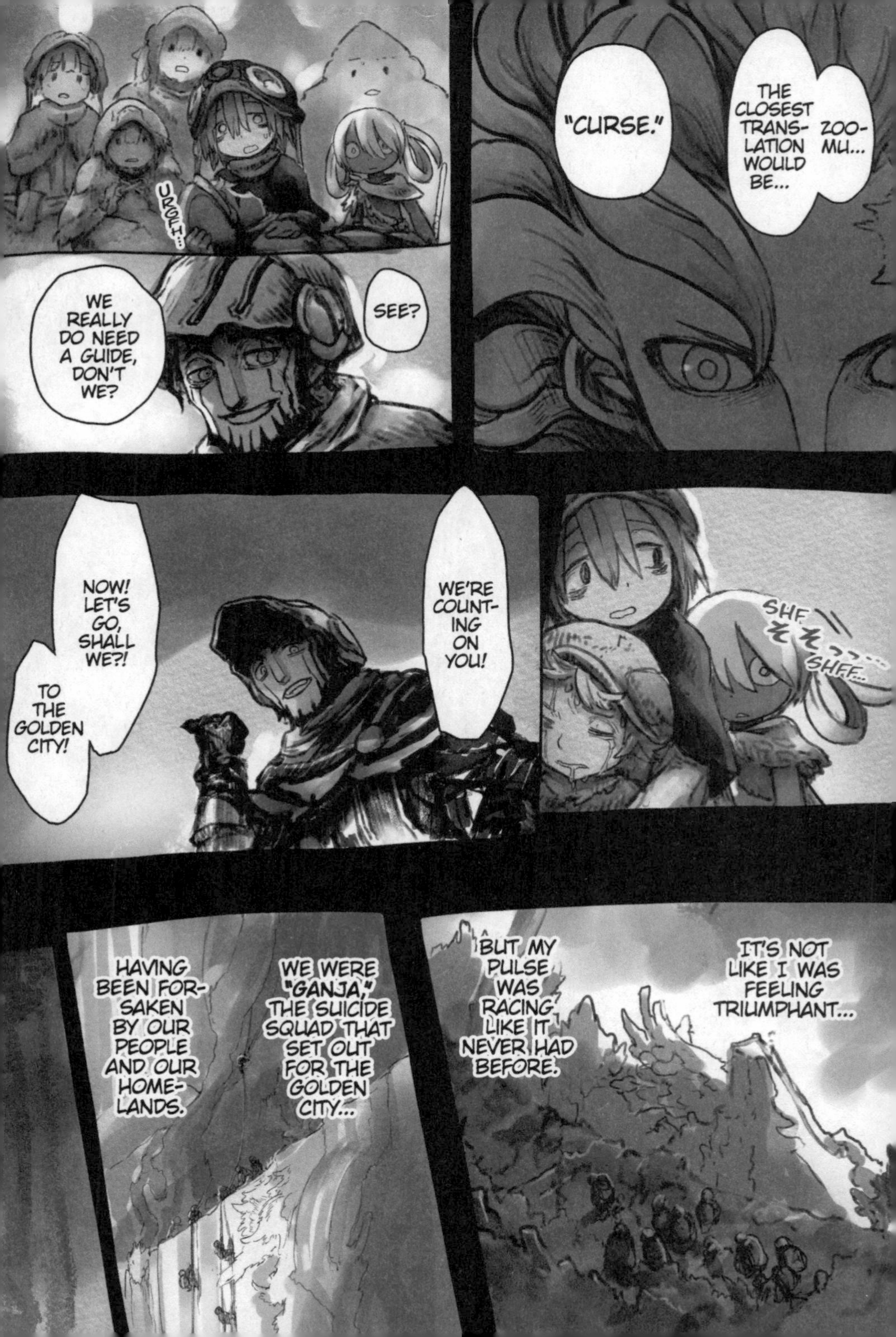
ZOO-MU...
THE CLOSEST TRANSLATION WOULD BE...
"CURSE."
URGH...
SEE?
WE REALLY DO NEED A GUIDE, DON'T WE?
SHF
そそっ...
SHFF...
WE'RE COUNTING ON YOU!
NOW! LET'S GO, SHALL WE?!
TO THE GOLDEN CITY!
IT'S NOT LIKE I WAS FEELING TRIUMPHANT...
BUT MY PULSE WAS RACING LIKE IT NEVER HAD BEFORE.
WE WERE "GANJA," THE SUICIDE SQUAD THAT SET OUT FOR THE GOLDEN CITY...
HAVING BEEN FORSAKEN BY OUR PEOPLE AND OUR HOMELANDS.

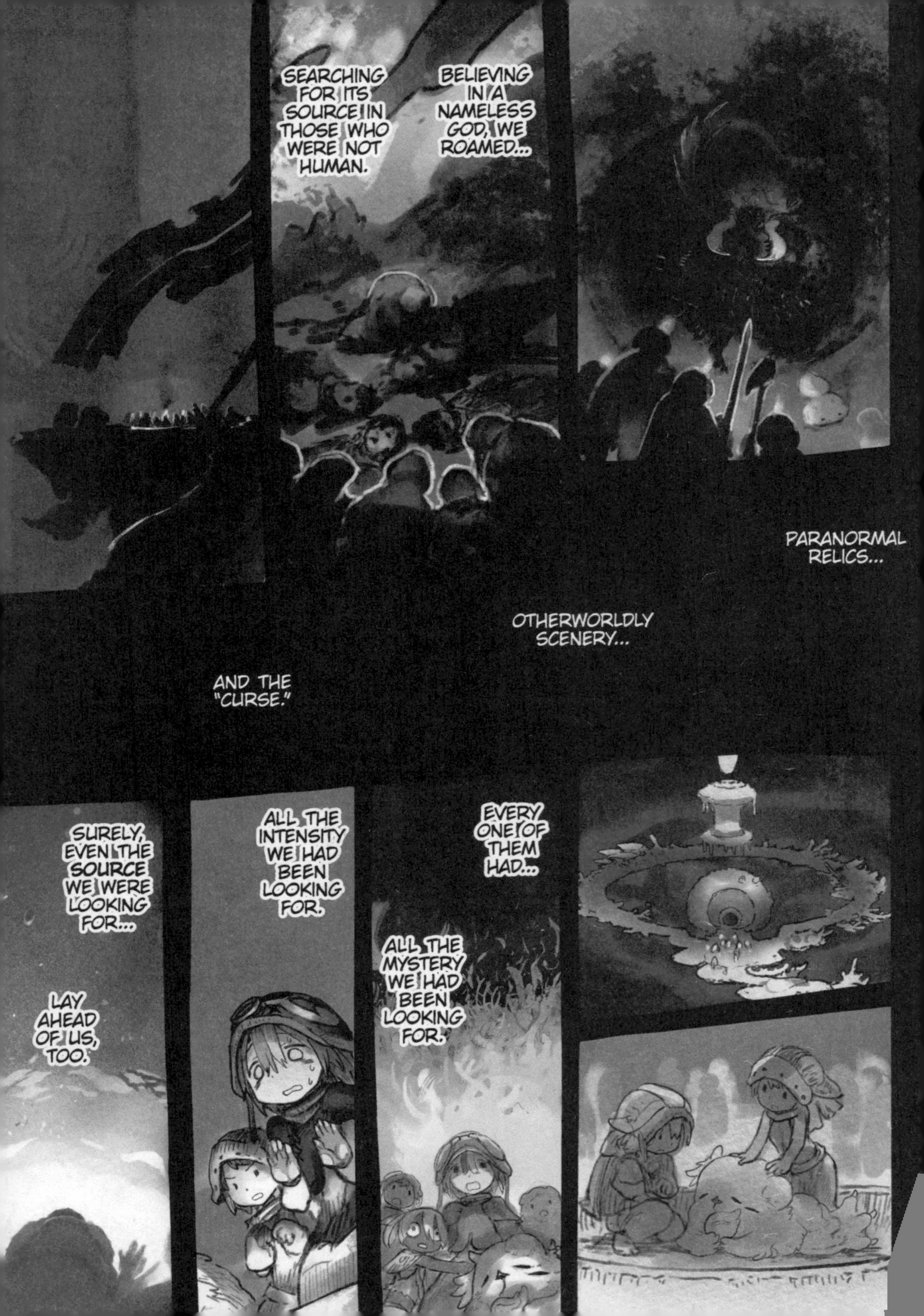
BELIEVING IN A NAMELESS GOD, WE ROAMED...
SEARCHING FOR ITS SOURCE IN THOSE WHO WERE NOT HUMAN.
PARANORMAL RELICS...
OTHERWORLDLY SCENERY...
AND THE "CURSE."
EVERY ONE OF THEM HAD...
ALL THE MYSTERY WE HAD BEEN LOOKING FOR.
ALL THE INTENSITY WE HAD BEEN LOOKING FOR.
SURELY, EVEN THE SOURCE WE WERE LOOKING FOR...
LAY AHEAD OF US, TOO.

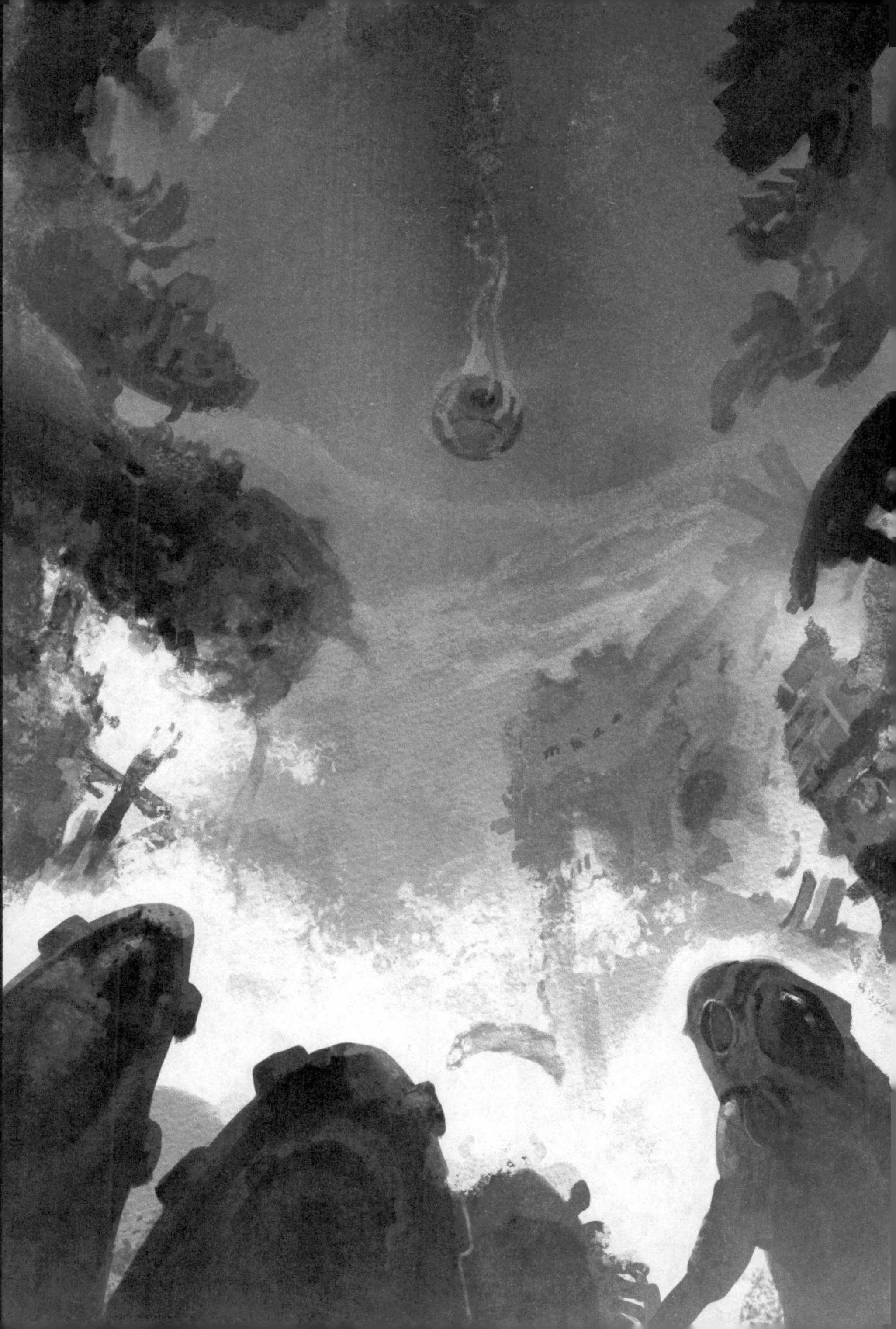

MADE IN ABYSS

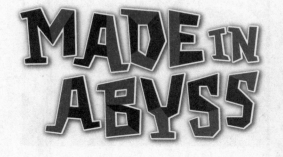

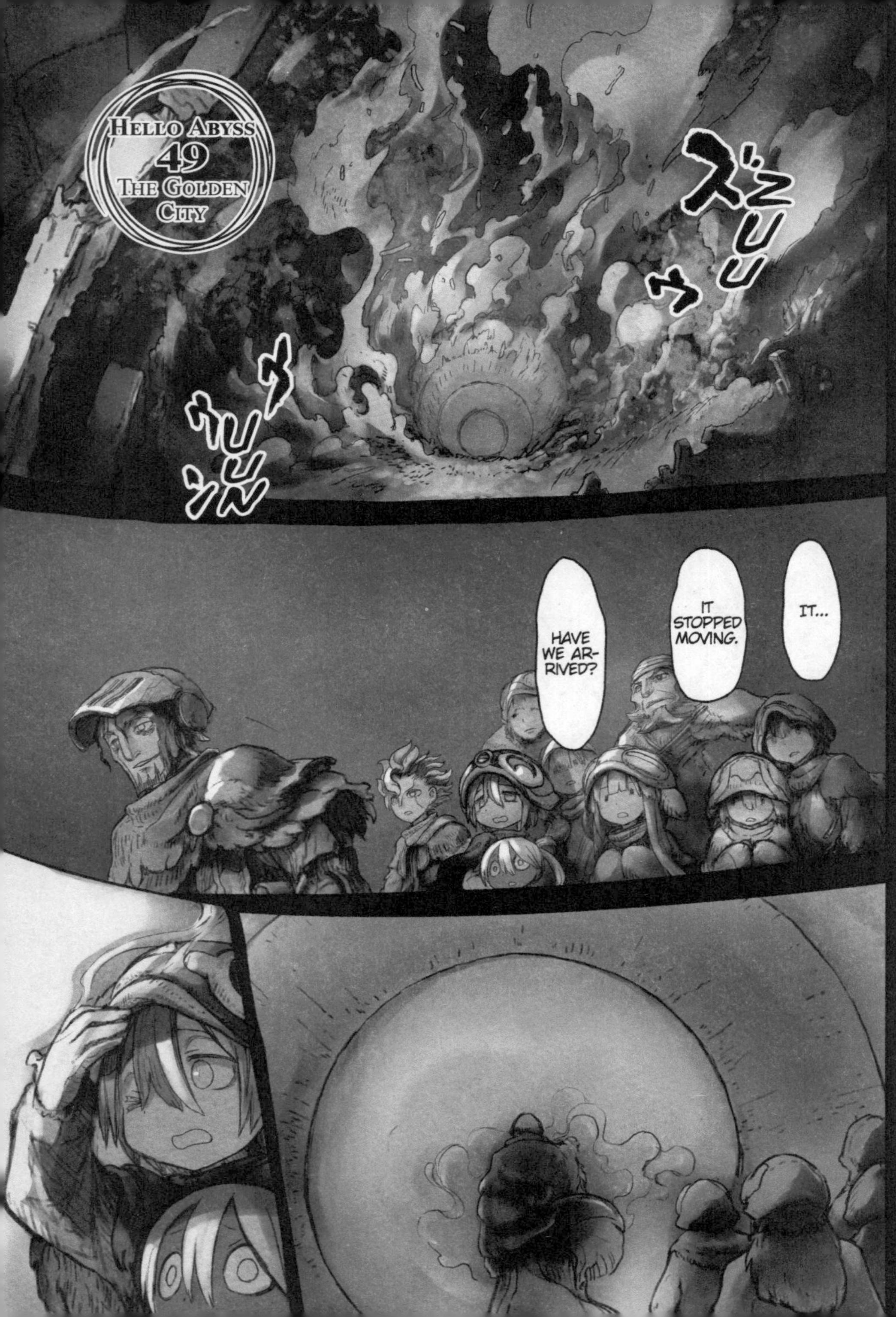
HELLO ABYSS
49
THE GOLDEN CITY
IT...
IT STOPPED MOVING.
HAVE WE AR-RIVED?

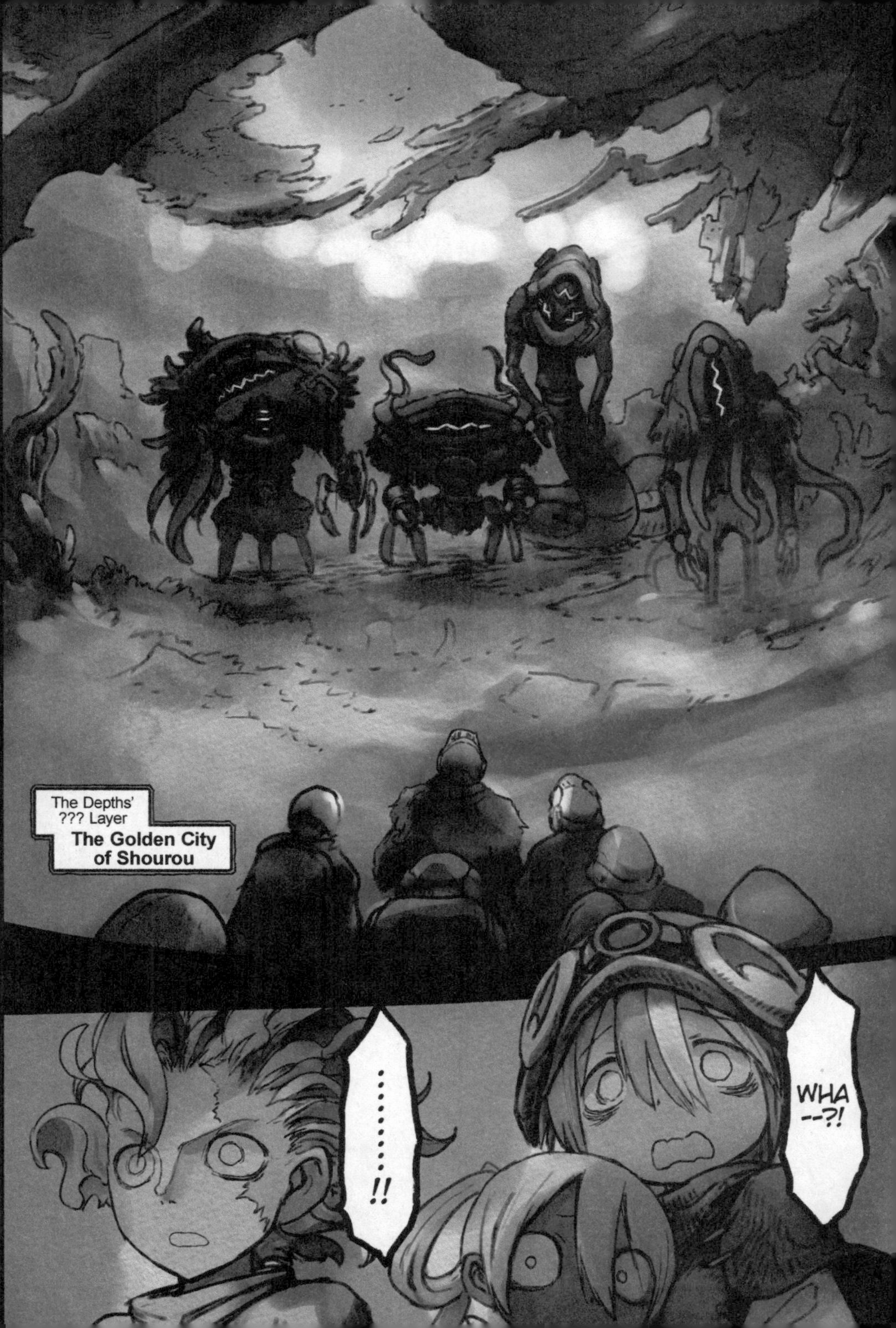
The Depths' ??? Layer
The Golden City of Shourou
WHA--?!
……!!

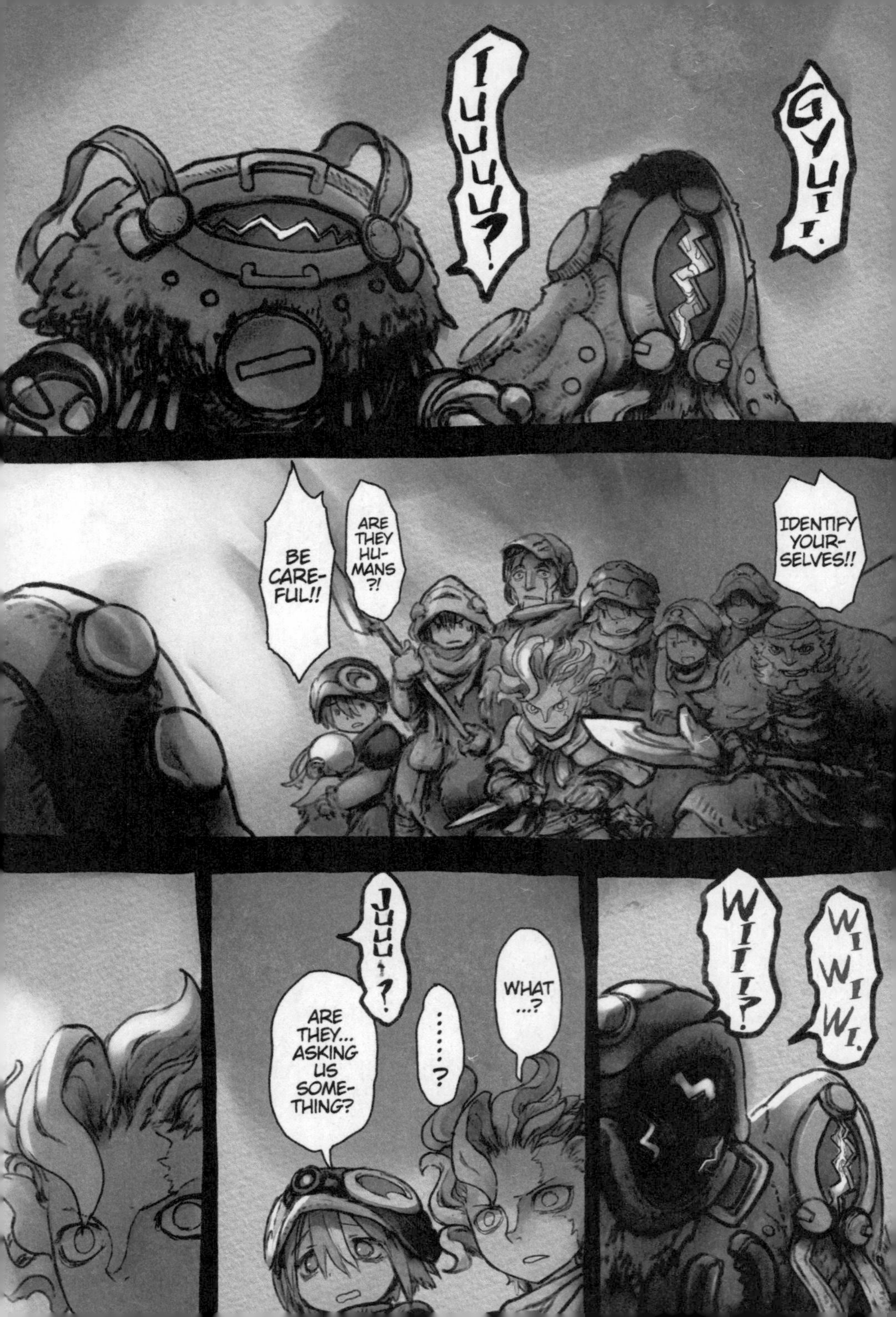
GYUII.
IUUUU?!
IDENTIFY YOUR-SELVES!!
ARE THEY HU-MANS?!
BE CARE-FUL!!
WIWIWI.
WIIII?!
JUUU↑?
WHAT...?
......?
ARE THEY... ASKING US SOME-THING?

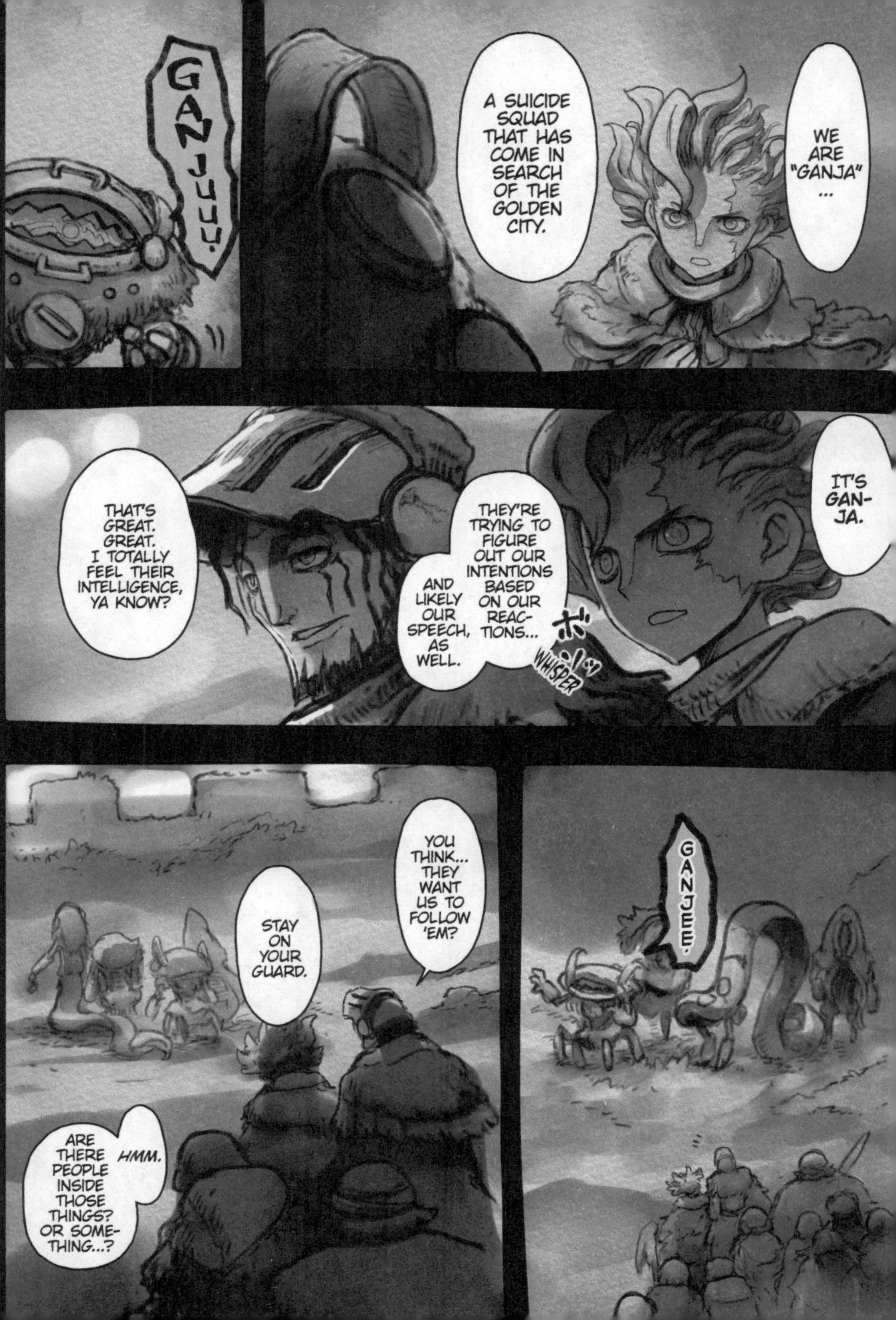
WE ARE "GANJA"...
A SUICIDE SQUAD THAT HAS COME IN SEARCH OF THE GOLDEN CITY.
GANJUUU!
IT'S GAN-JA.
THEY'RE TRYING TO FIGURE OUT OUR INTENTIONS BASED ON OUR REAC-TIONS...
AND LIKELY OUR SPEECH, AS WELL.
WHISPER
THAT'S GREAT. GREAT. I TOTALLY FEEL THEIR INTELLIGENCE, YA KNOW?
GANJEE.
YOU THINK... THEY WANT US TO FOLLOW 'EM?
STAY ON YOUR GUARD.
HMM.
ARE THERE PEOPLE INSIDE THOSE THINGS? OR SOME-THING...?

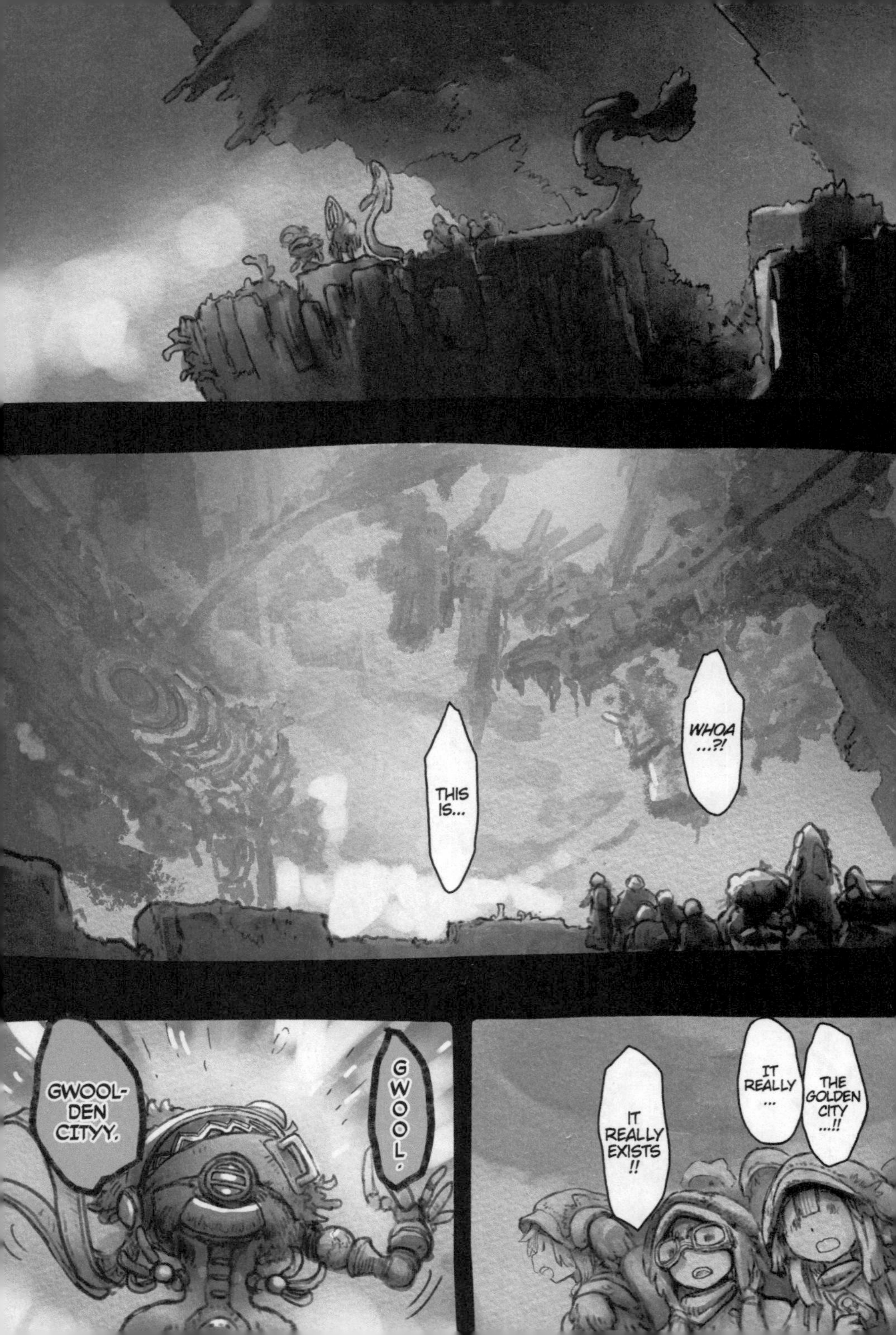
WHOA ...?!
THIS IS...
THE GOLDEN CITY ...!!
IT REALLY ...
IT REALLY EXISTS !!
GWOOL.
GWOOL-DEN CITYY.

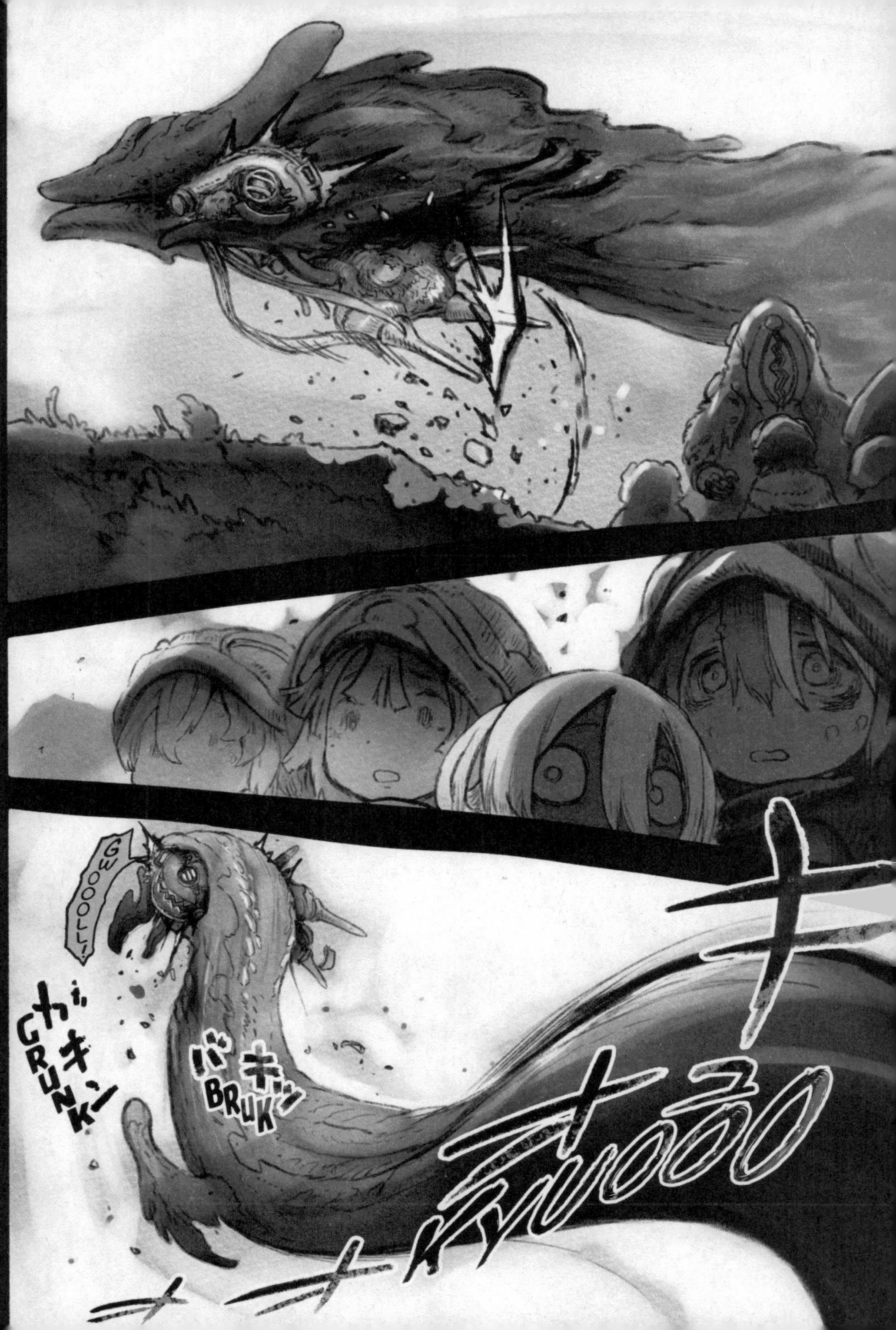
GWOOOOLL!
バキッ
BRUK
ガキン
GRUNK

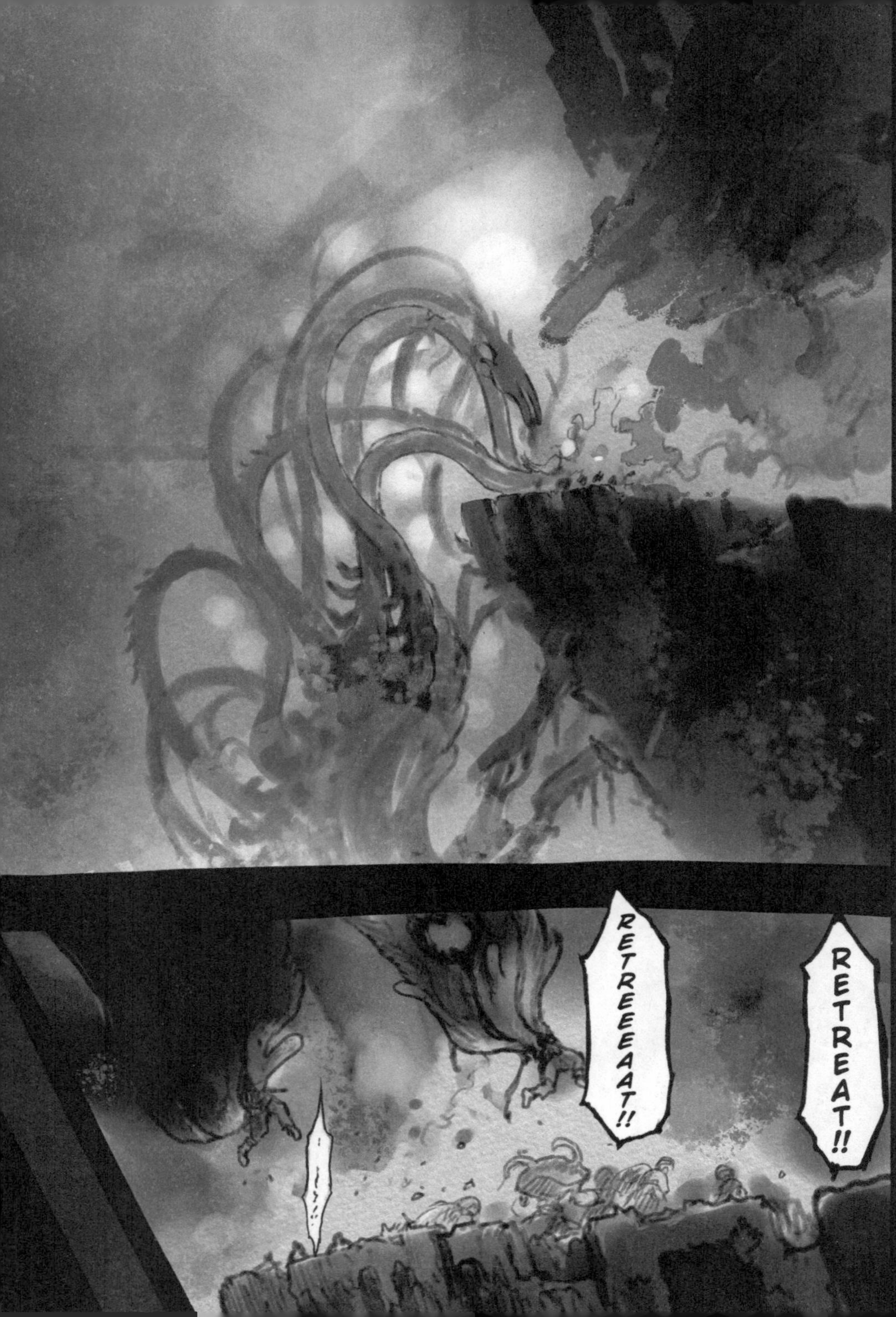
RETREAT!!
RETREEEAAT!!
..!?!!

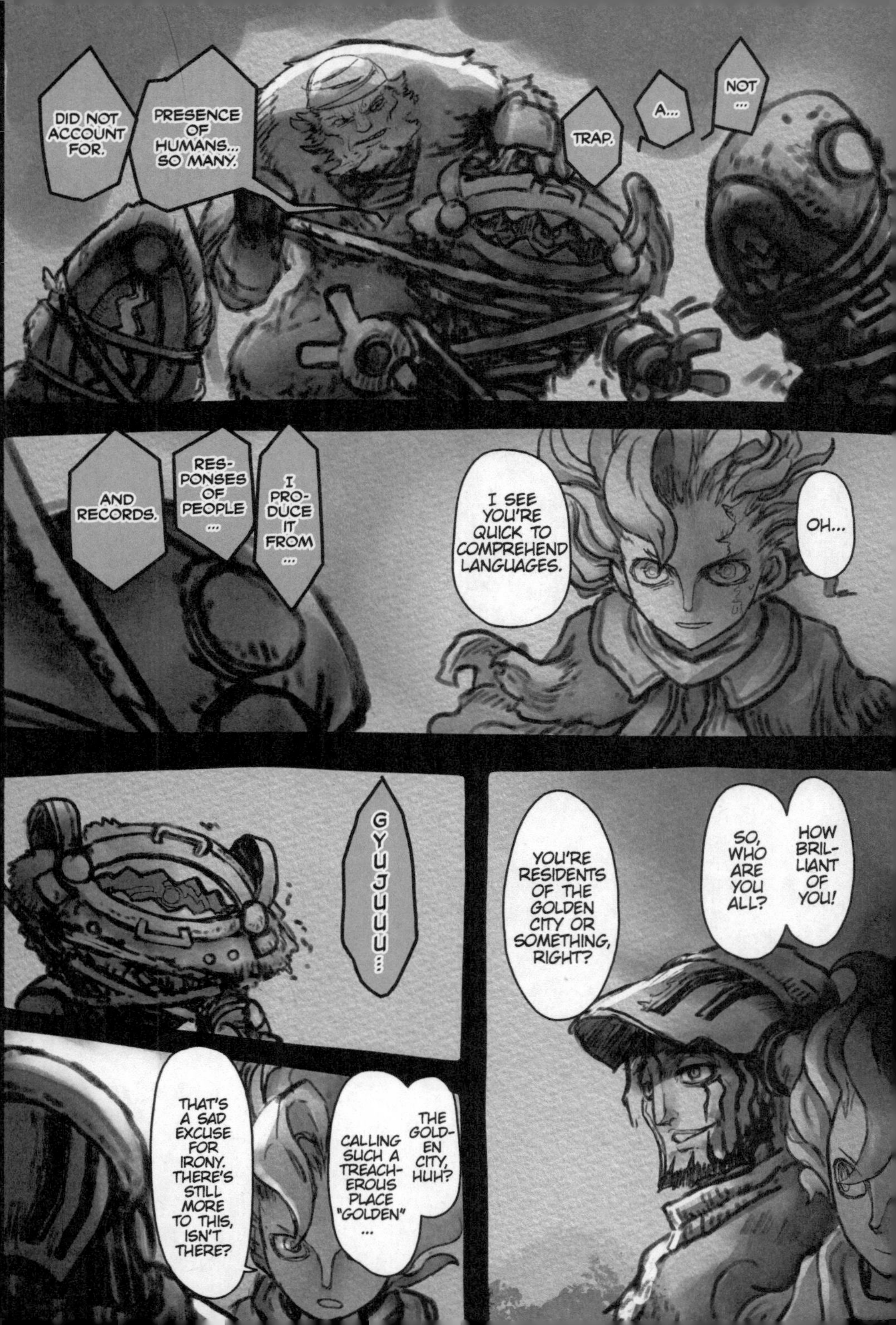
NOT...
A...
TRAP.
PRESENCE OF HUMANS... SO MANY.
DID NOT ACCOUNT FOR.
OH...
I SEE YOU'RE QUICK TO COMPREHEND LANGUAGES.
I PRO-DUCE IT FROM...
RES-PONSES OF PEOPLE...
AND RECORDS.
HOW BRIL-LIANT OF YOU!
SO, WHO ARE YOU ALL?
YOU'RE RESIDENTS OF THE GOLDEN CITY OR SOMETHING, RIGHT?
GYUJUUU...
THE GOLD-EN CITY, HUH?
CALLING SUCH A TREACH-EROUS PLACE "GOLDEN"...
THAT'S A SAD EXCUSE FOR IRONY. THERE'S STILL MORE TO THIS, ISN'T THERE?

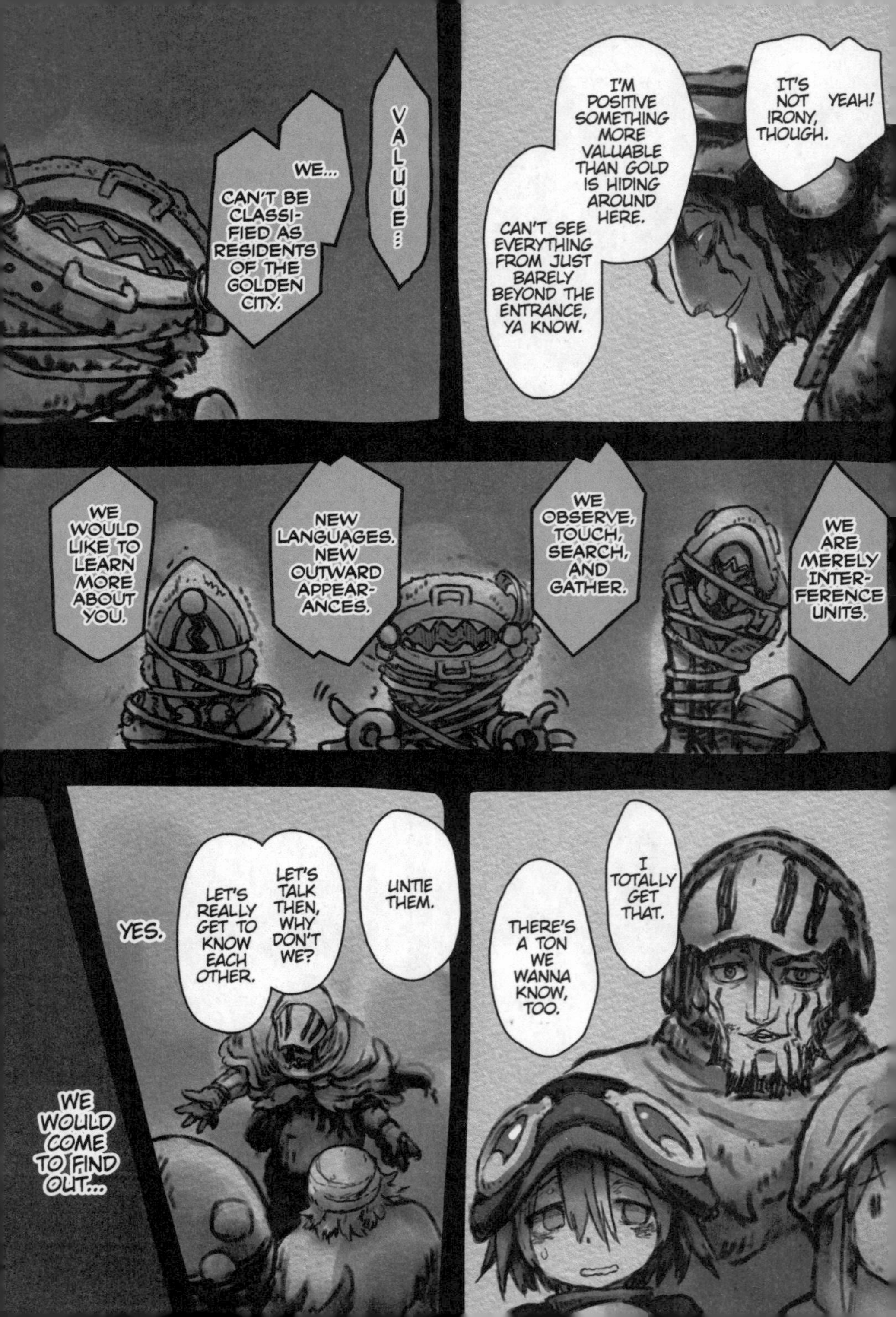
YEAH! IT'S NOT IRONY, THOUGH.
I'M POSITIVE SOMETHING MORE VALUABLE THAN GOLD IS HIDING AROUND HERE.
CAN'T SEE EVERYTHING FROM JUST BARELY BEYOND THE ENTRANCE, YA KNOW.
VALUUE...
WE... CAN'T BE CLASSIFIED AS RESIDENTS OF THE GOLDEN CITY.
WE ARE MERELY INTERFERENCE UNITS.
WE OBSERVE, TOUCH, SEARCH, AND GATHER.
NEW LANGUAGES. NEW OUTWARD APPEARANCES.
WE WOULD LIKE TO LEARN MORE ABOUT YOU.
I TOTALLY GET THAT.
THERE'S A TON WE WANNA KNOW, TOO.
UNTIE THEM.
LET'S TALK THEN, WHY DON'T WE?
LET'S REALLY GET TO KNOW EACH OTHER.
YES.
WE WOULD COME TO FIND OUT...

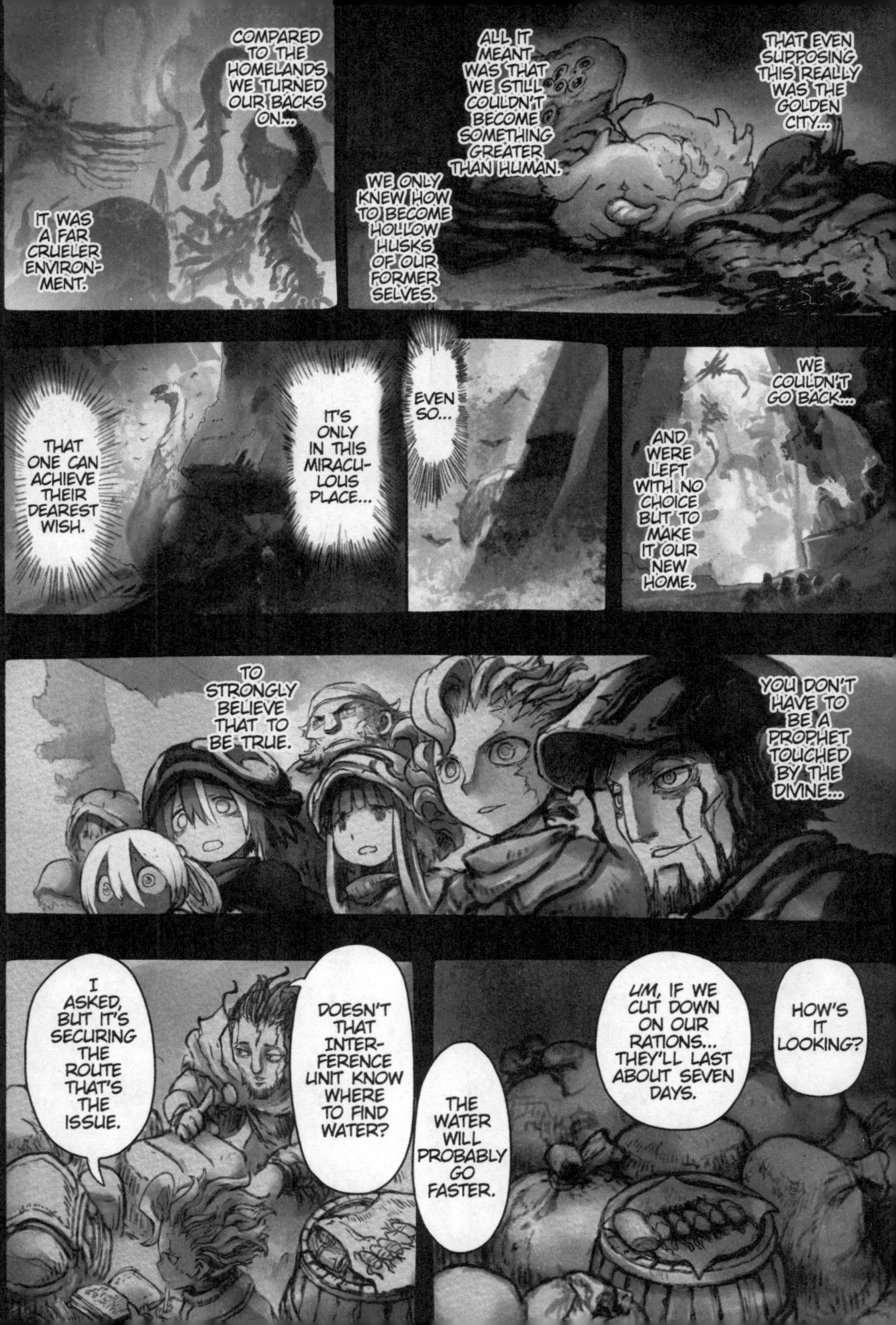
THAT EVEN SUPPOSING THIS REALLY WAS THE GOLDEN CITY...
ALL IT MEANT WAS THAT WE STILL COULDN'T BECOME SOMETHING GREATER THAN HUMAN.
WE ONLY KNEW HOW TO BECOME HOLLOW HUSKS OF OUR FORMER SELVES.
COMPARED TO THE HOMELANDS WE TURNED OUR BACKS ON...
IT WAS A FAR CRUELER ENVIRONMENT.
WE COULDN'T GO BACK...
AND WERE LEFT WITH NO CHOICE BUT TO MAKE IT OUR NEW HOME.
EVEN SO...
IT'S ONLY IN THIS MIRACULOUS PLACE...
THAT ONE CAN ACHIEVE THEIR DEAREST WISH.
YOU DON'T HAVE TO BE A PROPHET TOUCHED BY THE DIVINE...
TO STRONGLY BELIEVE THAT TO BE TRUE.
HOW'S IT LOOKING?
UM, IF WE CUT DOWN ON OUR RATIONS... THEY'LL LAST ABOUT SEVEN DAYS.
THE WATER WILL PROBABLY GO FASTER.
DOESN'T THAT INTERFERENCE UNIT KNOW WHERE TO FIND WATER?
I ASKED, BUT IT'S SECURING THE ROUTE THAT'S THE ISSUE.

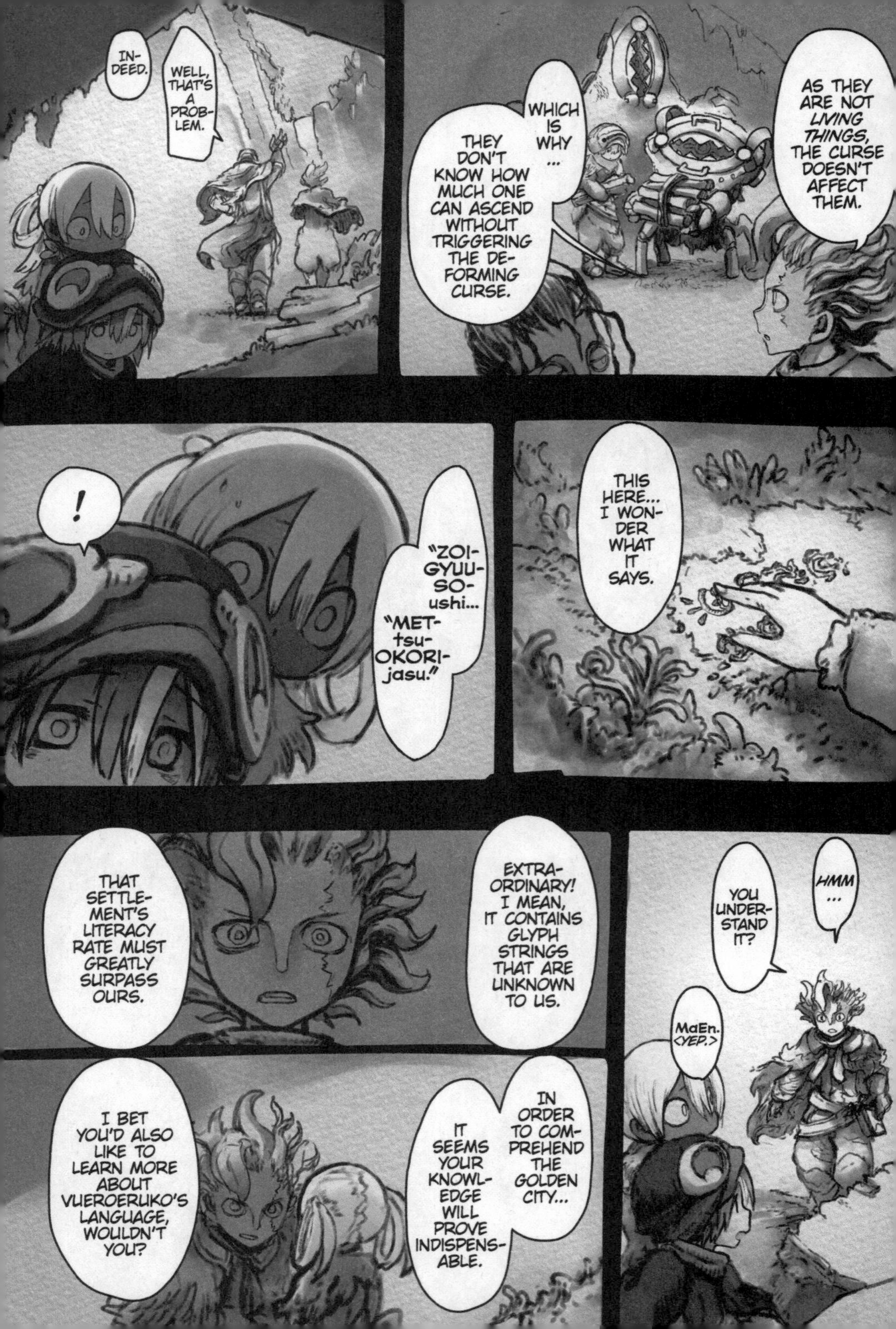
AS THEY ARE NOT *LIVING THINGS*, THE CURSE DOESN'T AFFECT THEM.
WHICH IS WHY...
THEY DON'T KNOW HOW MUCH ONE CAN ASCEND WITHOUT TRIGGERING THE DEFORMING CURSE.
WELL, THAT'S A PROBLEM.
INDEED.
THIS HERE... I WONDER WHAT IT SAYS.
"ZOI-GYUU-SO-ushi... "MET-tsu-OKORI-jasu."
!
HMM...
YOU UNDERSTAND IT?
MaEn. <YEP.>
EXTRAORDINARY! I MEAN, IT CONTAINS GLYPH STRINGS THAT ARE UNKNOWN TO US.
THAT SETTLEMENT'S LITERACY RATE MUST GREATLY SURPASS OURS.
IN ORDER TO COMPREHEND THE GOLDEN CITY...
IT SEEMS YOUR KNOWLEDGE WILL PROVE INDISPENSABLE.
I BET YOU'D ALSO LIKE TO LEARN MORE ABOUT VUEROERUKO'S LANGUAGE, WOULDN'T YOU?

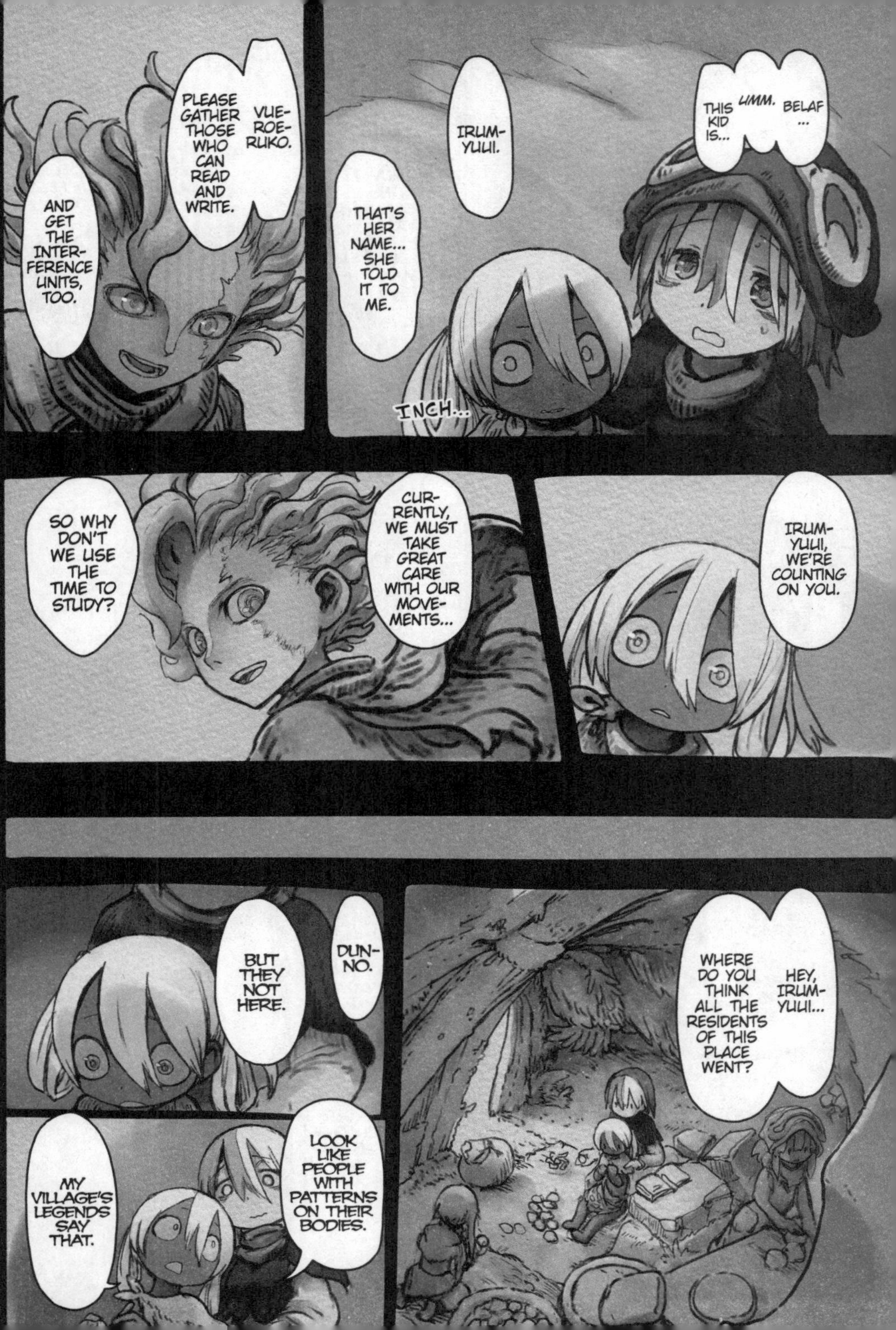
BELAF... UMM. THIS KID IS...
IRUMYUUI.
THAT'S HER NAME... SHE TOLD IT TO ME.
INCH...
VUEROERUKO.
PLEASE GATHER THOSE WHO CAN READ AND WRITE.
AND GET THE INTERFERENCE UNITS, TOO.
IRUMYUUI, WE'RE COUNTING ON YOU.
CURRENTLY, WE MUST TAKE GREAT CARE WITH OUR MOVEMENTS...
SO WHY DON'T WE USE THE TIME TO STUDY?
HEY, IRUMYUUI...
WHERE DO YOU THINK ALL THE RESIDENTS OF THIS PLACE WENT?
DUNNO.
BUT THEY NOT HERE.
LOOK LIKE PEOPLE WITH PATTERNS ON THEIR BODIES.
MY VILLAGE'S LEGENDS SAY THAT.

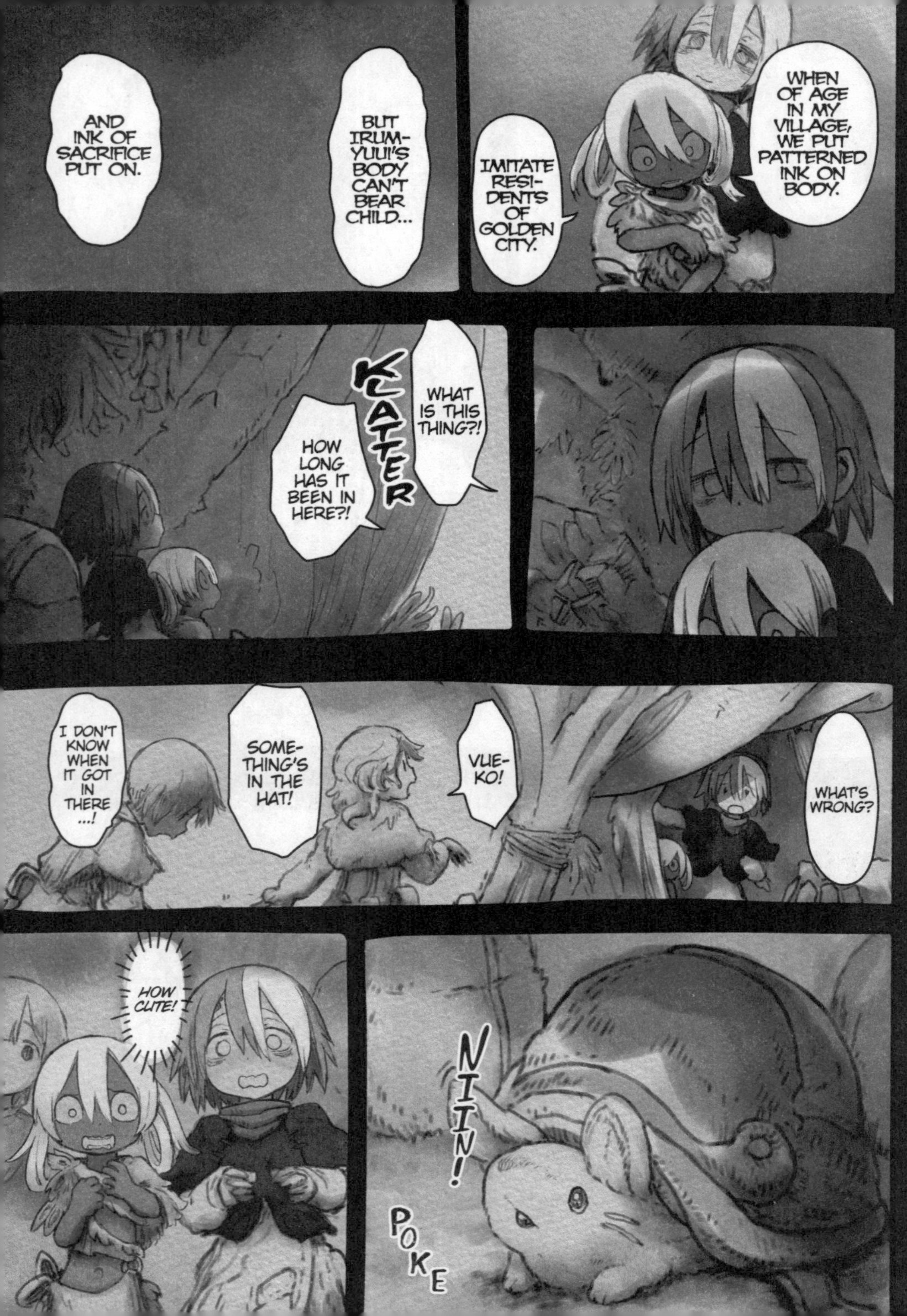
WHEN OF AGE IN MY VILLAGE, WE PUT PATTERNED INK ON BODY.
IMITATE RESIDENTS OF GOLDEN CITY.
BUT IRUMYUUI'S BODY CAN'T BEAR CHILD...
AND INK OF SACRIFICE PUT ON.
WHAT IS THIS THING?!
KLATTER
HOW LONG HAS IT BEEN IN HERE?!
WHAT'S WRONG?
VUEKO!
SOMETHING'S IN THE HAT!
I DON'T KNOW WHEN IT GOT IN THERE ...!
NIIIN!
POKE
HOW CUTE!

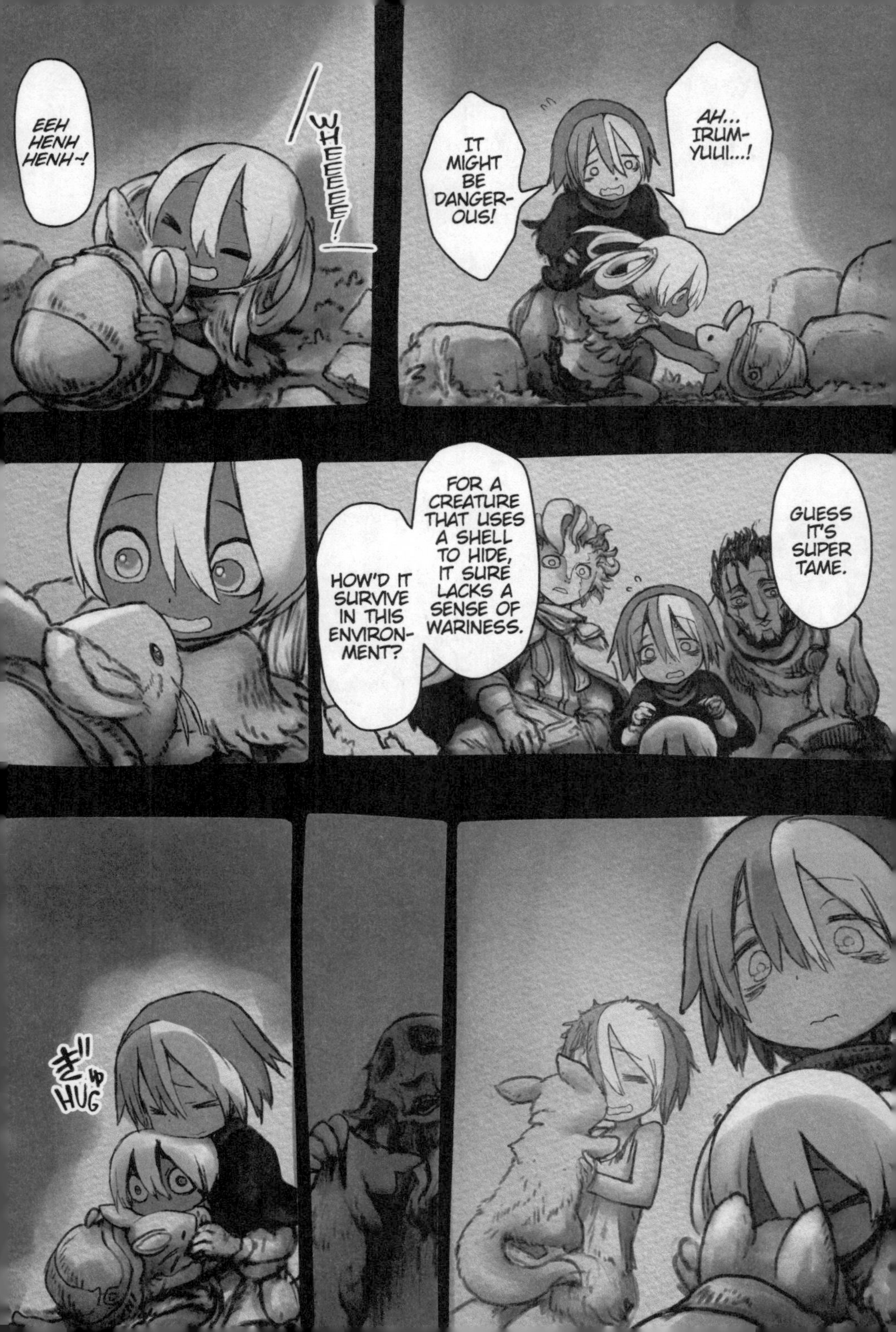
AH... IRUM-YUUI...!
IT MIGHT BE DANGER-OUS!
WHEEEEEE!
EEH HENH HENH~!
GUESS IT'S SUPER TAME.
FOR A CREATURE THAT USES A SHELL TO HIDE, IT SURE LACKS A SENSE OF WARINESS.
HOW'D IT SURVIVE IN THIS ENVIRONMENT?
ぎゅ HUG

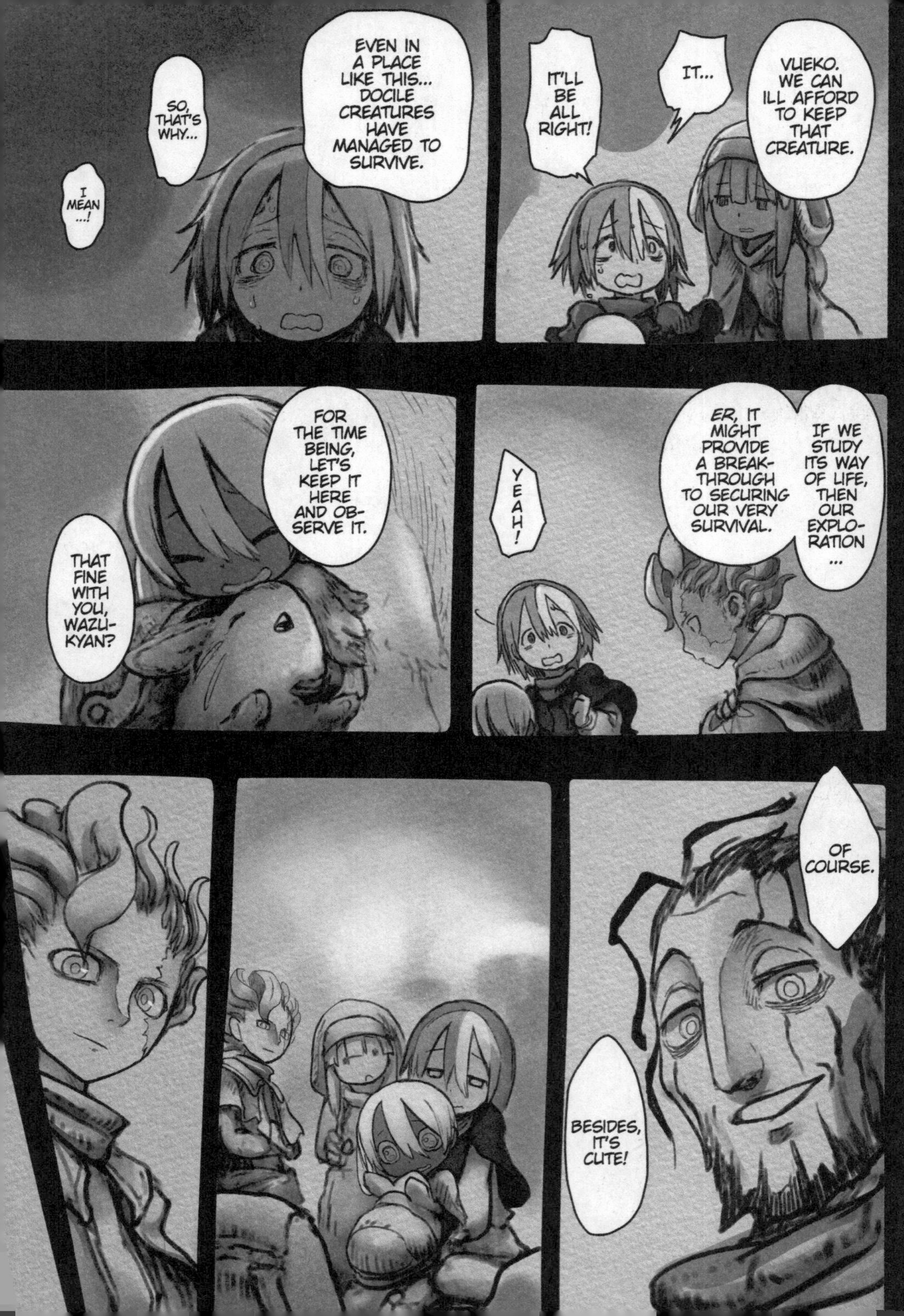
VUEKO. WE CAN ILL AFFORD TO KEEP THAT CREATURE.
IT...
IT'LL BE ALL RIGHT!
EVEN IN A PLACE LIKE THIS... DOCILE CREATURES HAVE MANAGED TO SURVIVE.
SO, THAT'S WHY...
I MEAN ...!
IF WE STUDY ITS WAY OF LIFE, THEN OUR EXPLO-RATION ...
ER, IT MIGHT PROVIDE A BREAK-THROUGH TO SECURING OUR VERY SURVIVAL.
YEAH!
FOR THE TIME BEING, LET'S KEEP IT HERE AND OB-SERVE IT.
THAT FINE WITH YOU, WAZU-KYAN?
OF COURSE.
BESIDES, IT'S CUTE!

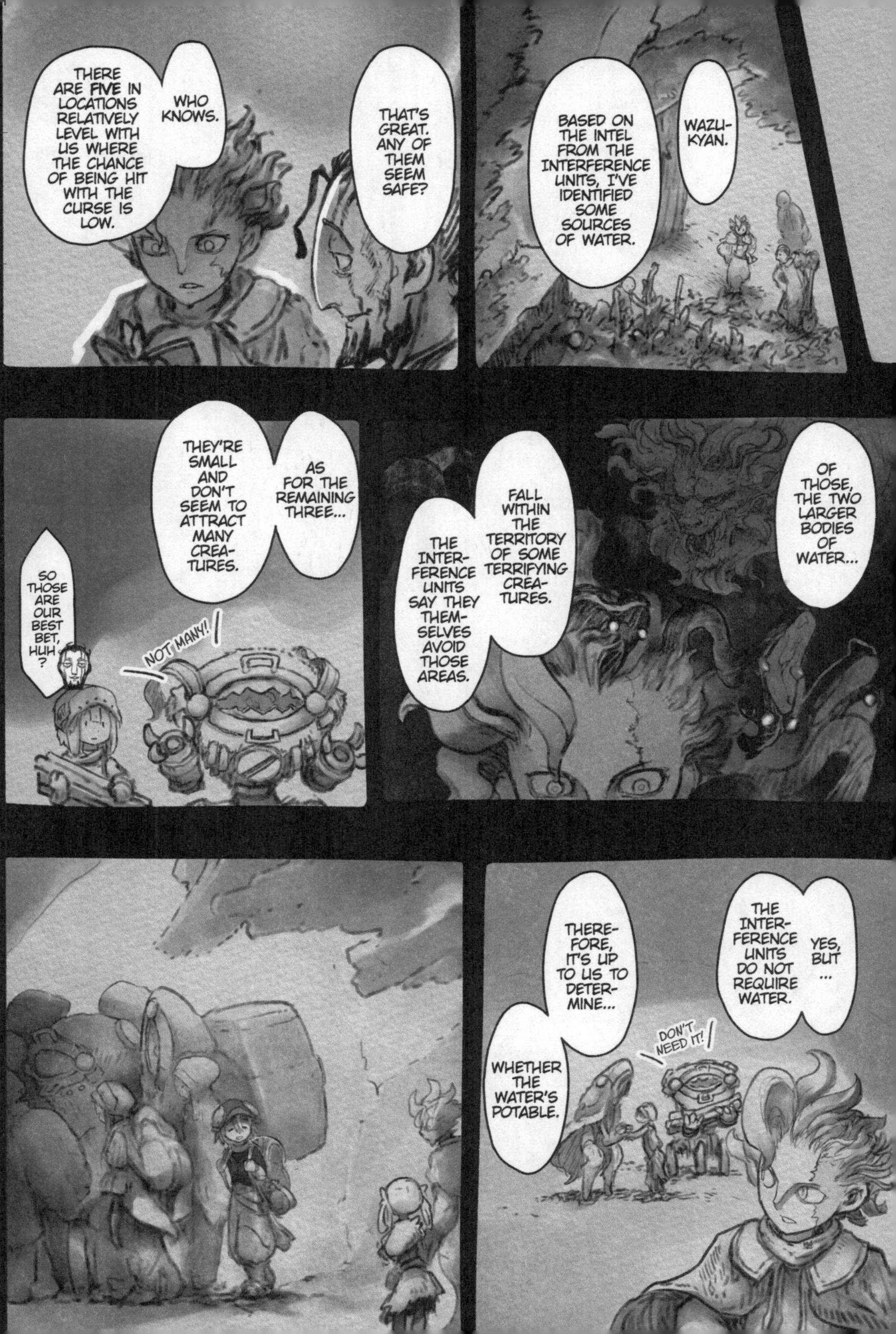
WAZUKYAN.
BASED ON THE INTEL FROM THE INTERFERENCE UNITS, I'VE IDENTIFIED SOME SOURCES OF WATER.
THAT'S GREAT. ANY OF THEM SEEM SAFE?
WHO KNOWS.
THERE ARE **FIVE** IN LOCATIONS RELATIVELY LEVEL WITH US WHERE THE CHANCE OF BEING HIT WITH THE CURSE IS LOW.
OF THOSE, THE TWO LARGER BODIES OF WATER...
FALL WITHIN THE TERRITORY OF SOME TERRIFYING CREATURES.
THE INTERFERENCE UNITS SAY THEY THEMSELVES AVOID THOSE AREAS.
AS FOR THE REMAINING THREE...
THEY'RE SMALL AND DON'T SEEM TO ATTRACT MANY CREATURES.
SO THOSE ARE OUR BEST BET, HUH?
NOT MANY!
YES, BUT ...
THE INTERFERENCE UNITS DO NOT REQUIRE WATER.
DON'T NEED IT!
THEREFORE, IT'S UP TO US TO DETERMINE...
WHETHER THE WATER'S POTABLE.

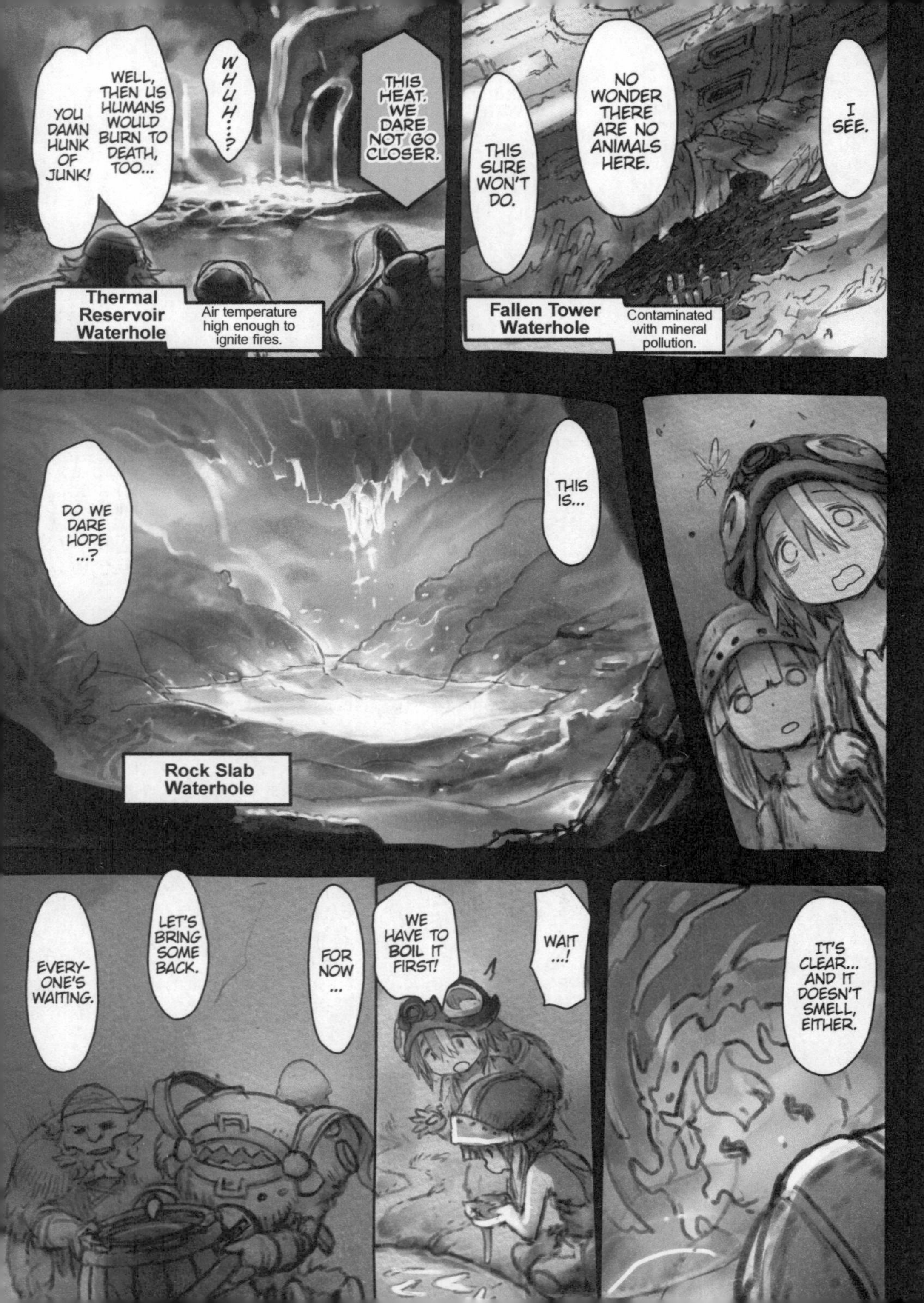
I SEE.
NO WONDER THERE ARE NO ANIMALS HERE.
THIS SURE WON'T DO.
Fallen Tower Waterhole
Contaminated with mineral pollution.
THIS HEAT. WE DARE NOT GO CLOSER.
WHUH...?
WELL, THEN US HUMANS WOULD BURN TO DEATH, TOO...
YOU DAMN HUNK OF JUNK!
Thermal Reservoir Waterhole
Air temperature high enough to ignite fires.
THIS IS...
DO WE DARE HOPE ...?
Rock Slab Waterhole
IT'S CLEAR... AND IT DOESN'T SMELL, EITHER.
WAIT ...!
WE HAVE TO BOIL IT FIRST!
FOR NOW ...
LET'S BRING SOME BACK.
EVERY-ONE'S WAITING.

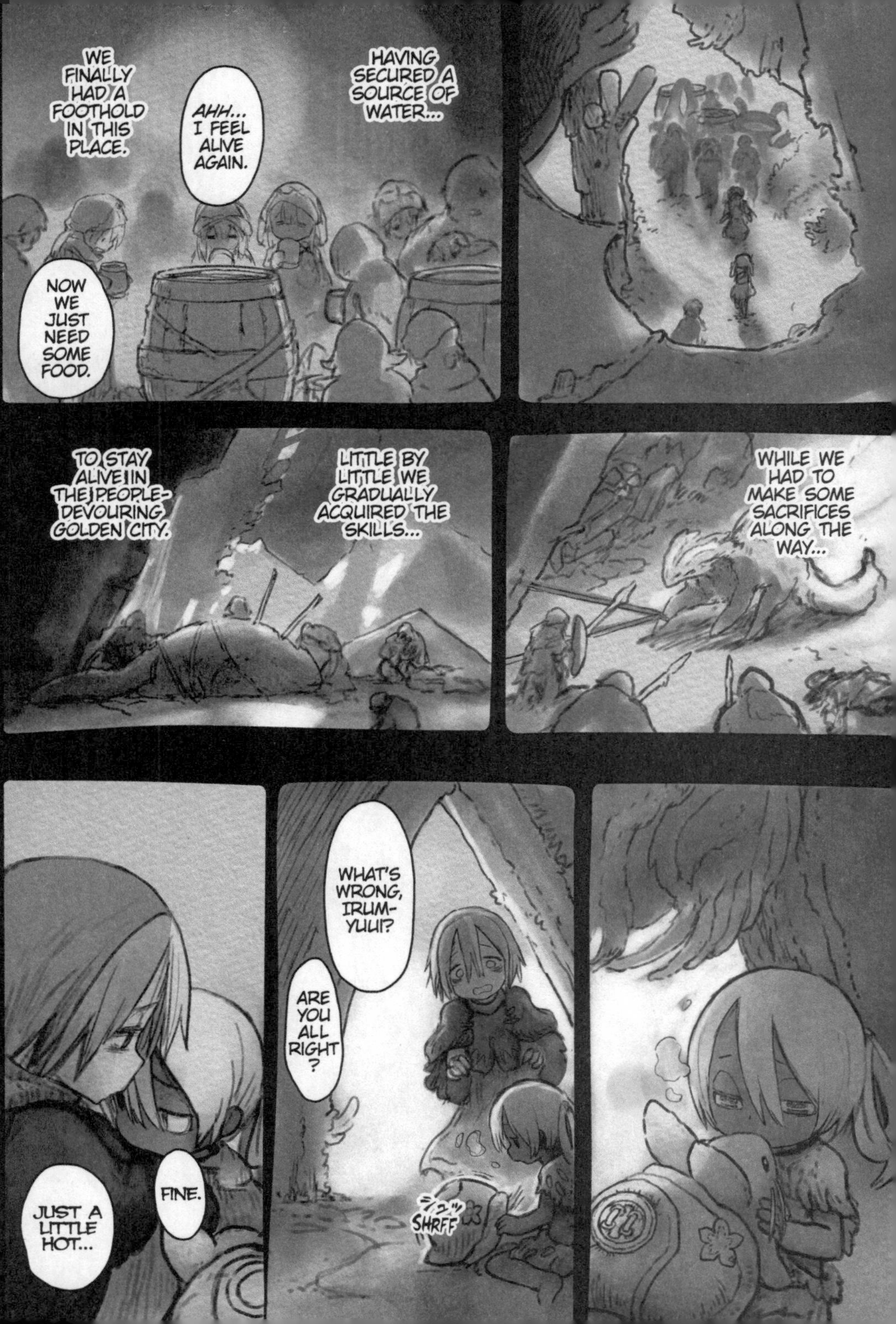
HAVING SECURED A SOURCE OF WATER...
AHH... I FEEL ALIVE AGAIN.
WE FINALLY HAD A FOOTHOLD IN THIS PLACE.
NOW WE JUST NEED SOME FOOD.
WHILE WE HAD TO MAKE SOME SACRIFICES ALONG THE WAY...
LITTLE BY LITTLE WE GRADUALLY ACQUIRED THE SKILLS...
TO STAY ALIVE IN THE PEOPLE-DEVOURING GOLDEN CITY.
WHAT'S WRONG, IRUM-YUUI?
ARE YOU ALL RIGHT?
SHRFF
FINE.
JUST A LITTLE HOT...

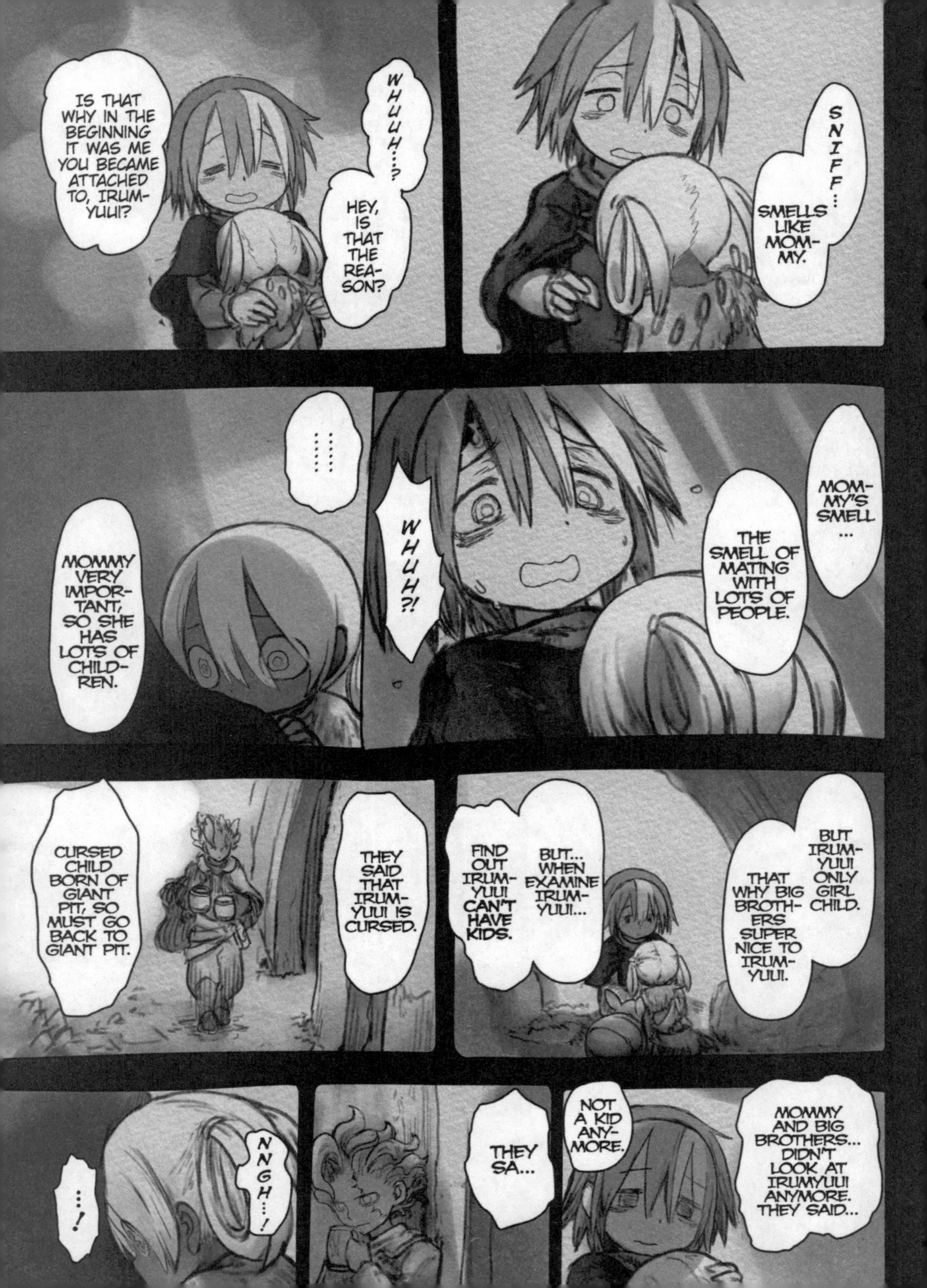

SNIFF...
SMELLS LIKE MOMMY.
WHUUH...?
IS THAT WHY IN THE BEGINNING IT WAS ME YOU BECAME ATTACHED TO, IRUMYUUI?
HEY, IS THAT THE REASON?
MOMMY'S SMELL...
THE SMELL OF MATING WITH LOTS OF PEOPLE.
WHUUH?!
......
MOMMY VERY IMPORTANT, SO SHE HAS LOTS OF CHILDREN.
BUT IRUMYUUI ONLY GIRL CHILD.
THAT WHY BIG BROTHERS SUPER NICE TO IRUMYUUI.
BUT... WHEN EXAMINE IRUMYUUI...
FIND OUT IRUMYUUI CAN'T HAVE KIDS.
THEY SAID THAT IRUMYUUI IS CURSED.
CURSED CHILD BORN OF GIANT PIT, SO MUST GO BACK TO GIANT PIT.
MOMMY AND BIG BROTHERS... DIDN'T LOOK AT IRUMYUUI ANYMORE. THEY SAID...
NOT A KID ANYMORE.
THEY SA...
NNGH...!
...!

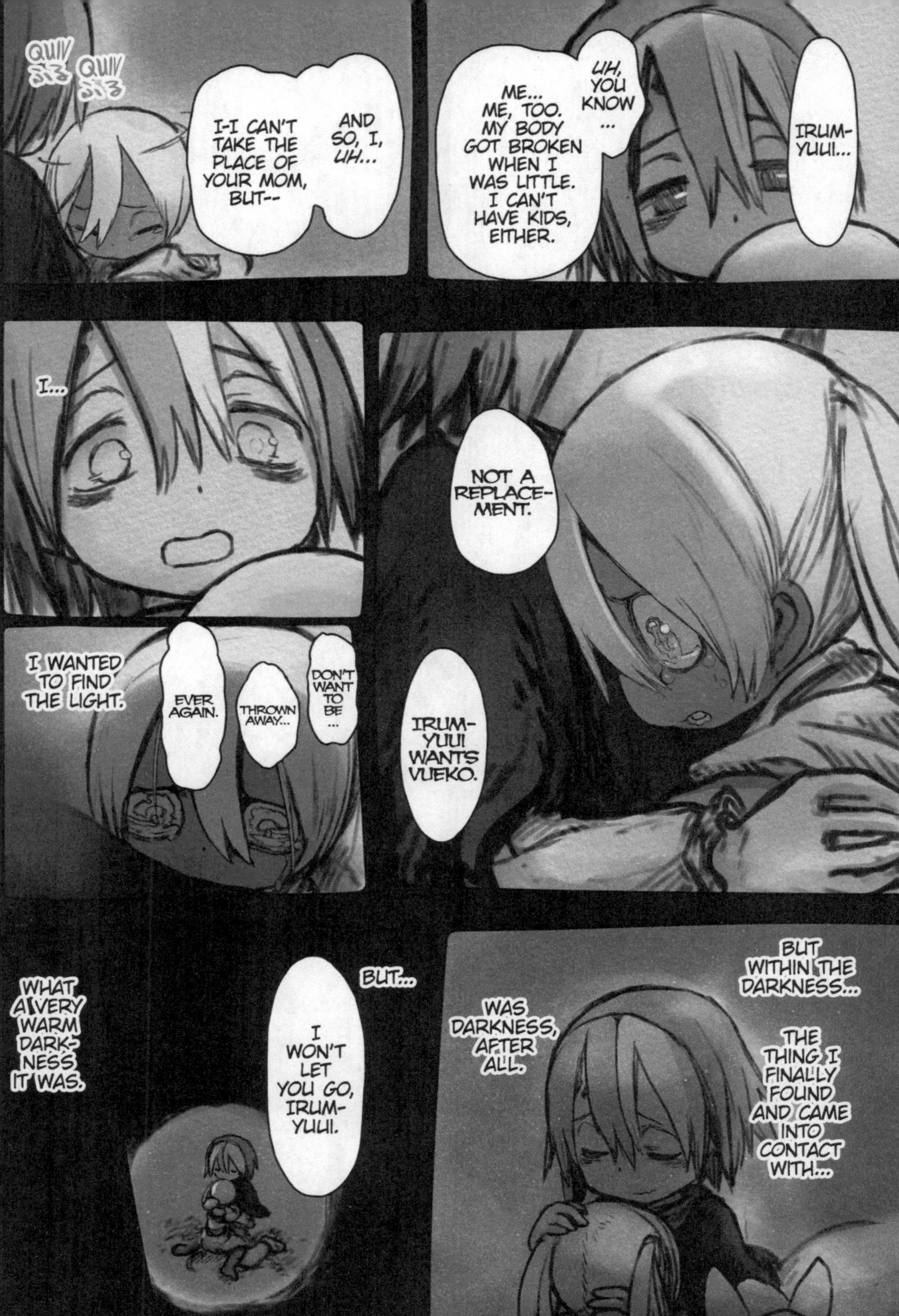
IRUM-YUUI...
UH, YOU KNOW ...
ME... ME, TOO. MY BODY GOT BROKEN WHEN I WAS LITTLE. I CAN'T HAVE KIDS, EITHER.
QUIV ふる QUIV ふる
AND SO, I, UH...
I-I CAN'T TAKE THE PLACE OF YOUR MOM, BUT--
NOT A REPLACEMENT.
IRUM-YUUI WANTS VUEKO.
I...
DON'T WANT TO BE ...
THROWN AWAY...
EVER AGAIN.
I WANTED TO FIND THE LIGHT.
BUT WITHIN THE DARKNESS...
THE THING I FINALLY FOUND AND CAME INTO CONTACT WITH...
WAS DARKNESS, AFTER ALL.
BUT...
I WON'T LET YOU GO, IRUM-YUUI.
WHAT A VERY WARM DARKNESS IT WAS.

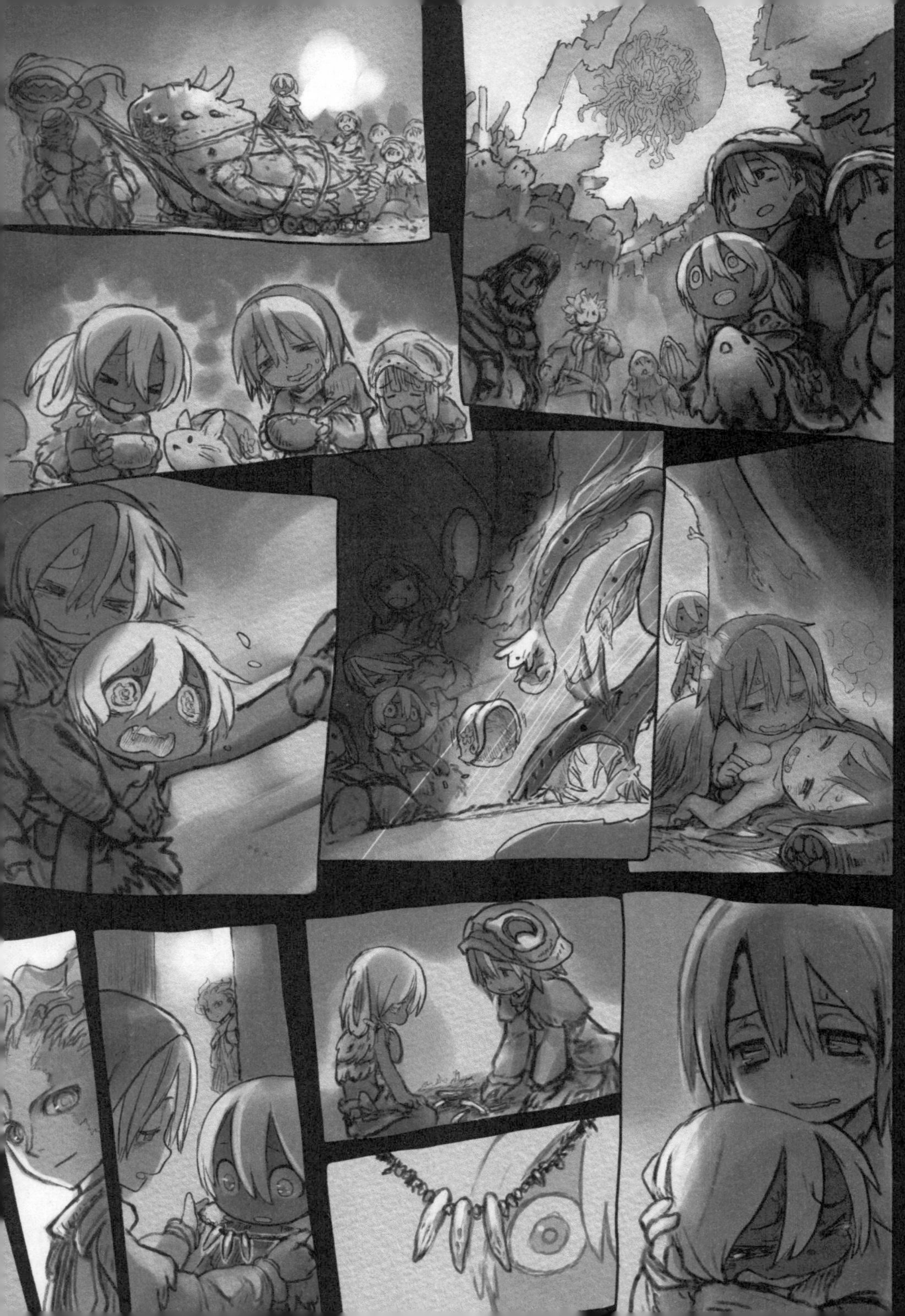

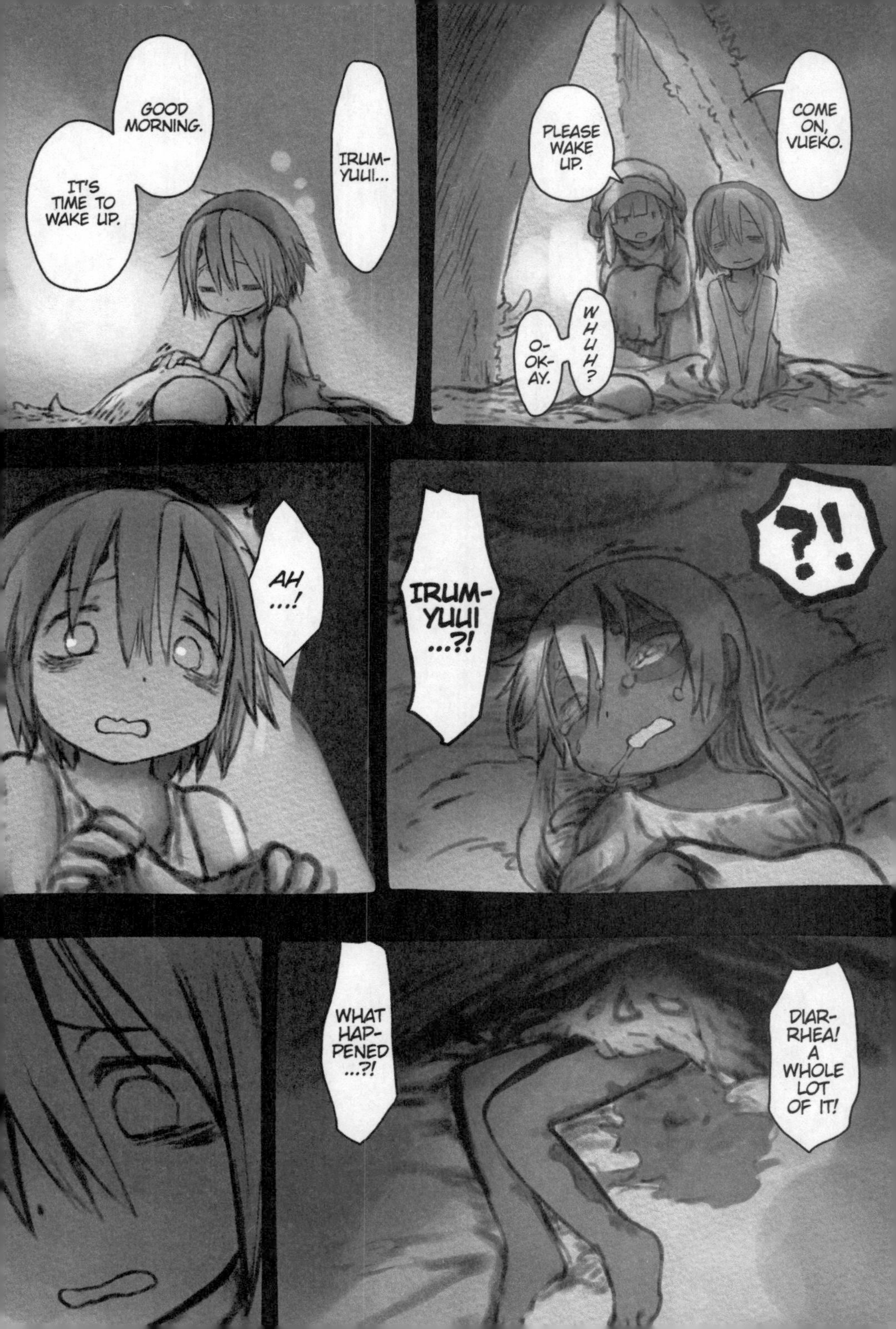
COME ON, VUEKO.
PLEASE WAKE UP.
WHUH?
O-OKAY.
IRUM-YUUI...
GOOD MORNING.
IT'S TIME TO WAKE UP.
?!
IRUM-YUUI ...?!
AH ...!
DIAR-RHEA! A WHOLE LOT OF IT!
WHAT HAP-PENED ...?!

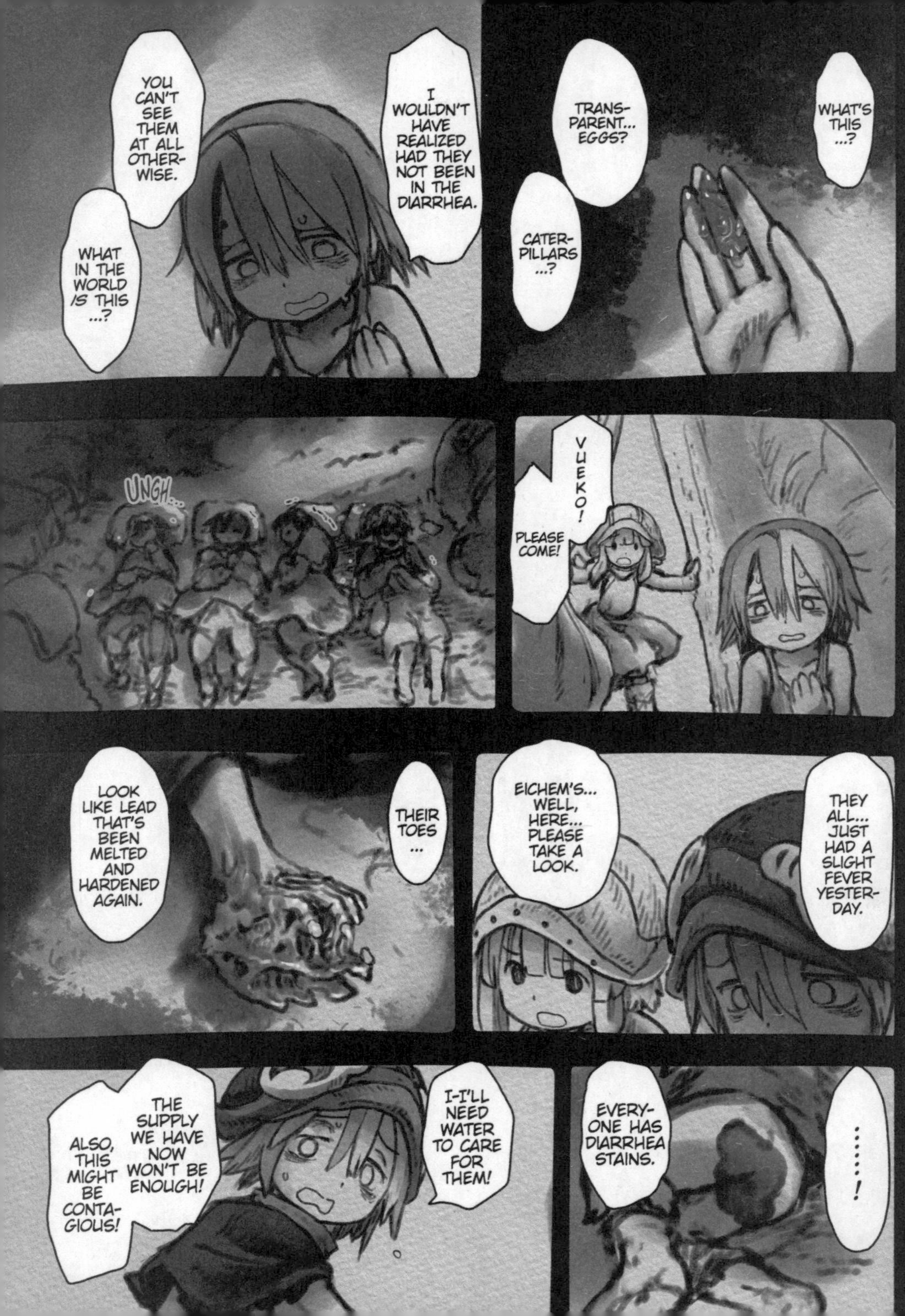

WHAT'S THIS ...?
TRANSPARENT... EGGS?
CATERPILLARS ...?
I WOULDN'T HAVE REALIZED HAD THEY NOT BEEN IN THE DIARRHEA.
YOU CAN'T SEE THEM AT ALL OTHERWISE.
WHAT IN THE WORLD IS THIS ...?
VUEKO!
PLEASE COME!
UNGH...
THEY ALL... JUST HAD A SLIGHT FEVER YESTERDAY.
EICHEM'S... WELL, HERE... PLEASE TAKE A LOOK.
THEIR TOES ...
LOOK LIKE LEAD THAT'S BEEN MELTED AND HARDENED AGAIN.
......!
EVERYONE HAS DIARRHEA STAINS.
I-I'LL NEED WATER TO CARE FOR THEM!
THE SUPPLY WE HAVE NOW WON'T BE ENOUGH!
ALSO, THIS MIGHT BE CONTAGIOUS!

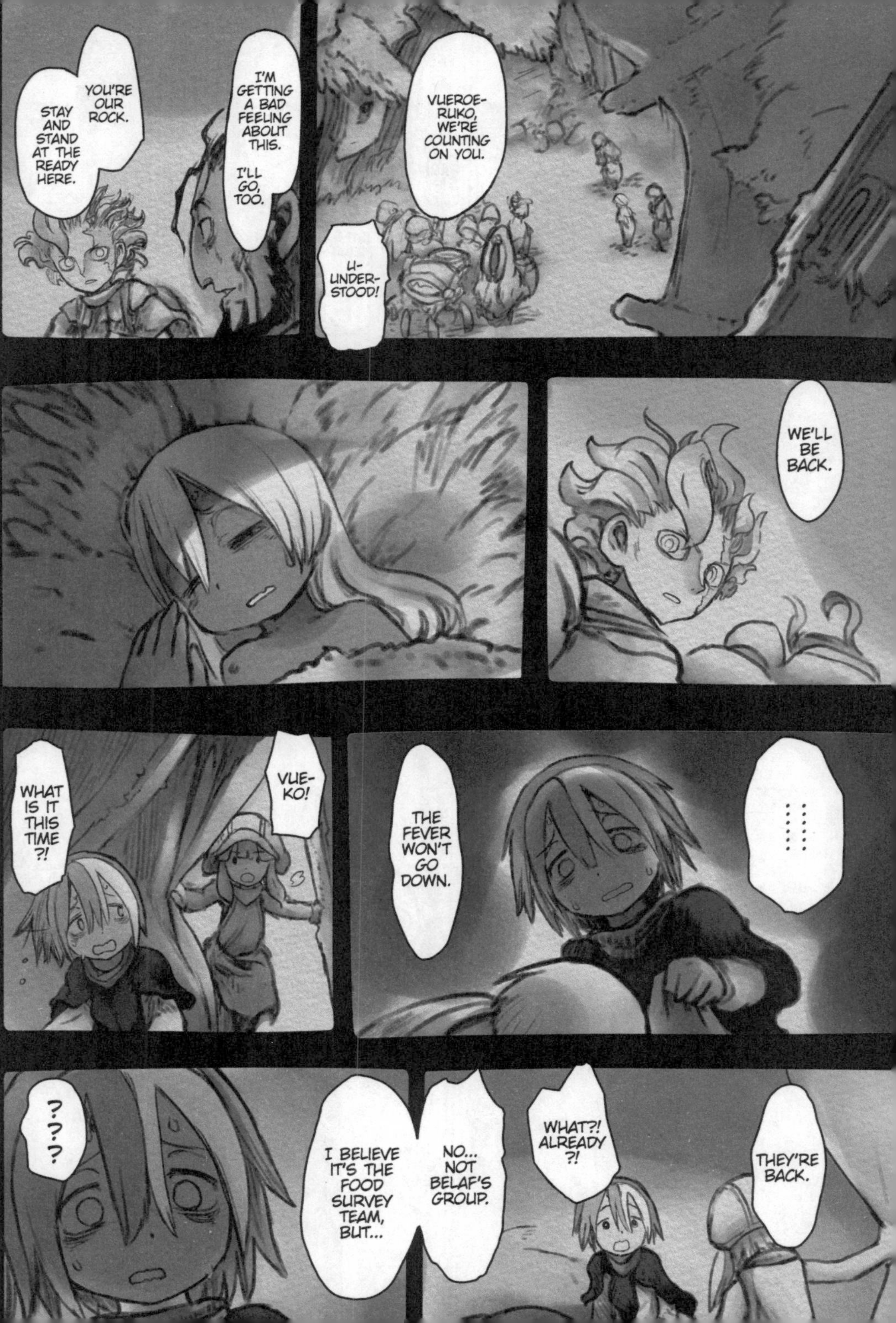
VUEROE-RUKO, WE'RE COUNTING ON YOU.
U-UNDERSTOOD!
I'M GETTING A BAD FEELING ABOUT THIS.
I'LL GO, TOO.
YOU'RE OUR ROCK.
STAY AND STAND AT THE READY HERE.
WE'LL BE BACK.
......
THE FEVER WON'T GO DOWN.
VUE-KO!
WHAT IS IT THIS TIME?!
THEY'RE BACK.
WHAT?! ALREADY?!
NO... NOT BELAF'S GROUP.
I BELIEVE IT'S THE FOOD SURVEY TEAM, BUT...
?.?.?

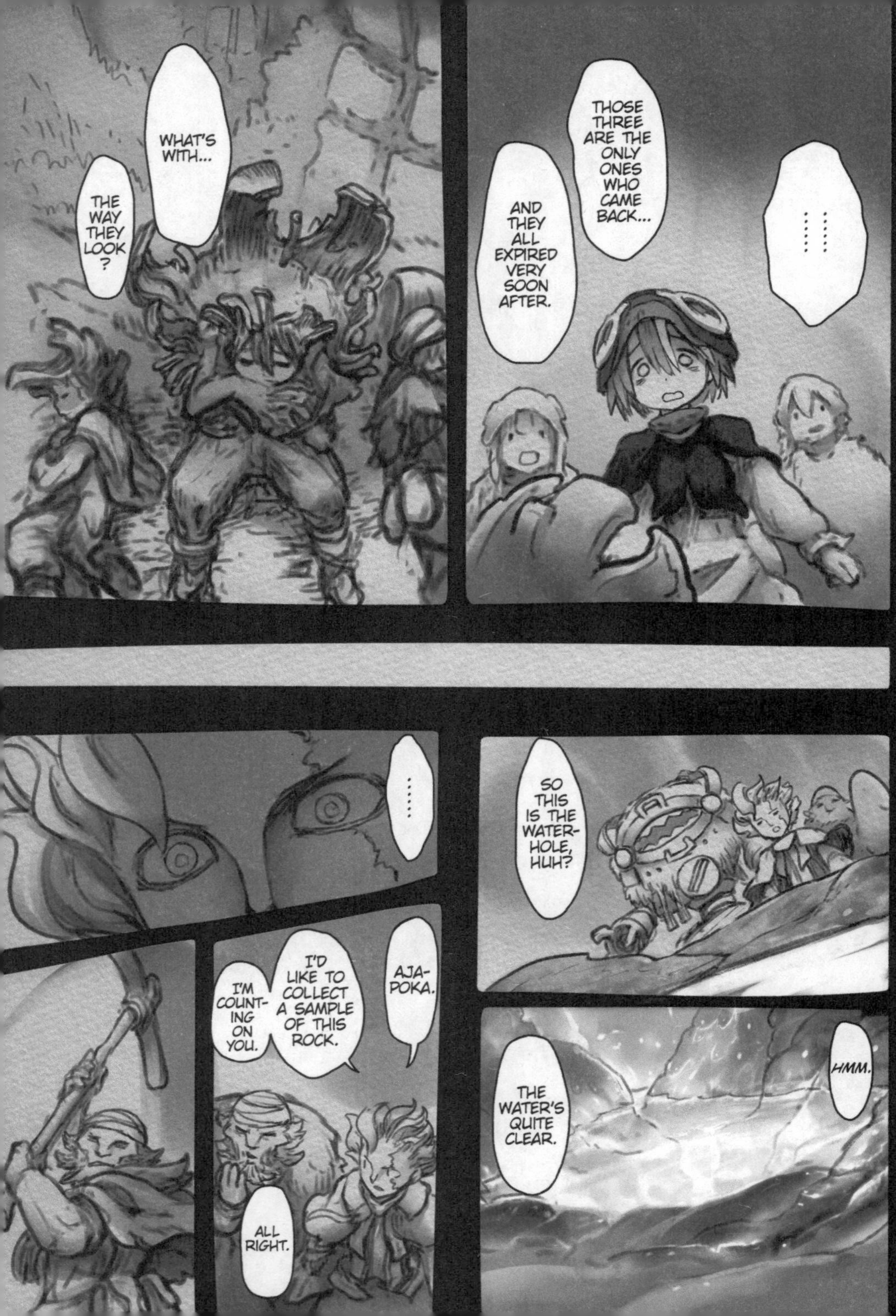
......
THOSE THREE ARE THE ONLY ONES WHO CAME BACK...
AND THEY ALL EXPIRED VERY SOON AFTER.
WHAT'S WITH...
THE WAY THEY LOOK?
SO THIS IS THE WATER-HOLE, HUH?
......
HMM.
THE WATER'S QUITE CLEAR.
AJA-POKA.
I'D LIKE TO COLLECT A SAMPLE OF THIS ROCK.
I'M COUNT-ING ON YOU.
ALL RIGHT.

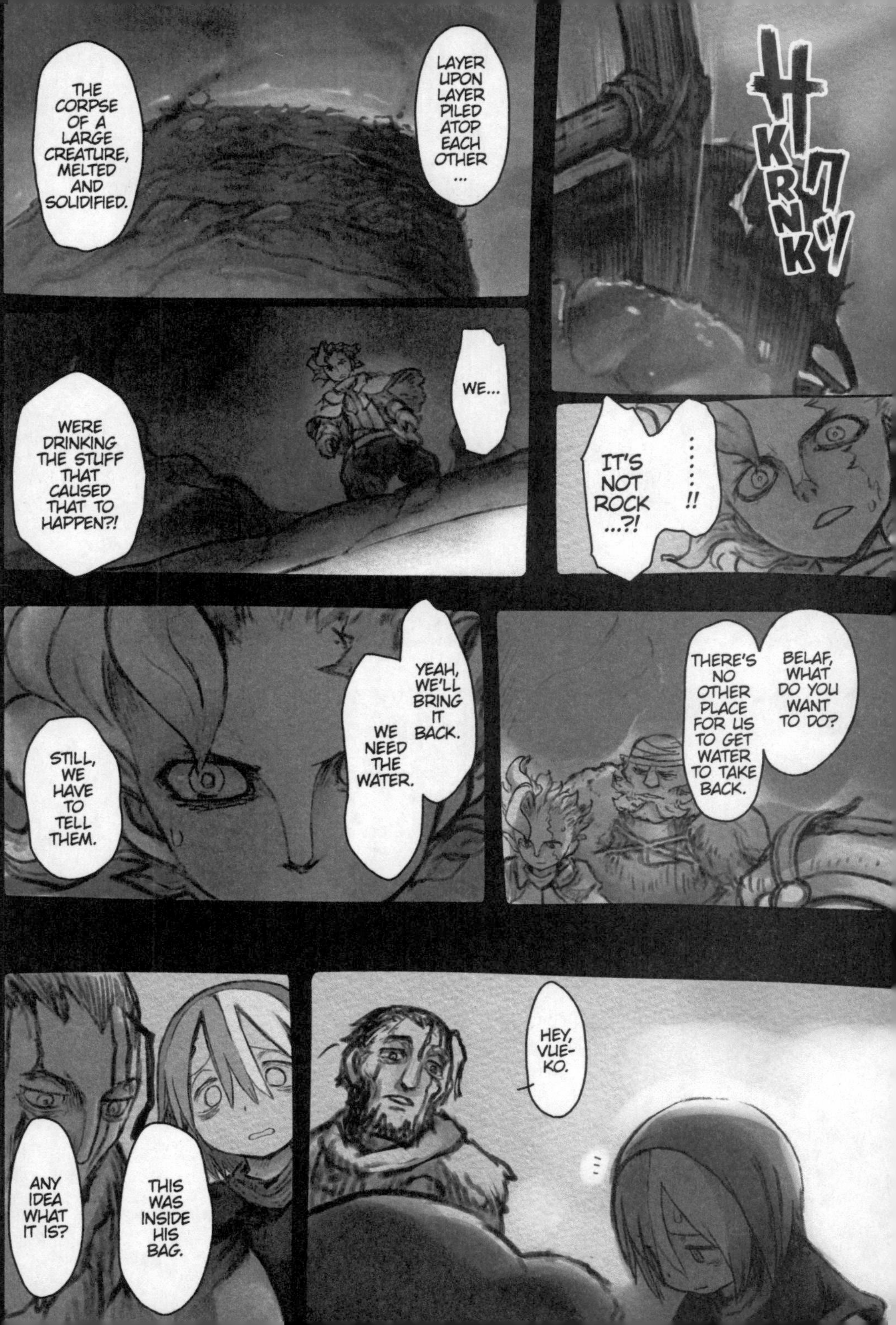
KRNK
......!!
IT'S NOT ROCK...?!
LAYER UPON LAYER PILED ATOP EACH OTHER...
THE CORPSE OF A LARGE CREATURE, MELTED AND SOLIDIFIED.
WE...
WERE DRINKING THE STUFF THAT CAUSED THAT TO HAPPEN?!
BELAF, WHAT DO YOU WANT TO DO?
THERE'S NO OTHER PLACE FOR US TO GET WATER TO TAKE BACK.
YEAH, WE'LL BRING IT BACK.
WE NEED THE WATER.
STILL, WE HAVE TO TELL THEM.
HEY, VUEKO.
THIS WAS INSIDE HIS BAG.
ANY IDEA WHAT IT IS?

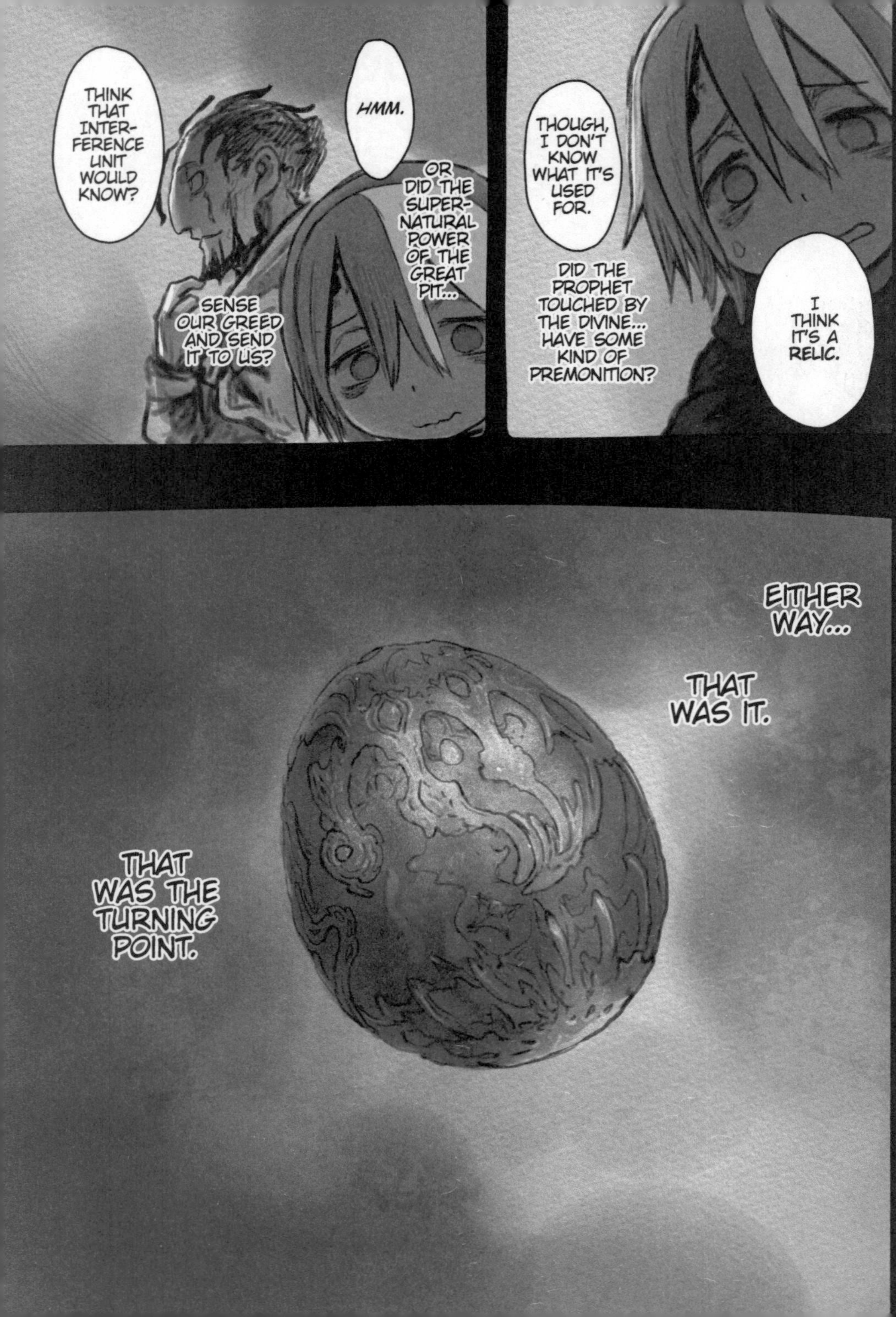
I THINK IT'S A RELIC.
THOUGH, I DON'T KNOW WHAT IT'S USED FOR.
DID THE PROPHET TOUCHED BY THE DIVINE... HAVE SOME KIND OF PREMONITION?
HMM.
OR DID THE SUPER-NATURAL POWER OF THE GREAT PIT...
SENSE OUR GREED AND SEND IT TO US?
THINK THAT INTER-FERENCE UNIT WOULD KNOW?
EITHER WAY...
THAT WAS IT.
THAT WAS THE TURNING POINT.

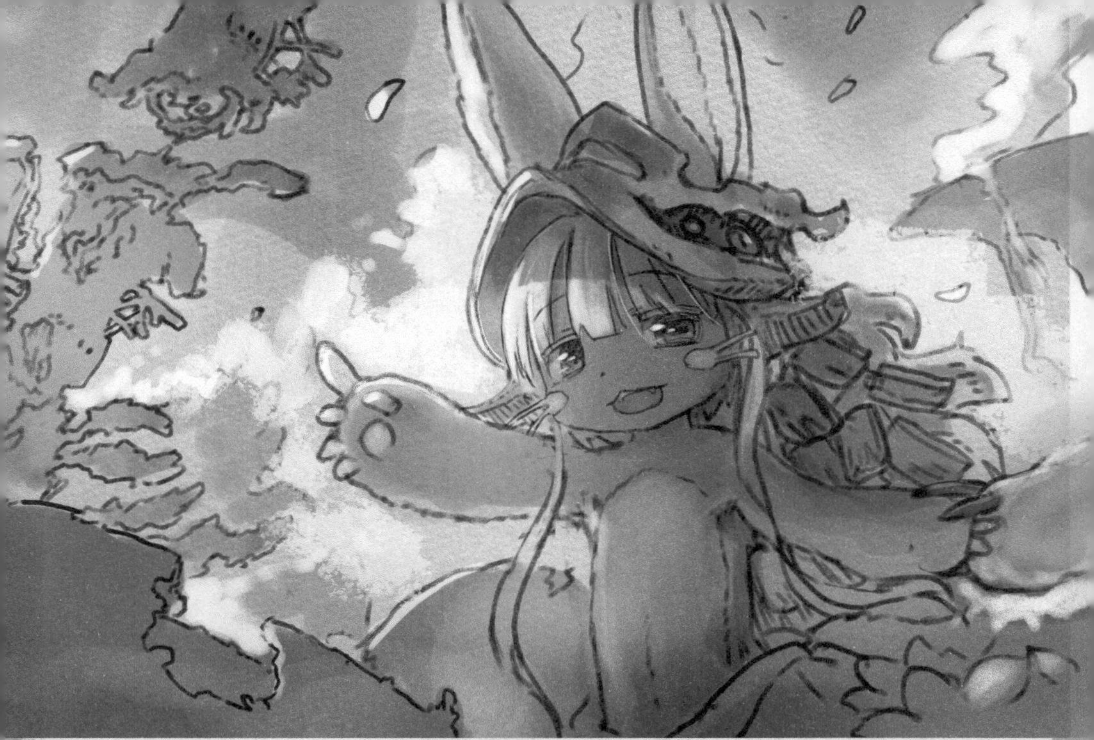

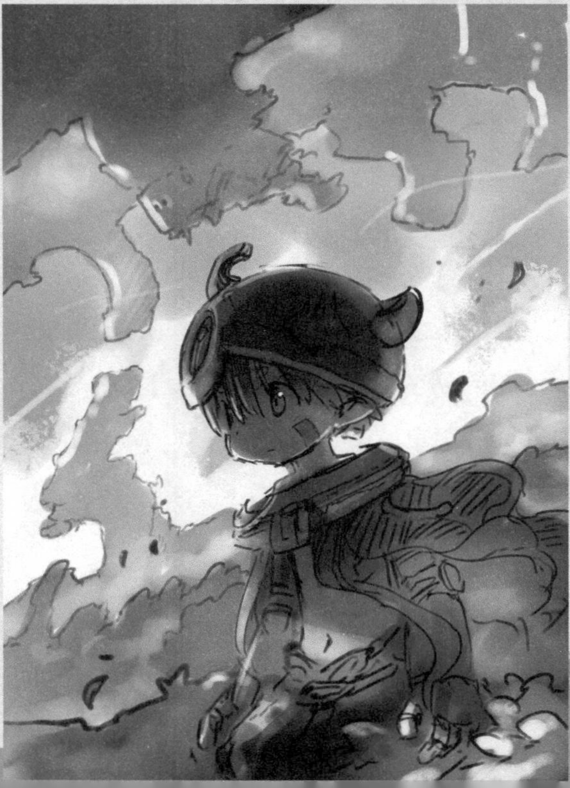

Live paintings from
Napoli COMICON 2019.

Top: Nanachi (about 40 minutes).
Bottom: Reg (during the rehearsal).

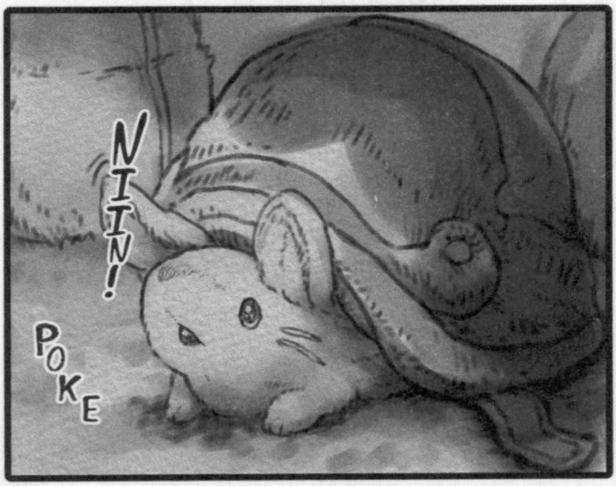
NIIIN!
POKE

MADE IN ABYSS

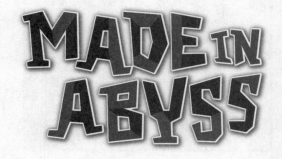

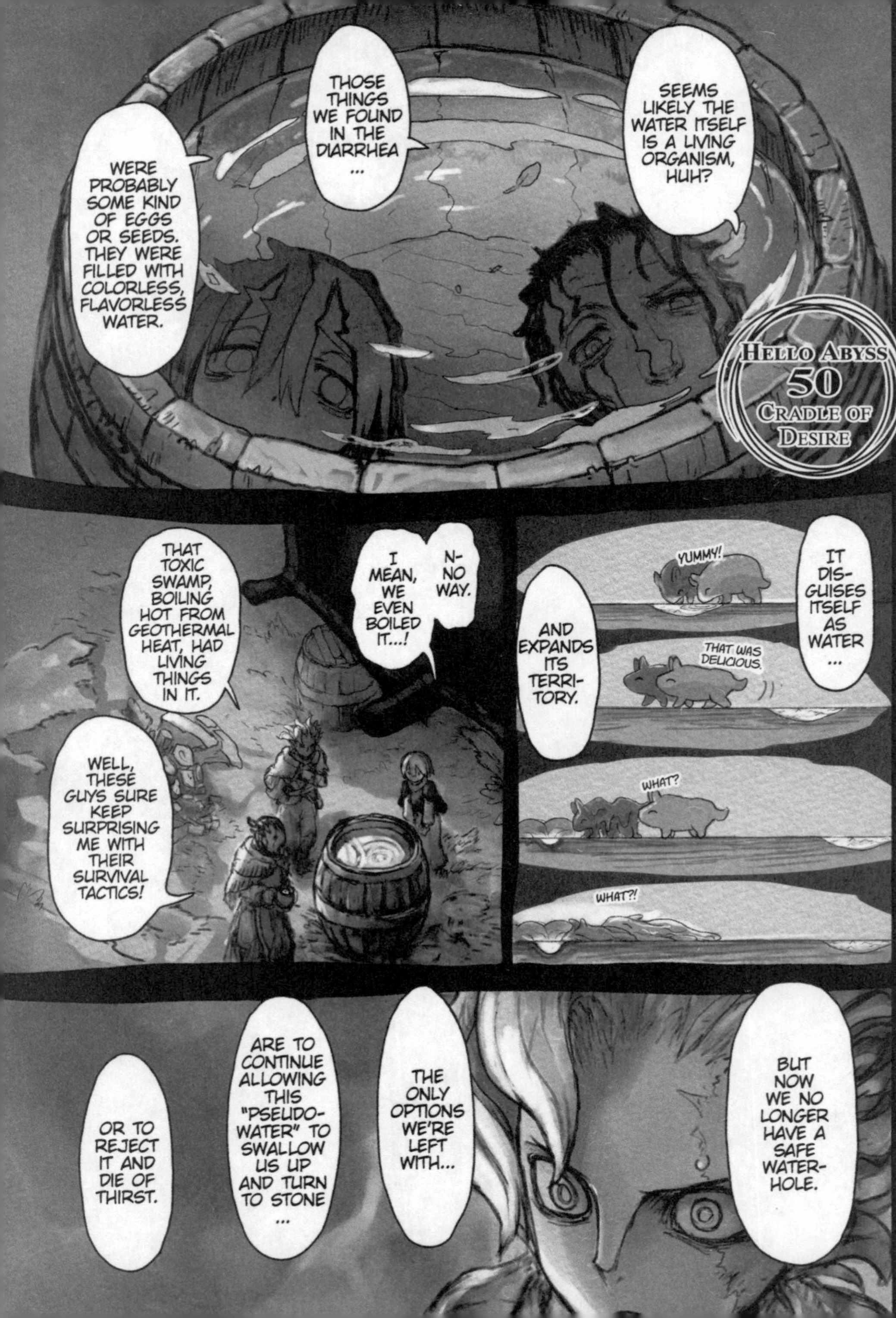
HELLO ABYSS 50 CRADLE OF DESIRE
SEEMS LIKELY THE WATER ITSELF IS A LIVING ORGANISM, HUH?
THOSE THINGS WE FOUND IN THE DIARRHEA ...
WERE PROBABLY SOME KIND OF EGGS OR SEEDS. THEY WERE FILLED WITH COLORLESS, FLAVORLESS WATER.
IT DISGUISES ITSELF AS WATER ...
AND EXPANDS ITS TERRITORY.
YUMMY!
THAT WAS DELICIOUS.
WHAT?
WHAT?!
N-NO WAY.
I MEAN, WE EVEN BOILED IT...!
THAT TOXIC SWAMP, BOILING HOT FROM GEOTHERMAL HEAT, HAD LIVING THINGS IN IT.
WELL, THESE GUYS SURE KEEP SURPRISING ME WITH THEIR SURVIVAL TACTICS!
BUT NOW WE NO LONGER HAVE A SAFE WATERHOLE.
THE ONLY OPTIONS WE'RE LEFT WITH...
ARE TO CONTINUE ALLOWING THIS "PSEUDO-WATER" TO SWALLOW US UP AND TURN TO STONE ...
OR TO REJECT IT AND DIE OF THIRST.

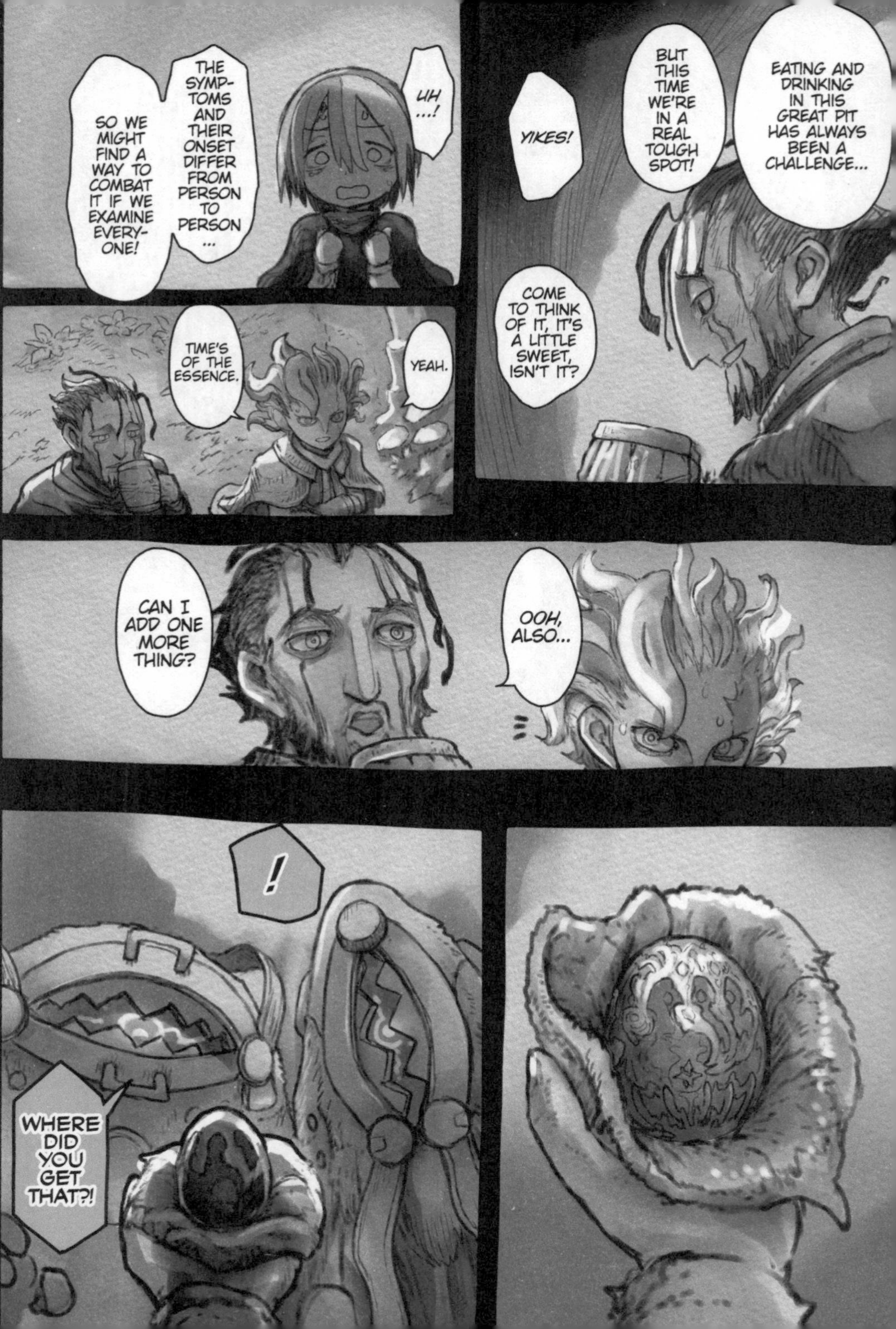
EATING AND DRINKING IN THIS GREAT PIT HAS ALWAYS BEEN A CHALLENGE...
BUT THIS TIME WE'RE IN A REAL TOUGH SPOT!
YIKES!
COME TO THINK OF IT, IT'S A LITTLE SWEET, ISN'T IT?
UH...!
THE SYMPTOMS AND THEIR ONSET DIFFER FROM PERSON TO PERSON...
SO WE MIGHT FIND A WAY TO COMBAT IT IF WE EXAMINE EVERYONE!
YEAH.
TIME'S OF THE ESSENCE.
OOH, ALSO...
CAN I ADD ONE MORE THING?
!
WHERE DID YOU GET THAT?!

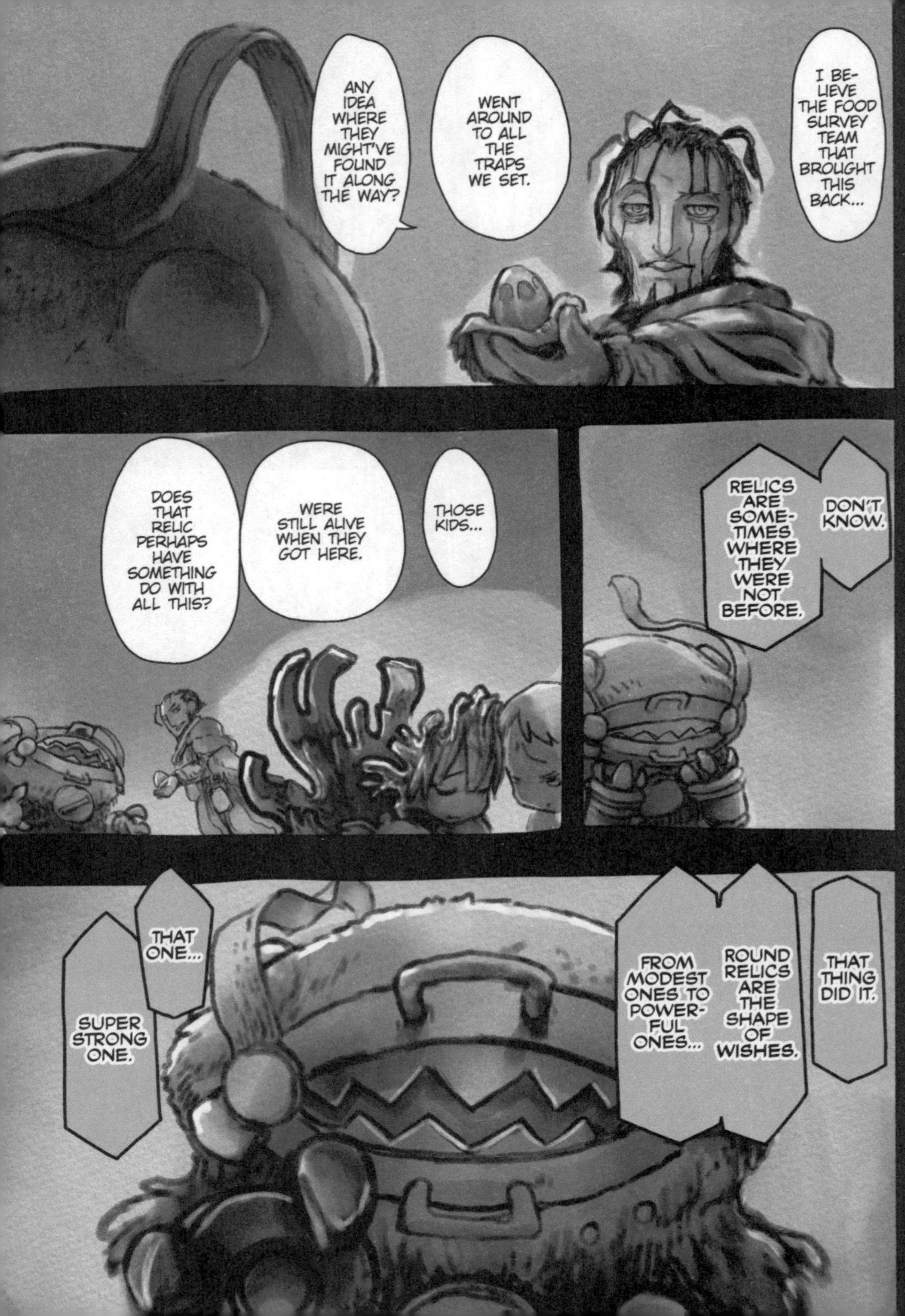
I BELIEVE THE FOOD SURVEY TEAM THAT BROUGHT THIS BACK...
WENT AROUND TO ALL THE TRAPS WE SET.
ANY IDEA WHERE THEY MIGHT'VE FOUND IT ALONG THE WAY?
DON'T KNOW.
RELICS ARE SOMETIMES WHERE THEY WERE NOT BEFORE.
THOSE KIDS...
WERE STILL ALIVE WHEN THEY GOT HERE.
DOES THAT RELIC PERHAPS HAVE SOMETHING DO WITH ALL THIS?
THAT THING DID IT.
ROUND RELICS ARE THE SHAPE OF WISHES.
FROM MODEST ONES TO POWERFUL ONES...
THAT ONE...
SUPER STRONG ONE.

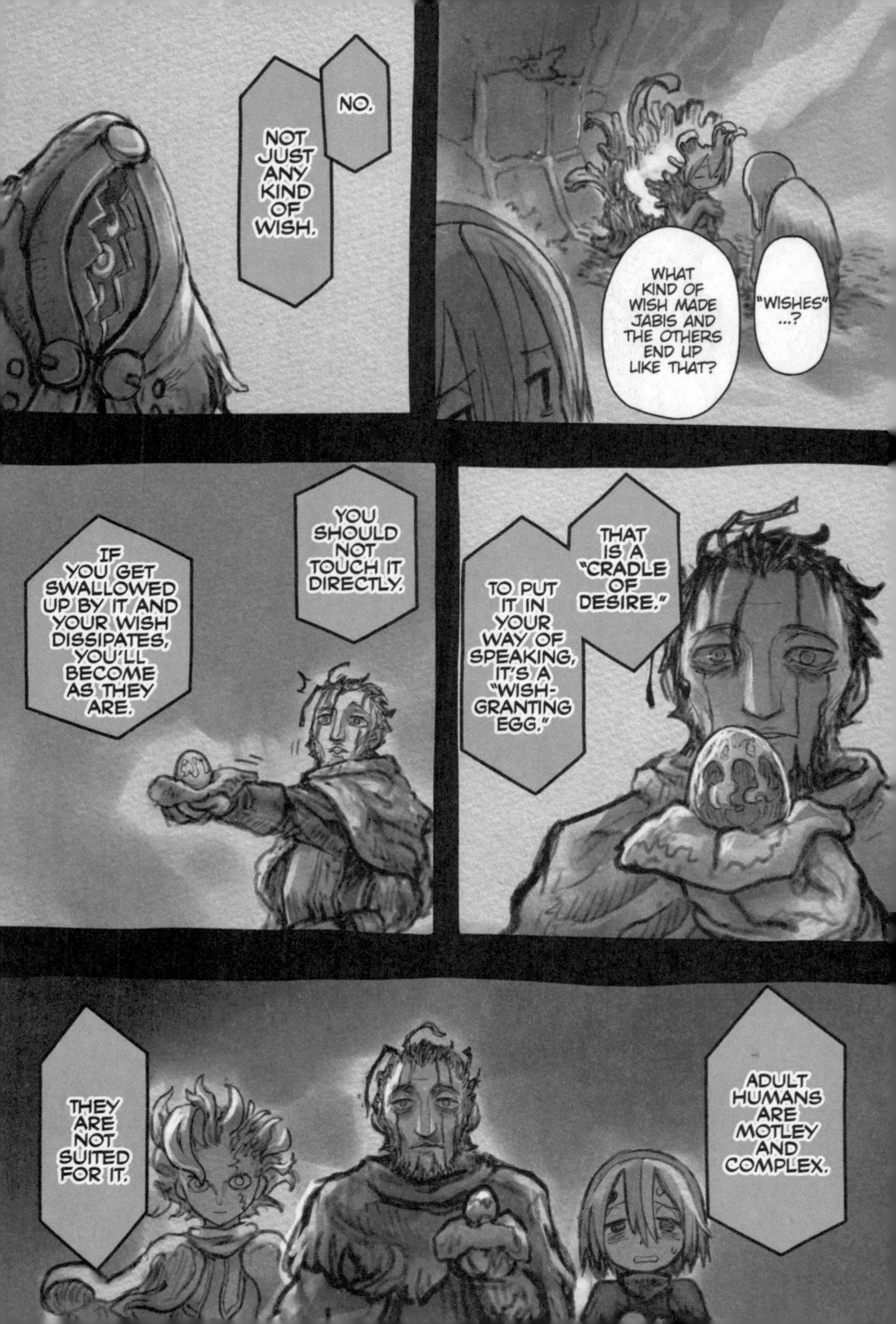
"WISHES"...?
WHAT KIND OF WISH MADE JABIS AND THE OTHERS END UP LIKE THAT?
NO.
NOT JUST ANY KIND OF WISH.
THAT IS A "CRADLE OF DESIRE."
TO PUT IT IN YOUR WAY OF SPEAKING, IT'S A "WISH-GRANTING EGG."
YOU SHOULD NOT TOUCH IT DIRECTLY.
IF YOU GET SWALLOWED UP BY IT AND YOUR WISH DISSIPATES, YOU'LL BECOME AS THEY ARE.
ADULT HUMANS ARE MOTLEY AND COMPLEX.
THEY ARE NOT SUITED FOR IT.

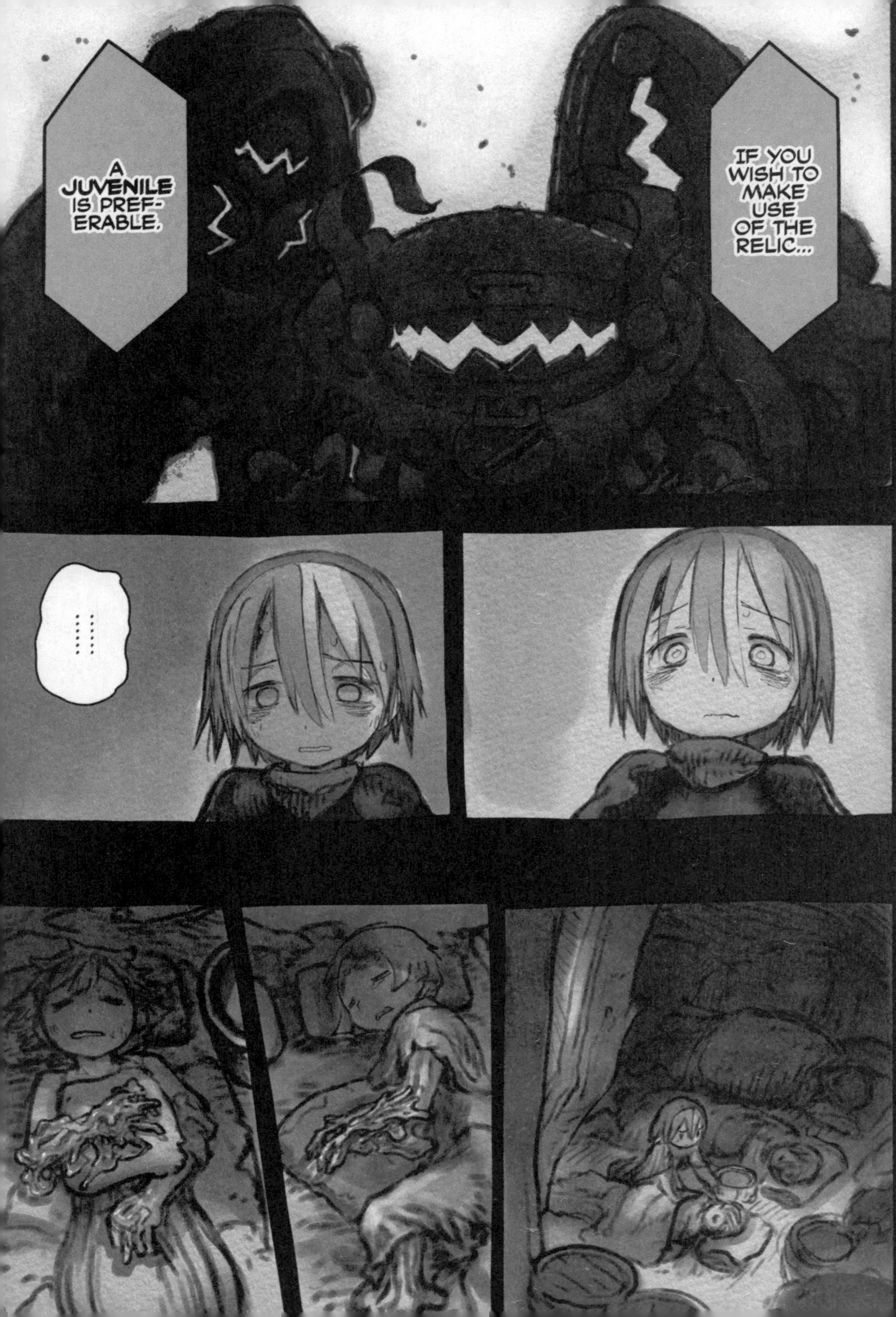
IF YOU WISH TO MAKE USE OF THE RELIC...
A JUVENILE IS PREF-ERABLE.
......

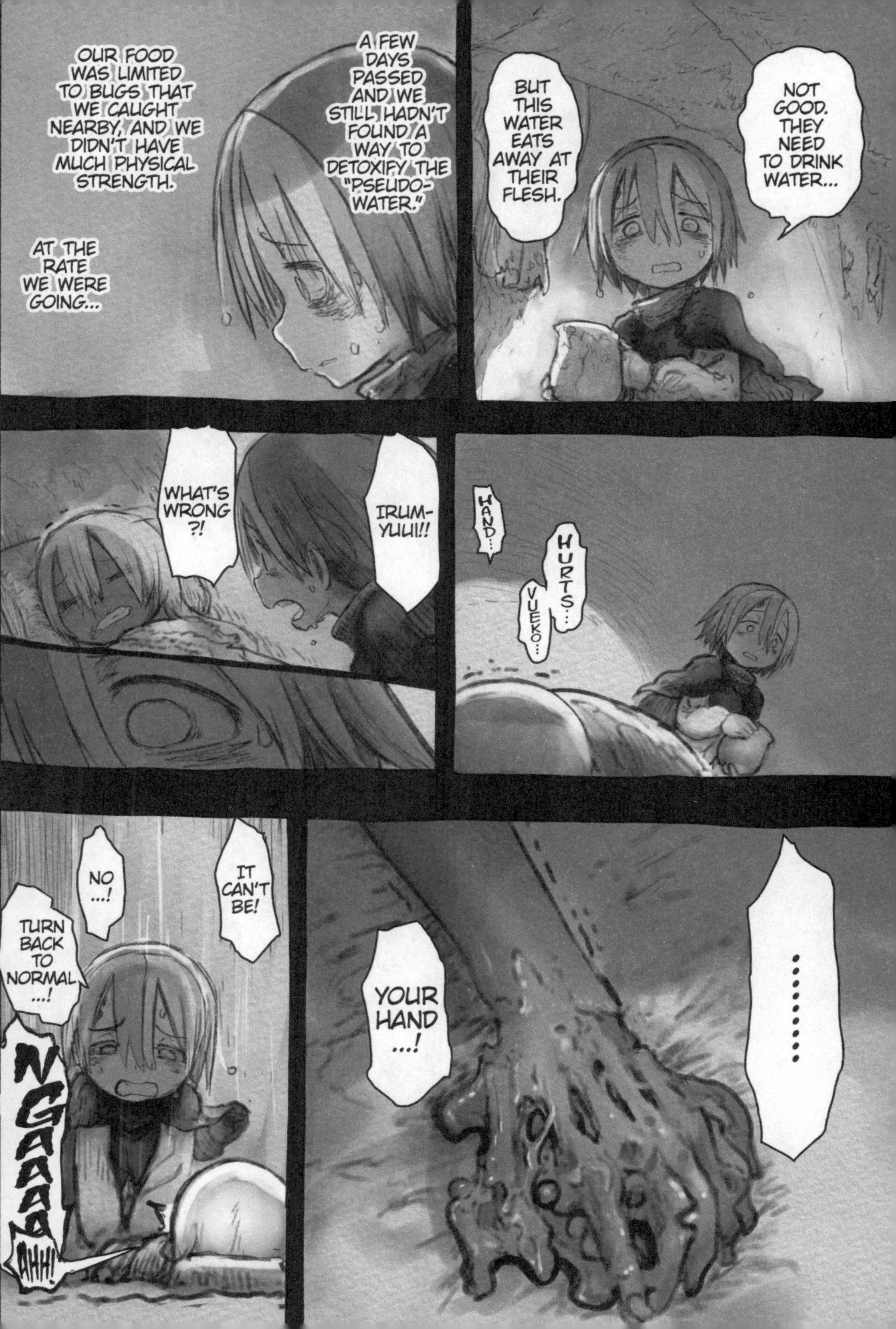
NOT GOOD. THEY NEED TO DRINK WATER...
BUT THIS WATER EATS AWAY AT THEIR FLESH.
A FEW DAYS PASSED AND WE STILL HADN'T FOUND A WAY TO DETOXIFY THE "PSEUDO-WATER."
OUR FOOD WAS LIMITED TO BUGS THAT WE CAUGHT NEARBY, AND WE DIDN'T HAVE MUCH PHYSICAL STRENGTH.
AT THE RATE WE WERE GOING...
HAND...
HURTS...
VUEKO...
IRUM-YUUI!!
WHAT'S WRONG?!
....
YOUR HAND...!
IT CAN'T BE!
NO...!
TURN BACK TO NORMAL...!
NGAAAAAHH!

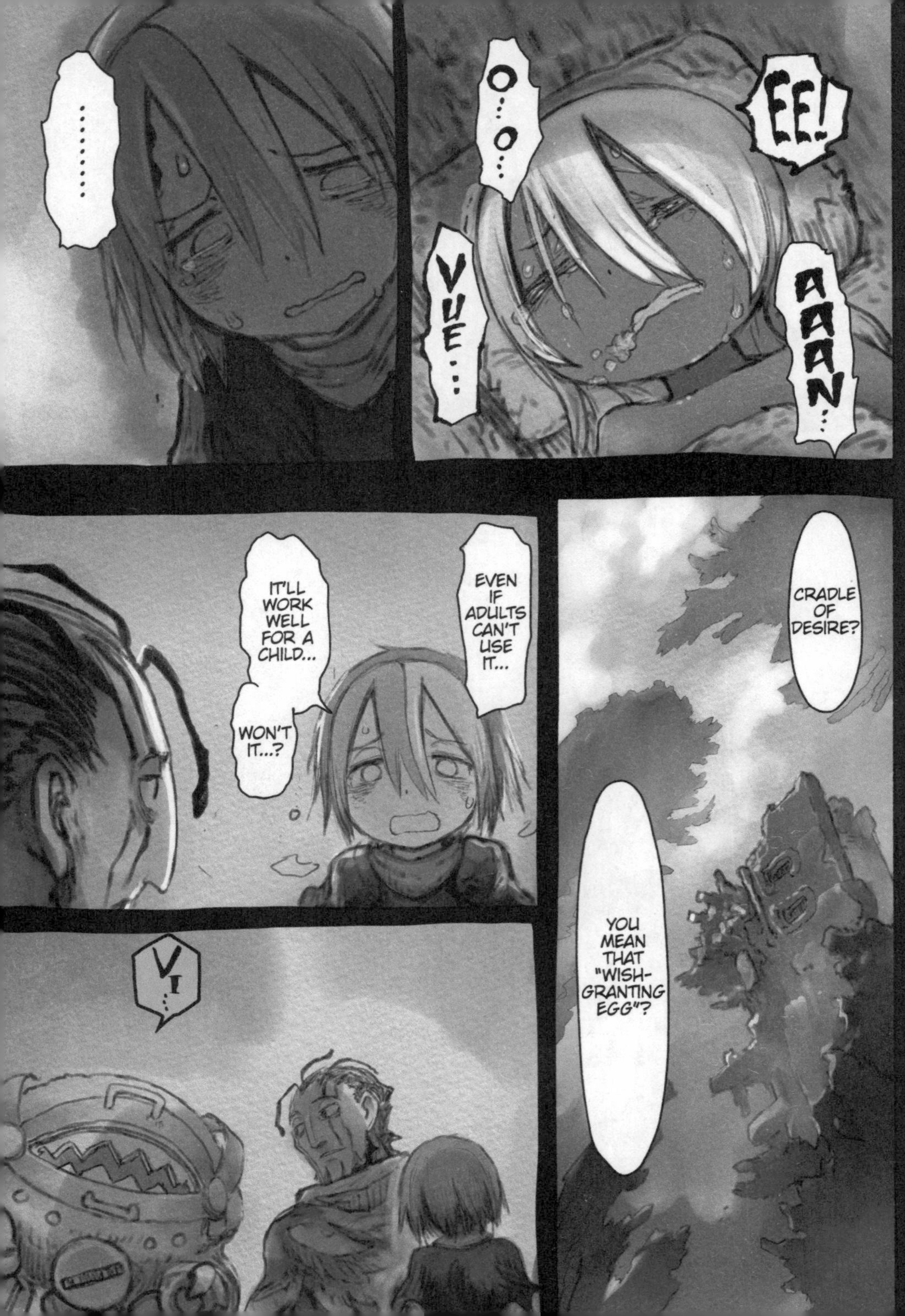
EE!
O...O...
AAAN...
VUE...
......
CRADLE OF DESIRE?
YOU MEAN THAT "WISH-GRANTING EGG"?
EVEN IF ADULTS CAN'T USE IT...
IT'LL WORK WELL FOR A CHILD...
WON'T IT...?
VI...

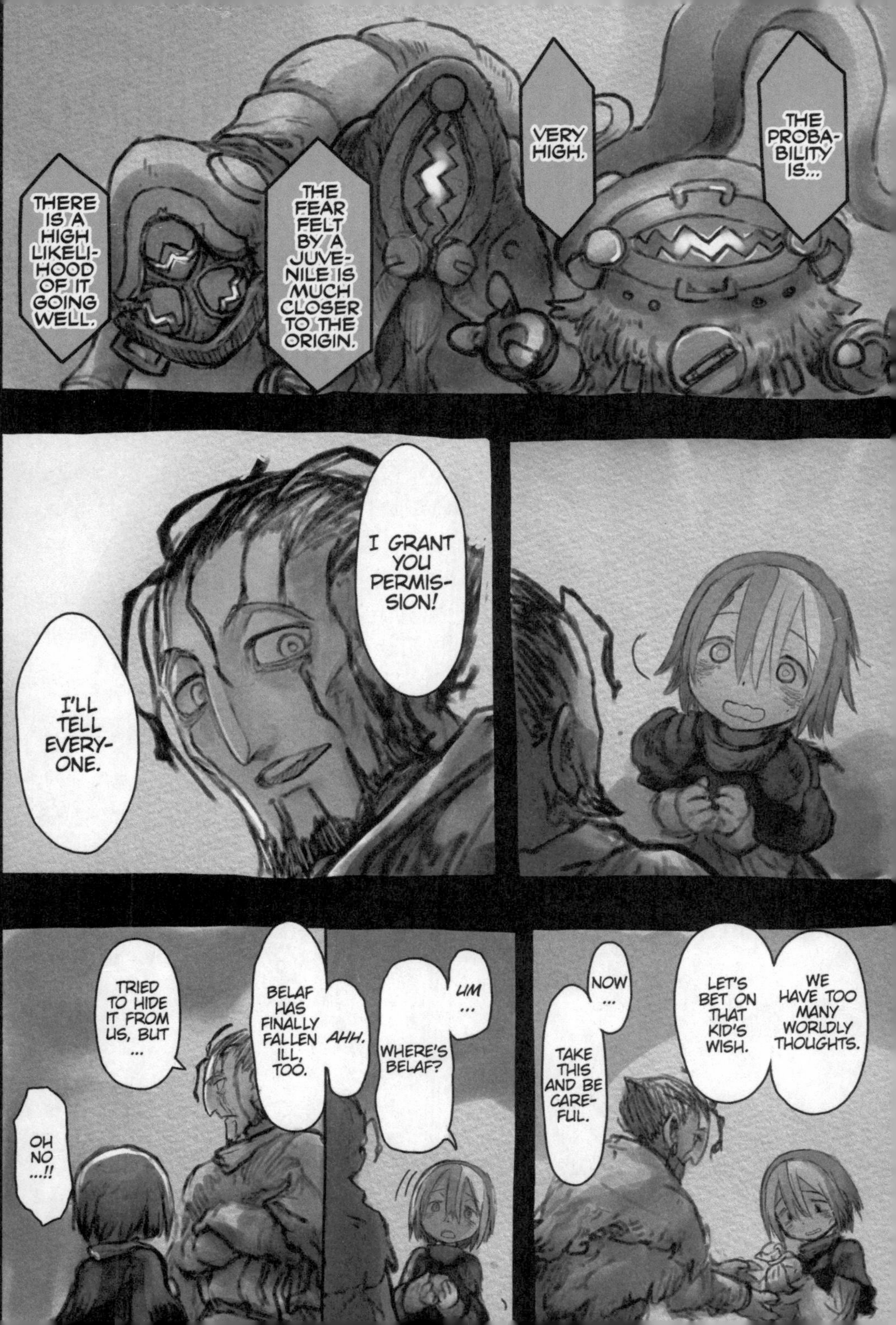
THE PROBABILITY IS...
VERY HIGH.
THE FEAR FELT BY A JUVENILE IS MUCH CLOSER TO THE ORIGIN.
THERE IS A HIGH LIKELIHOOD OF IT GOING WELL.
I GRANT YOU PERMISSION!
I'LL TELL EVERYONE.
WE HAVE TOO MANY WORLDLY THOUGHTS.
LET'S BET ON THAT KID'S WISH.
NOW ...
TAKE THIS AND BE CAREFUL.
UM ...
WHERE'S BELAF?
AHH.
BELAF HAS FINALLY FALLEN ILL, TOO.
TRIED TO HIDE IT FROM US, BUT ...
OH NO ...!!

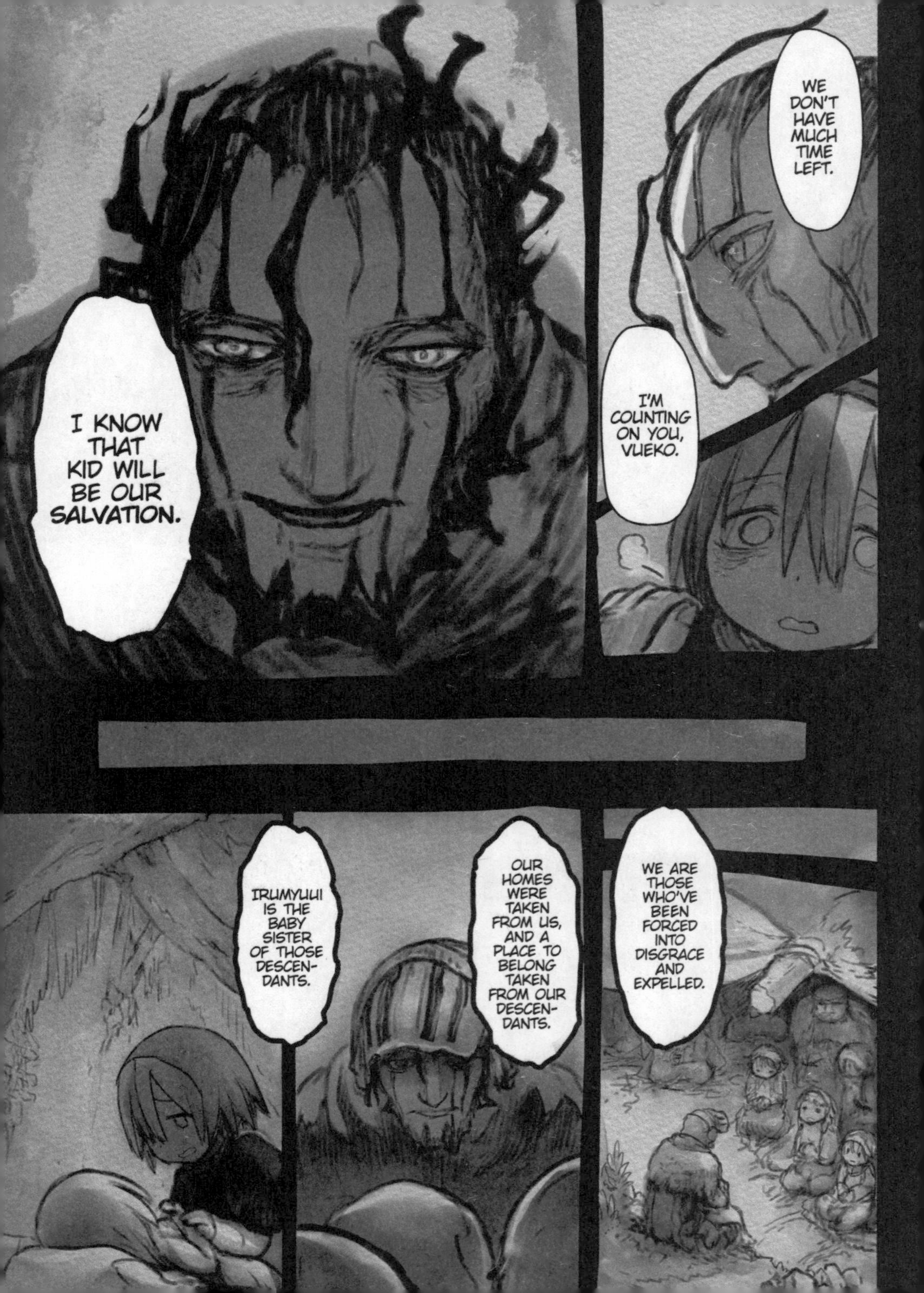
WE DON'T HAVE MUCH TIME LEFT.
I'M COUNTING ON YOU, VUEKO.
I KNOW THAT KID WILL BE OUR SALVATION.
WE ARE THOSE WHO'VE BEEN FORCED INTO DISGRACE AND EXPELLED.
OUR HOMES WERE TAKEN FROM US, AND A PLACE TO BELONG TAKEN FROM OUR DESCENDANTS.
IRUMYUUI IS THE BABY SISTER OF THOSE DESCENDANTS.

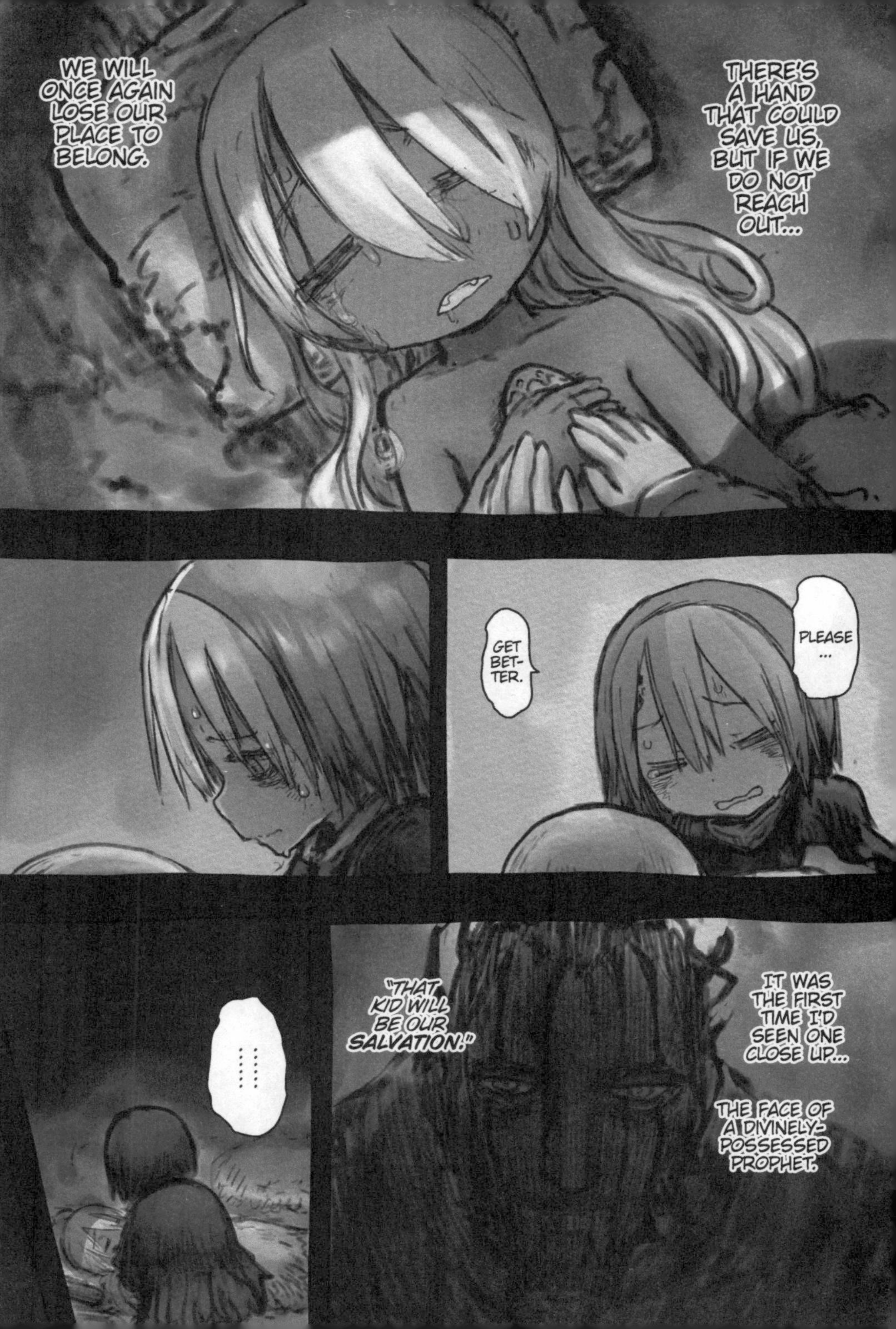
THERE'S A HAND THAT COULD SAVE US, BUT IF WE DO NOT REACH OUT...
WE WILL ONCE AGAIN LOSE OUR PLACE TO BELONG.
PLEASE...
GET BETTER.
IT WAS THE FIRST TIME I'D SEEN ONE CLOSE UP...
THE FACE OF A DIVINELY-POSSESSED PROPHET.
"THAT KID WILL BE OUR SALVATION."
......

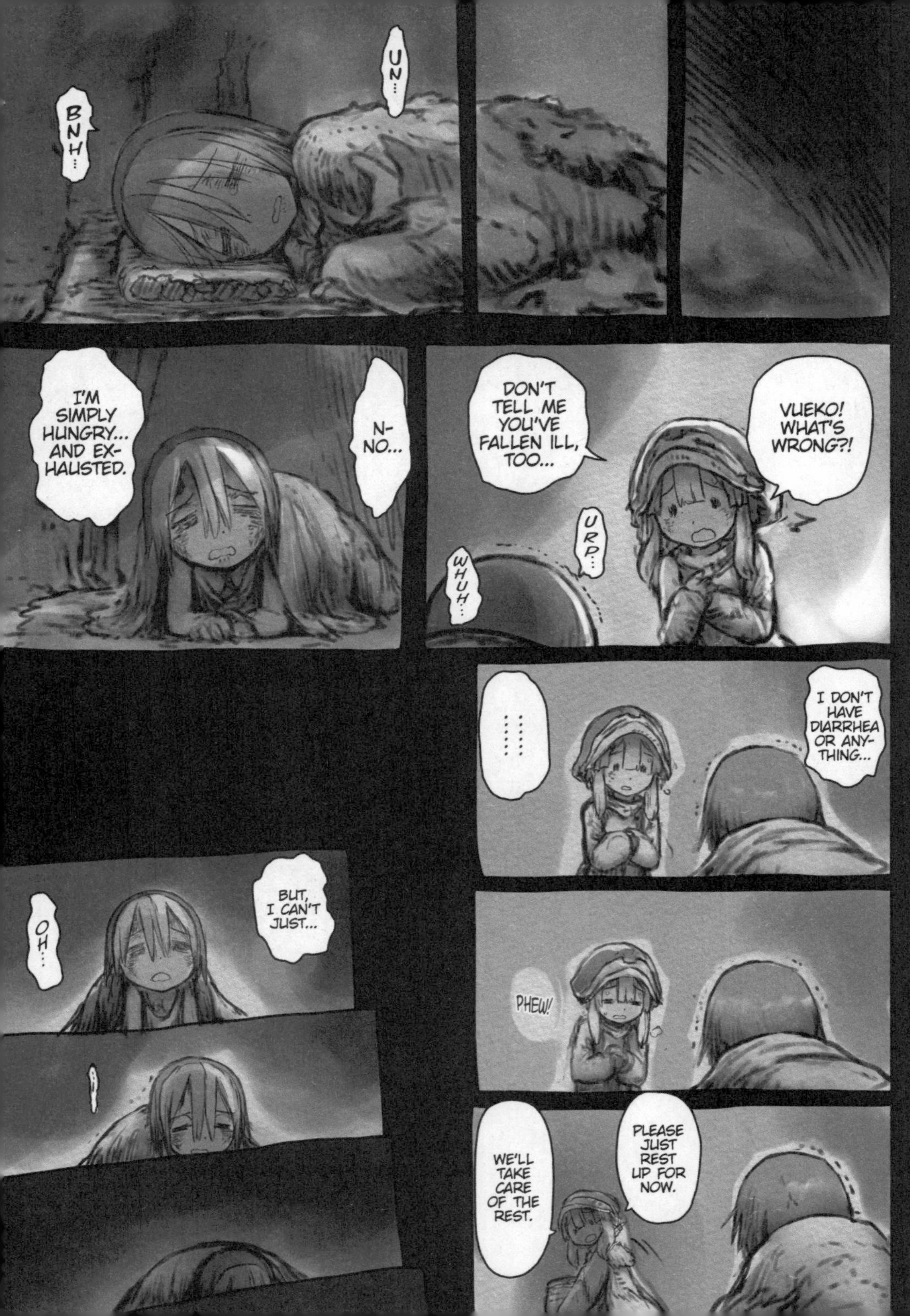
UN...
BNH...
VUEKO! WHAT'S WRONG?!
DON'T TELL ME YOU'VE FALLEN ILL, TOO...
URP...
WHUH...
N-NO...
I'M SIMPLY HUNGRY... AND EX-HAUSTED.
I DON'T HAVE DIARRHEA OR ANY-THING...
......
PHEW!
PLEASE JUST REST UP FOR NOW.
WE'LL TAKE CARE OF THE REST.
BUT, I CAN'T JUST...
OH...

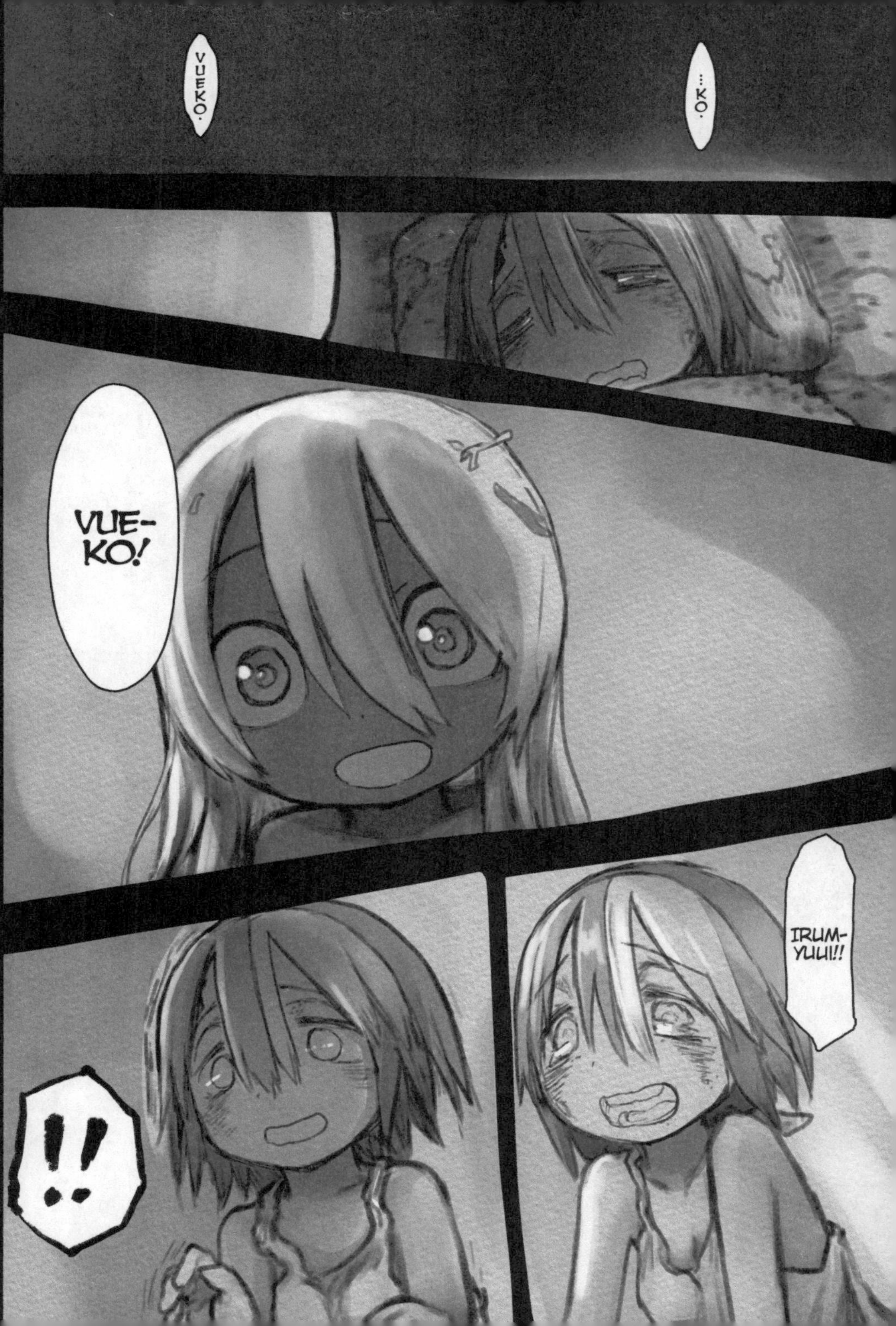
...KO.
VUEKO.
VUE-KO!
IRUM-YUUI!!
!!

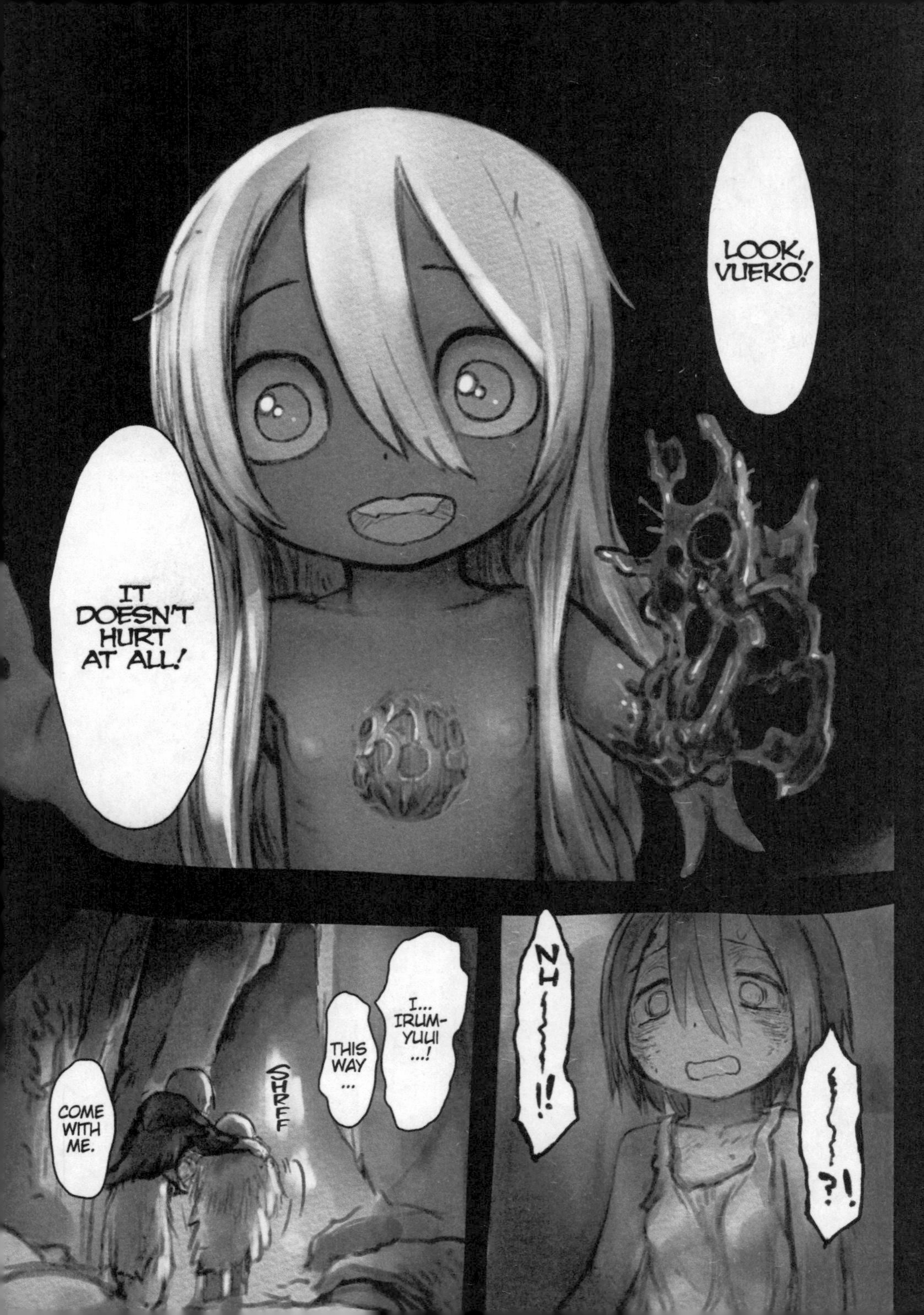
LOOK, VUEKO!
IT DOESN'T HURT AT ALL!
NH———!!
———?!
I... IRUM-YUUI...!
THIS WAY...
SHRFF
COME WITH ME.

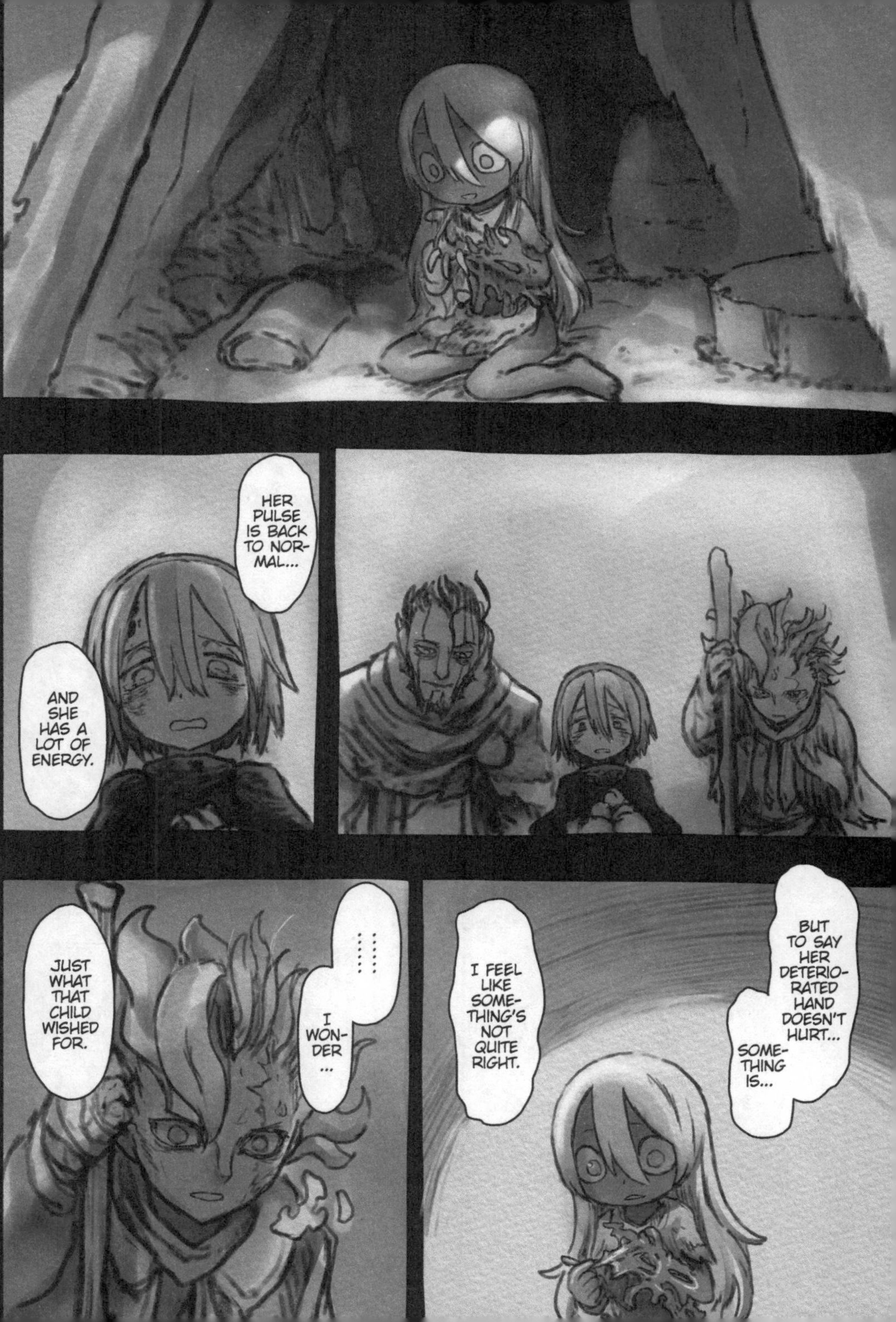
HER PULSE IS BACK TO NOR-MAL...
AND SHE HAS A LOT OF ENERGY.
BUT TO SAY HER DETERIO-RATED HAND DOESN'T HURT...
SOME-THING IS...
I FEEL LIKE SOME-THING'S NOT QUITE RIGHT.
......
I WON-DER ...
JUST WHAT THAT CHILD WISHED FOR.

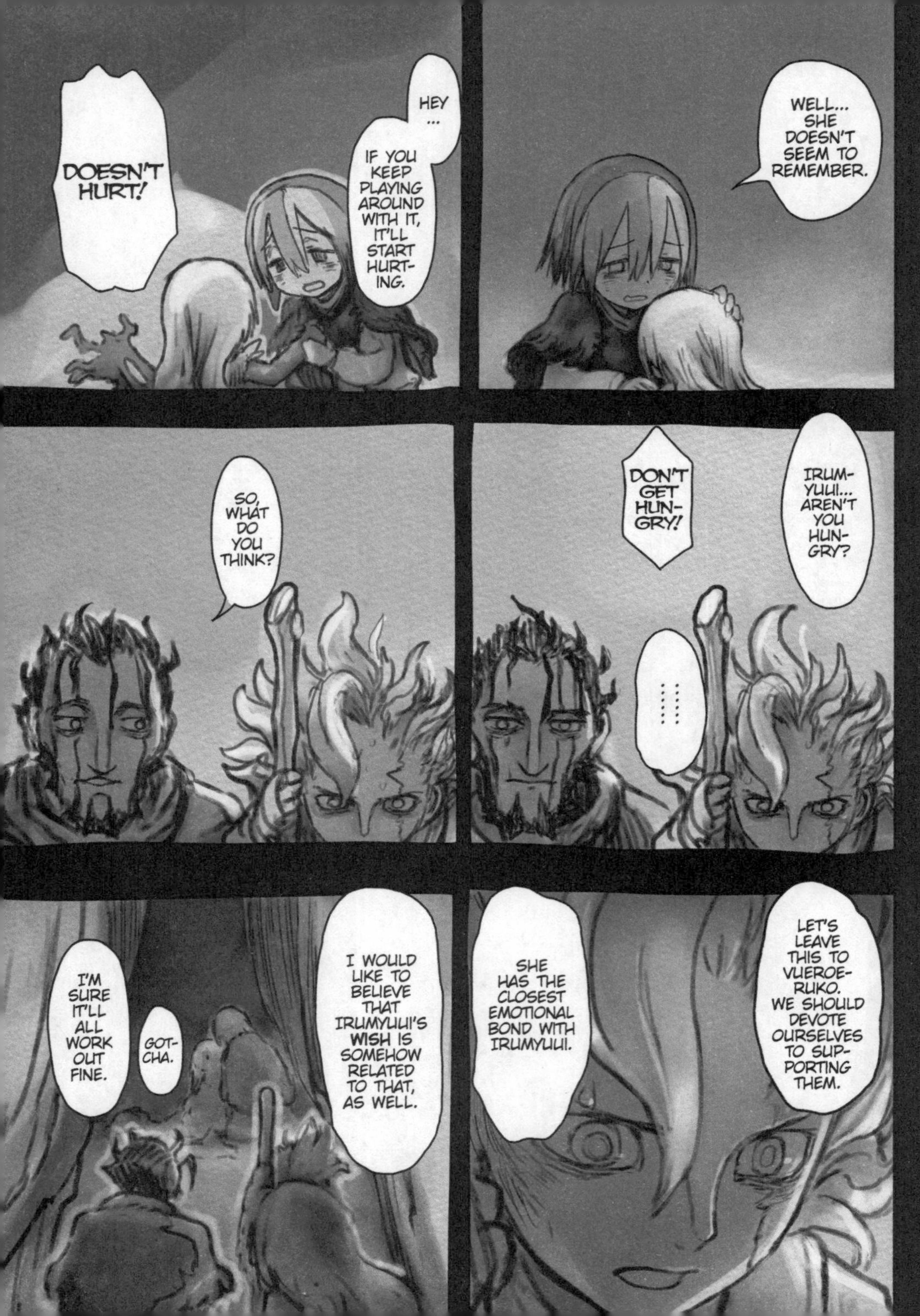
WELL... SHE DOESN'T SEEM TO REMEMBER.
HEY ...
IF YOU KEEP PLAYING AROUND WITH IT, IT'LL START HURTING.
DOESN'T HURT!
IRUMYUUI... AREN'T YOU HUNGRY?
DON'T GET HUNGRY!
......
SO, WHAT DO YOU THINK?
LET'S LEAVE THIS TO VUEROERUKO. WE SHOULD DEVOTE OURSELVES TO SUPPORTING THEM.
SHE HAS THE CLOSEST EMOTIONAL BOND WITH IRUMYUUI.
I WOULD LIKE TO BELIEVE THAT IRUMYUUI'S WISH IS SOMEHOW RELATED TO THAT, AS WELL.
GOTCHA.
I'M SURE IT'LL ALL WORK OUT FINE.

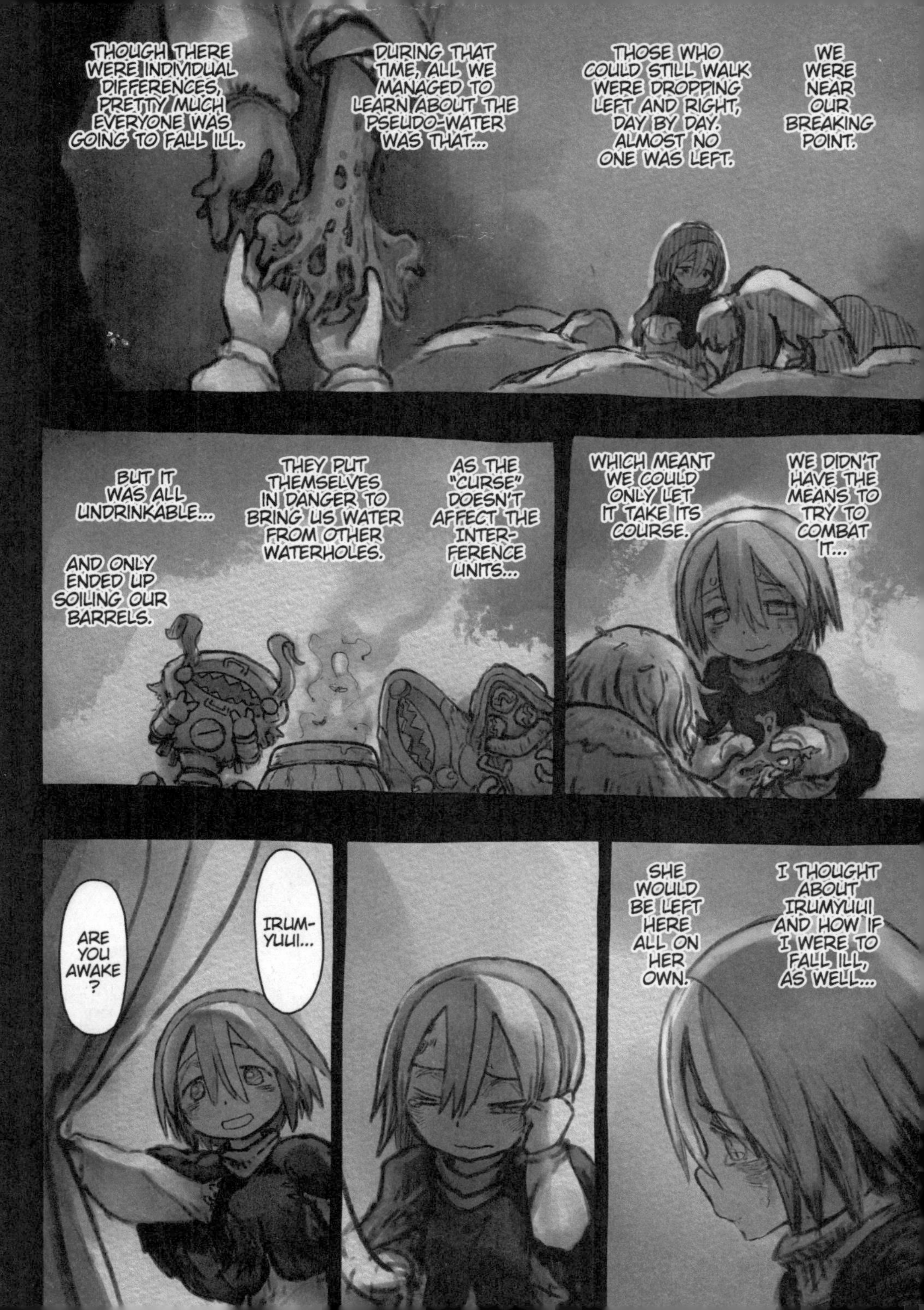
WE WERE NEAR OUR BREAKING POINT.
THOSE WHO COULD STILL WALK WERE DROPPING LEFT AND RIGHT, DAY BY DAY. ALMOST NO ONE WAS LEFT.
DURING THAT TIME, ALL WE MANAGED TO LEARN ABOUT THE PSEUDO-WATER WAS THAT...
THOUGH THERE WERE INDIVIDUAL DIFFERENCES, PRETTY MUCH EVERYONE WAS GOING TO FALL ILL.
WE DIDN'T HAVE THE MEANS TO TRY TO COMBAT IT...
WHICH MEANT WE COULD ONLY LET IT TAKE ITS COURSE.
AS THE "CURSE" DOESN'T AFFECT THE INTER-FERENCE UNITS...
THEY PUT THEMSELVES IN DANGER TO BRING US WATER FROM OTHER WATERHOLES.
BUT IT WAS ALL UNDRINKABLE...
AND ONLY ENDED UP SOILING OUR BARRELS.
I THOUGHT ABOUT IRUMYUUI AND HOW IF I WERE TO FALL ILL, AS WELL...
SHE WOULD BE LEFT HERE ALL ON HER OWN.
IRUM-YUUI...
ARE YOU AWAKE ?

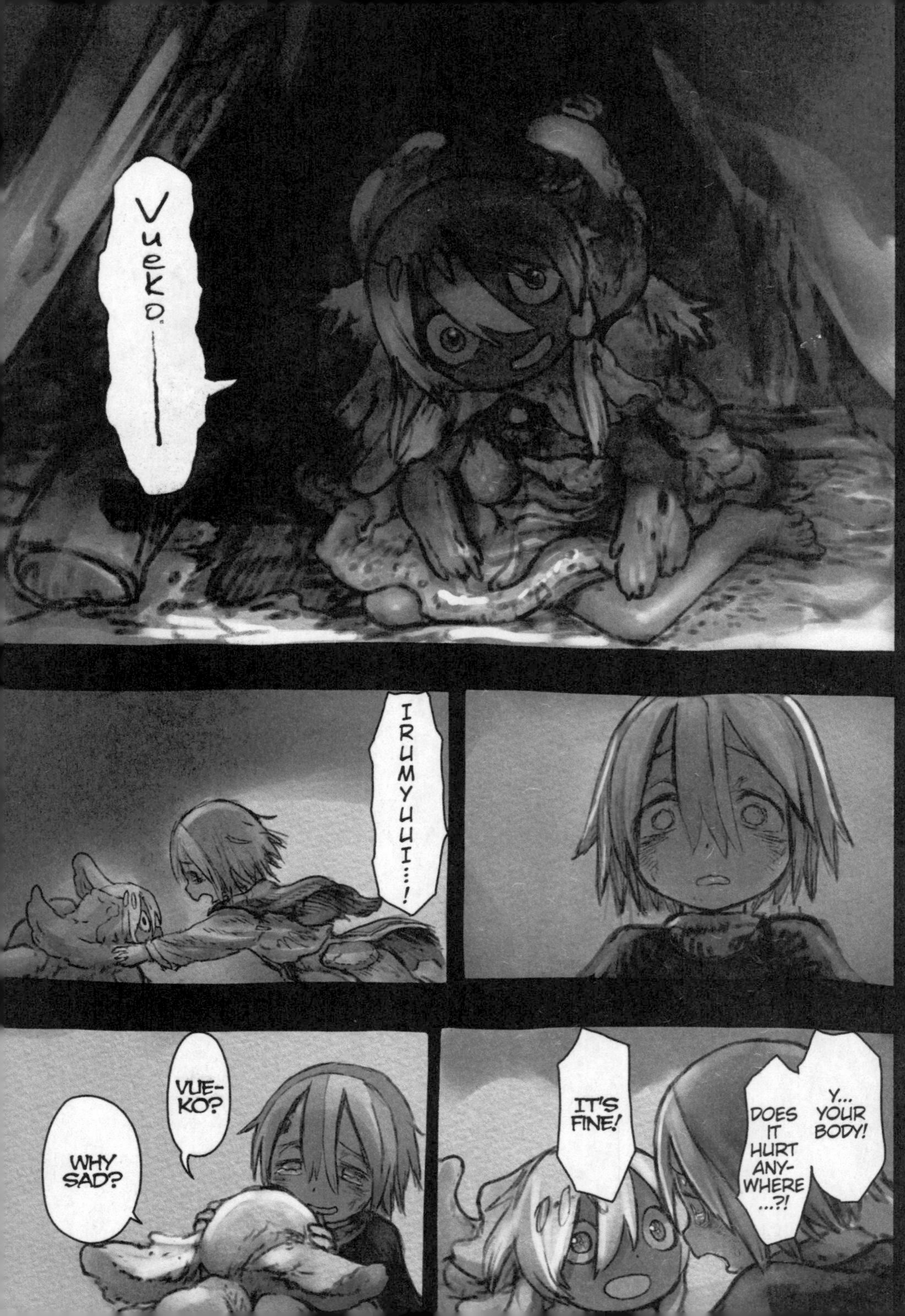
Vueko——
IRUMYUUI...!
Y... YOUR BODY!
DOES IT HURT ANYWHERE...?!
IT'S FINE!
VUEKO?
WHY SAD?

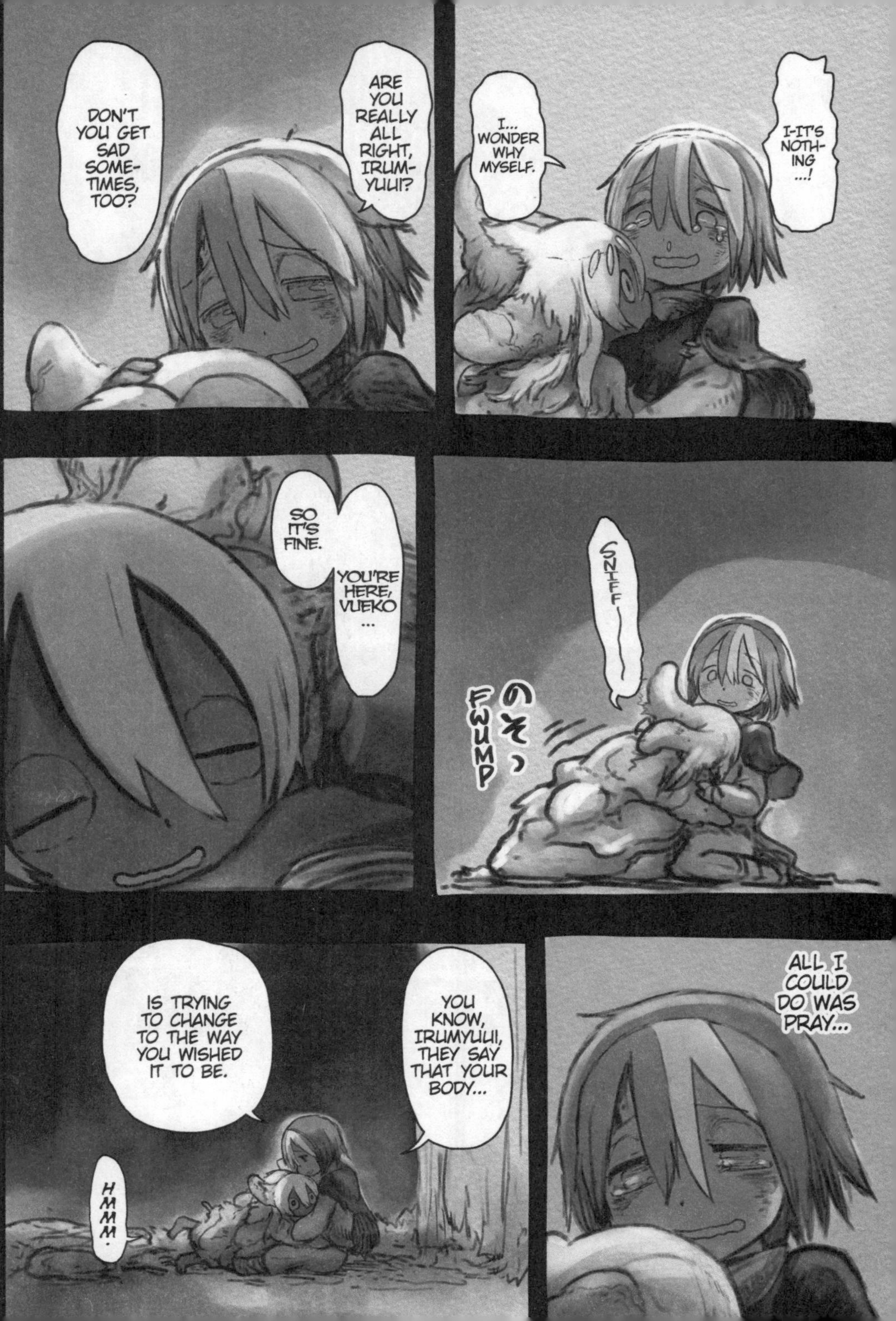
I-IT'S NOTHING...!
I... WONDER WHY MYSELF.
ARE YOU REALLY ALL RIGHT, IRUMYUUI?
DON'T YOU GET SAD SOMETIMES, TOO?
SNIFF
のそっ FWUMP
SO IT'S FINE.
YOU'RE HERE, VUEKO...
ALL I COULD DO WAS PRAY...
YOU KNOW, IRUMYUUI, THEY SAY THAT YOUR BODY...
IS TRYING TO CHANGE TO THE WAY YOU WISHED IT TO BE.
HMMM.

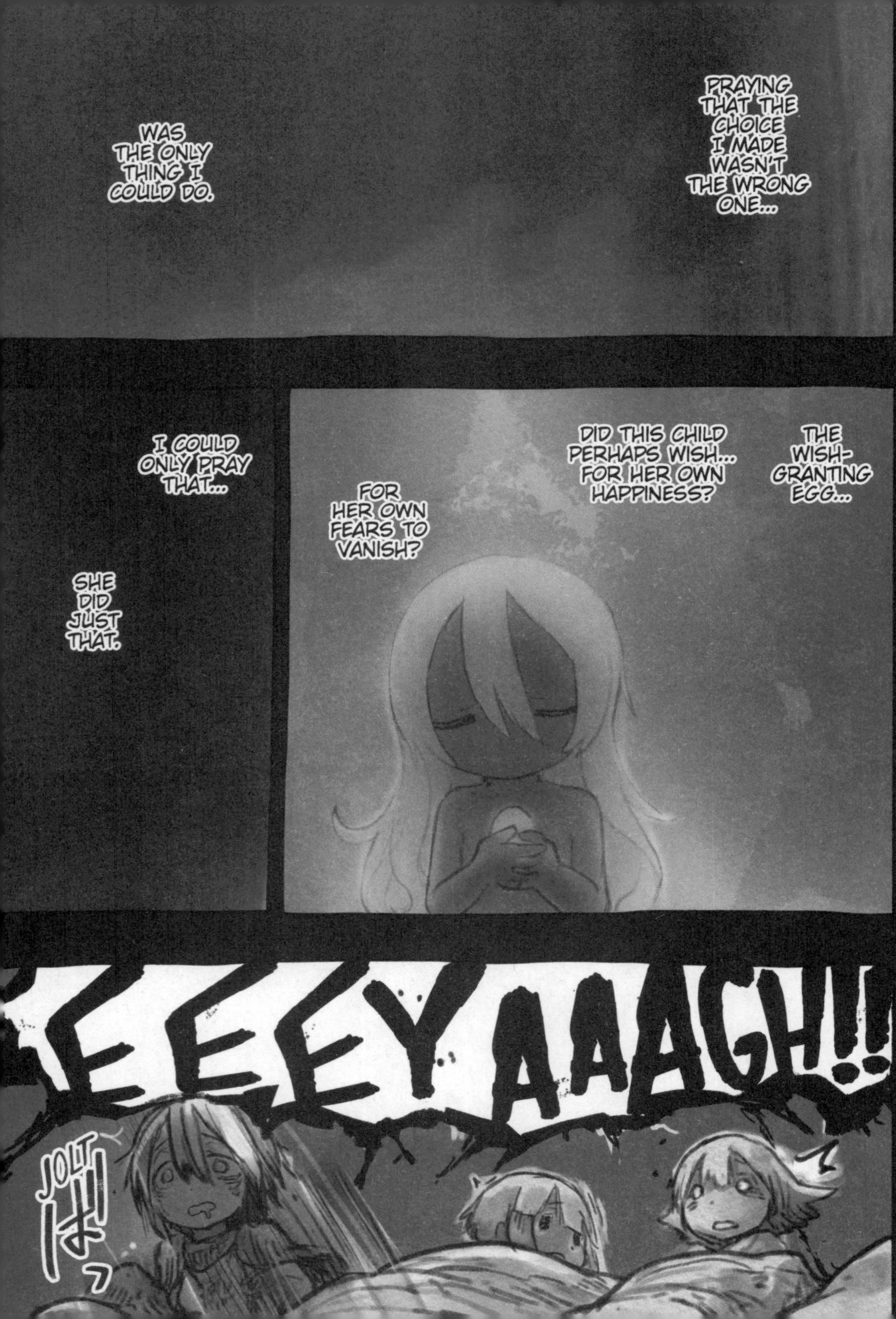
PRAYING THAT THE CHOICE I MADE WASN'T THE WRONG ONE...
WAS THE ONLY THING I COULD DO.
THE WISH-GRANTING EGG...
DID THIS CHILD PERHAPS WISH... FOR HER OWN HAPPINESS?
FOR HER OWN FEARS TO VANISH?
I COULD ONLY PRAY THAT...
SHE DID JUST THAT.
EEEYAAAGH!!
JOLT

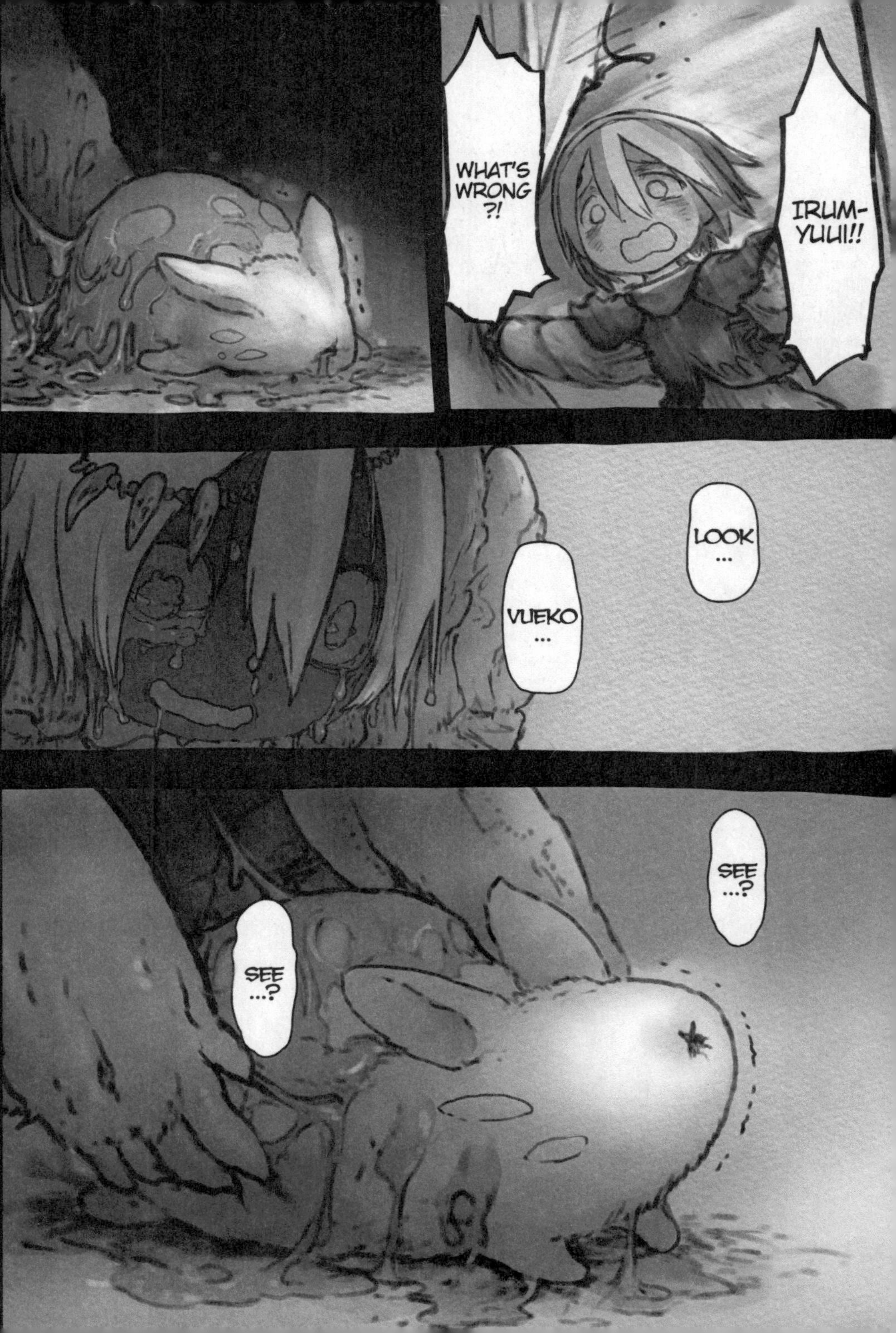
IRUM-YUUI!!
WHAT'S WRONG?!
LOOK...
VUEKO...
SEE...?
SEE...?

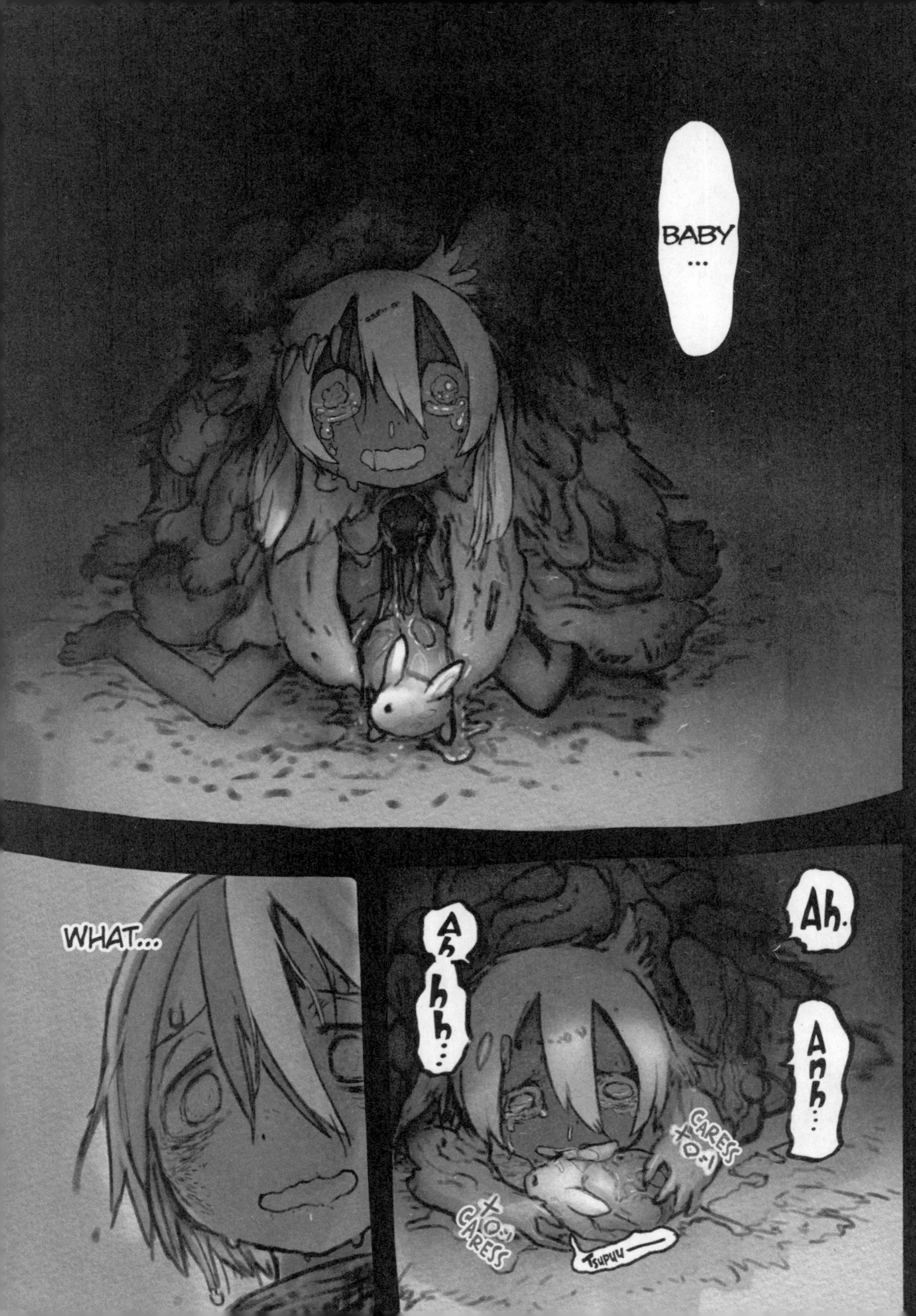
BABY
...
Ah.
Anh...
Ahh...
CARESS
CARESS
Tsupuu—
WHAT...

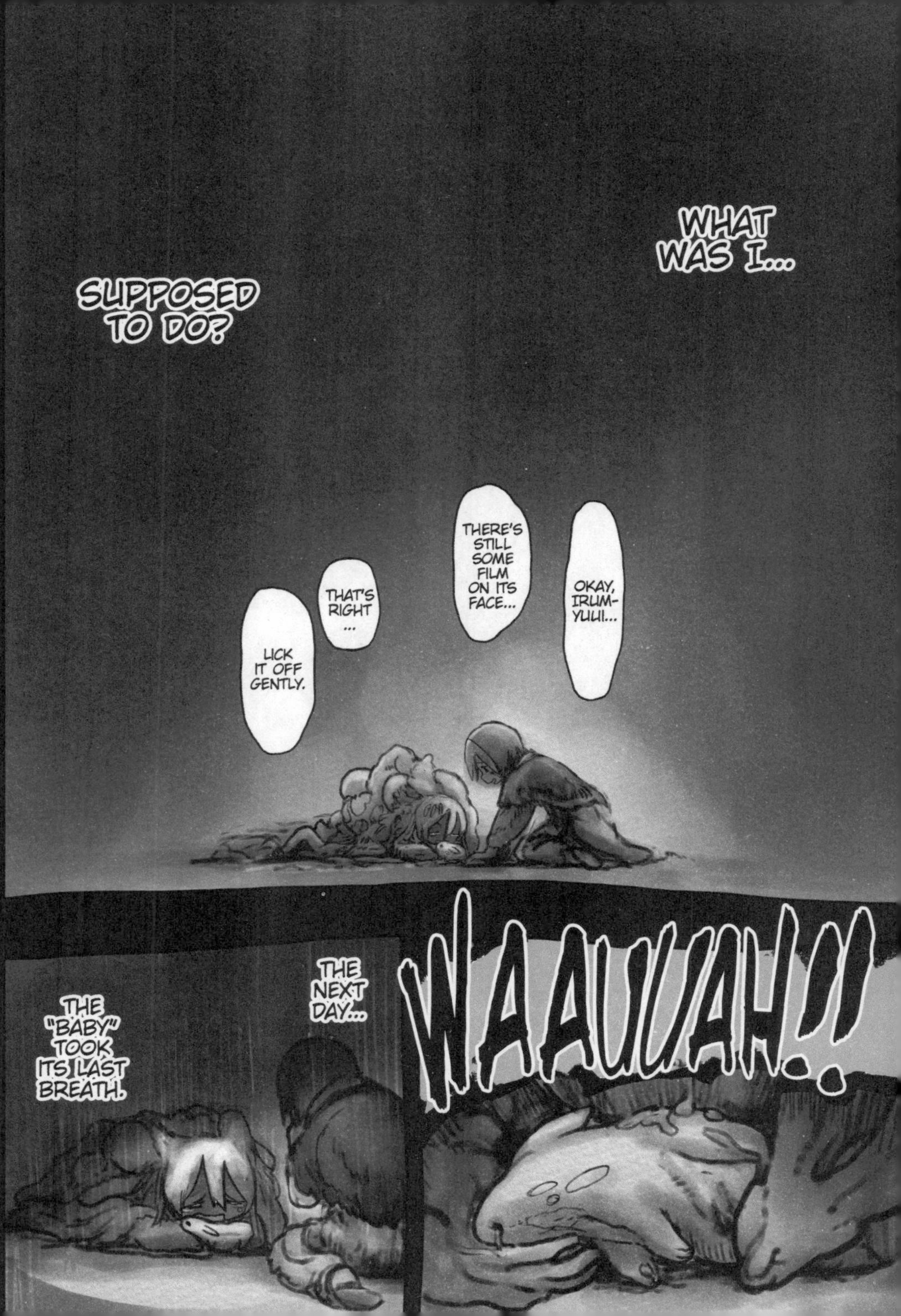
WHAT WAS I...
SUPPOSED TO DO?
OKAY, IRUM-YUUI...
THERE'S STILL SOME FILM ON ITS FACE...
THAT'S RIGHT ...
LICK IT OFF GENTLY.
WAAUUAH!!
THE NEXT DAY...
THE "BABY" TOOK ITS LAST BREATH.

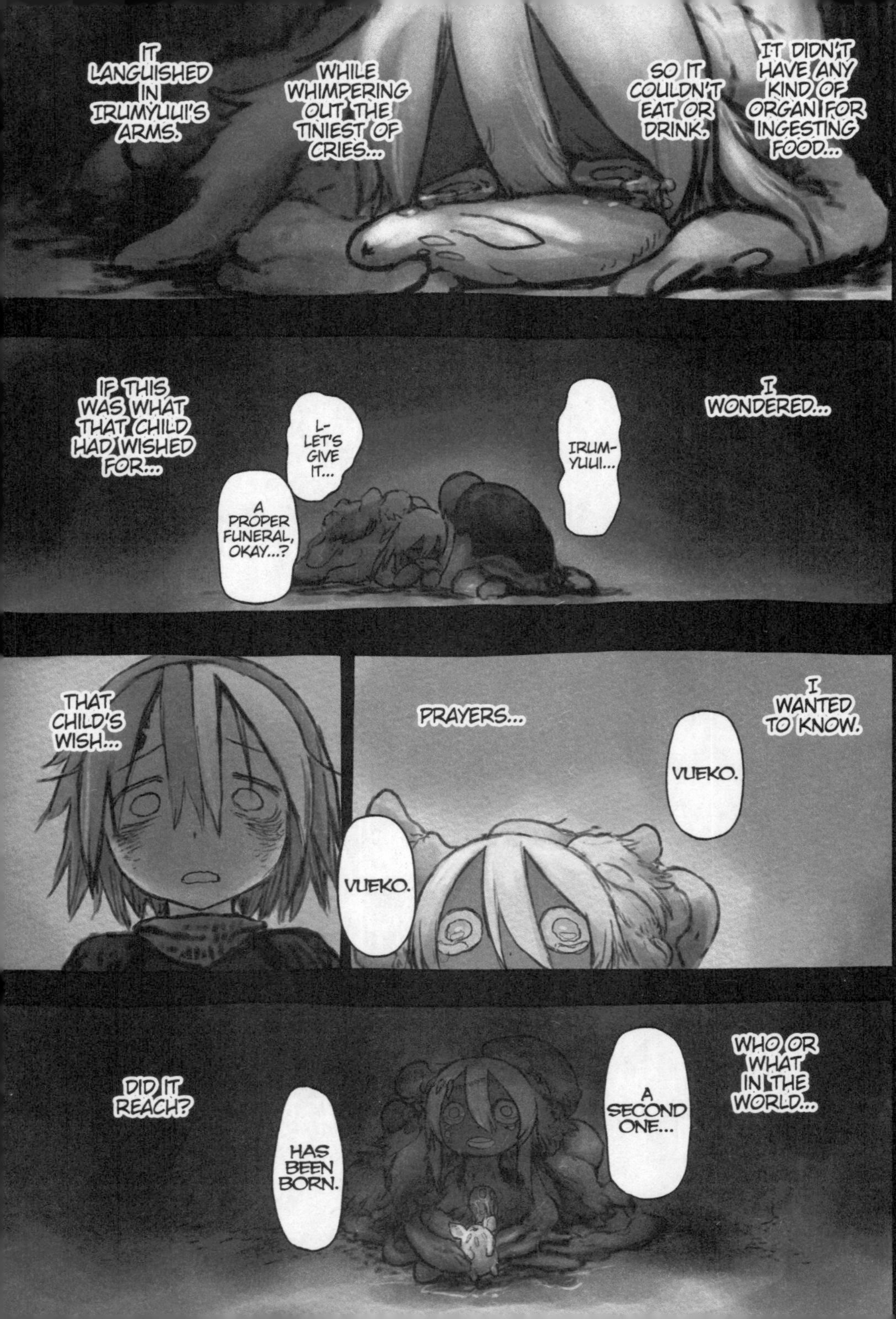
IT DIDN'T HAVE ANY KIND OF ORGAN FOR INGESTING FOOD...
SO IT COULDN'T EAT OR DRINK.
WHILE WHIMPERING OUT THE TINIEST OF CRIES...
IT LANGUISHED IN IRUMYUUI'S ARMS.
I WONDERED...
IRUM-YUUI...
L-LET'S GIVE IT...
A PROPER FUNERAL, OKAY...?
IF THIS WAS WHAT THAT CHILD HAD WISHED FOR...
I WANTED TO KNOW.
VUEKO.
PRAYERS...
VUEKO.
THAT CHILD'S WISH...
WHO OR WHAT IN THE WORLD...
A SECOND ONE...
HAS BEEN BORN.
DID IT REACH?

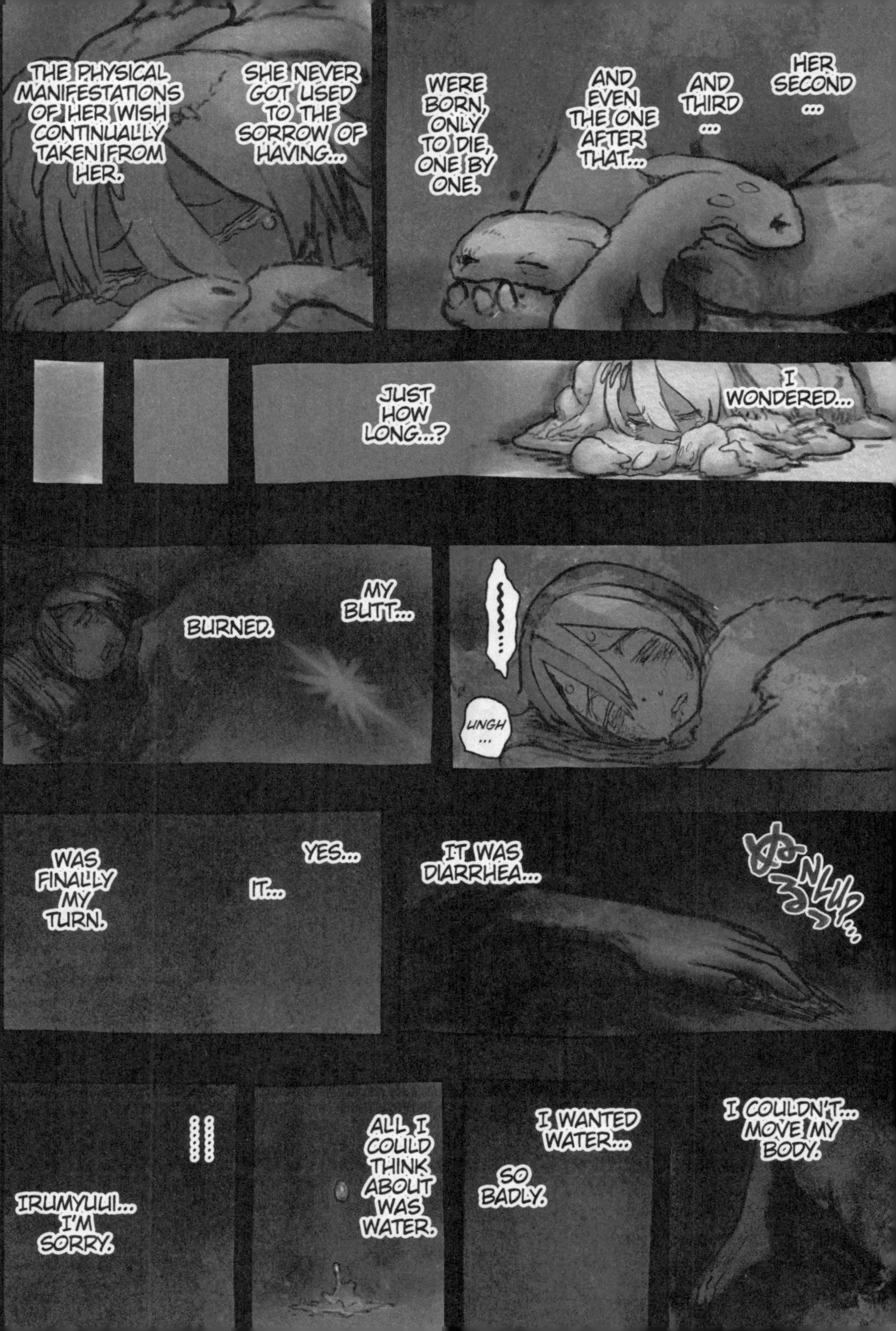
HER SECOND ...
AND THIRD ...
AND EVEN THE ONE AFTER THAT...
WERE BORN, ONLY TO DIE, ONE BY ONE.
SHE NEVER GOT USED TO THE SORROW OF HAVING...
THE PHYSICAL MANIFESTATIONS OF HER WISH CONTINUALLY TAKEN FROM HER.
I WONDERED...
JUST HOW LONG...?
......
UNGH ...
MY BUTT...
BURNED.
ぬるっ
NLUP...
IT WAS DIARRHEA...
YES...
IT...
WAS FINALLY MY TURN.
I COULDN'T... MOVE MY BODY.
I WANTED WATER...
SO BADLY.
ALL I COULD THINK ABOUT WAS WATER.
......
IRUMYUUI... I'M SORRY.

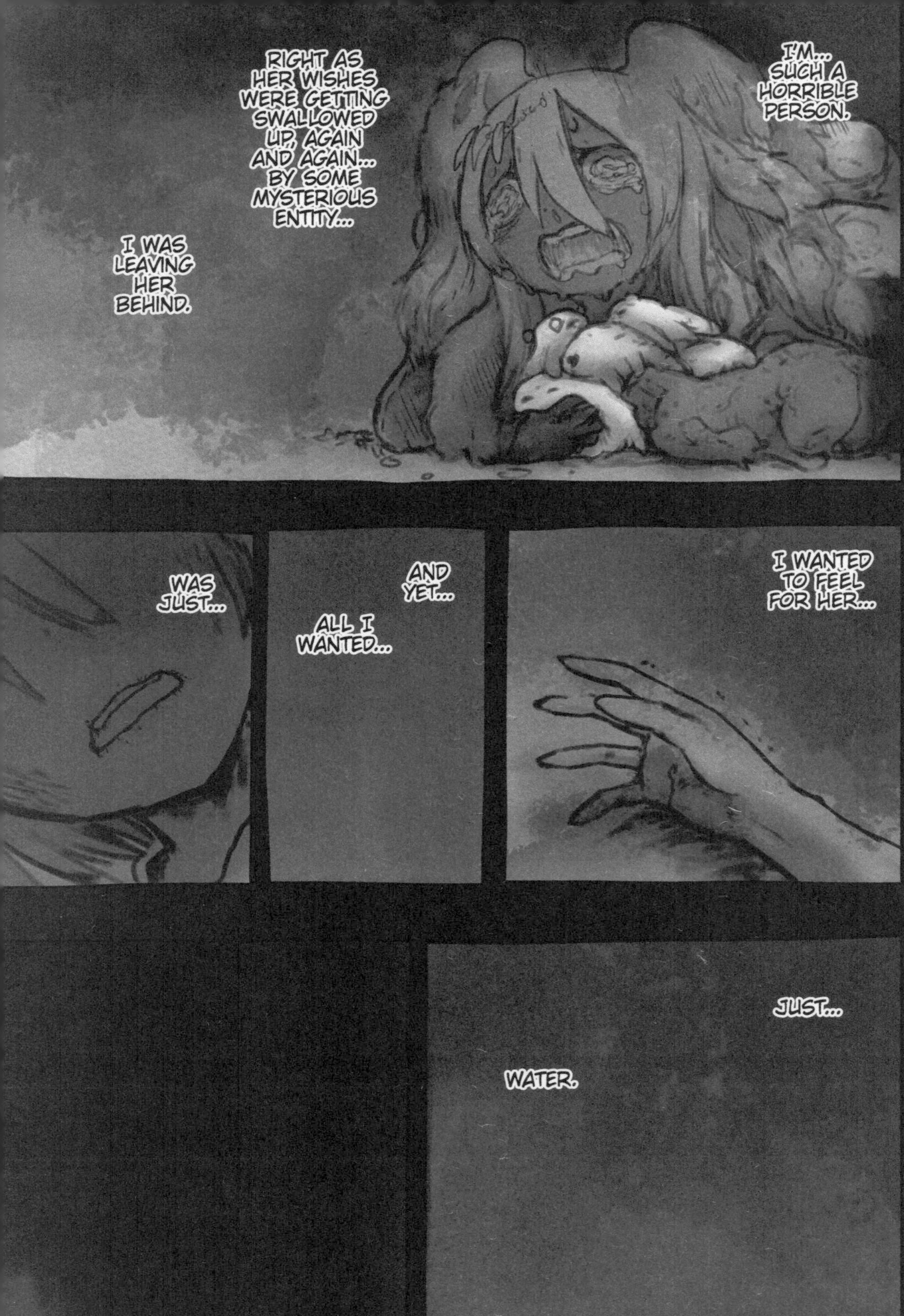
I'M... SUCH A HORRIBLE PERSON.
RIGHT AS HER WISHES WERE GETTING SWALLOWED UP, AGAIN AND AGAIN... BY SOME MYSTERIOUS ENTITY...
I WAS LEAVING HER BEHIND.
I WANTED TO FEEL FOR HER...
AND YET...
ALL I WANTED...
WAS JUST...
JUST...
WATER.

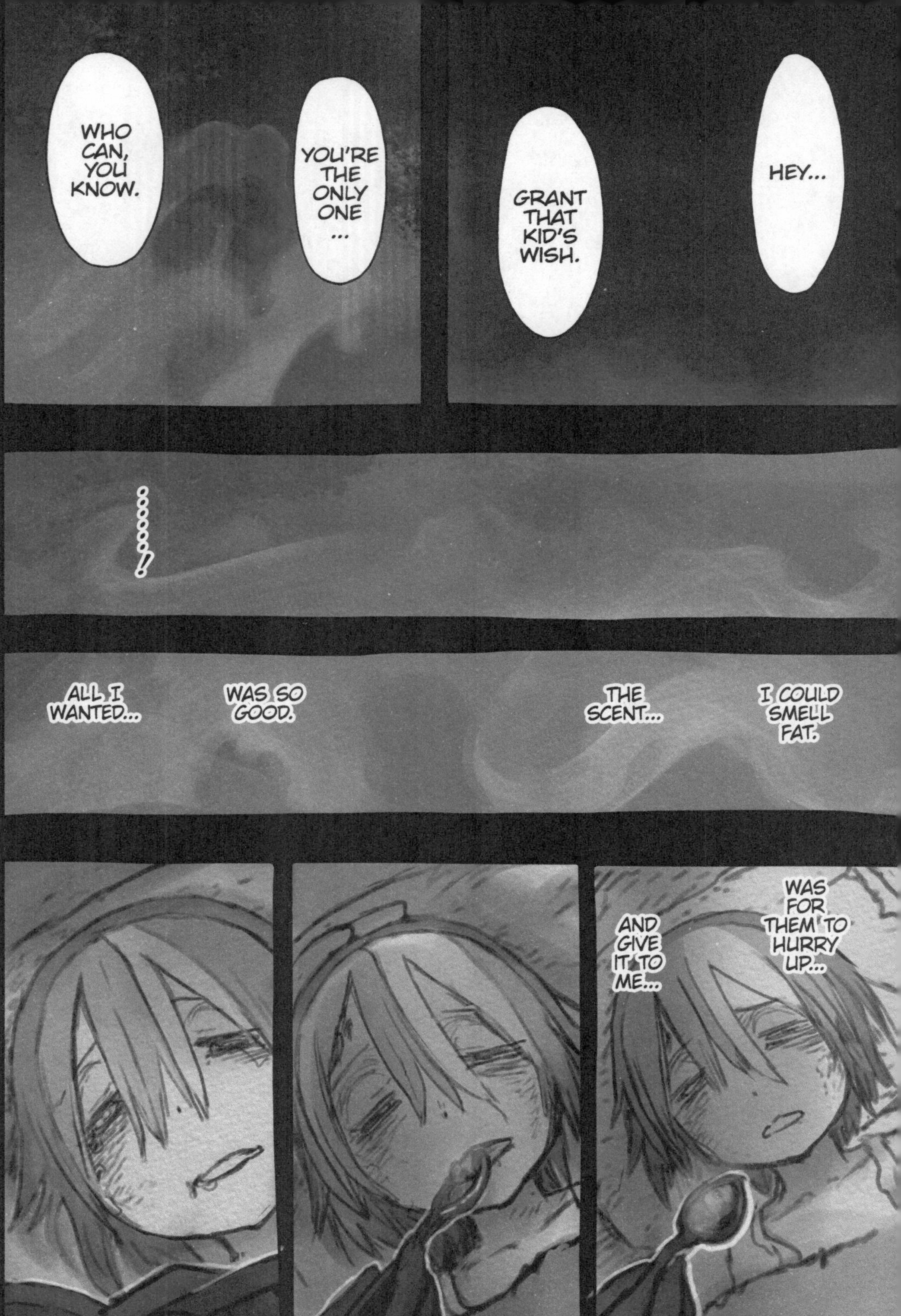
HEY...
GRANT THAT KID'S WISH.
YOU'RE THE ONLY ONE ...
WHO CAN, YOU KNOW.
......!
I COULD SMELL FAT.
THE SCENT...
WAS SO GOOD.
ALL I WANTED...
WAS FOR THEM TO HURRY UP...
AND GIVE IT TO ME...

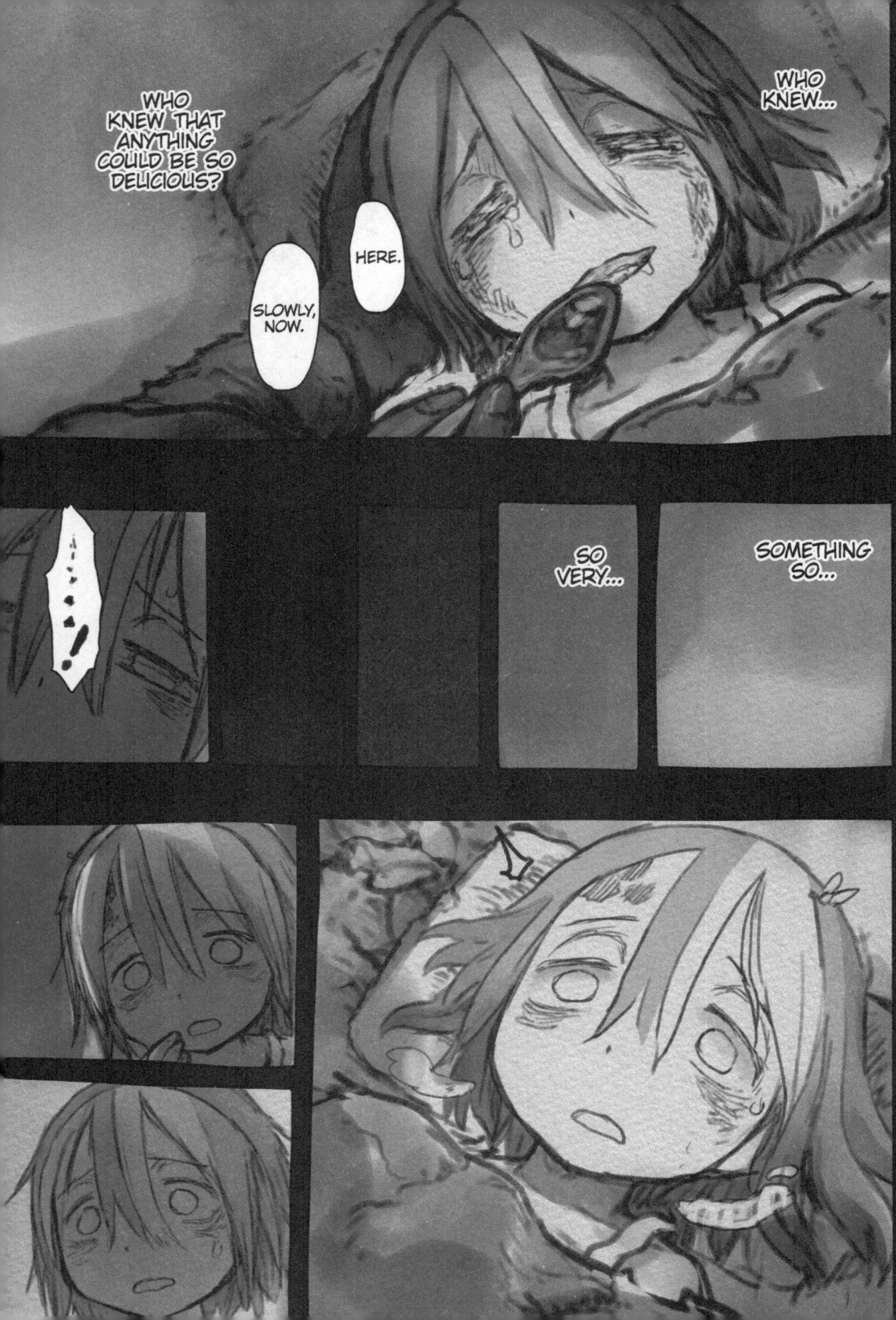
WHO KNEW...
WHO KNEW THAT ANYTHING COULD BE SO DELICIOUS?
HERE.
SLOWLY, NOW.
SOMETHING SO...
SO VERY...
...!

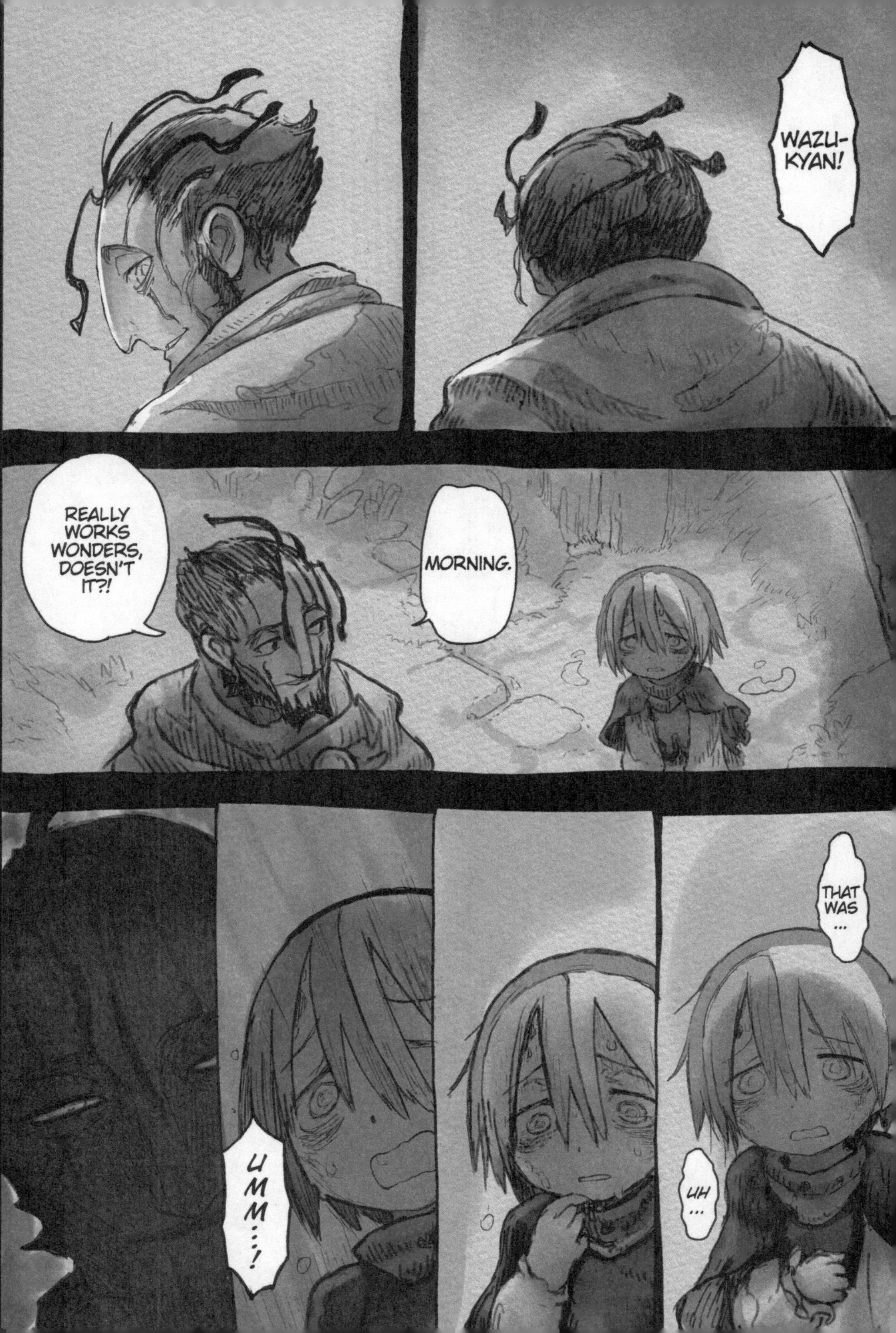
WAZU-KYAN!
MORNING.
REALLY WORKS WONDERS, DOESN'T IT?!
THAT WAS ...
UH ...
UMM...!

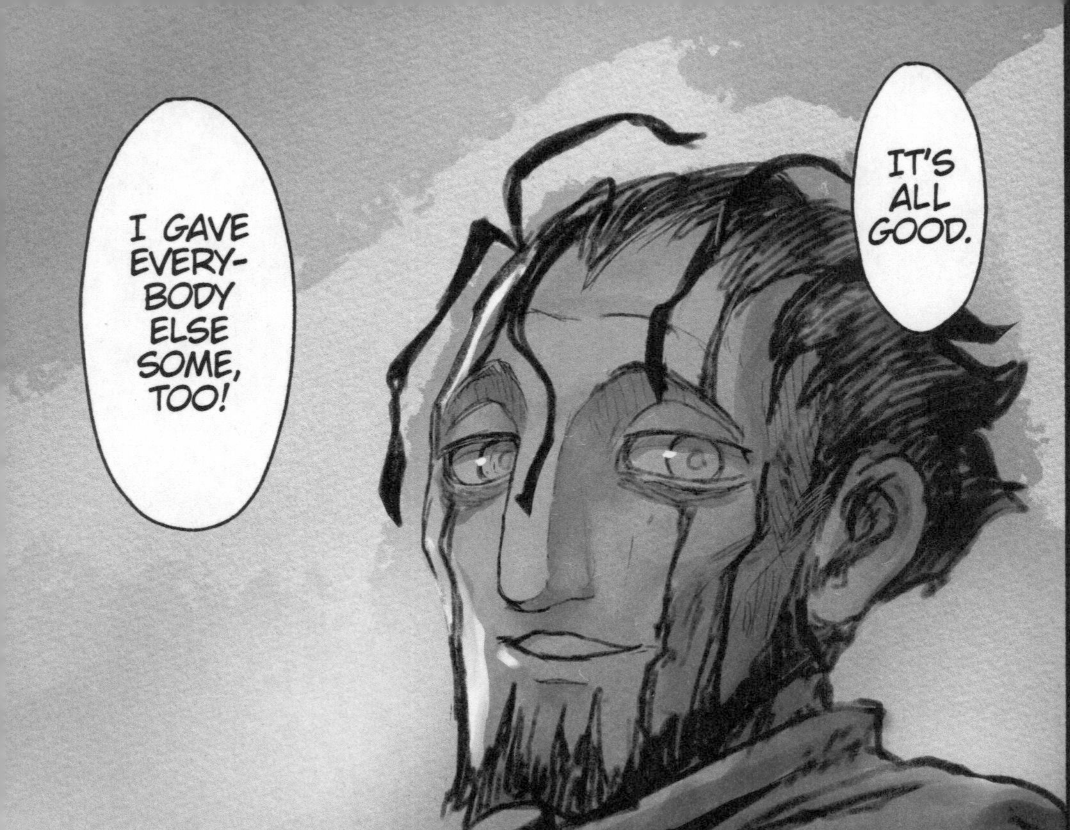
IT'S ALL GOOD.
I GAVE EVERY-BODY ELSE SOME, TOO!
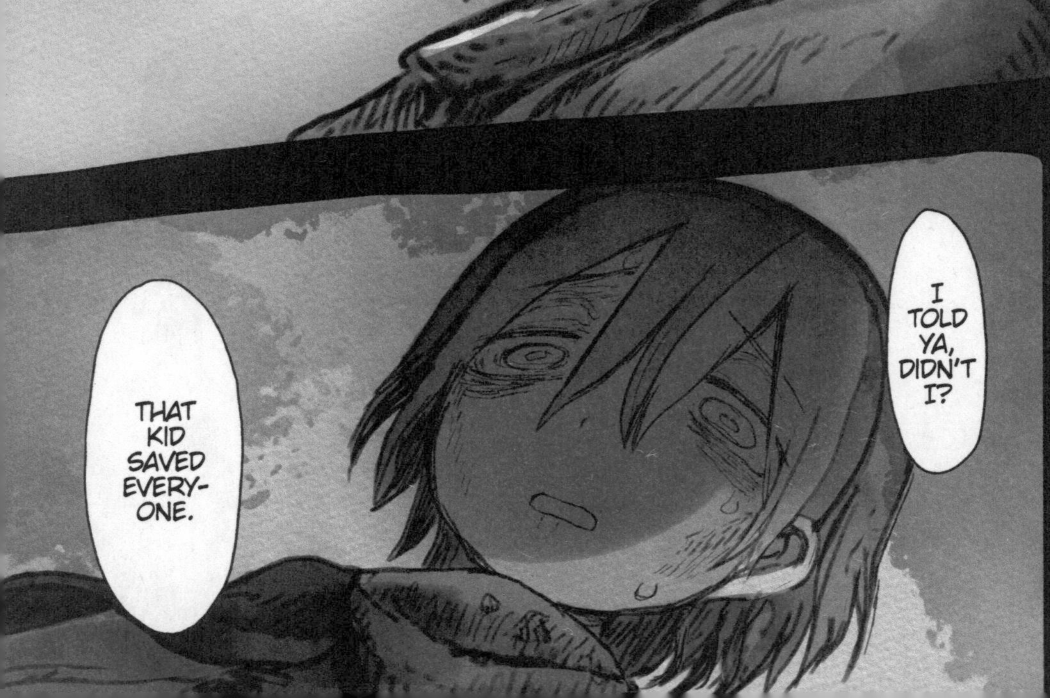
I TOLD YA, DIDN'T I?
THAT KID SAVED EVERY-ONE.

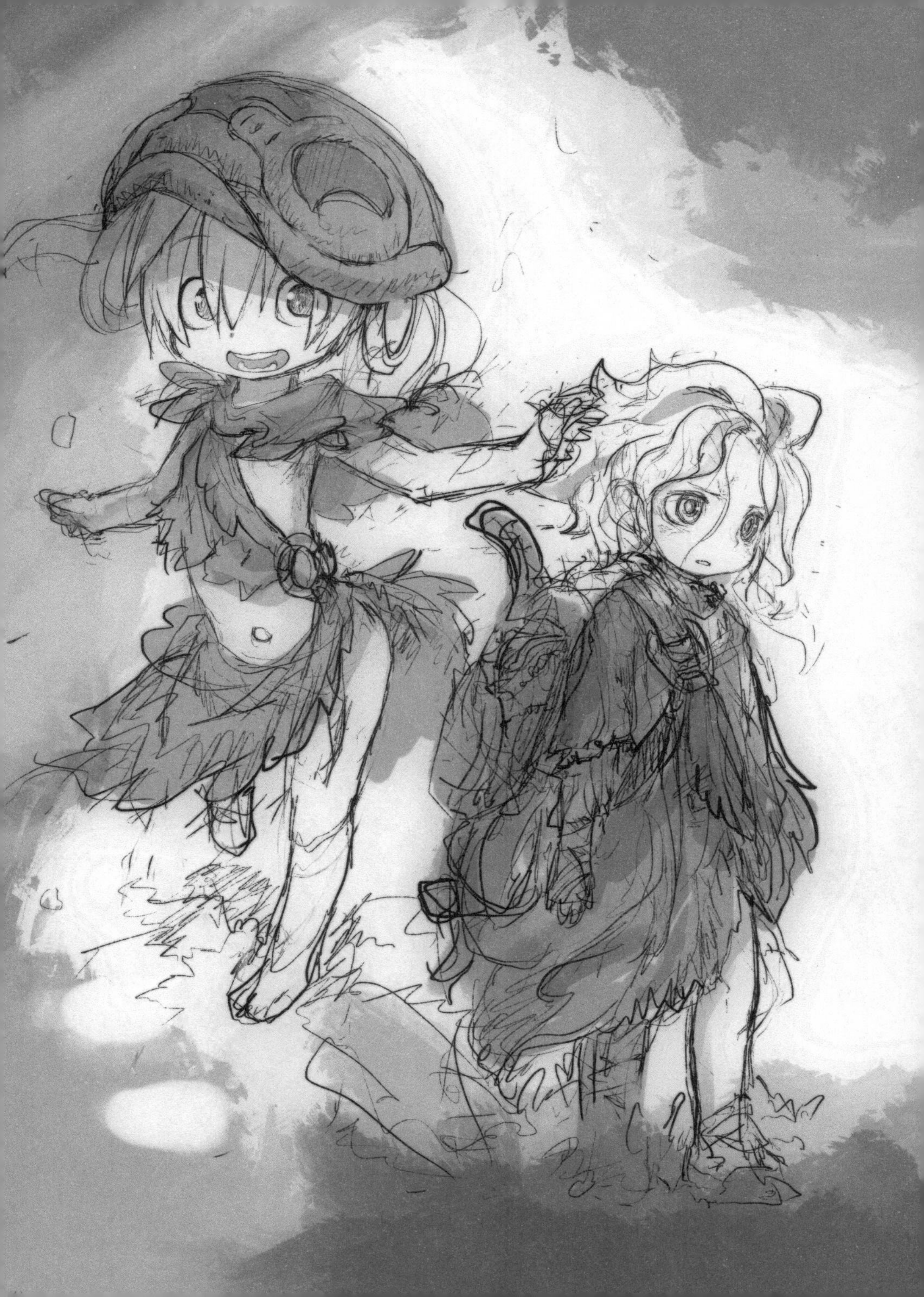

MADE IN ABYSS

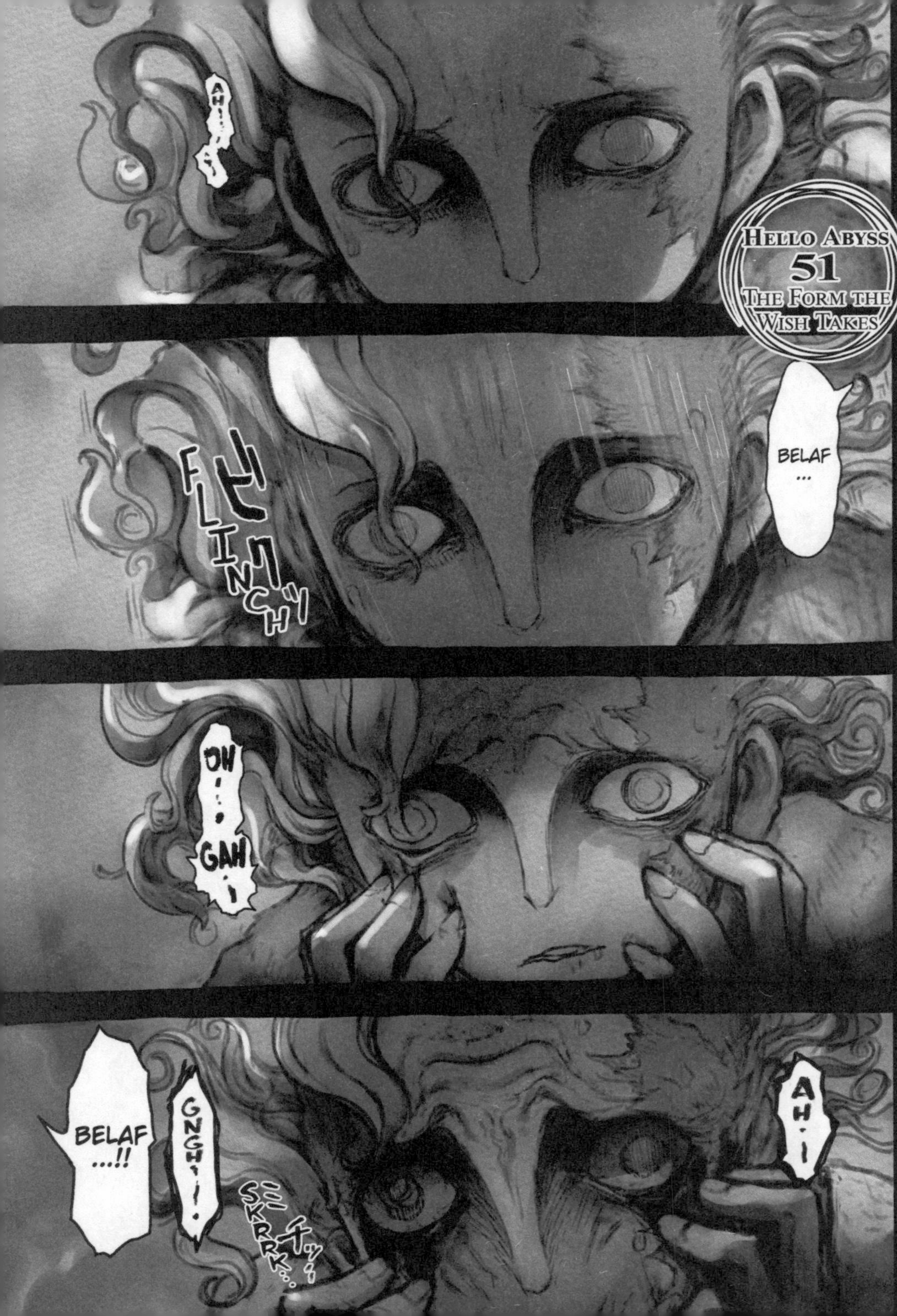
HELLO ABYSS
51
THE FORM THE WISH TAKES
AH...
BELAF...
FLINCH
OH... GAH
AH
GNGH!
SKRRK...
BELAF...!!

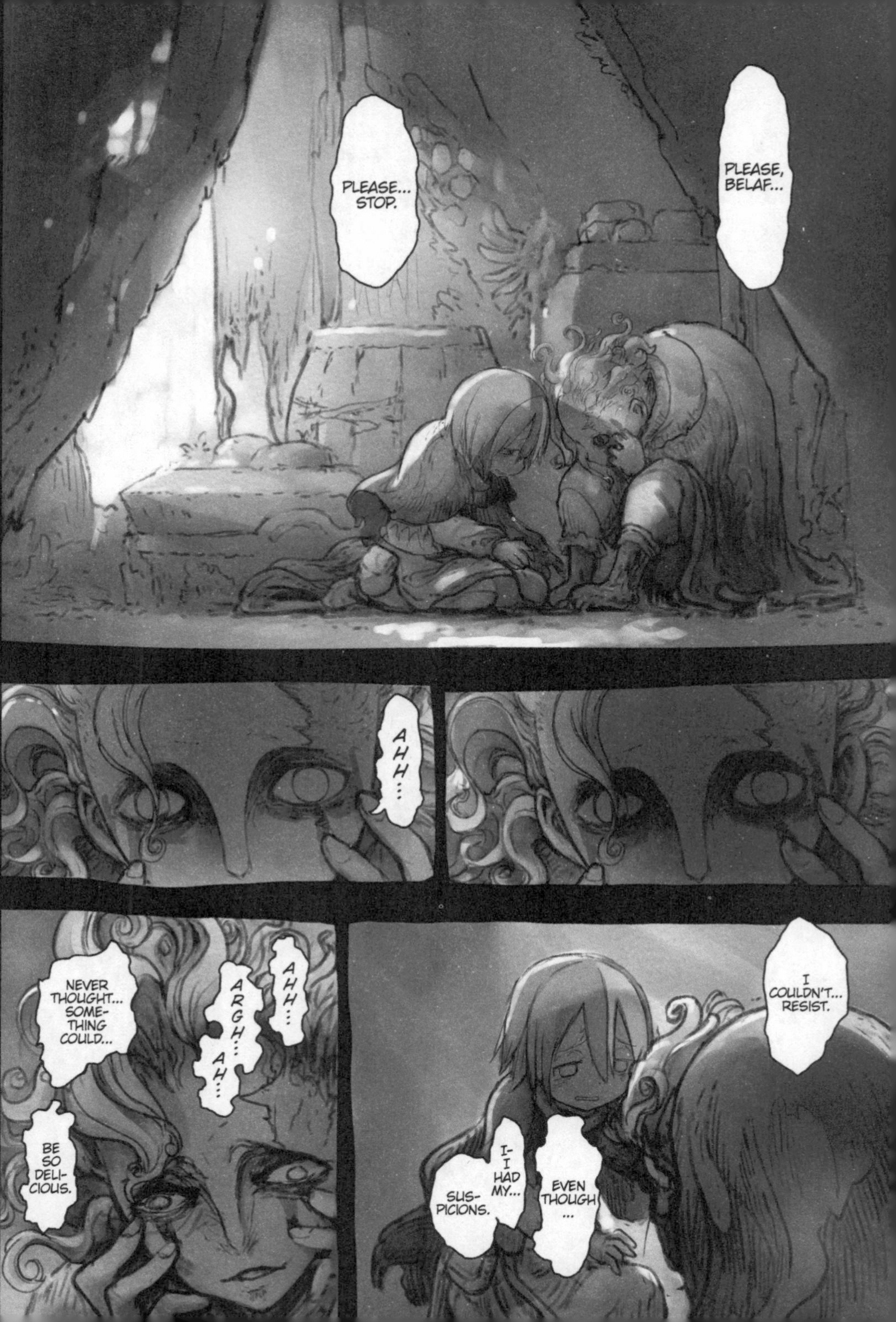
PLEASE, BELAF...
PLEASE... STOP.
AHH...
I COULDN'T... RESIST.
EVEN THOUGH ...
I-I HAD MY...
SUS-PICIONS.
AHH...
ARGH... AH...
NEVER THOUGHT... SOME-THING COULD...
BE SO DELI-CIOUS.

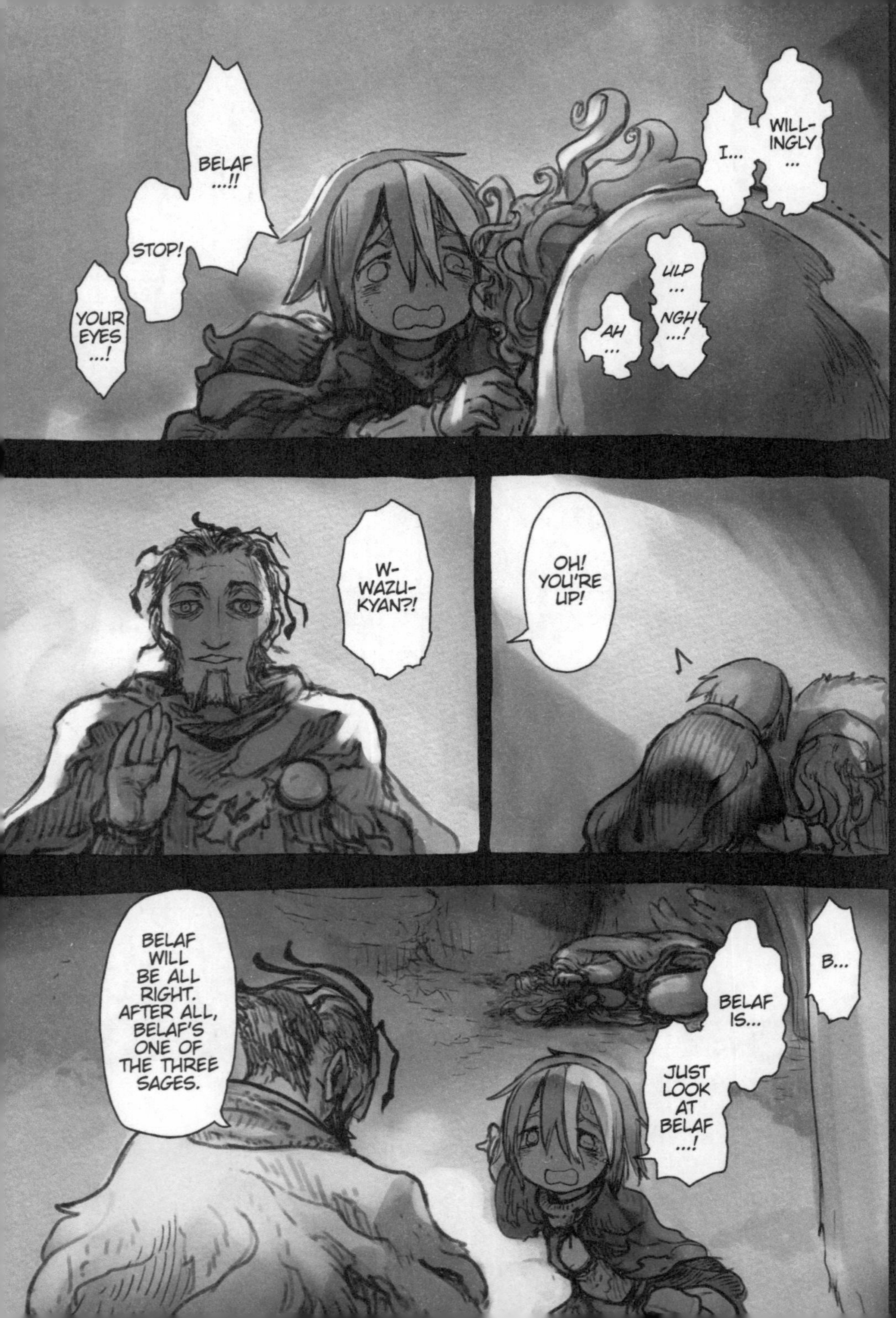
I... WILL-INGLY...
ULP... NGH...!
AH...
BELAF...!!
STOP!
YOUR EYES...!
OH! YOU'RE UP!
W-WAZU-KYAN?!
B...
BELAF IS...
JUST LOOK AT BELAF...!
BELAF WILL BE ALL RIGHT. AFTER ALL, BELAF'S ONE OF THE THREE SAGES.

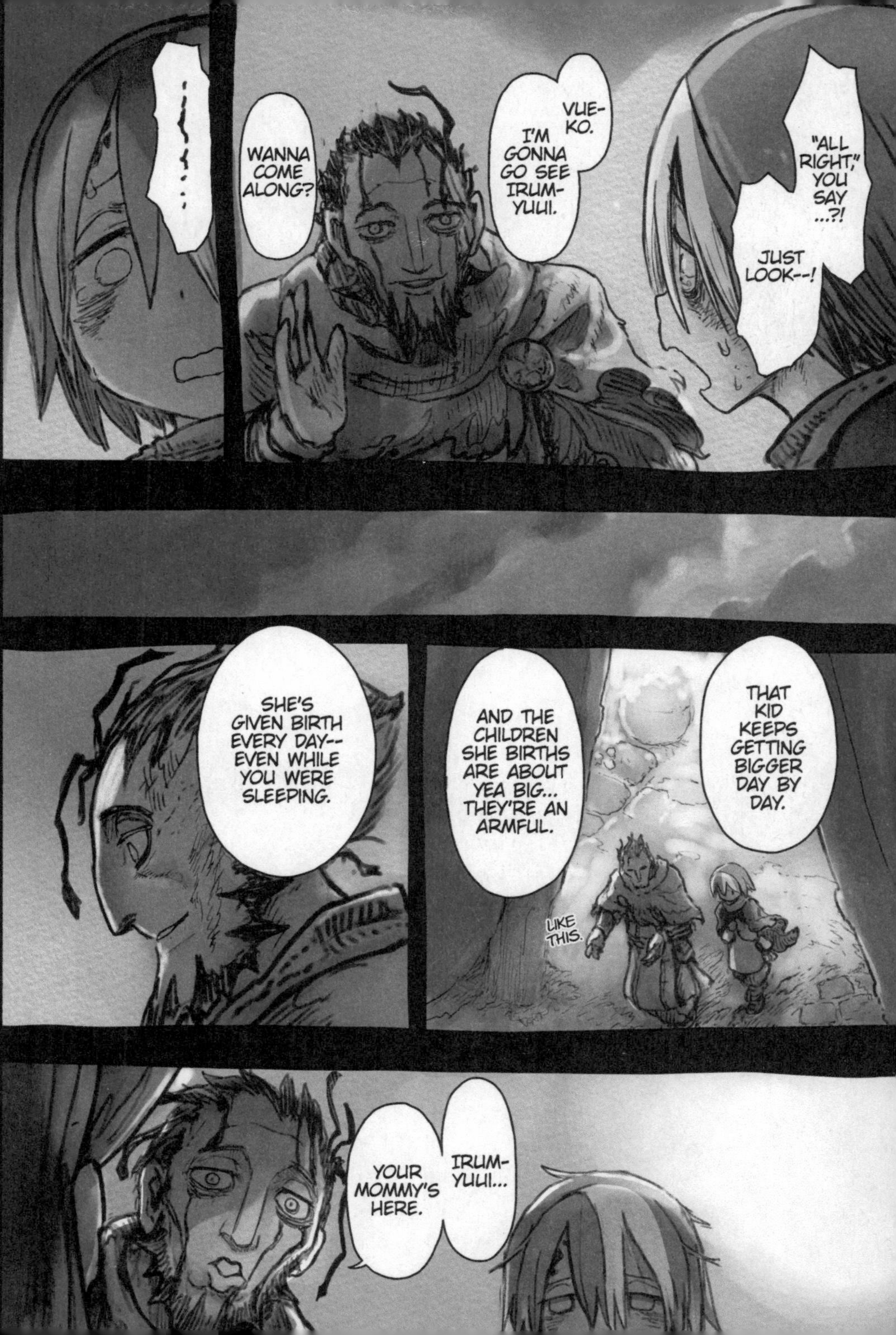

"ALL RIGHT," YOU SAY ...?!
JUST LOOK--!
VUEKO. I'M GONNA GO SEE IRUM-YUUI.
WANNA COME ALONG?
......
THAT KID KEEPS GETTING BIGGER DAY BY DAY.
AND THE CHILDREN SHE BIRTHS ARE ABOUT YEA BIG... THEY'RE AN ARMFUL.
LIKE THIS.
SHE'S GIVEN BIRTH EVERY DAY--EVEN WHILE YOU WERE SLEEPING.
IRUM-YUUI...
YOUR MOMMY'S HERE.

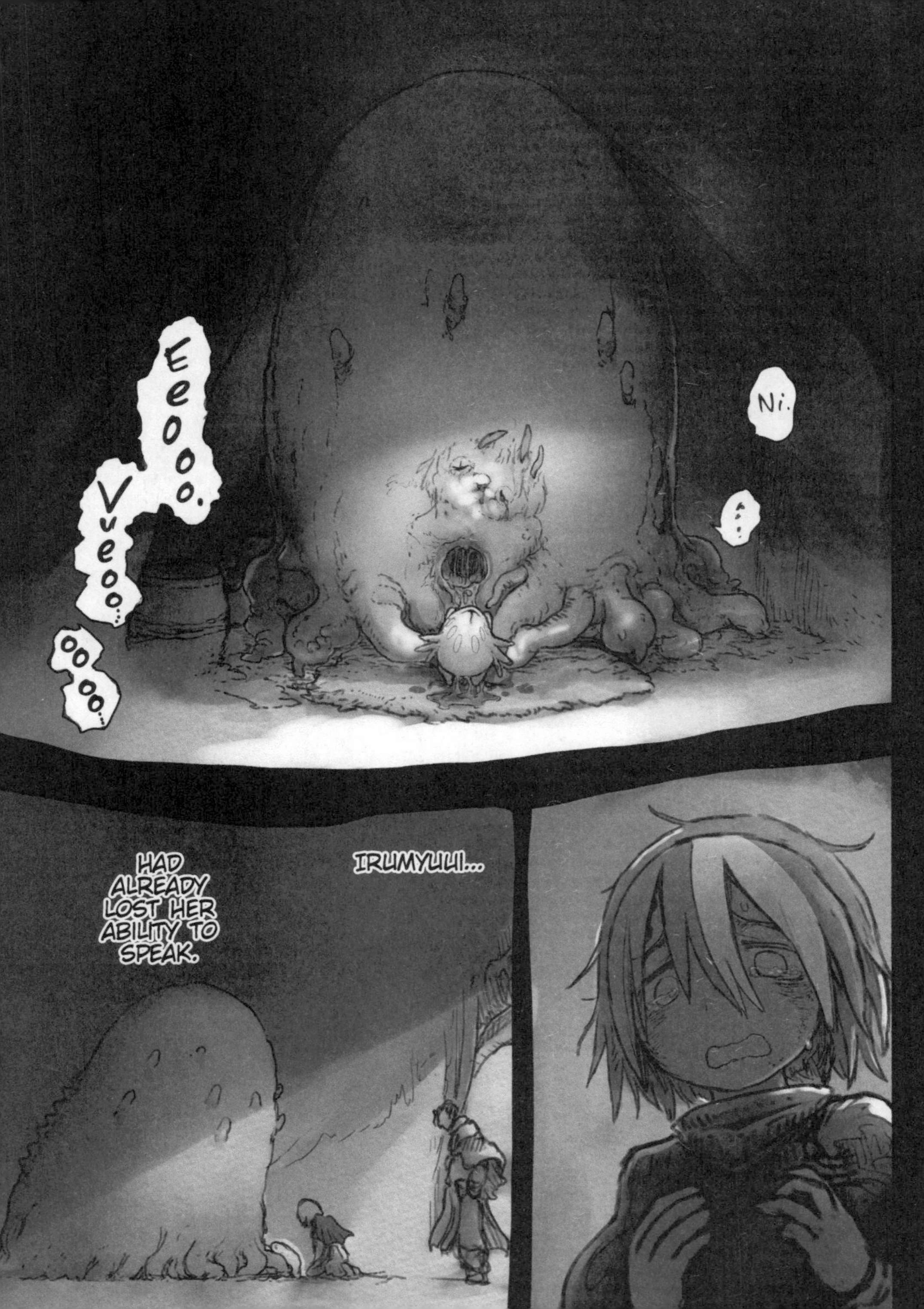
Ni.
...
Eeooo.
Vueoo...
oo oo...
IRUMYUUI...
HAD ALREADY LOST HER ABILITY TO SPEAK.

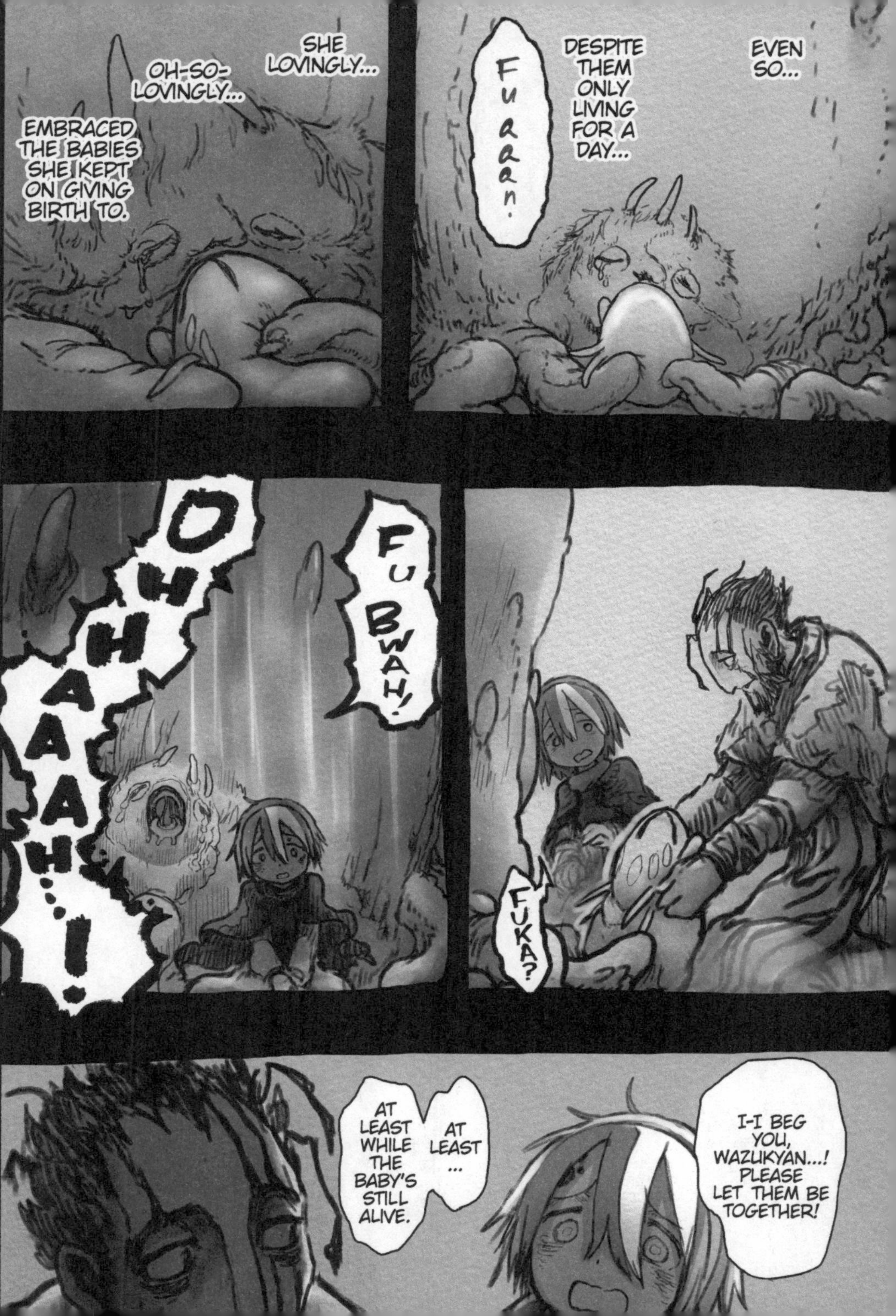
EVEN SO...
DESPITE THEM ONLY LIVING FOR A DAY...
Fuaaan.
SHE LOVINGLY...
OH-SO-LOVINGLY...
EMBRACED THE BABIES SHE KEPT ON GIVING BIRTH TO.
FUKA?
FU BWAH!
OHHAAAAAH...!
I-I BEG YOU, WAZUKYAN...! PLEASE LET THEM BE TOGETHER!
AT LEAST...
AT LEAST WHILE THE BABY'S STILL ALIVE.

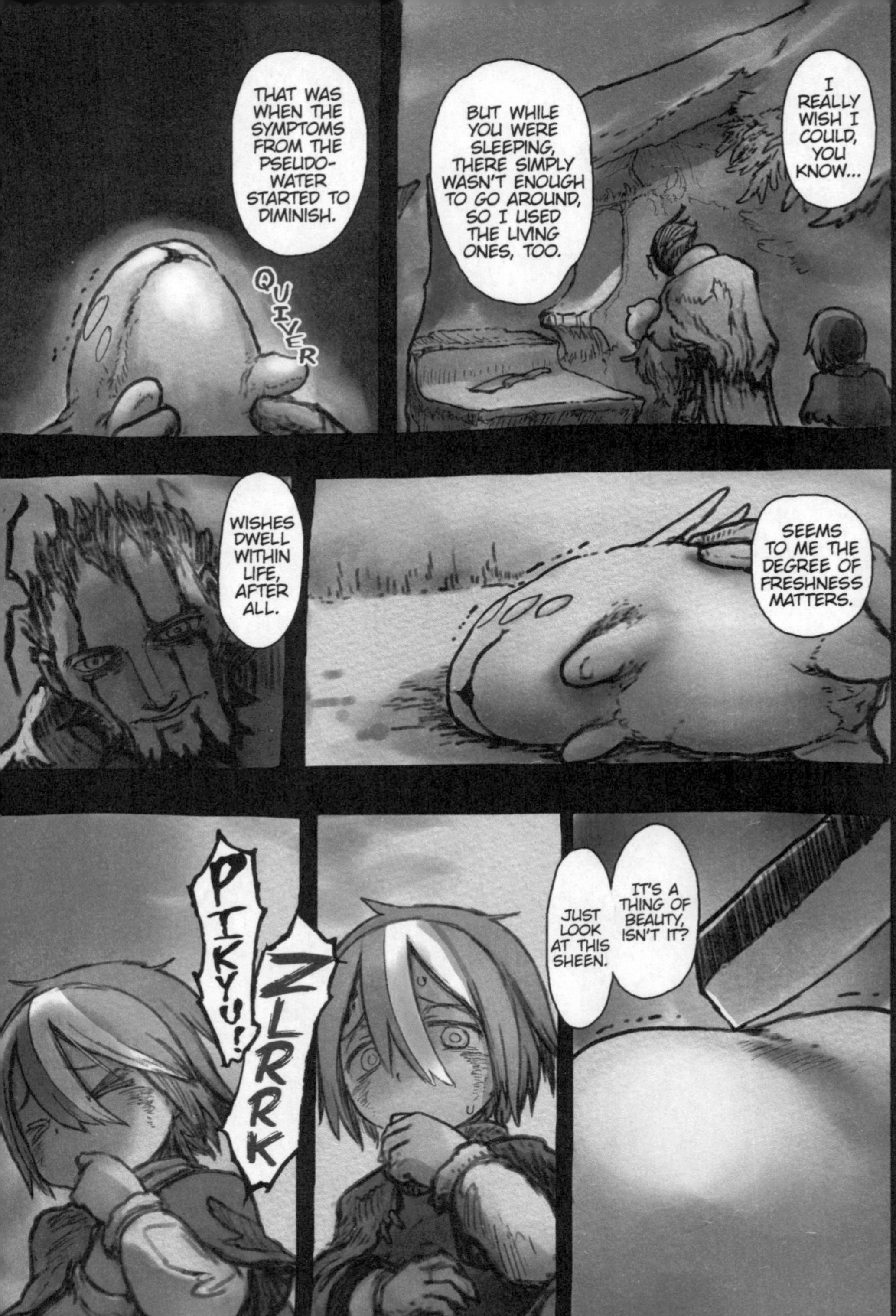
I REALLY WISH I COULD, YOU KNOW...
BUT WHILE YOU WERE SLEEPING, THERE SIMPLY WASN'T ENOUGH TO GO AROUND, SO I USED THE LIVING ONES, TOO.
THAT WAS WHEN THE SYMPTOMS FROM THE PSEUDO-WATER STARTED TO DIMINISH.
QUIVER
SEEMS TO ME THE DEGREE OF FRESHNESS MATTERS.
WISHES DWELL WITHIN LIFE, AFTER ALL.
IT'S A THING OF BEAUTY, ISN'T IT?
JUST LOOK AT THIS SHEEN.
ZLRRK
PIKYU!

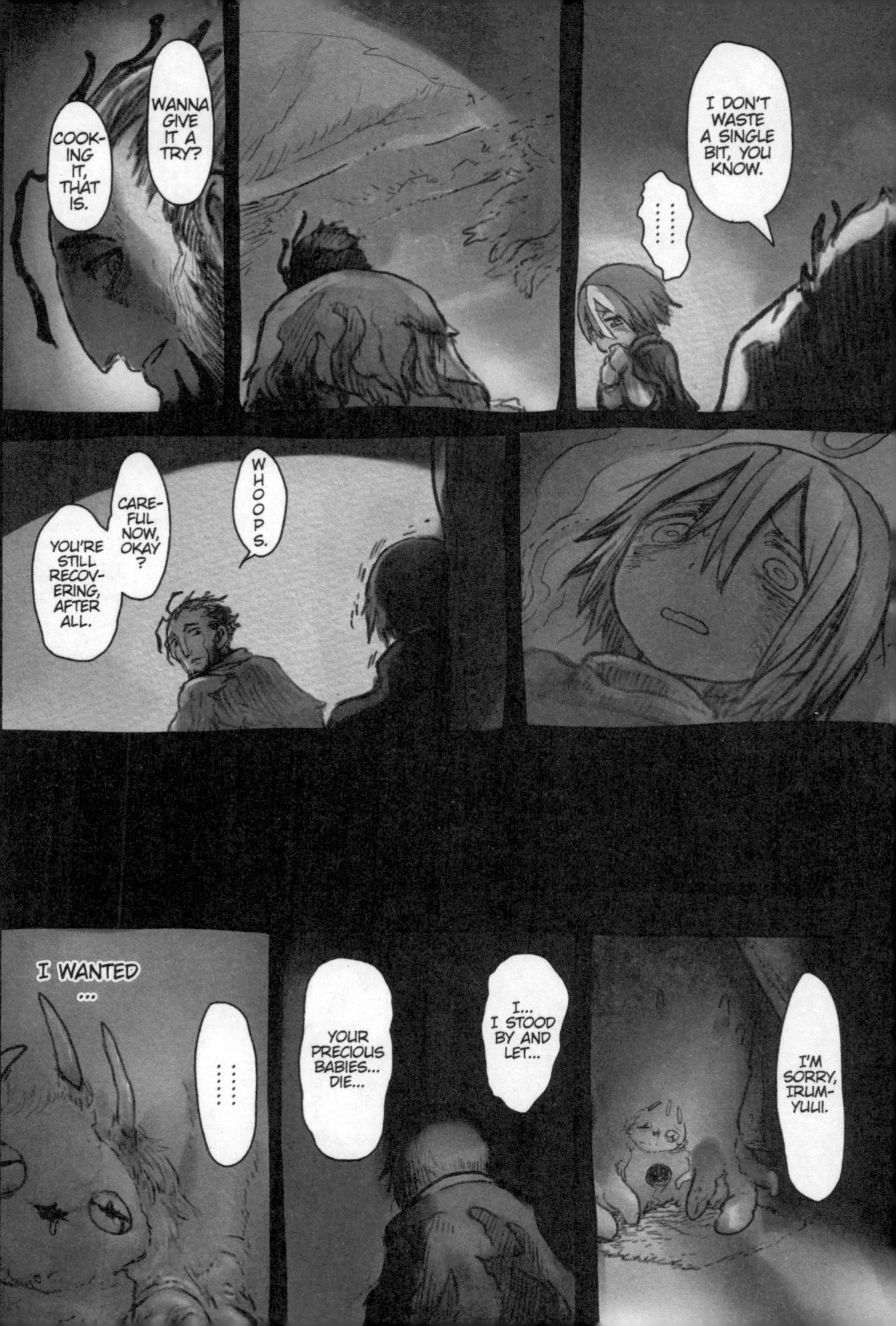
I DON'T WASTE A SINGLE BIT, YOU KNOW.
……
WANNA GIVE IT A TRY?
COOKING IT, THAT IS.
WHOOPS.
CAREFUL NOW, OKAY?
YOU'RE STILL RECOVERING, AFTER ALL.
I'M SORRY, IRUMYUUI.
I... I STOOD BY AND LET...
YOUR PRECIOUS BABIES... DIE...
I WANTED...
……

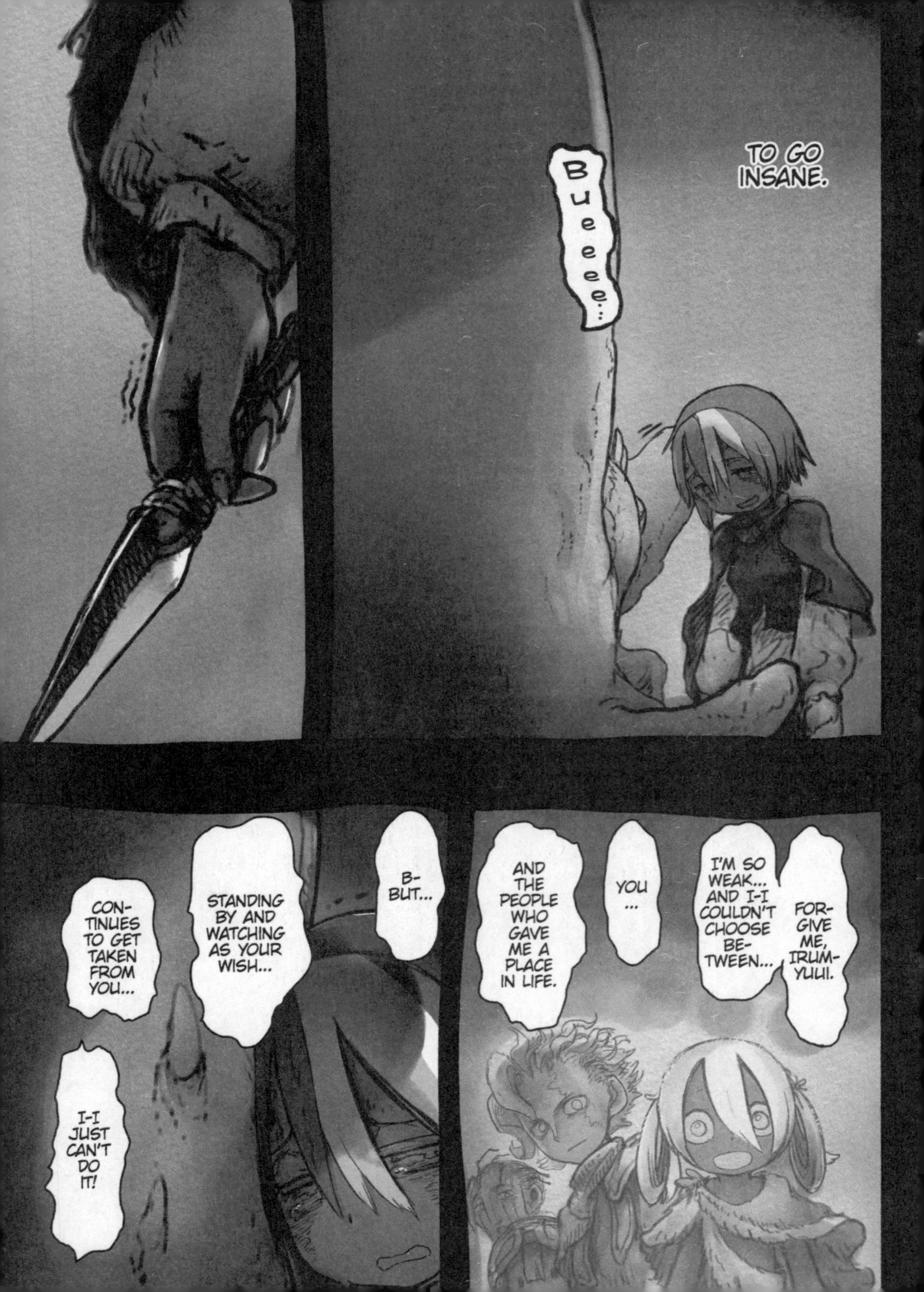
TO GO INSANE.
Bueeee...
FORGIVE ME, IRUMYUUI.
I'M SO WEAK... AND I-I COULDN'T CHOOSE BETWEEN...
YOU...
AND THE PEOPLE WHO GAVE ME A PLACE IN LIFE.
B-BUT...
STANDING BY AND WATCHING AS YOUR WISH...
CONTINUES TO GET TAKEN FROM YOU...
I-I JUST CAN'T DO IT!

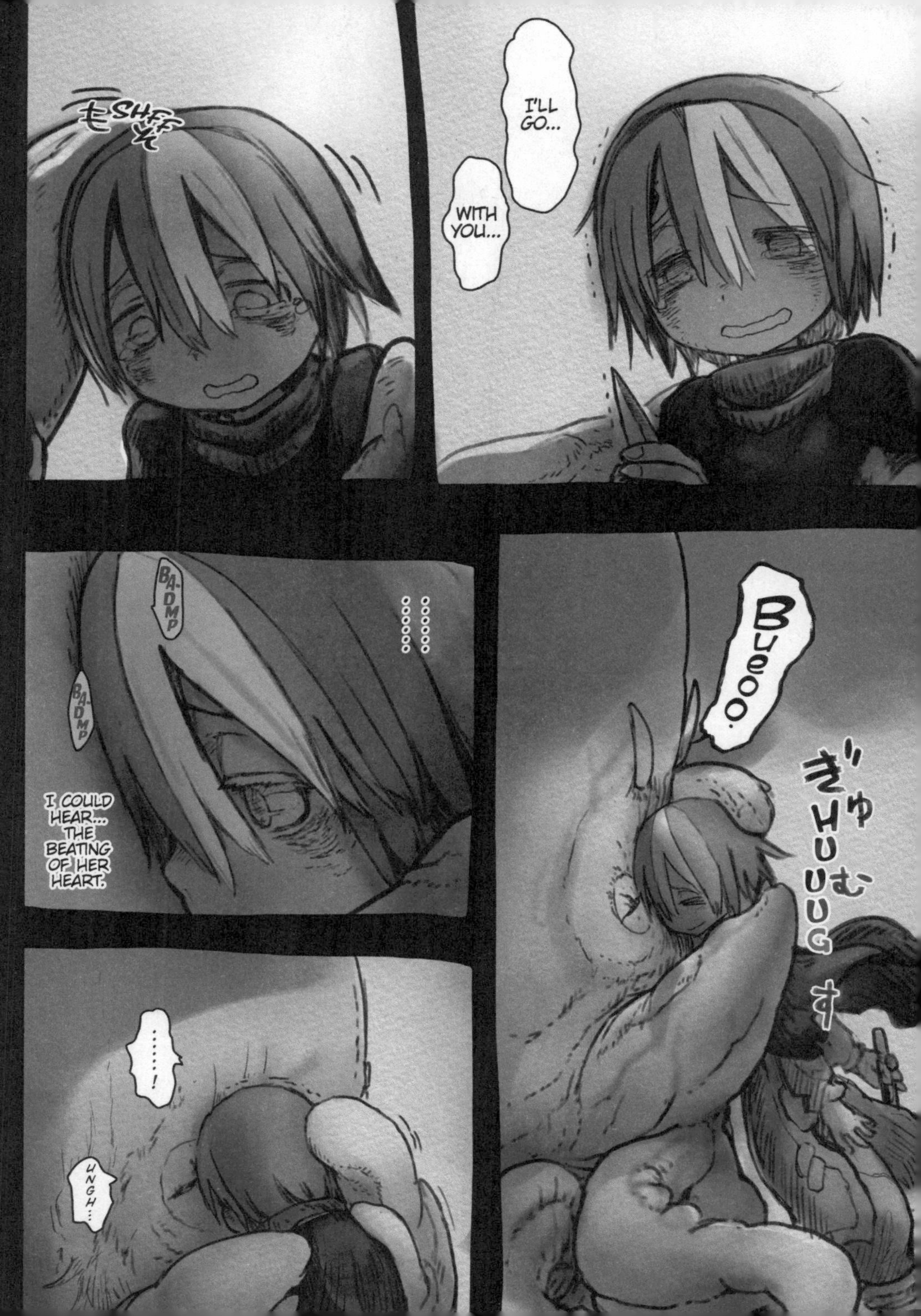
I'LL GO...
WITH YOU...
SHFF
Bueooo.
HUUUG
BA-DMP
BA-DMP
I COULD HEAR... THE BEATING OF HER HEART.
......!
UNGH...

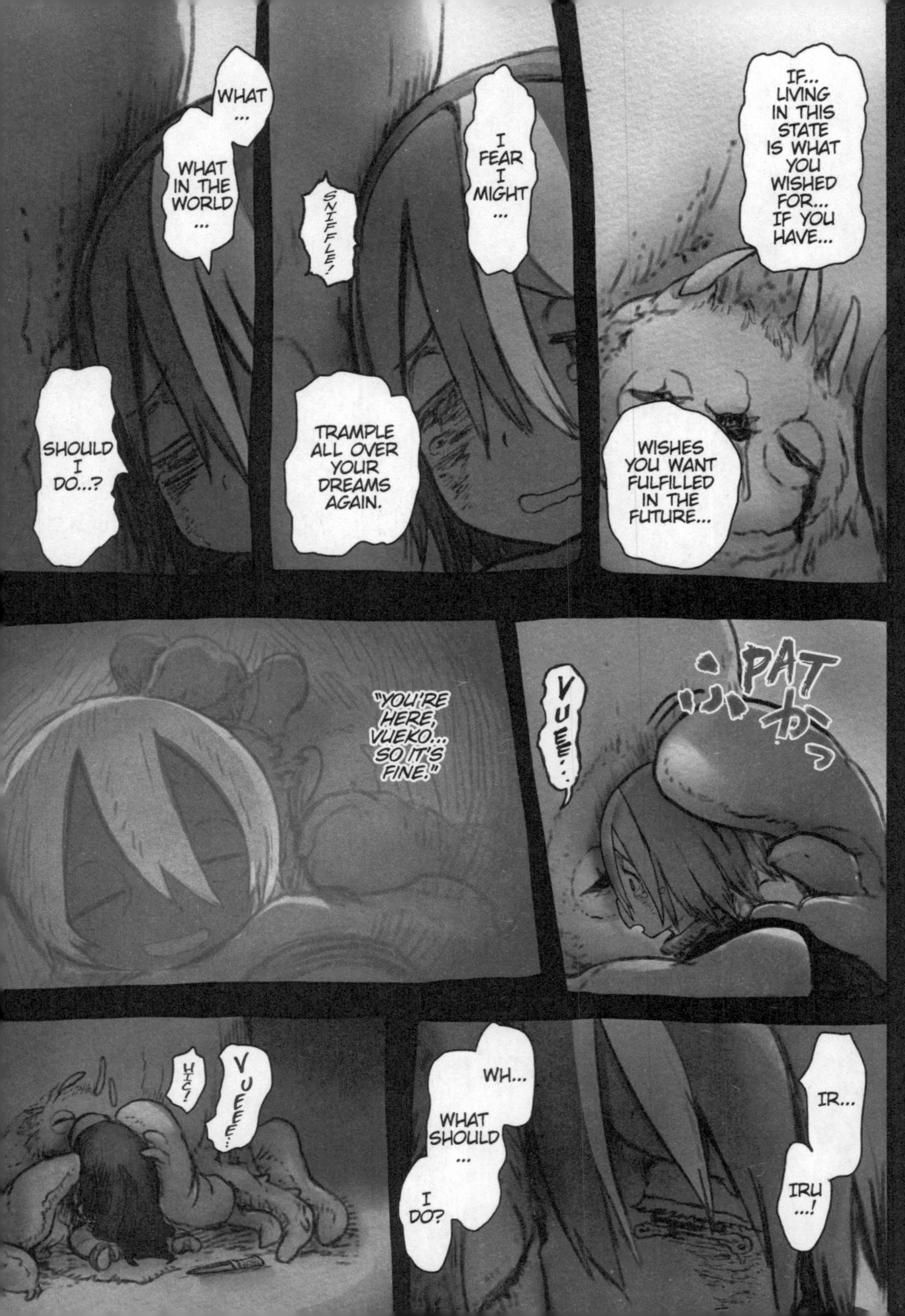
IF... LIVING IN THIS STATE IS WHAT YOU WISHED FOR... IF YOU HAVE...
WISHES YOU WANT FULFILLED IN THE FUTURE...
I FEAR I MIGHT ...
SNIFFLE!
TRAMPLE ALL OVER YOUR DREAMS AGAIN.
WHAT ...
WHAT IN THE WORLD ...
SHOULD I DO...?
PAT
VUEE...
"YOU'RE HERE, VUEKO... SO IT'S FINE."
IR...
IRU ...!
WH...
WHAT SHOULD ...
I DO?
VUEEE...
HIC!

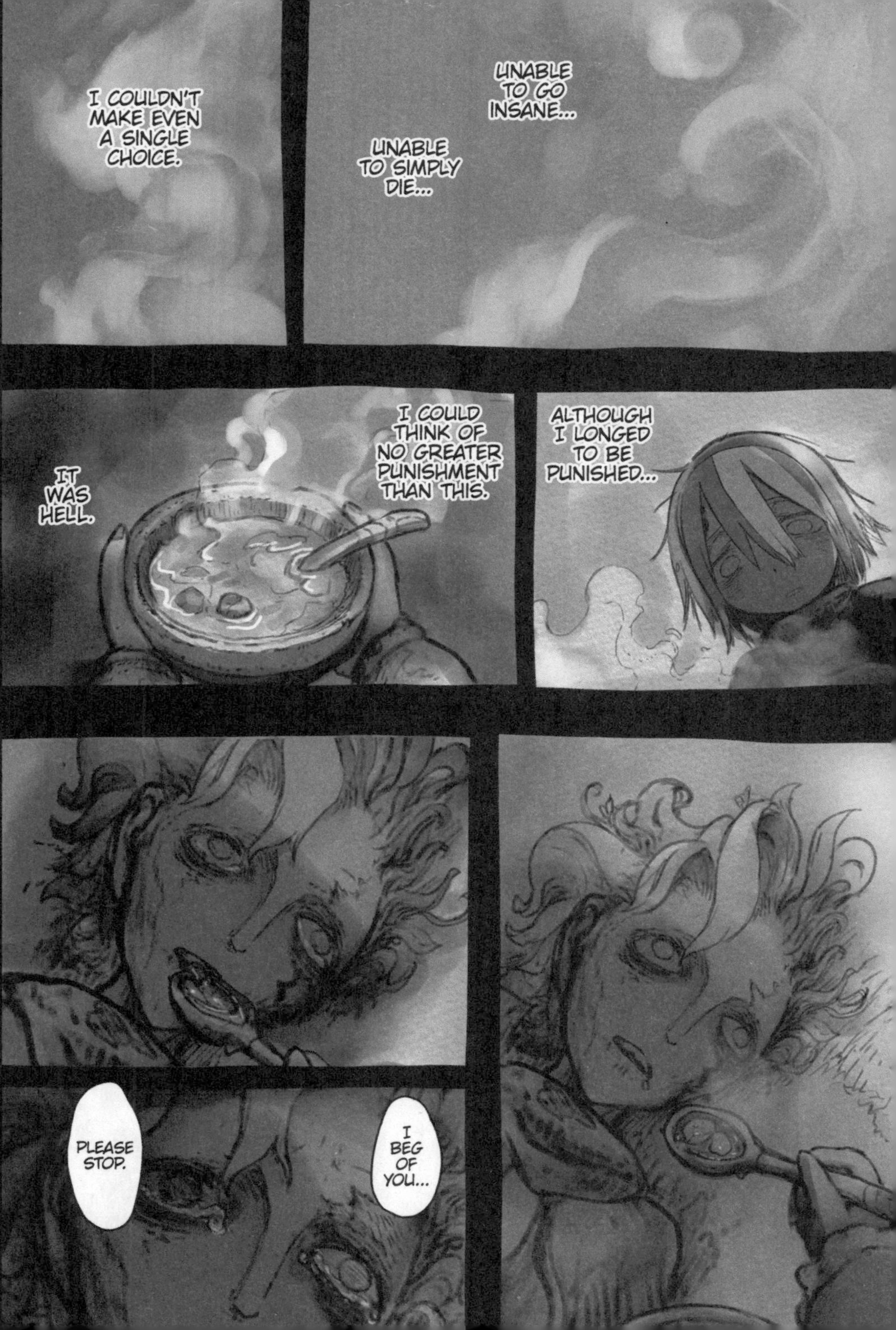
UNABLE TO GO INSANE...
UNABLE TO SIMPLY DIE...
I COULDN'T MAKE EVEN A SINGLE CHOICE.
ALTHOUGH I LONGED TO BE PUNISHED...
I COULD THINK OF NO GREATER PUNISHMENT THAN THIS.
IT WAS HELL.
I BEG OF YOU...
PLEASE STOP.

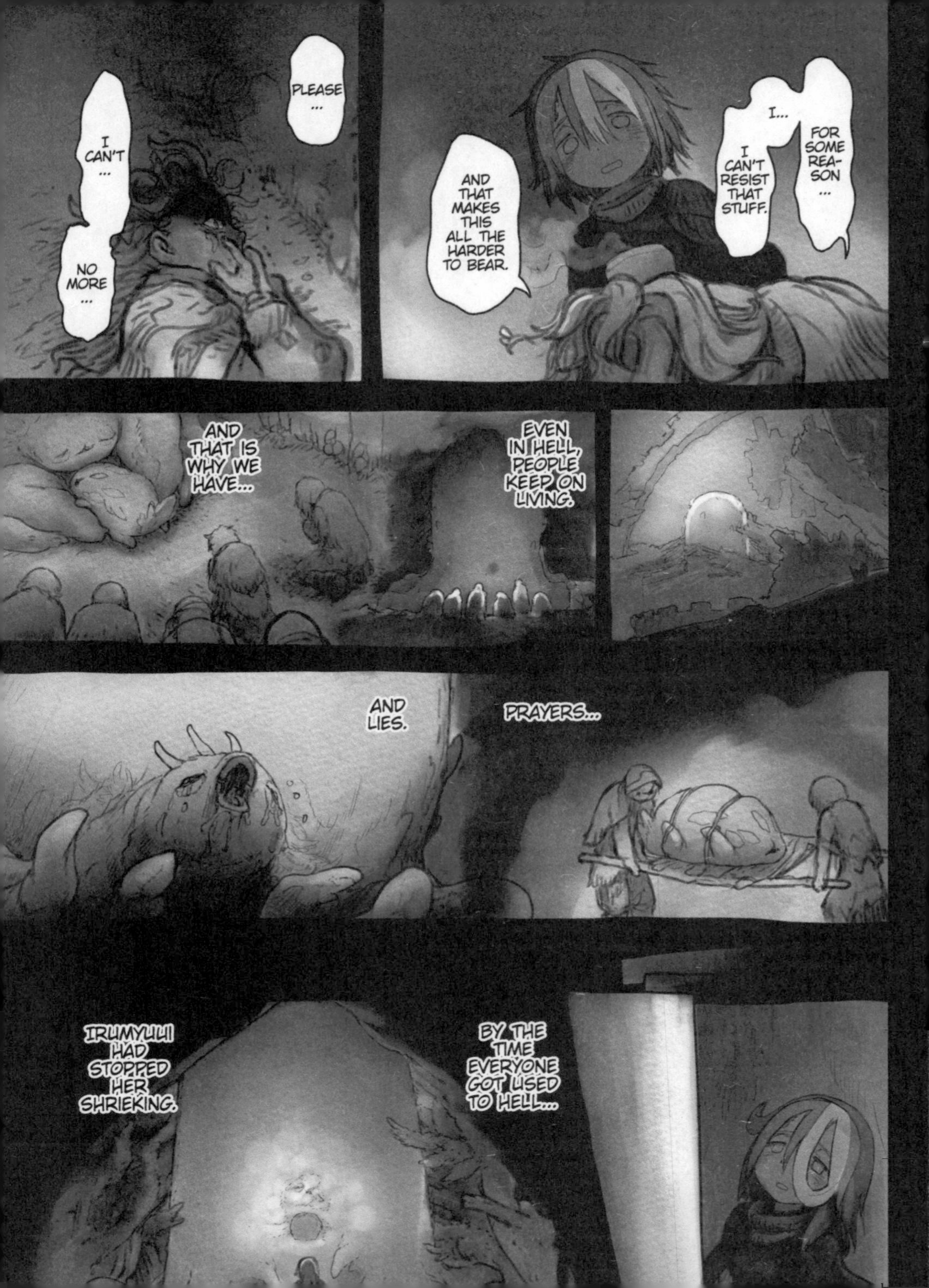
FOR SOME REA-SON...
I... I CAN'T RESIST THAT STUFF.
AND THAT MAKES THIS ALL THE HARDER TO BEAR.
PLEASE...
I CAN'T...
NO MORE...
EVEN IN HELL, PEOPLE KEEP ON LIVING.
AND THAT IS WHY WE HAVE...
PRAYERS...
AND LIES.
BY THE TIME EVERYONE GOT USED TO HELL...
IRUMYUUI HAD STOPPED HER SHRIEKING.

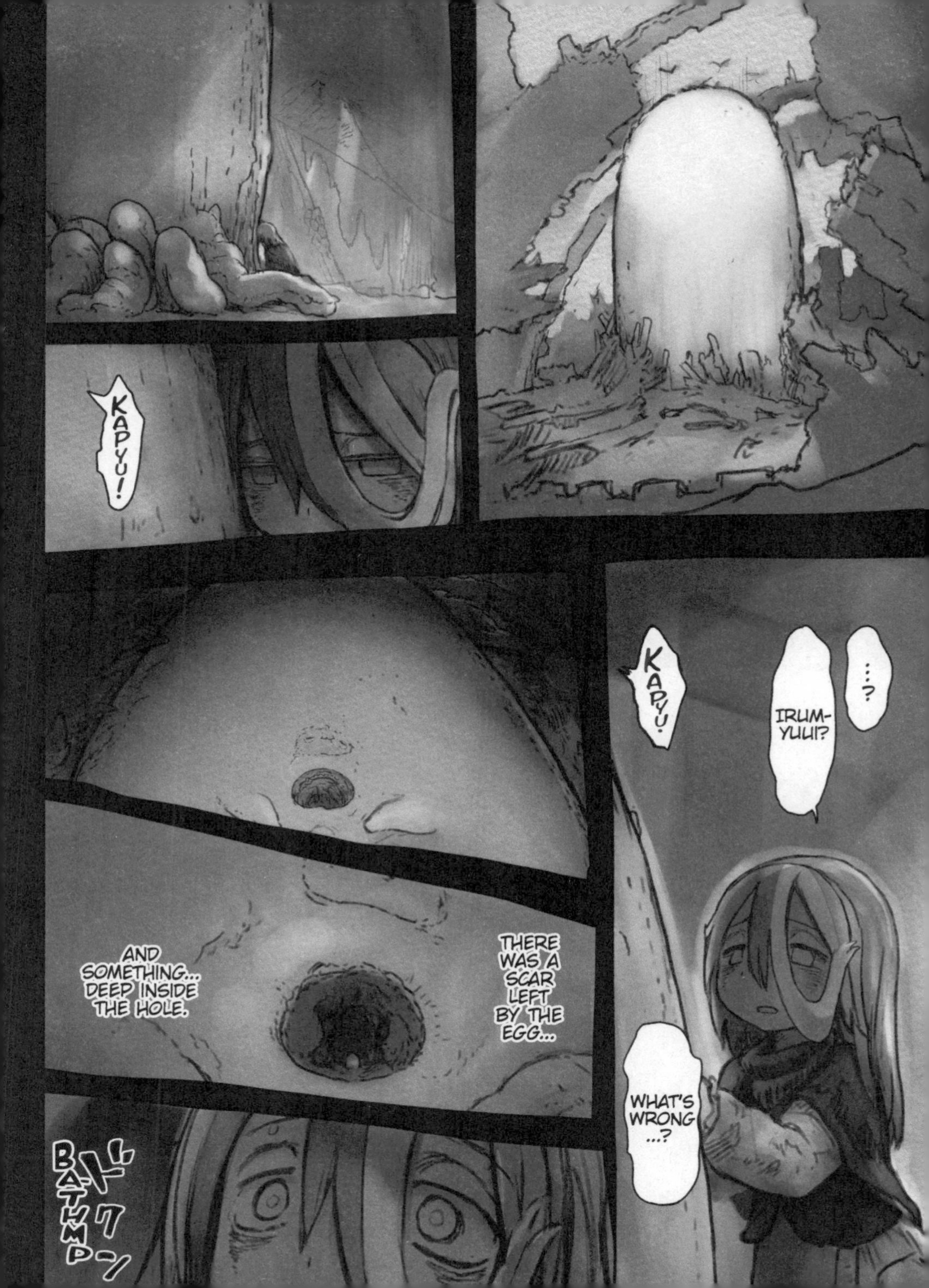
KAPYU!
...?
IRUM-YUUI?
KAPYU.
WHAT'S WRONG ...?
THERE WAS A SCAR LEFT BY THE EGG...
AND SOMETHING... DEEP INSIDE THE HOLE.
BA-THUMP

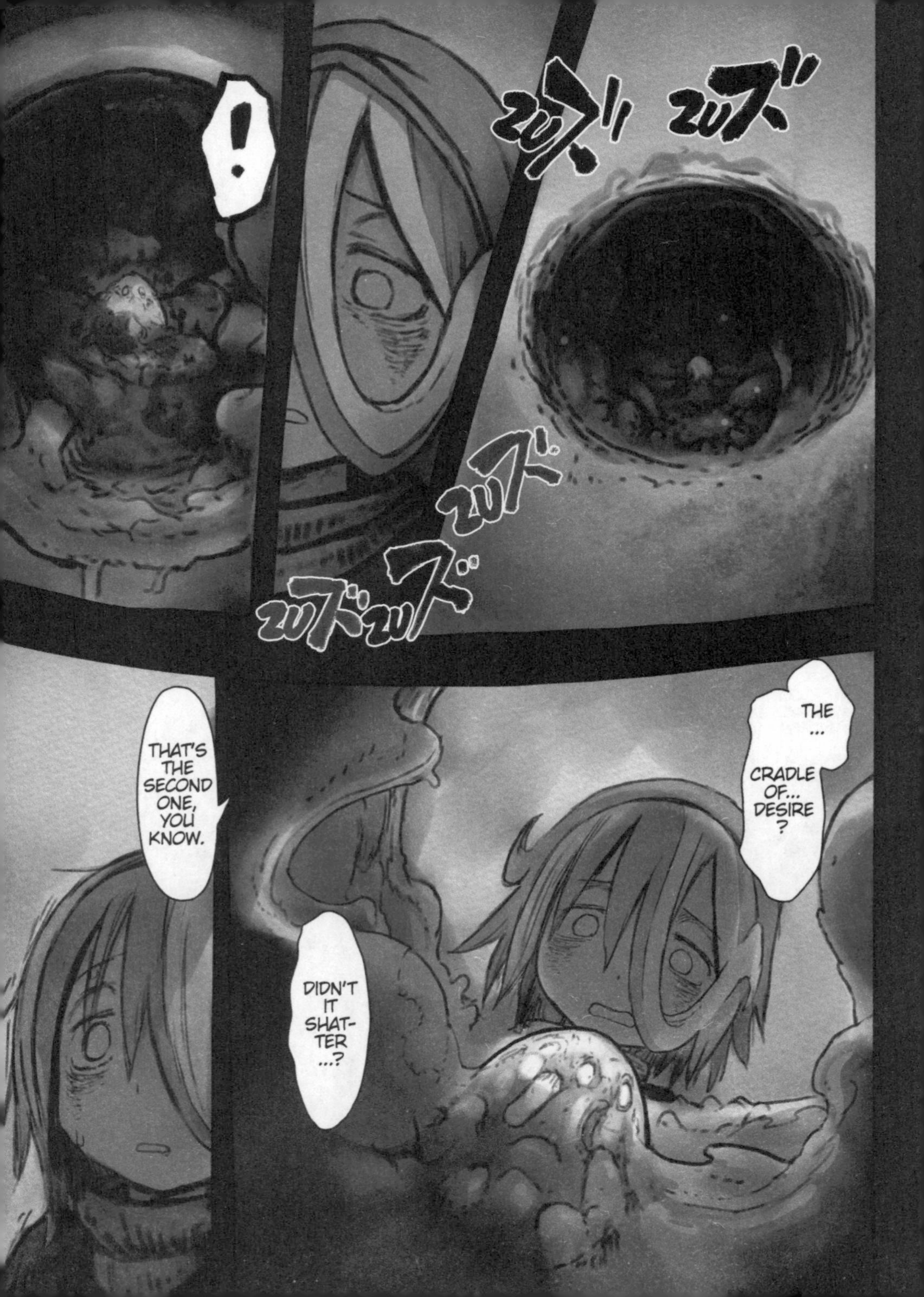
ZUズ ZUズ
ZUズ
ZUズZUズ
!
THE... CRADLE OF... DESIRE?
DIDN'T IT SHATTER...?
THAT'S THE SECOND ONE, YOU KNOW.

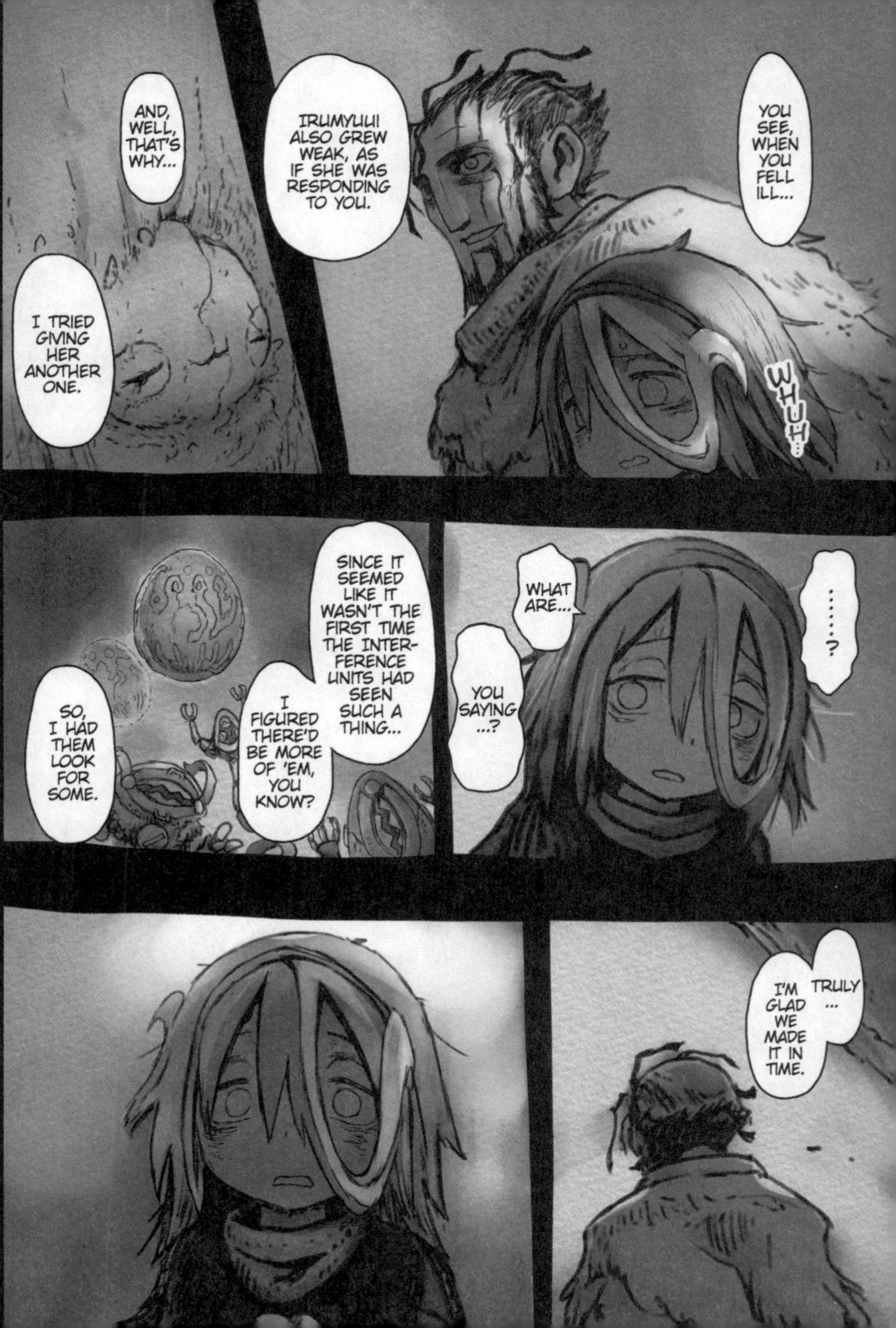
YOU SEE, WHEN YOU FELL ILL...
WHUH...
IRUMYUUI ALSO GREW WEAK, AS IF SHE WAS RESPONDING TO YOU.
AND, WELL, THAT'S WHY...
I TRIED GIVING HER ANOTHER ONE.
......?
WHAT ARE...
YOU SAYING ...?
SINCE IT SEEMED LIKE IT WASN'T THE FIRST TIME THE INTER-FERENCE UNITS HAD SEEN SUCH A THING...
I FIGURED THERE'D BE MORE OF 'EM, YOU KNOW?
SO, I HAD THEM LOOK FOR SOME.
TRULY...
I'M GLAD WE MADE IT IN TIME.

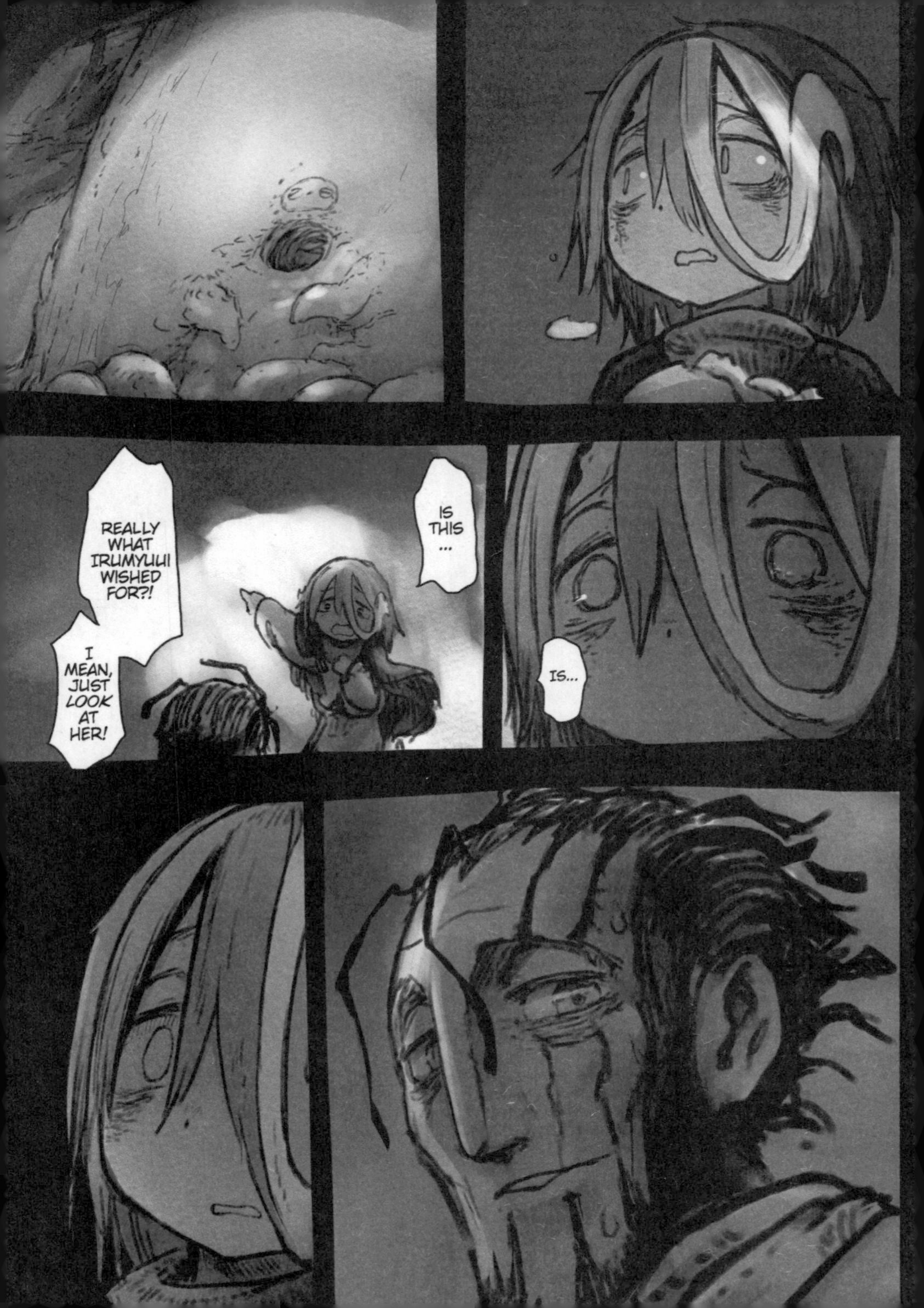
IS...
IS THIS ...
REALLY WHAT IRUMYUUI WISHED FOR?!
I MEAN, JUST LOOK AT HER!

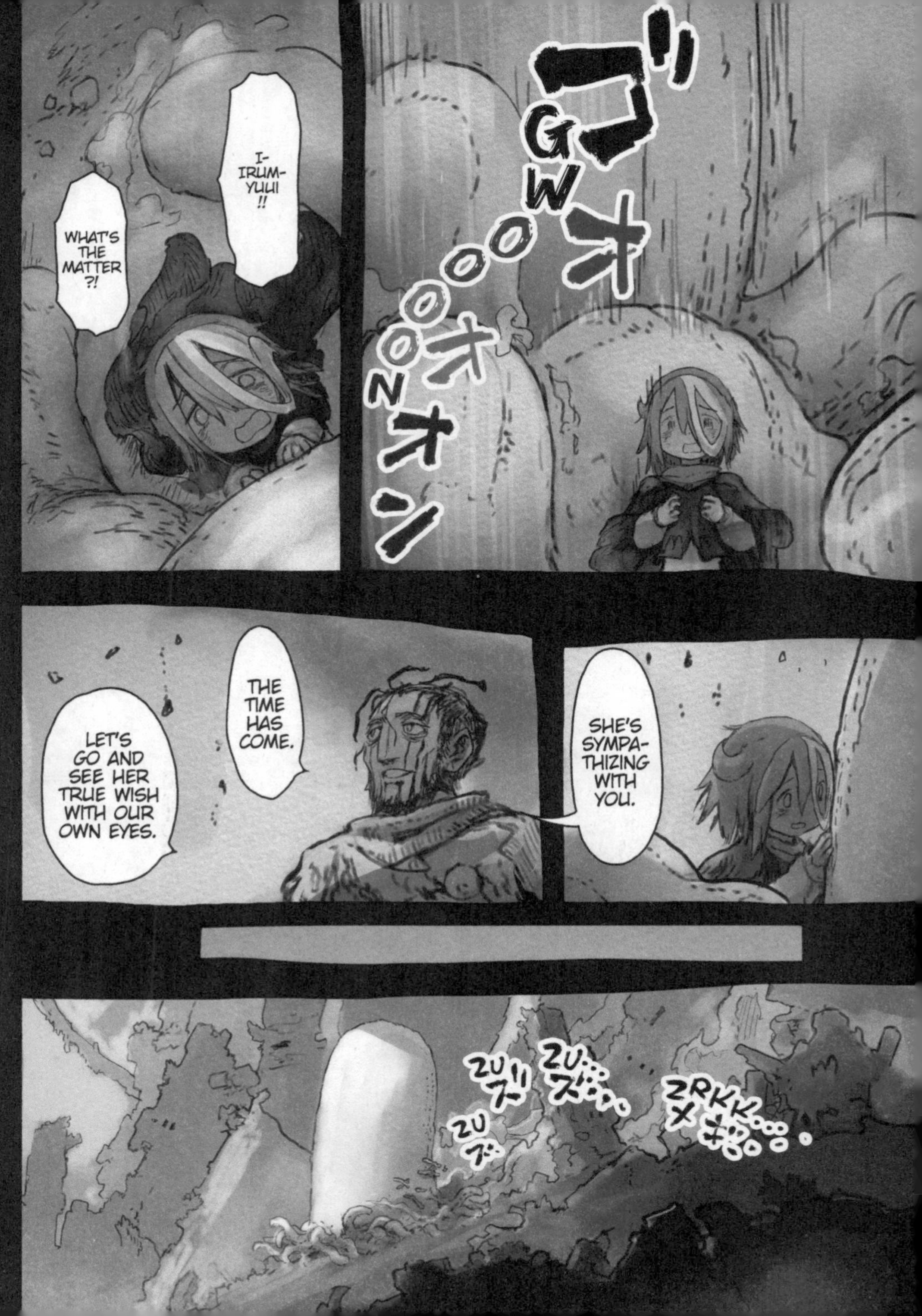
GWOOOOON
I-IRUMYUUI!!
WHAT'S THE MATTER?!
SHE'S SYMPATHIZING WITH YOU.
THE TIME HAS COME.
LET'S GO AND SEE HER TRUE WISH WITH OUR OWN EYES.
ZU!!
ZU...
ZU
ZRKK...

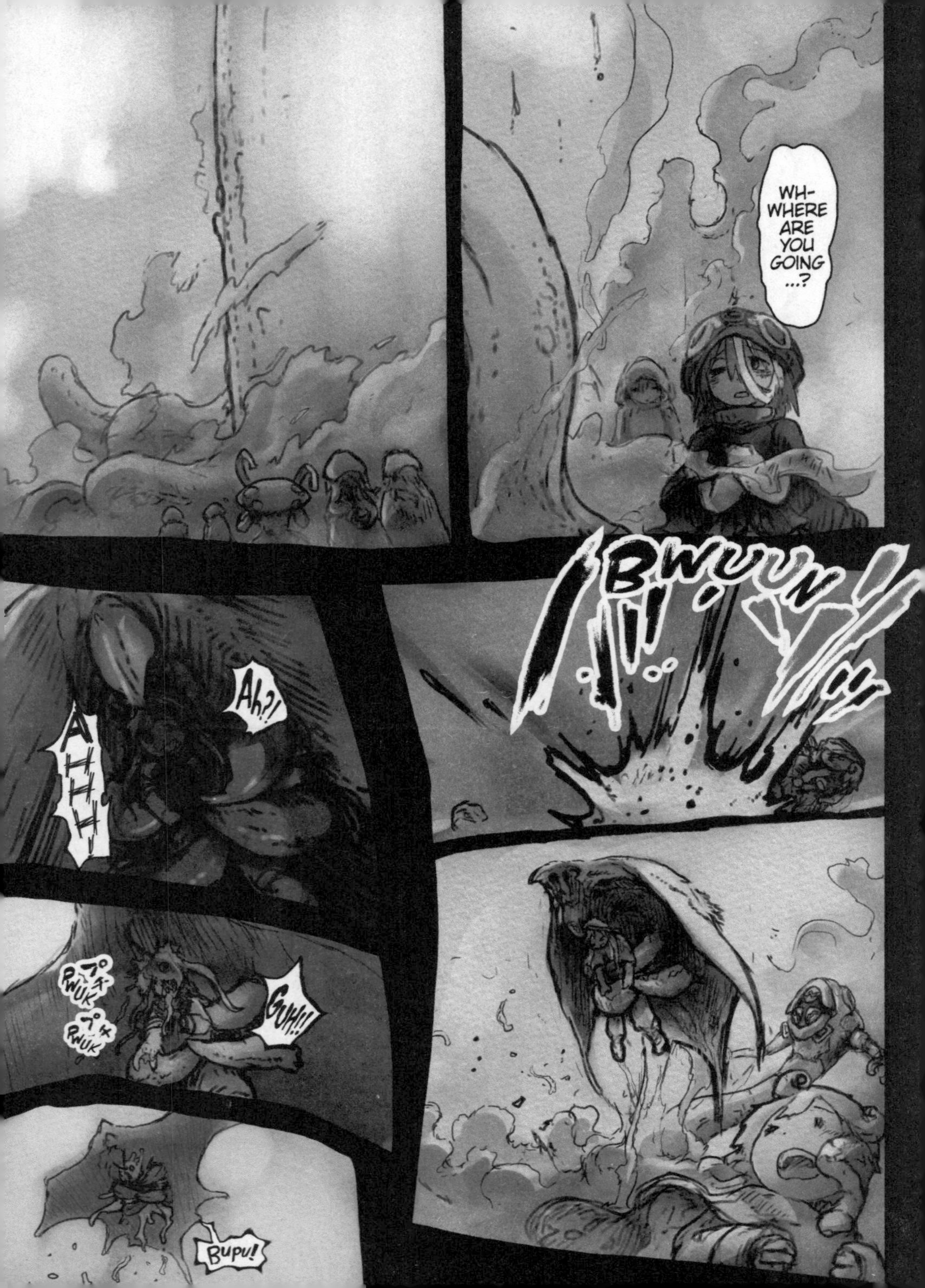
WH-WHERE ARE YOU GOING ...?
BWUUN!
Ah?!
AHHHH
GUH!!
プチ PWUK
プチ PWUK
Bupu!

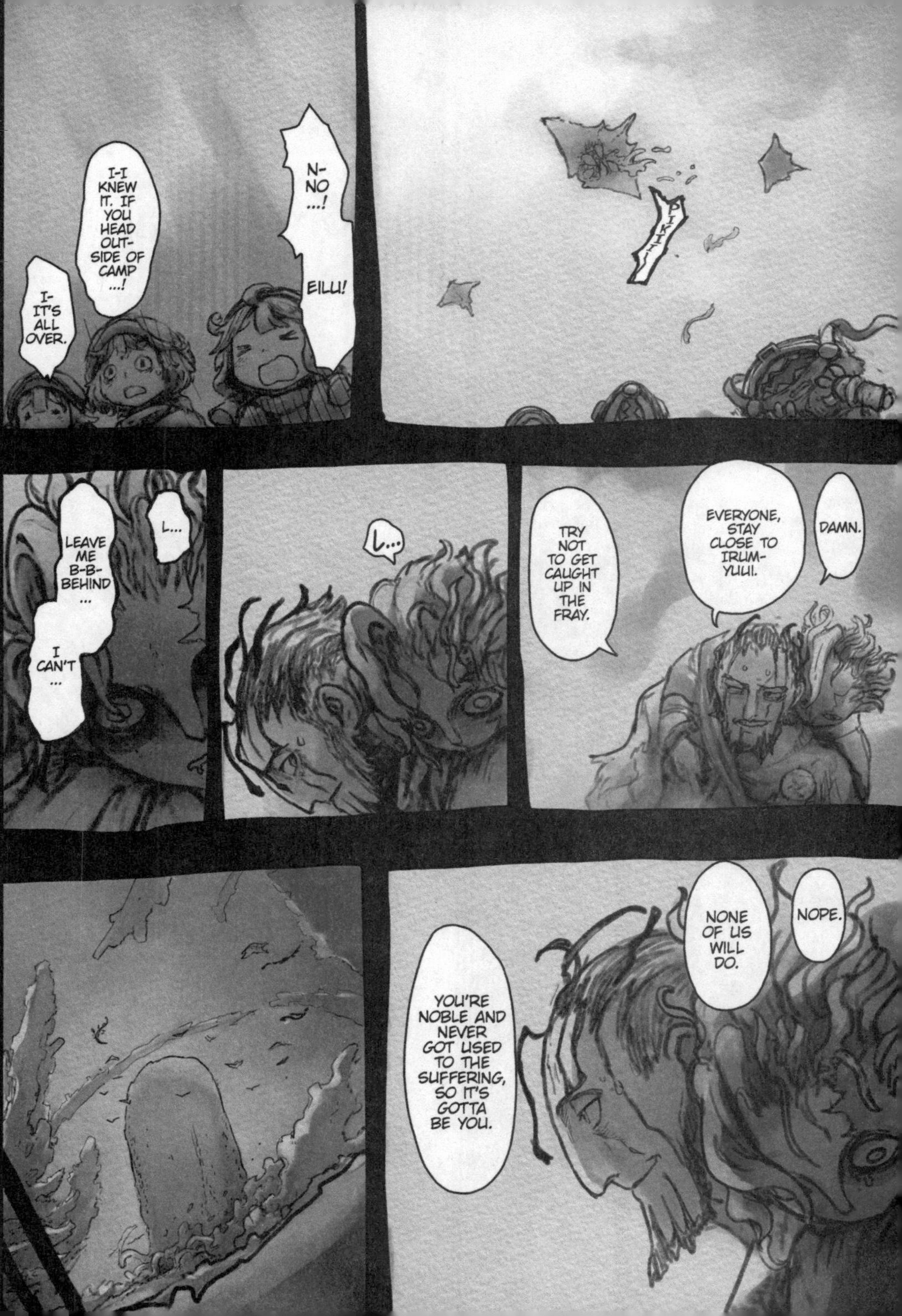
PIKII!
N-NO...! EILU!
I-I KNEW IT. IF YOU HEAD OUTSIDE OF CAMP...!
I- IT'S ALL OVER.
DAMN.
EVERYONE, STAY CLOSE TO IRUMYUUI.
TRY NOT TO GET CAUGHT UP IN THE FRAY.
L...
L...
LEAVE ME B-B-BEHIND...
I CAN'T...
NOPE.
NONE OF US WILL DO.
YOU'RE NOBLE AND NEVER GOT USED TO THE SUFFERING, SO IT'S GOTTA BE YOU.

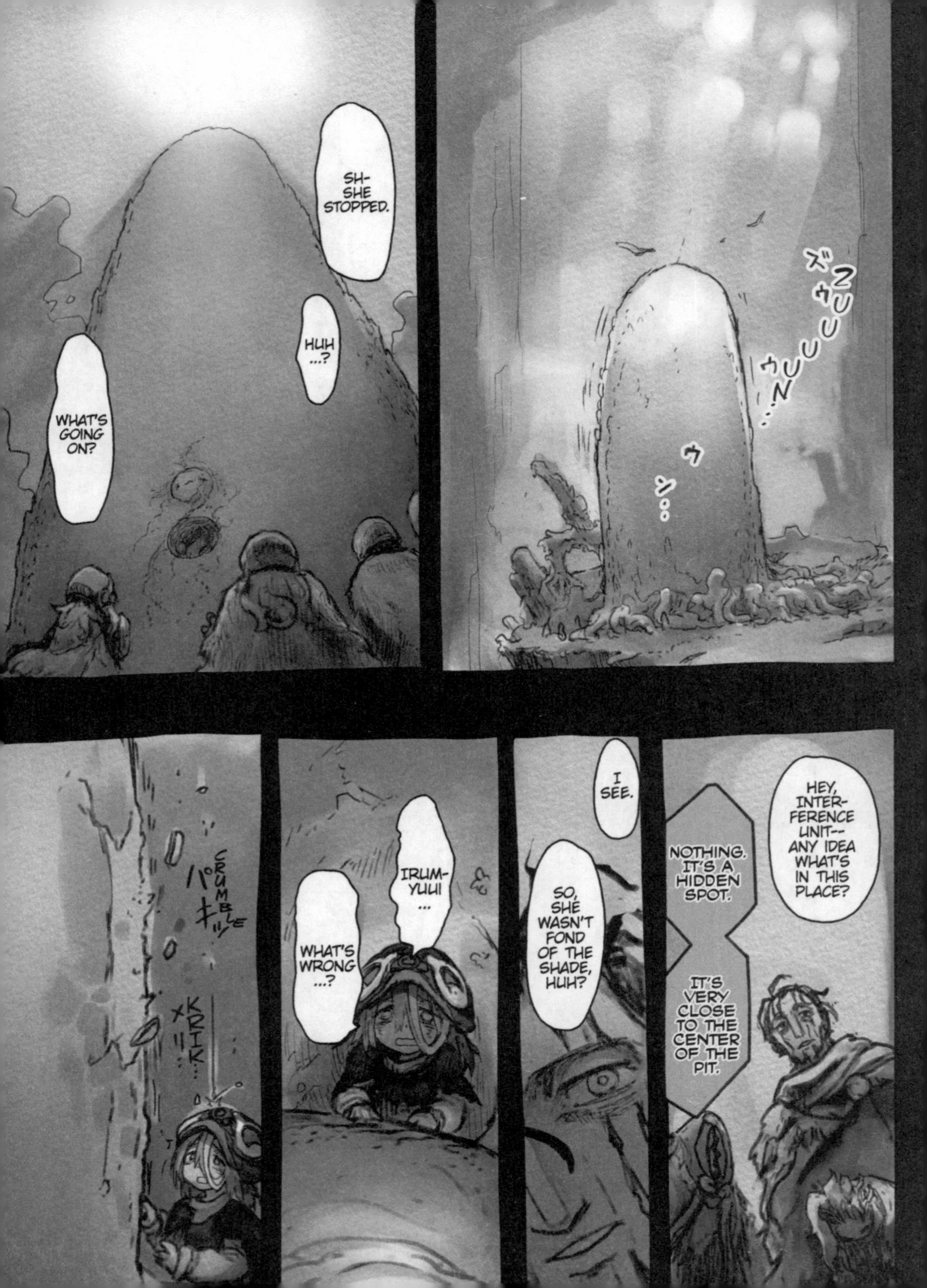
ZUUUUUN...
SH-SHE STOPPED.
HUH...?
WHAT'S GOING ON?
HEY, INTERFERENCE UNIT--ANY IDEA WHAT'S IN THIS PLACE?
NOTHING. IT'S A HIDDEN SPOT.
IT'S VERY CLOSE TO THE CENTER OF THE PIT.
I SEE.
SO, SHE WASN'T FOND OF THE SHADE, HUH?
IRUMYUUI...
WHAT'S WRONG...?
CRUMBLE
KRIK...

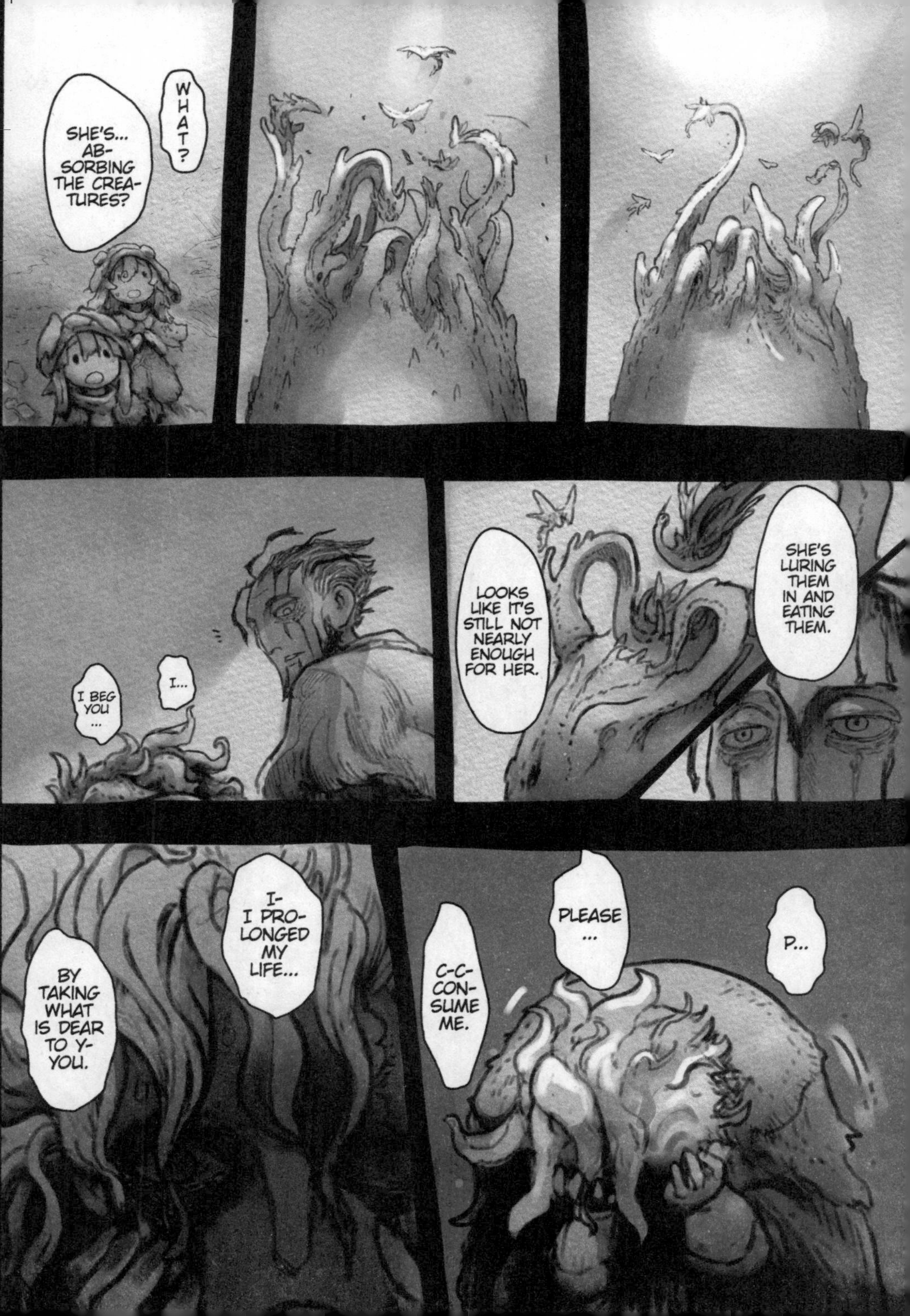
WHAT?
SHE'S... ABSORBING THE CREATURES?
SHE'S LURING THEM IN AND EATING THEM.
LOOKS LIKE IT'S STILL NOT NEARLY ENOUGH FOR HER.
I...
I BEG YOU ...
P...
PLEASE ...
C-C-CONSUME ME.
I- I PROLONGED MY LIFE...
BY TAKING WHAT IS DEAR TO Y-YOU.

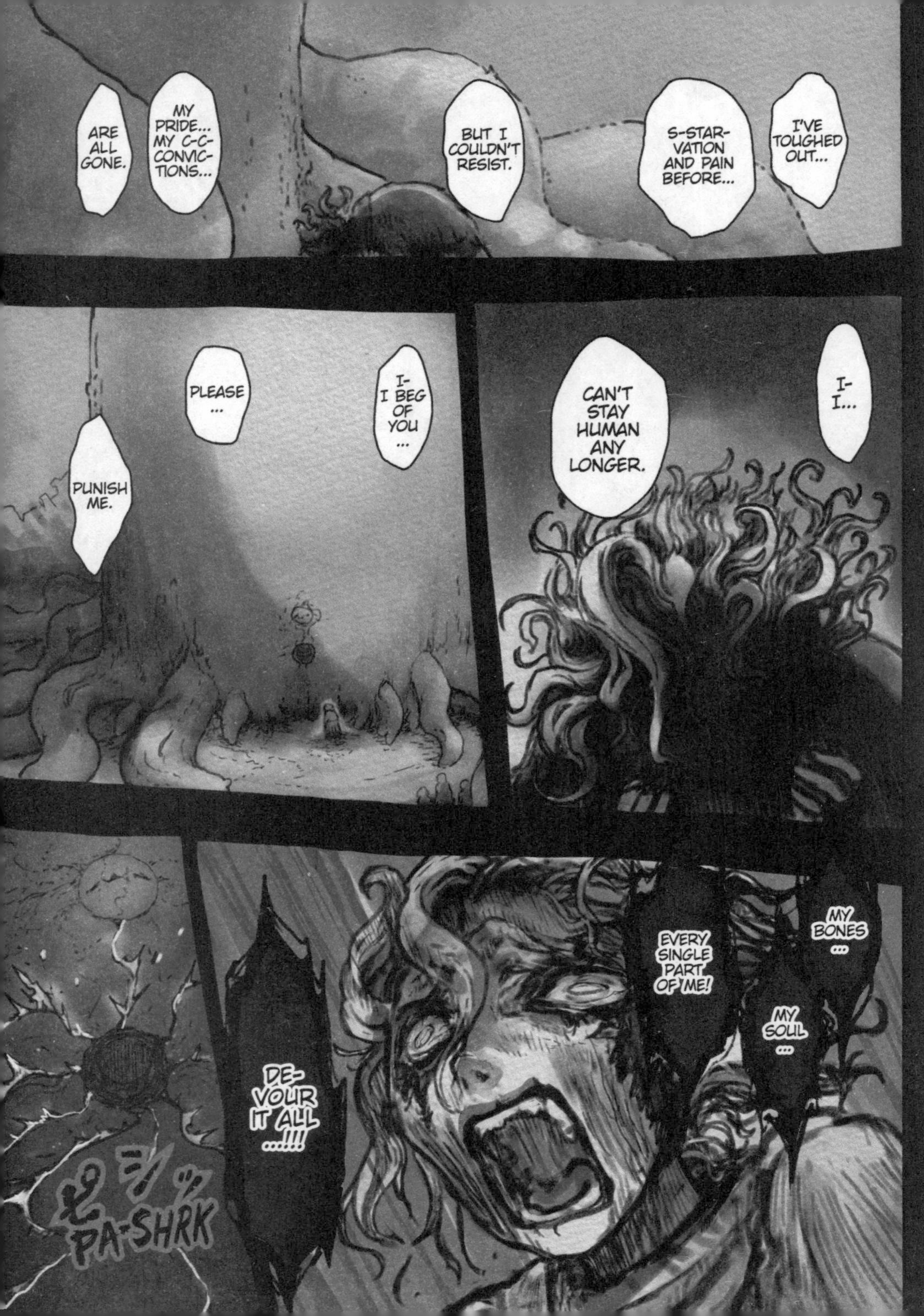
I'VE TOUGHED OUT...
S-STARVATION AND PAIN BEFORE...
BUT I COULDN'T RESIST.
MY PRIDE... MY C-C-CONVICTIONS...
ARE ALL GONE.
I- I...
CAN'T STAY HUMAN ANY LONGER.
I- I BEG OF YOU...
PLEASE...
PUNISH ME.
MY BONES...
EVERY SINGLE PART OF ME!
MY SOUL...
DEVOUR IT ALL...!!!!
PA-SHRK

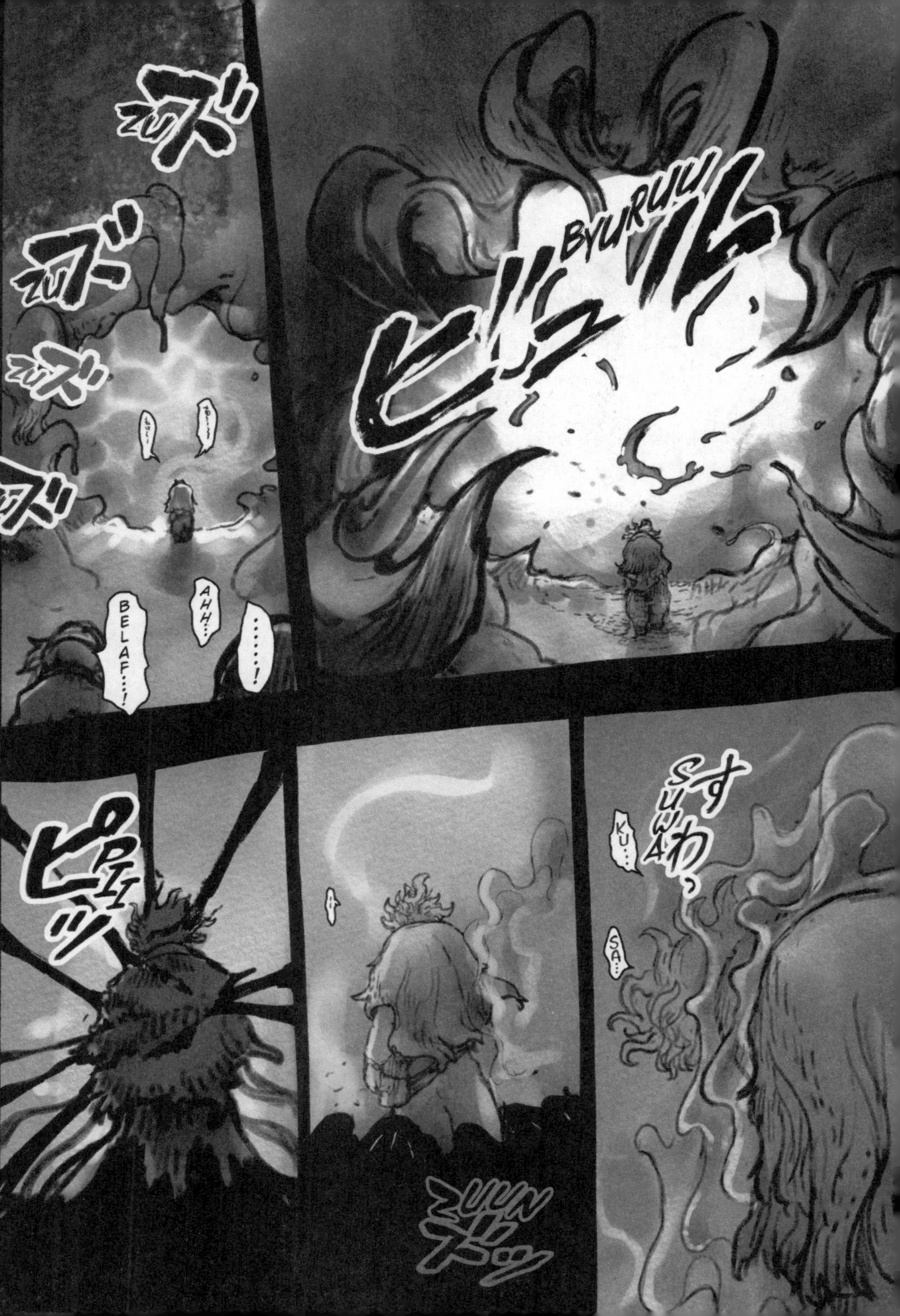
ビュルル
BYURUYU
ズ
ZU
ブ
ZU
ズ
ZU
ズ
ZU
AHH...
.....!
BELAF...!
すわっ
SUWA
KU...
SA...
ZUUN
ピッ
PII

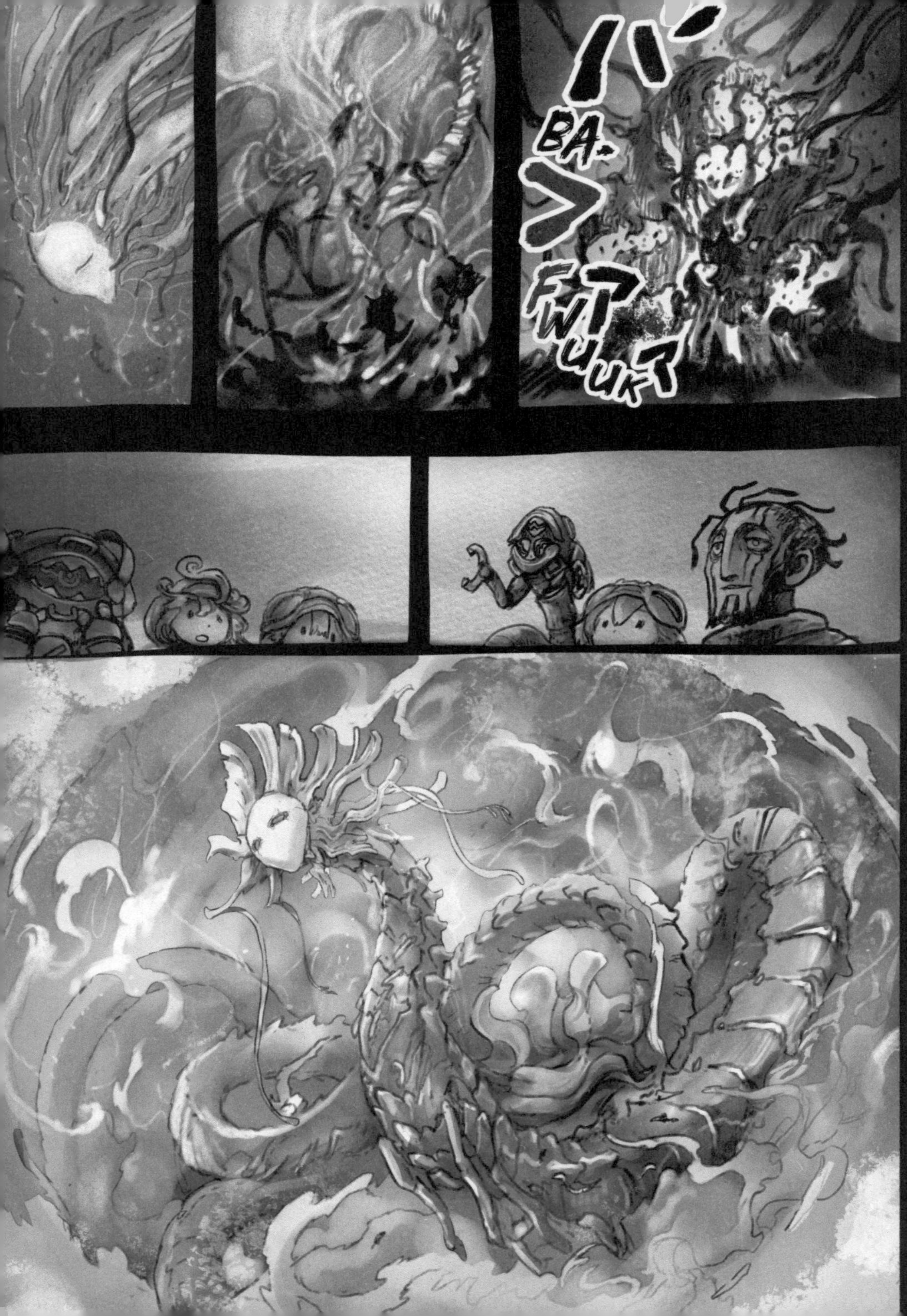

バ
BA-
FWUUK

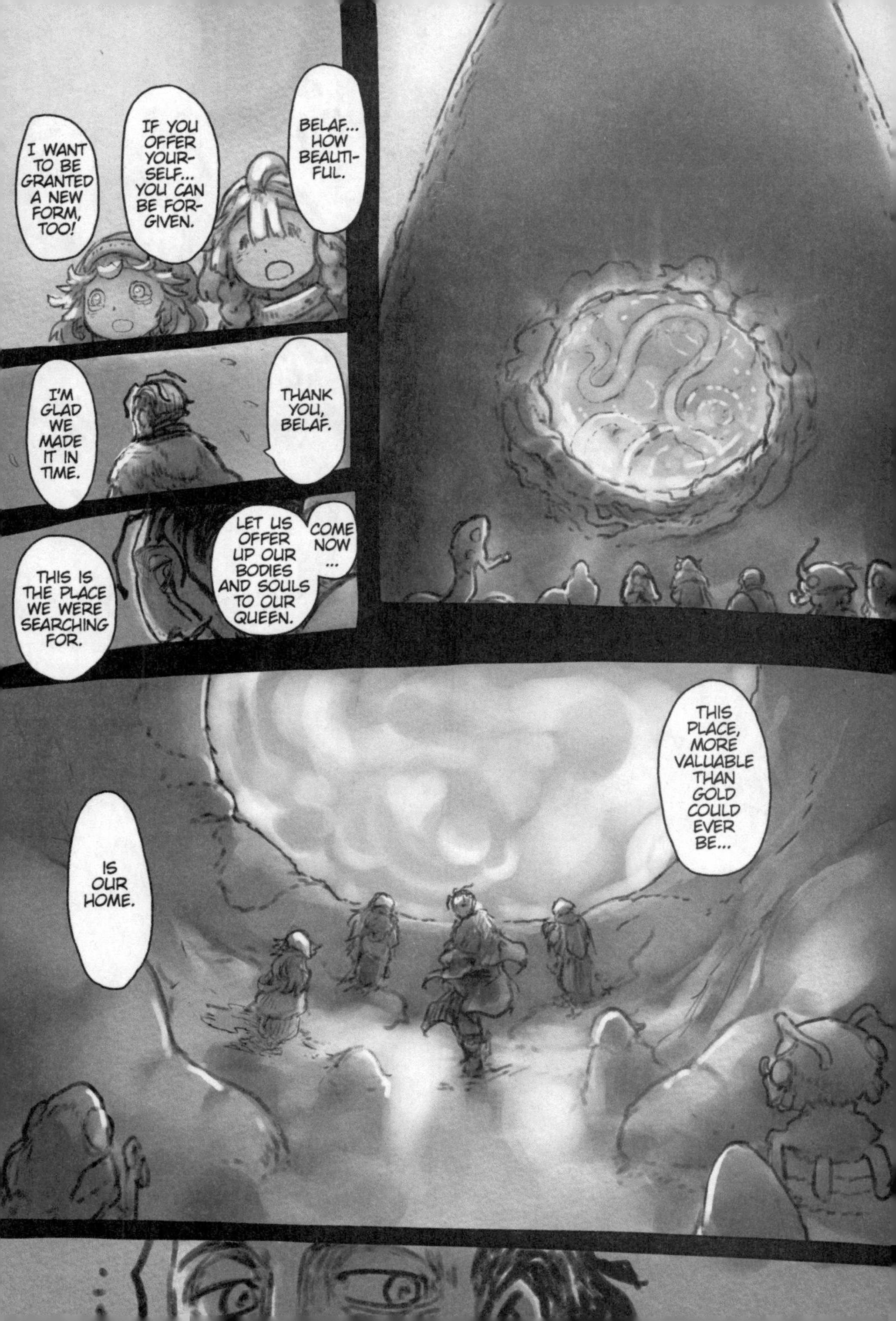
BELAF... HOW BEAUTIFUL.
IF YOU OFFER YOURSELF... YOU CAN BE FORGIVEN.
I WANT TO BE GRANTED A NEW FORM, TOO!
THANK YOU, BELAF.
I'M GLAD WE MADE IT IN TIME.
COME NOW...
LET US OFFER UP OUR BODIES AND SOULS TO OUR QUEEN.
THIS IS THE PLACE WE WERE SEARCHING FOR.
THIS PLACE, MORE VALUABLE THAN GOLD COULD EVER BE...
IS OUR HOME.

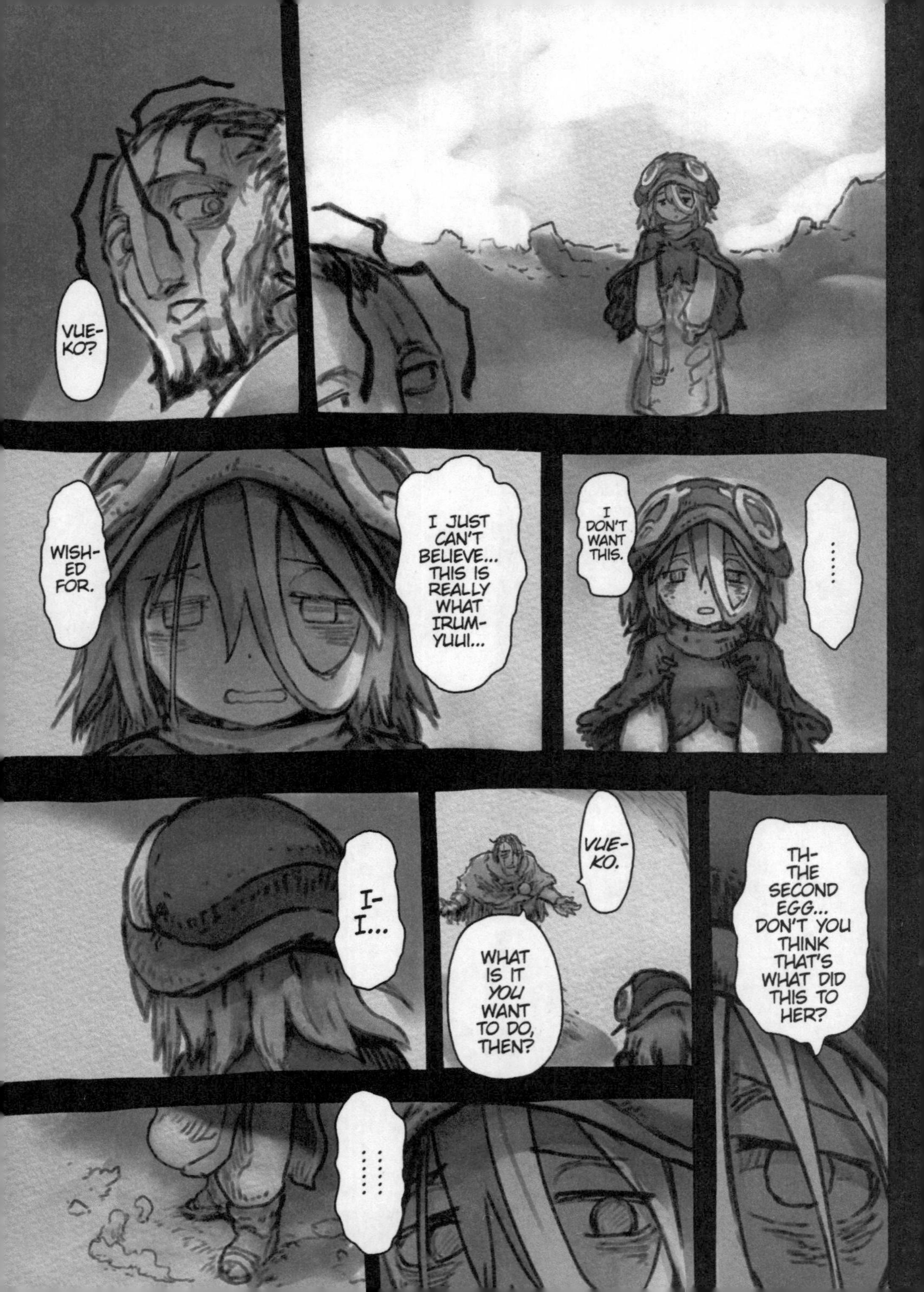
VUEKO?
......
I DON'T WANT THIS.
I JUST CAN'T BELIEVE... THIS IS REALLY WHAT IRUMYUUI...
WISHED FOR.
TH-THE SECOND EGG... DON'T YOU THINK THAT'S WHAT DID THIS TO HER?
VUEKO.
WHAT IS IT *YOU* WANT TO DO, THEN?
I-I...
......

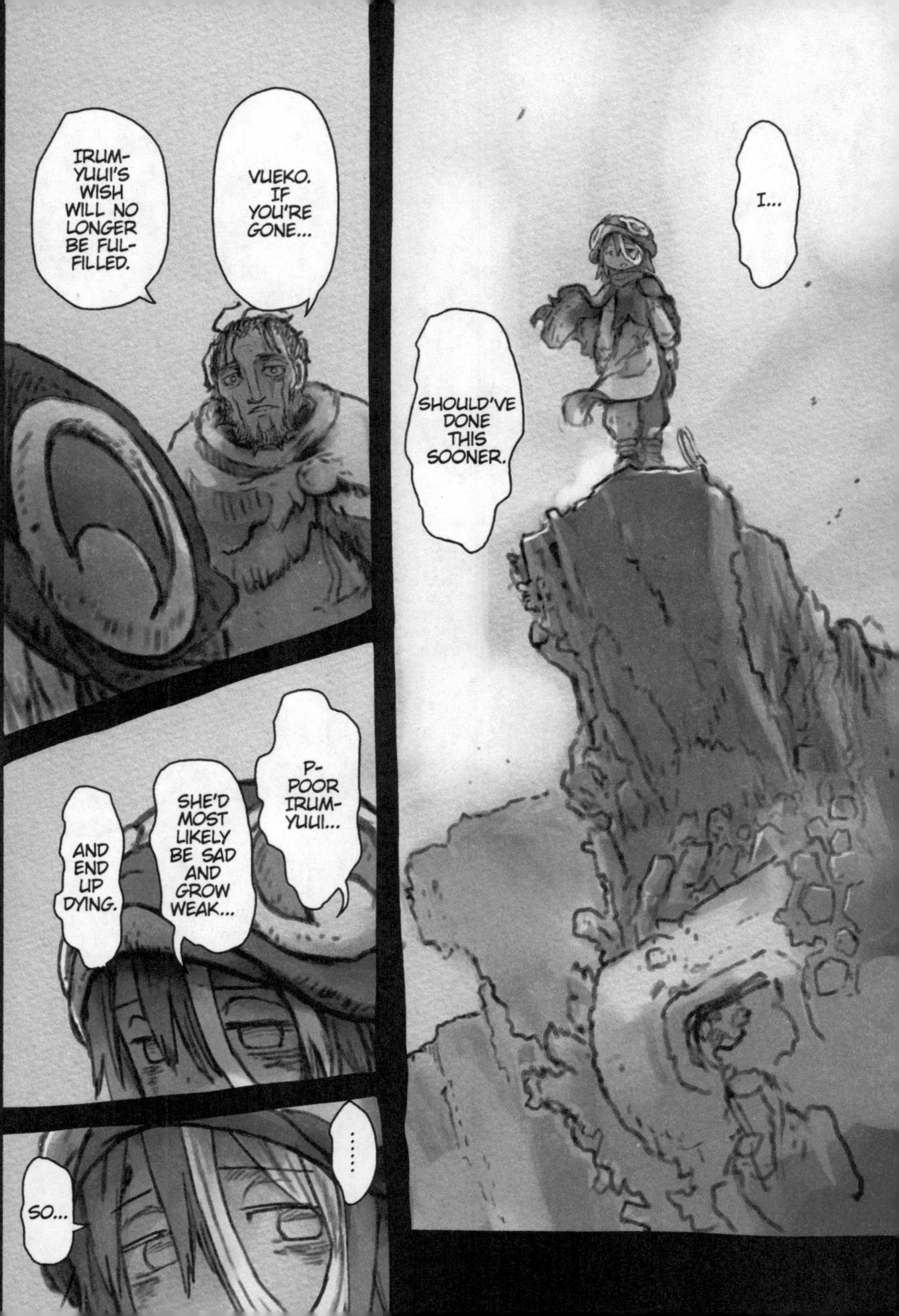
I...
SHOULD'VE DONE THIS SOONER.
VUEKO. IF YOU'RE GONE...
IRUM-YUUI'S WISH WILL NO LONGER BE FUL-FILLED.
P-POOR IRUM-YUUI...
SHE'D MOST LIKELY BE SAD AND GROW WEAK...
AND END UP DYING.
......
SO...

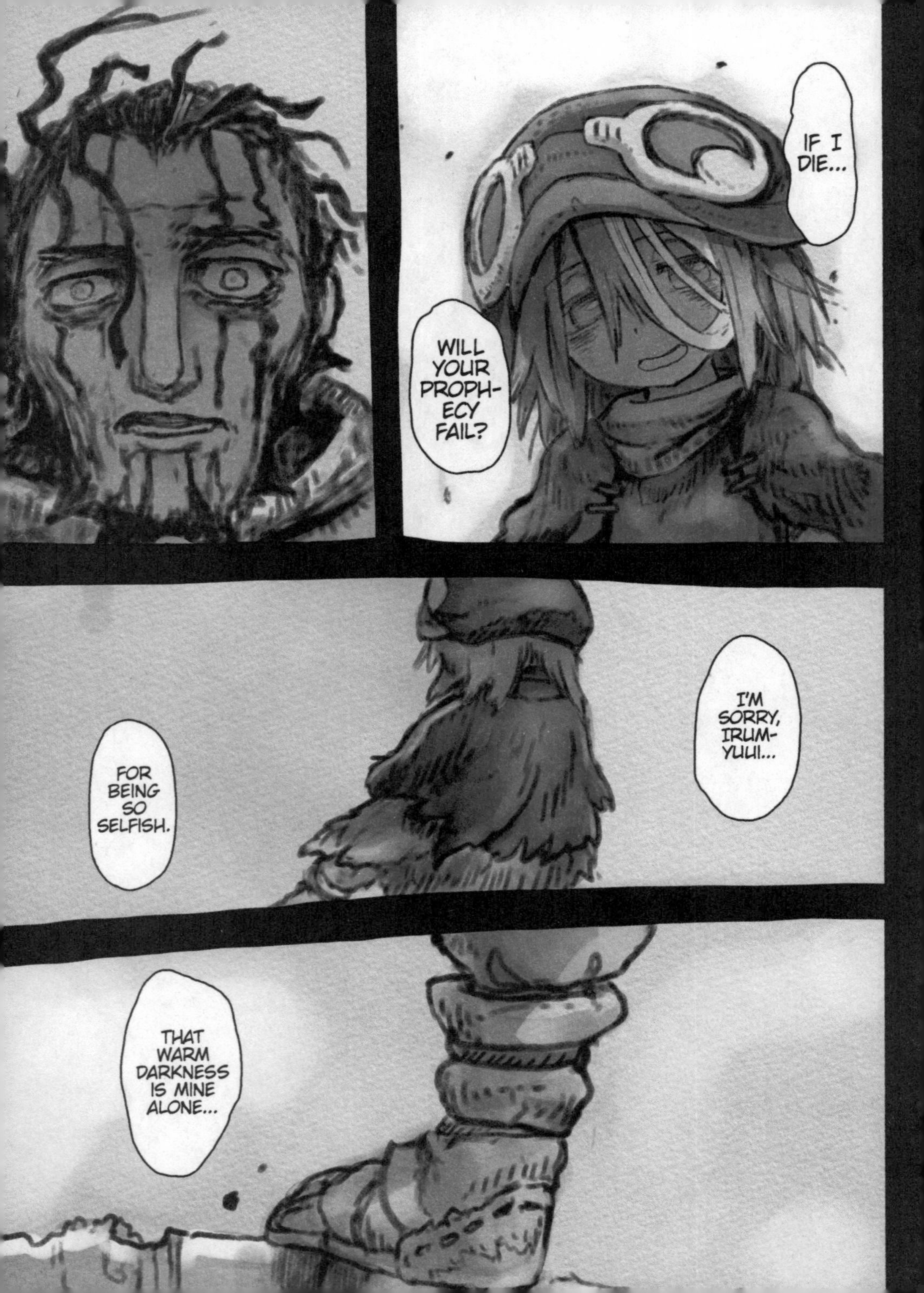
IF I DIE...
WILL YOUR PROPHECY FAIL?
I'M SORRY, IRUMYUUI...
FOR BEING SO SELFISH.
THAT WARM DARKNESS IS MINE ALONE...

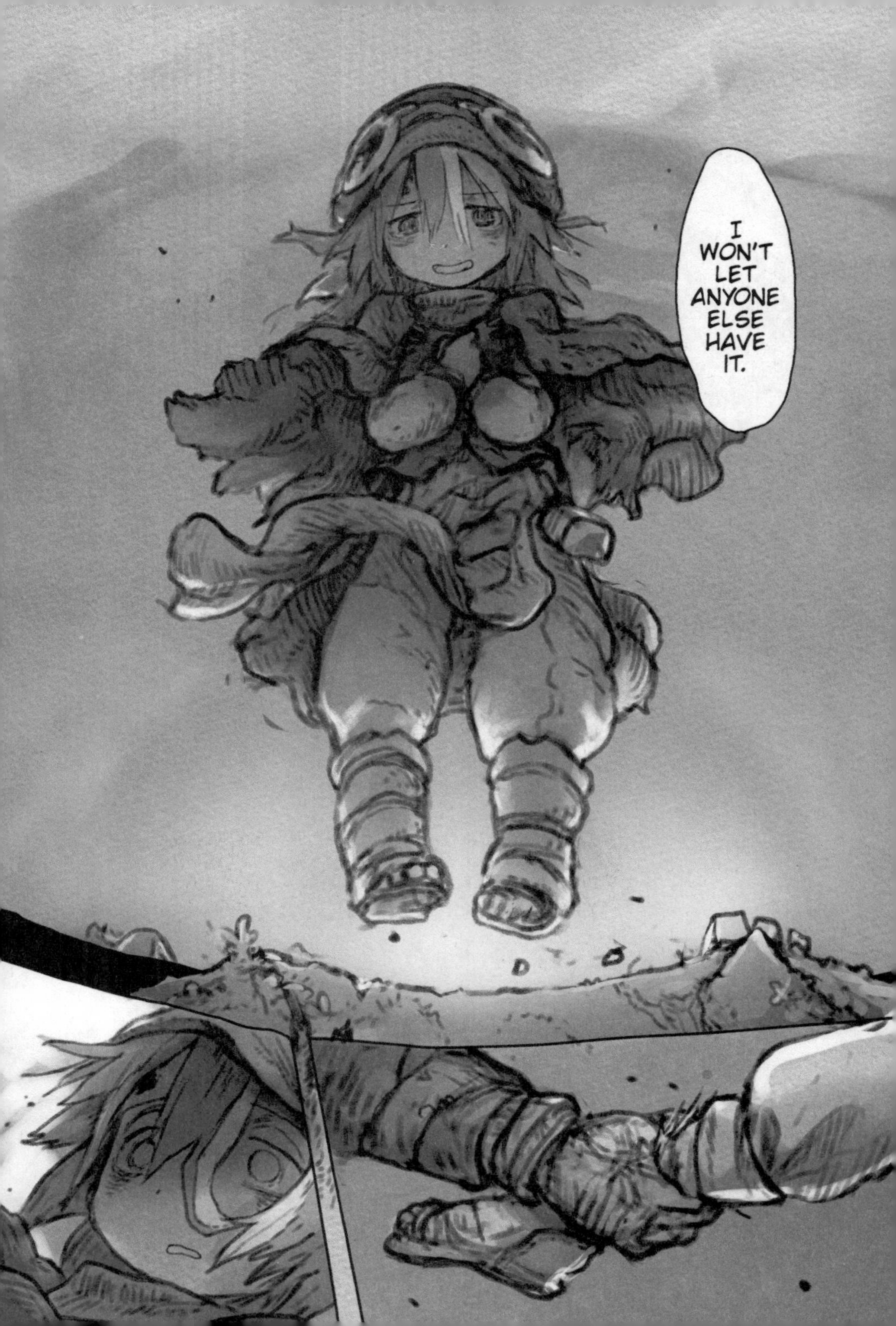
I WON'T LET ANYONE ELSE HAVE IT.

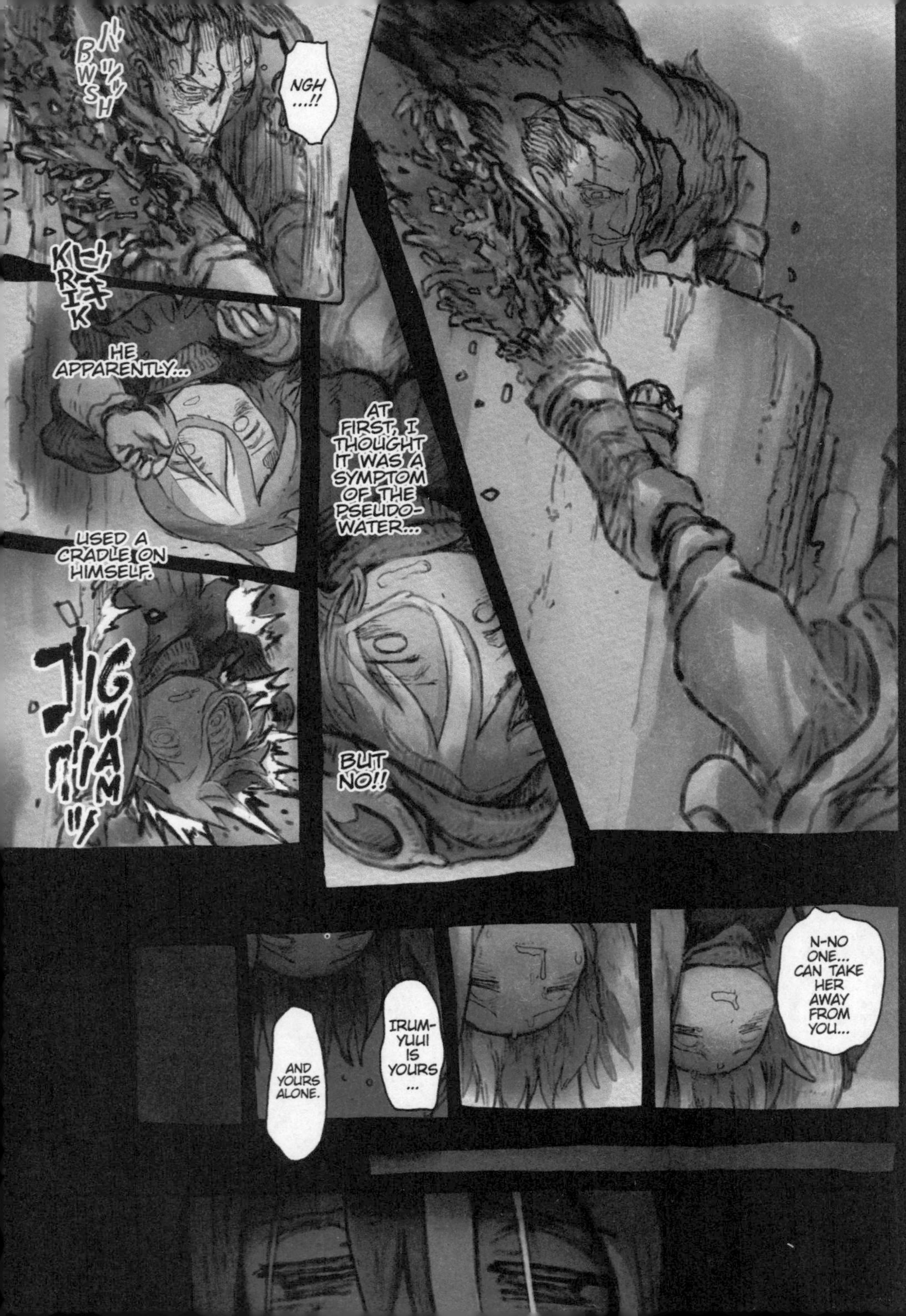
NGH ...!!
BWSH
AT FIRST, I THOUGHT IT WAS A SYMPTOM OF THE PSEUDO-WATER...
BUT NO!!
KRIK
HE APPARENTLY...
USED A CRADLE ON HIMSELF.
JIGWAM
N-NO ONE... CAN TAKE HER AWAY FROM YOU...
IRUMYUUI IS YOURS ...
AND YOURS ALONE.

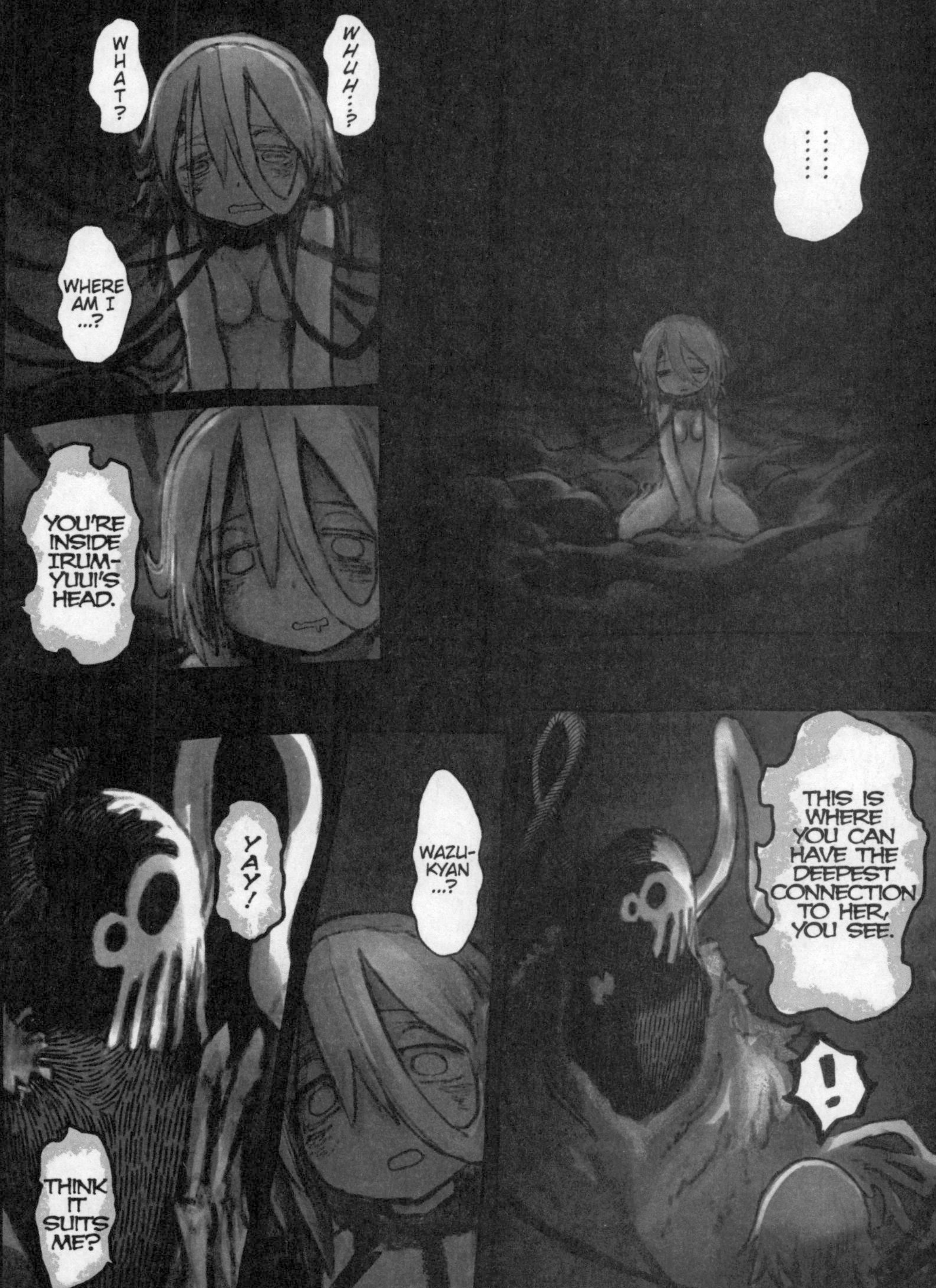
......
WHUH...?
WHAT?
WHERE AM I ...?
YOU'RE INSIDE IRUM-YUUI'S HEAD.
THIS IS WHERE YOU CAN HAVE THE DEEPEST CONNECTION TO HER, YOU SEE.
!
WAZU-KYAN ...?
YAY!
THINK IT SUITS ME?

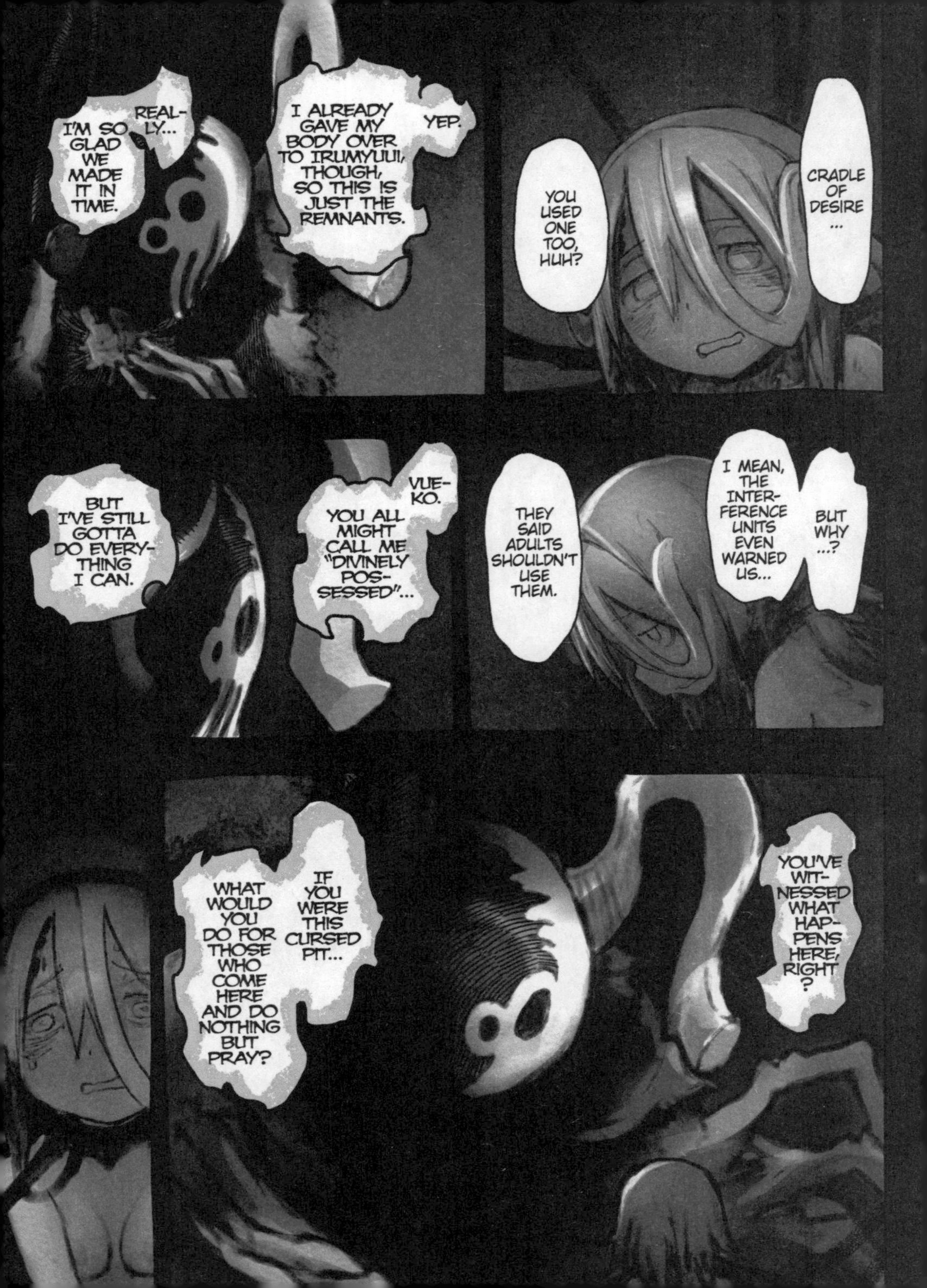
CRADLE OF DESIRE ...
YOU USED ONE TOO, HUH?
YEP.
I ALREADY GAVE MY BODY OVER TO IRUMYUUI, THOUGH, SO THIS IS JUST THE REMNANTS.
REALLY...
I'M SO GLAD WE MADE IT IN TIME.
BUT WHY ...?
I MEAN, THE INTERFERENCE UNITS EVEN WARNED US...
THEY SAID ADULTS SHOULDN'T USE THEM.
VUEKO.
YOU ALL MIGHT CALL ME "DIVINELY POSSESSED"...
BUT I'VE STILL GOTTA DO EVERYTHING I CAN.
YOU'VE WITNESSED WHAT HAPPENS HERE, RIGHT?
IF YOU WERE THIS CURSED PIT...
WHAT WOULD YOU DO FOR THOSE WHO COME HERE AND DO NOTHING BUT PRAY?

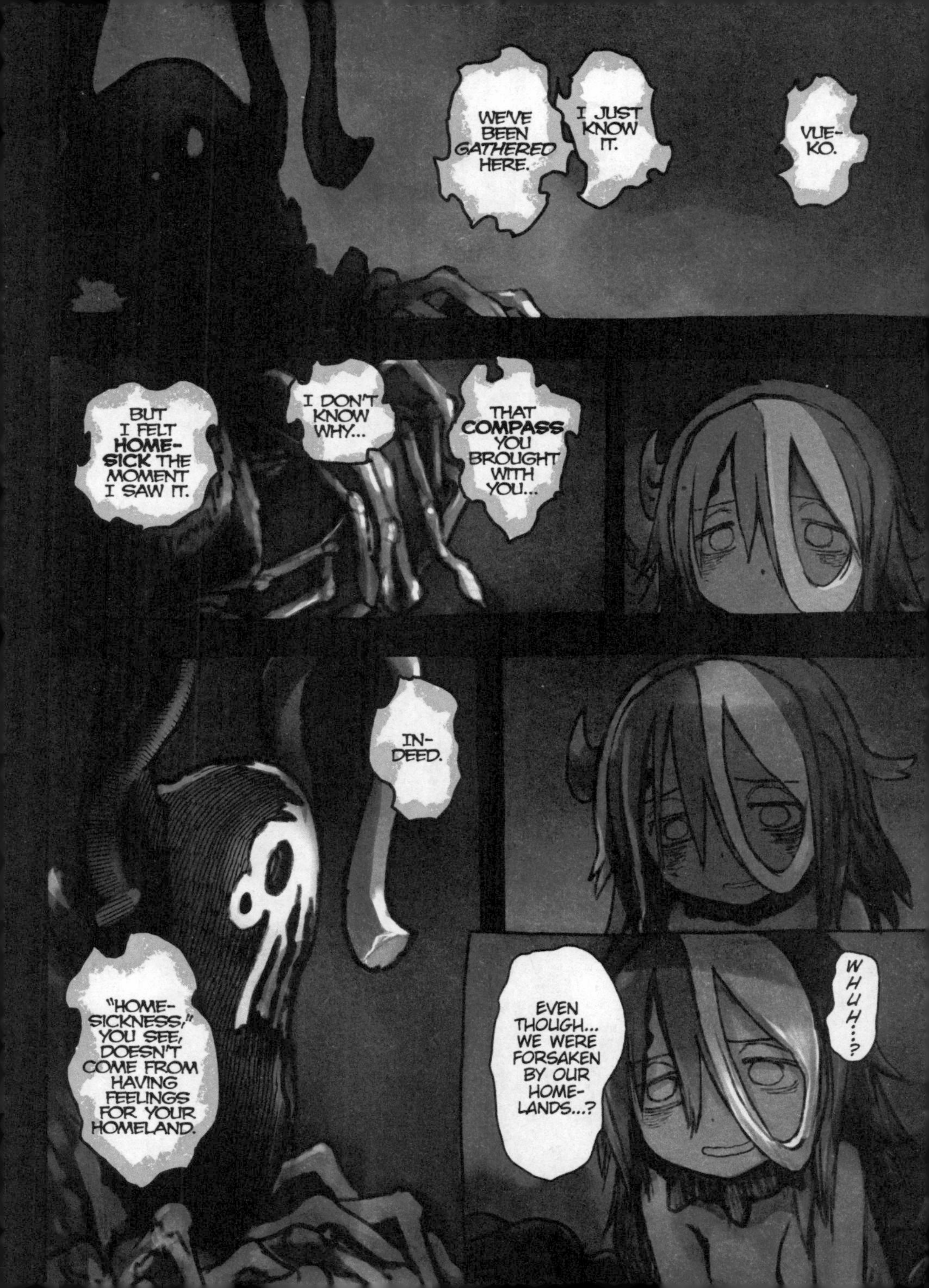
VUE-KO.
I JUST KNOW IT.
WE'VE BEEN GATHERED HERE.
THAT **COMPASS** YOU BROUGHT WITH YOU...
I DON'T KNOW WHY...
BUT I FELT **HOME-SICK** THE MOMENT I SAW IT.
WHUH...?
EVEN THOUGH... WE WERE FORSAKEN BY OUR HOME-LANDS...?
IN-DEED.
"HOME-SICKNESS," YOU SEE, DOESN'T COME FROM HAVING FEELINGS FOR YOUR HOMELAND.

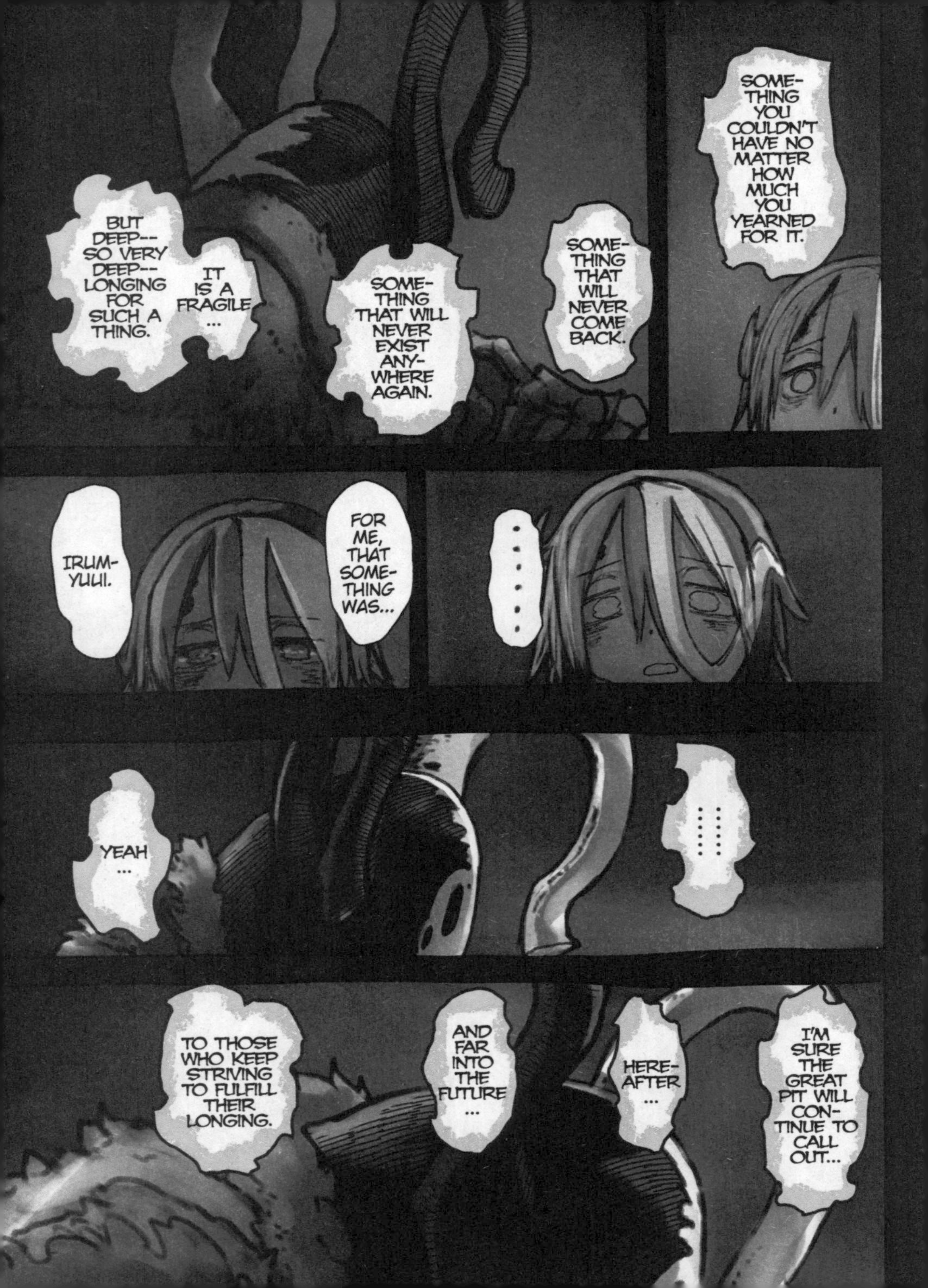
SOME-THING YOU COULDN'T HAVE NO MATTER HOW MUCH YOU YEARNED FOR IT.
SOME-THING THAT WILL NEVER COME BACK.
SOME-THING THAT WILL NEVER EXIST ANY-WHERE AGAIN.
IT IS A FRAGILE ...
BUT DEEP-- SO VERY DEEP-- LONGING FOR SUCH A THING.
......
FOR ME, THAT SOME-THING WAS...
IRUM-YUUI.
......
YEAH ...
I'M SURE THE GREAT PIT WILL CON-TINUE TO CALL OUT...
HERE-AFTER ...
AND FAR INTO THE FUTURE ...
TO THOSE WHO KEEP STRIVING TO FULFILL THEIR LONGING.

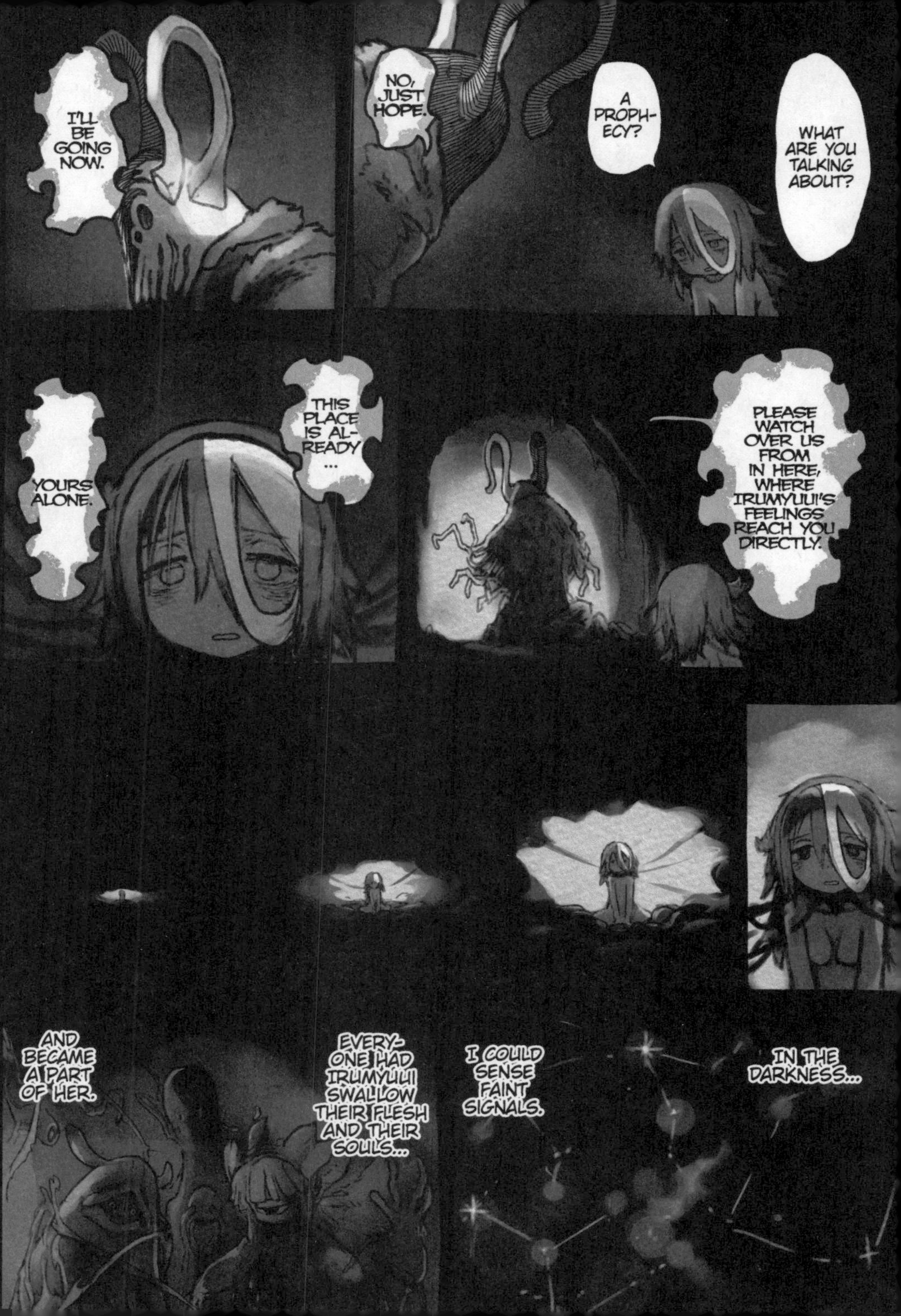
WHAT ARE YOU TALKING ABOUT?
A PROPHECY?
NO, JUST HOPE.
I'LL BE GOING NOW.
PLEASE WATCH OVER US FROM IN HERE, WHERE IRUMYUUI'S FEELINGS REACH YOU DIRECTLY.
THIS PLACE IS ALREADY...
YOURS ALONE.
IN THE DARKNESS...
I COULD SENSE FAINT SIGNALS.
EVERYONE HAD IRUMYUUI SWALLOW THEIR FLESH AND THEIR SOULS...
AND BECAME A PART OF HER.

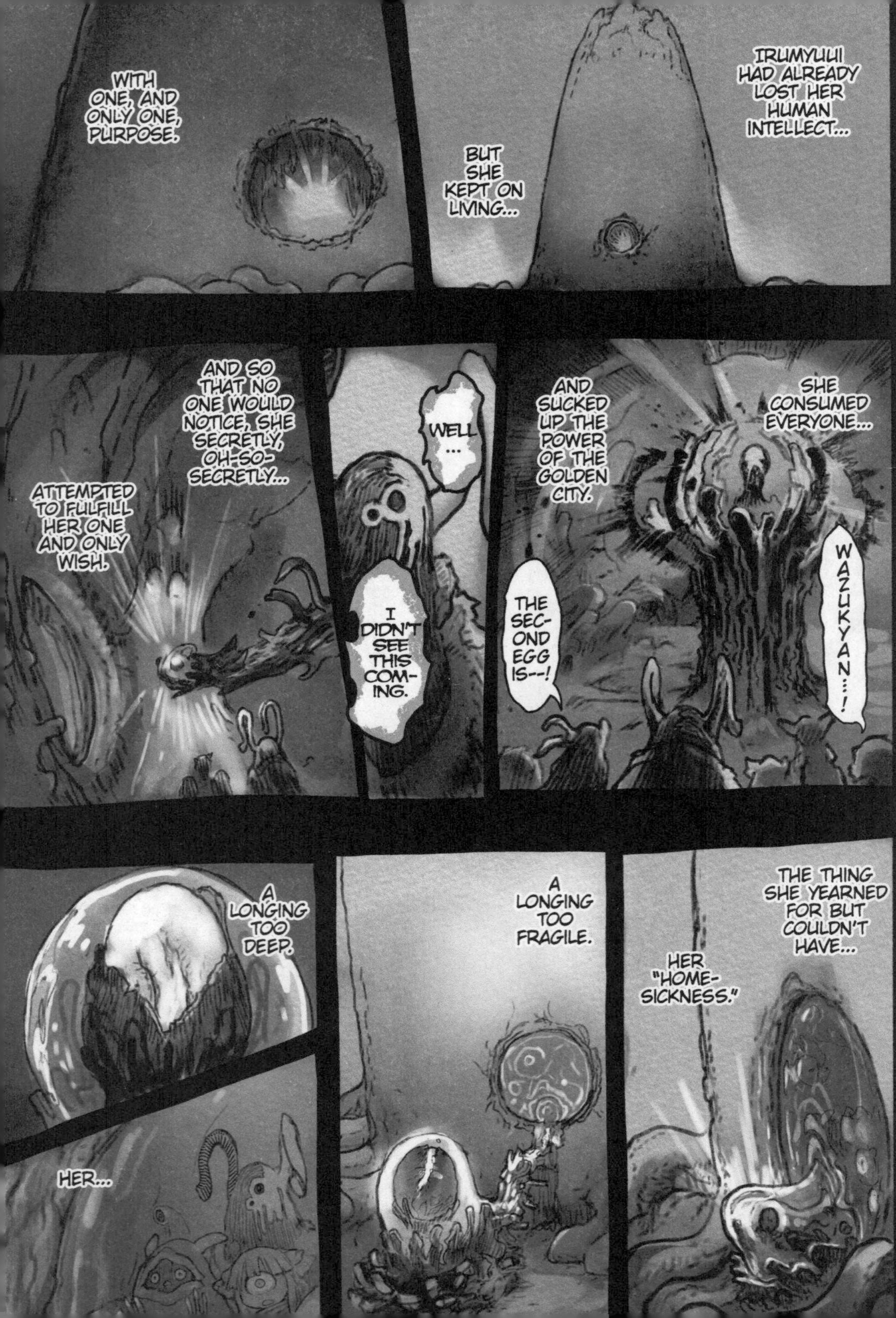

IRUMYUUI HAD ALREADY LOST HER HUMAN INTELLECT...
BUT SHE KEPT ON LIVING...
WITH ONE, AND ONLY ONE, PURPOSE.
SHE CONSUMED EVERYONE...
AND SUCKED UP THE POWER OF THE GOLDEN CITY.
WAZUKYAN...!
THE SECOND EGG IS--!
WELL...
I DIDN'T SEE THIS COMING.
AND SO THAT NO ONE WOULD NOTICE, SHE SECRETLY, OH-SO-SECRETLY...
ATTEMPTED TO FULFILL HER ONE AND ONLY WISH.
THE THING SHE YEARNED FOR BUT COULDN'T HAVE...
HER "HOMESICKNESS."
A LONGING TOO FRAGILE.
A LONGING TOO DEEP.
HER...

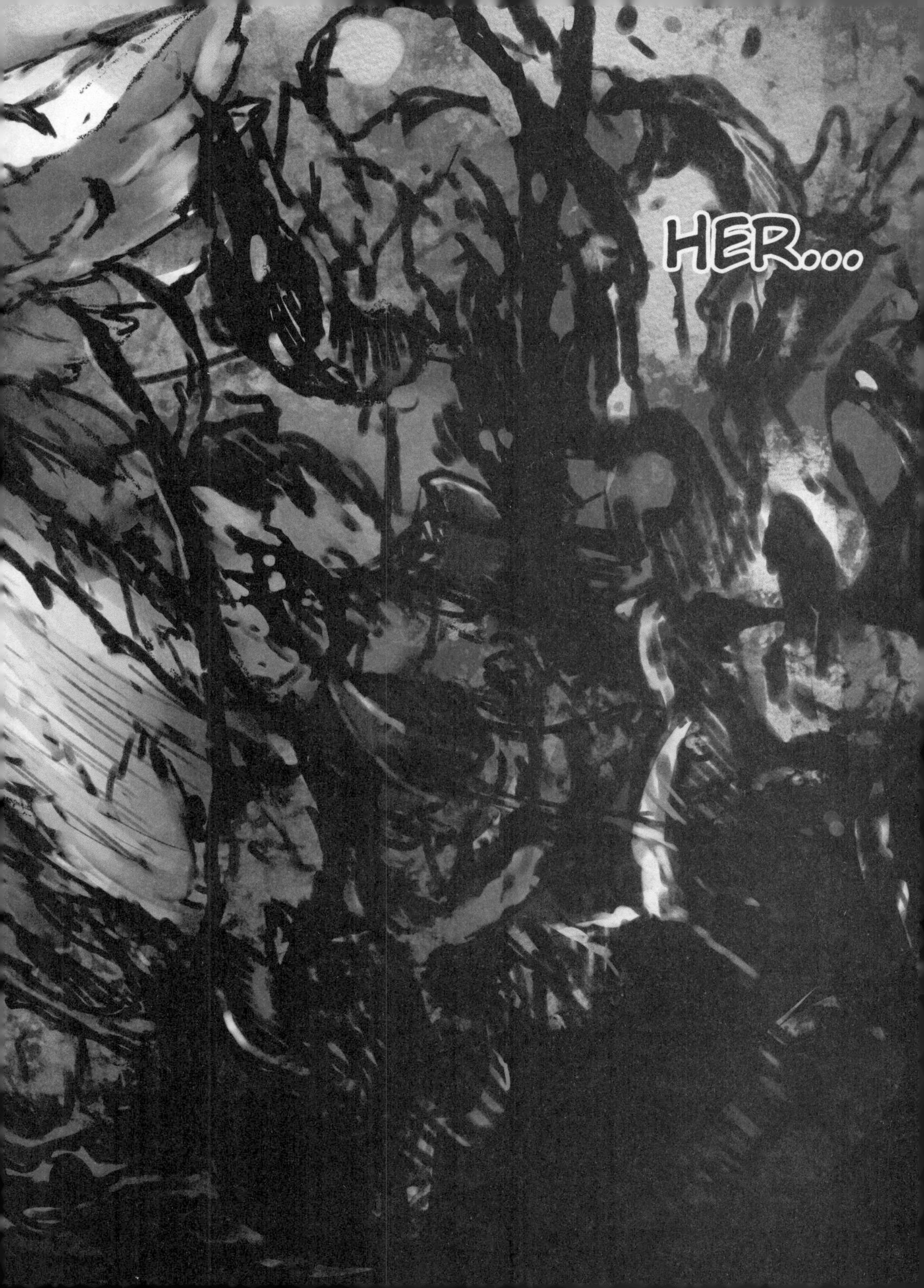
HER...

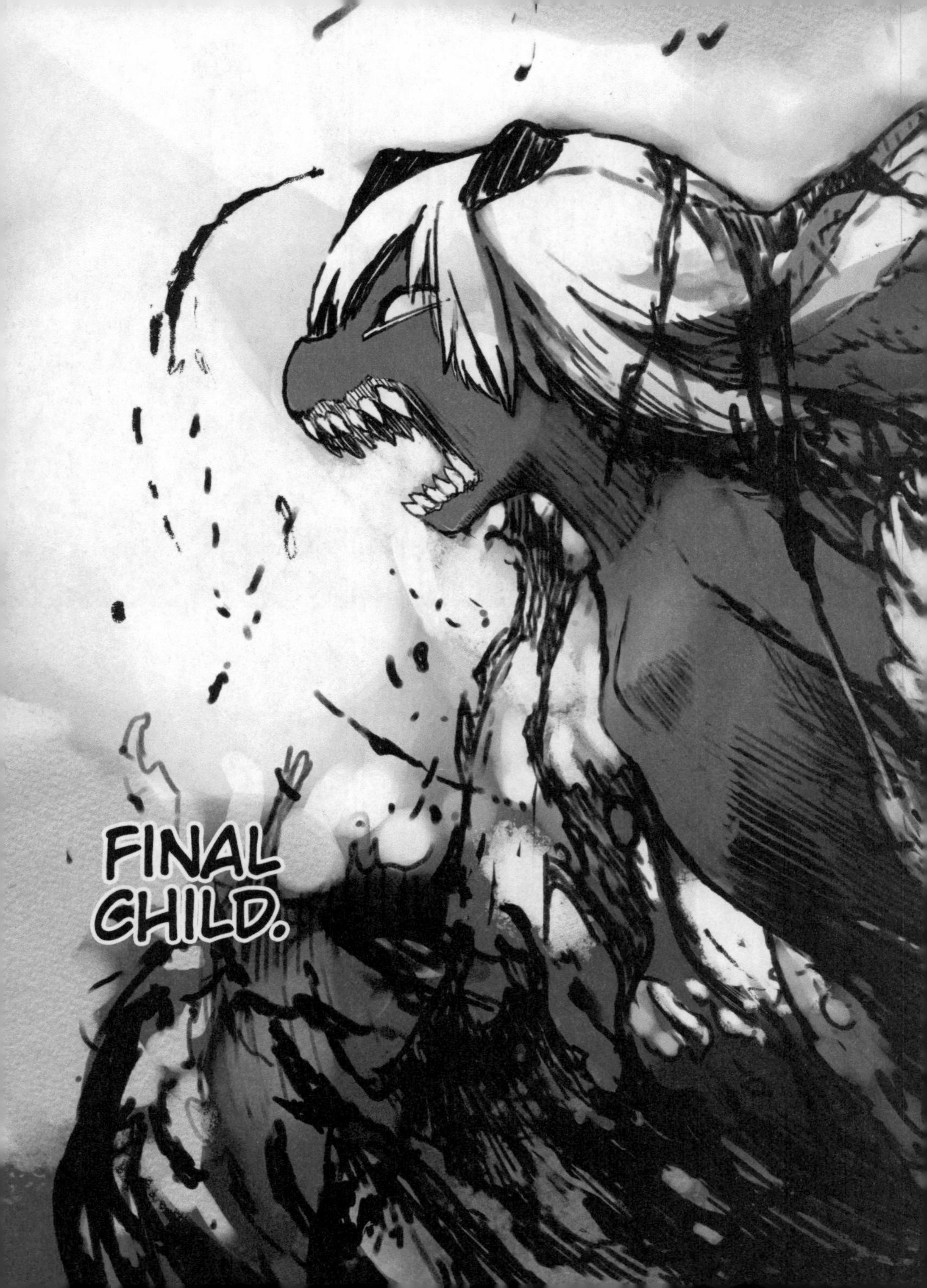
FINAL CHILD.

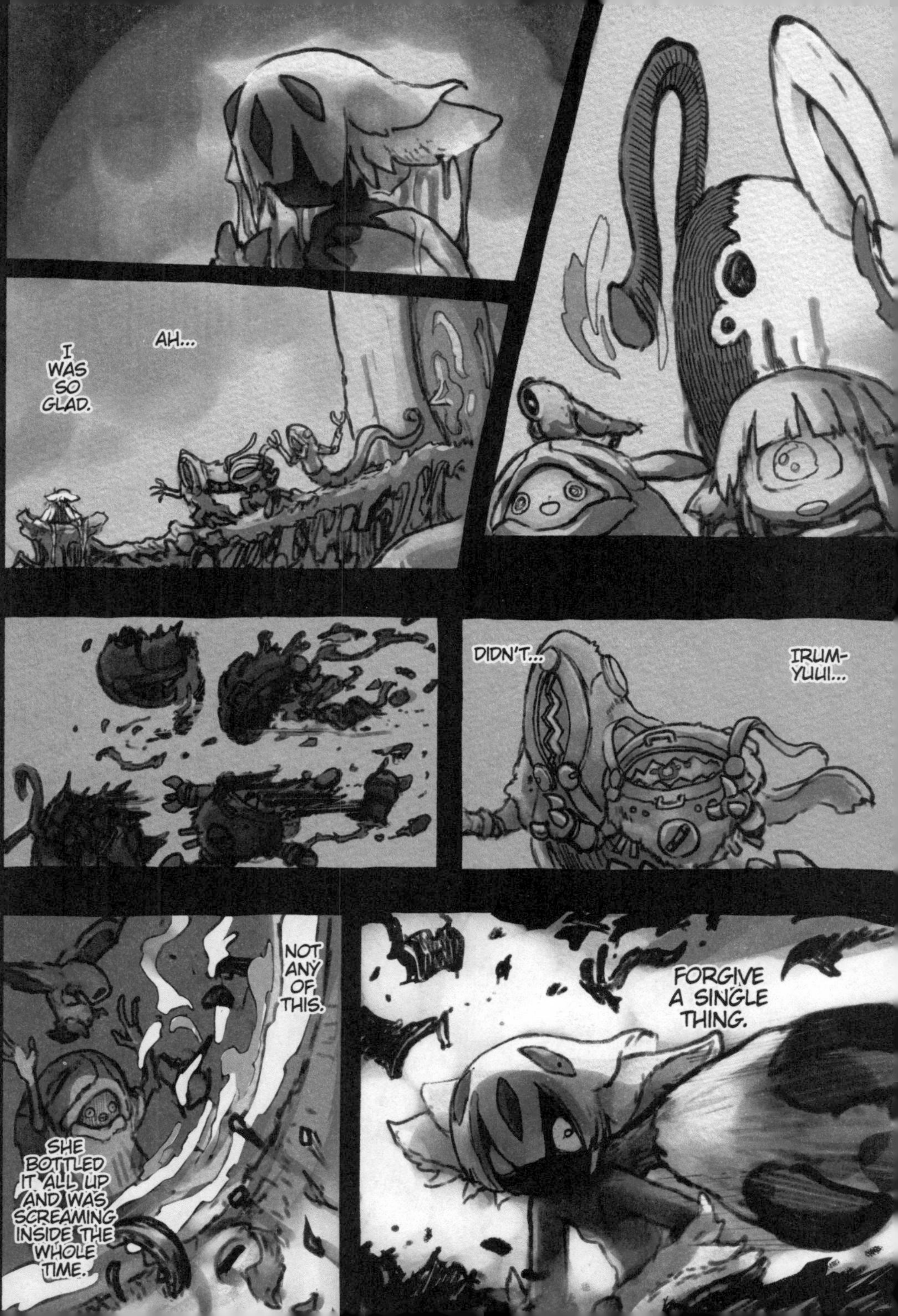
AH...
I WAS SO GLAD.
IRUM-YUUI...
DIDN'T...
FORGIVE A SINGLE THING.
NOT ANY OF THIS.
SHE BOTTLED IT ALL UP AND WAS SCREAMING INSIDE THE WHOLE TIME.

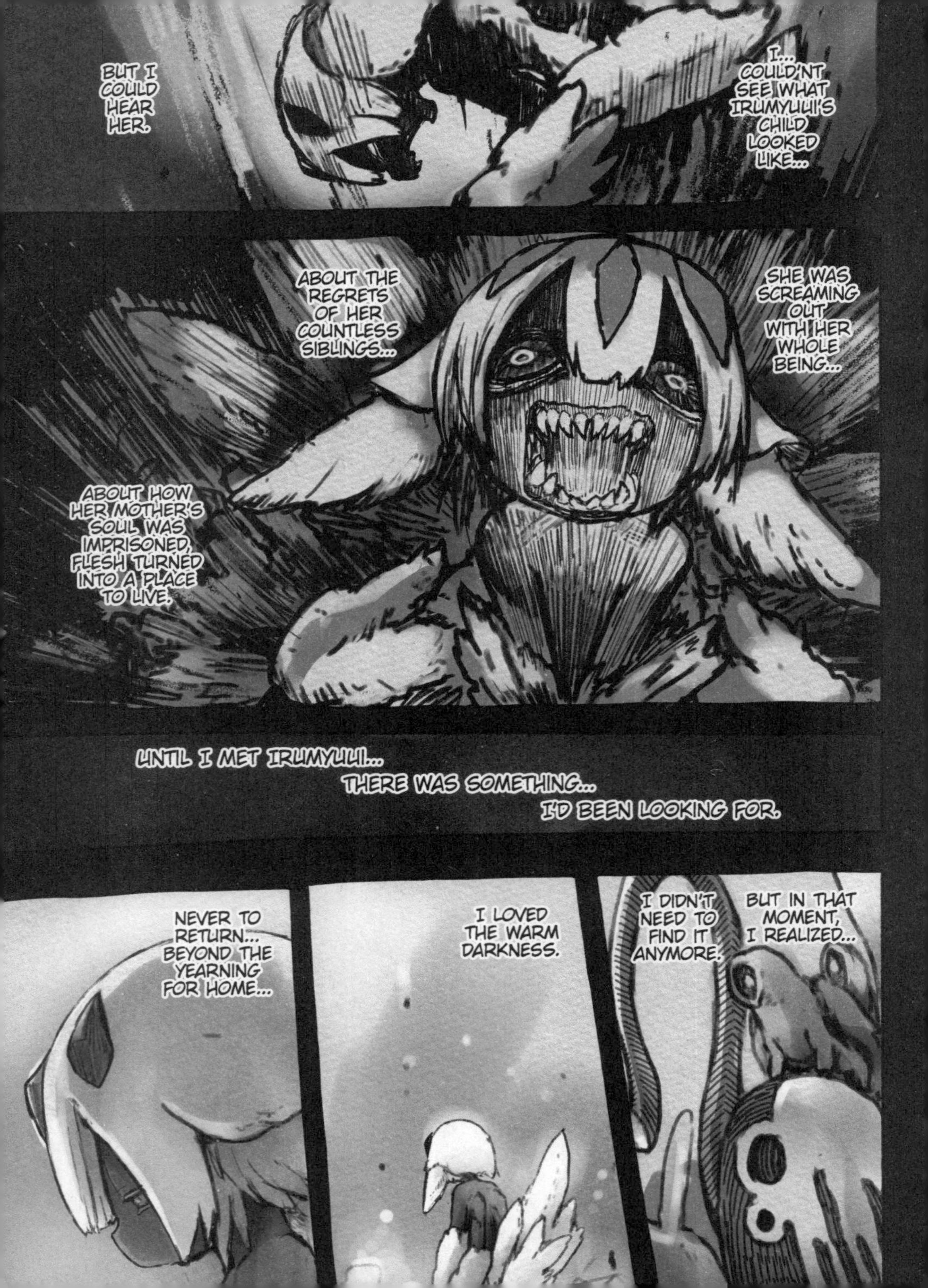
I... COULD'NT SEE WHAT IRUMYUUI'S CHILD LOOKED LIKE...
BUT I COULD HEAR HER.
SHE WAS SCREAMING OUT WITH HER WHOLE BEING...
ABOUT THE REGRETS OF HER COUNTLESS SIBLINGS...
ABOUT HOW HER MOTHER'S SOUL WAS IMPRISONED, FLESH TURNED INTO A PLACE TO LIVE.
UNTIL I MET IRUMYUUI...
THERE WAS SOMETHING...
I'D BEEN LOOKING FOR.
BUT IN THAT MOMENT, I REALIZED...
I DIDN'T NEED TO FIND IT ANYMORE.
I LOVED THE WARM DARKNESS.
NEVER TO RETURN... BEYOND THE YEARNING FOR HOME...

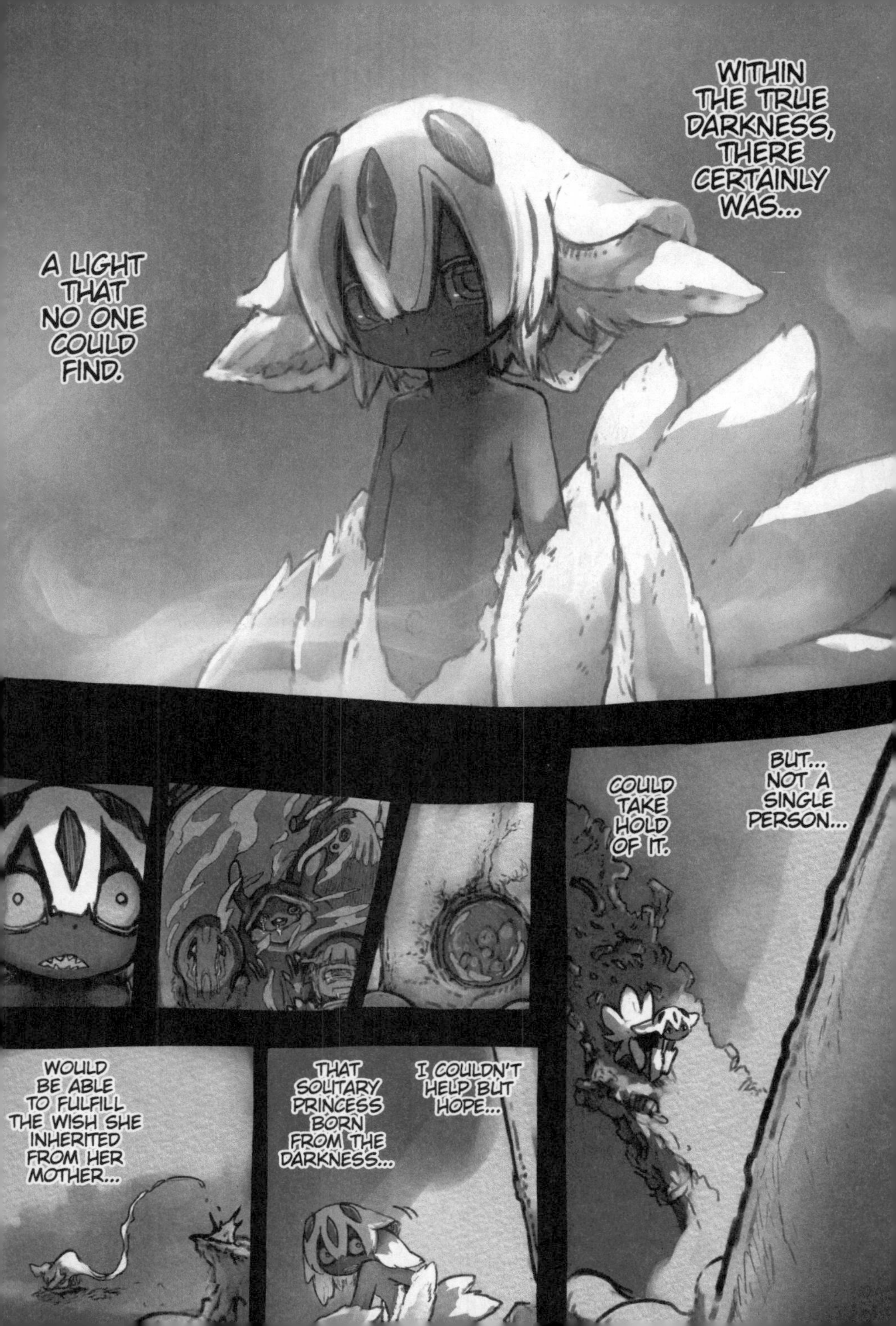
WITHIN THE TRUE DARKNESS, THERE CERTAINLY WAS...
A LIGHT THAT NO ONE COULD FIND.
BUT... NOT A SINGLE PERSON...
COULD TAKE HOLD OF IT.
I COULDN'T HELP BUT HOPE...
THAT SOLITARY PRINCESS BORN FROM THE DARKNESS...
WOULD BE ABLE TO FULFILL THE WISH SHE INHERITED FROM HER MOTHER...

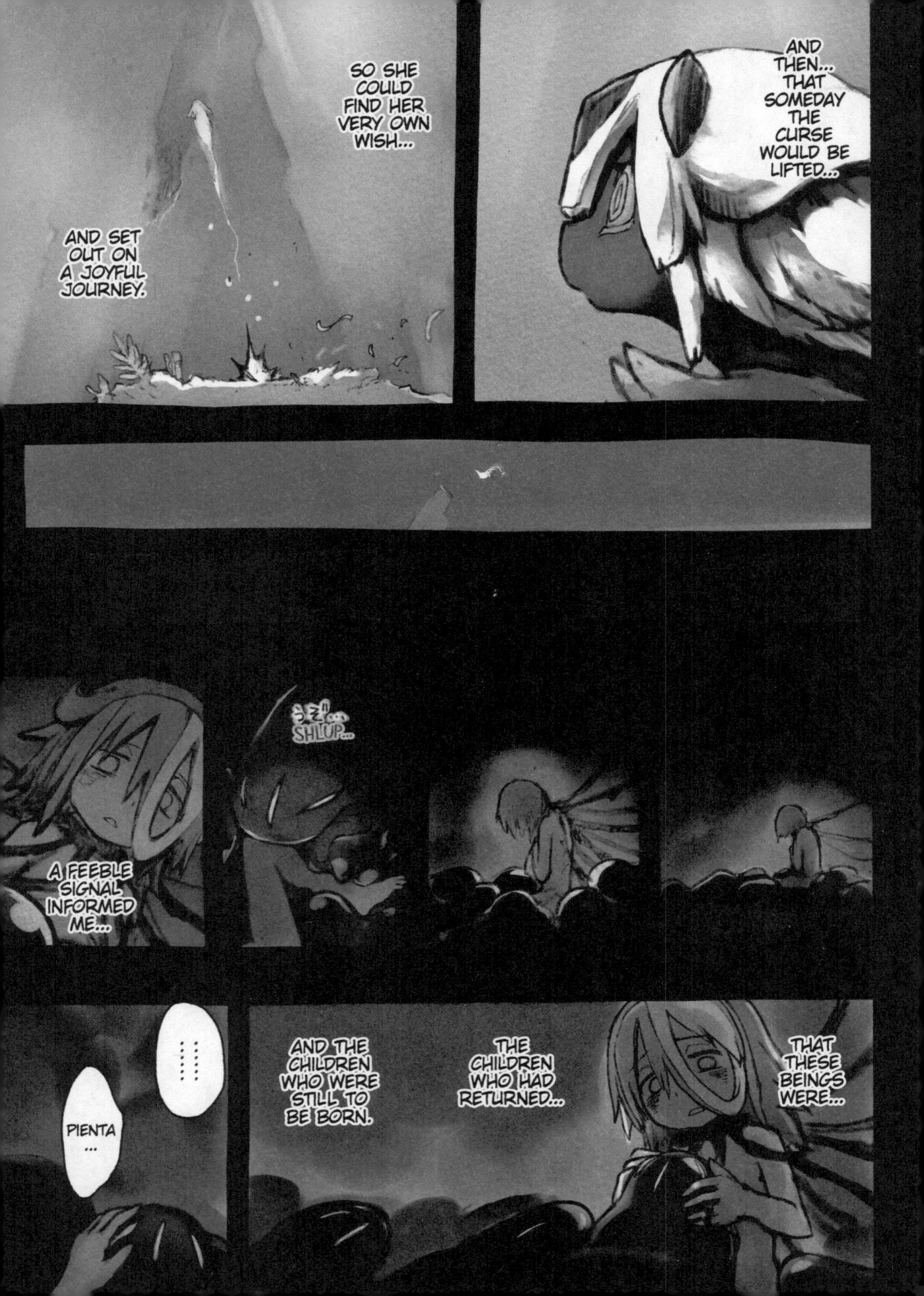
AND THEN... THAT SOMEDAY THE CURSE WOULD BE LIFTED...
SO SHE COULD FIND HER VERY OWN WISH...
AND SET OUT ON A JOYFUL JOURNEY.
SHLUP...
A FEEBLE SIGNAL INFORMED ME...
THAT THESE BEINGS WERE...
THE CHILDREN WHO HAD RETURNED...
AND THE CHILDREN WHO WERE STILL TO BE BORN.
......
PIENTA ...

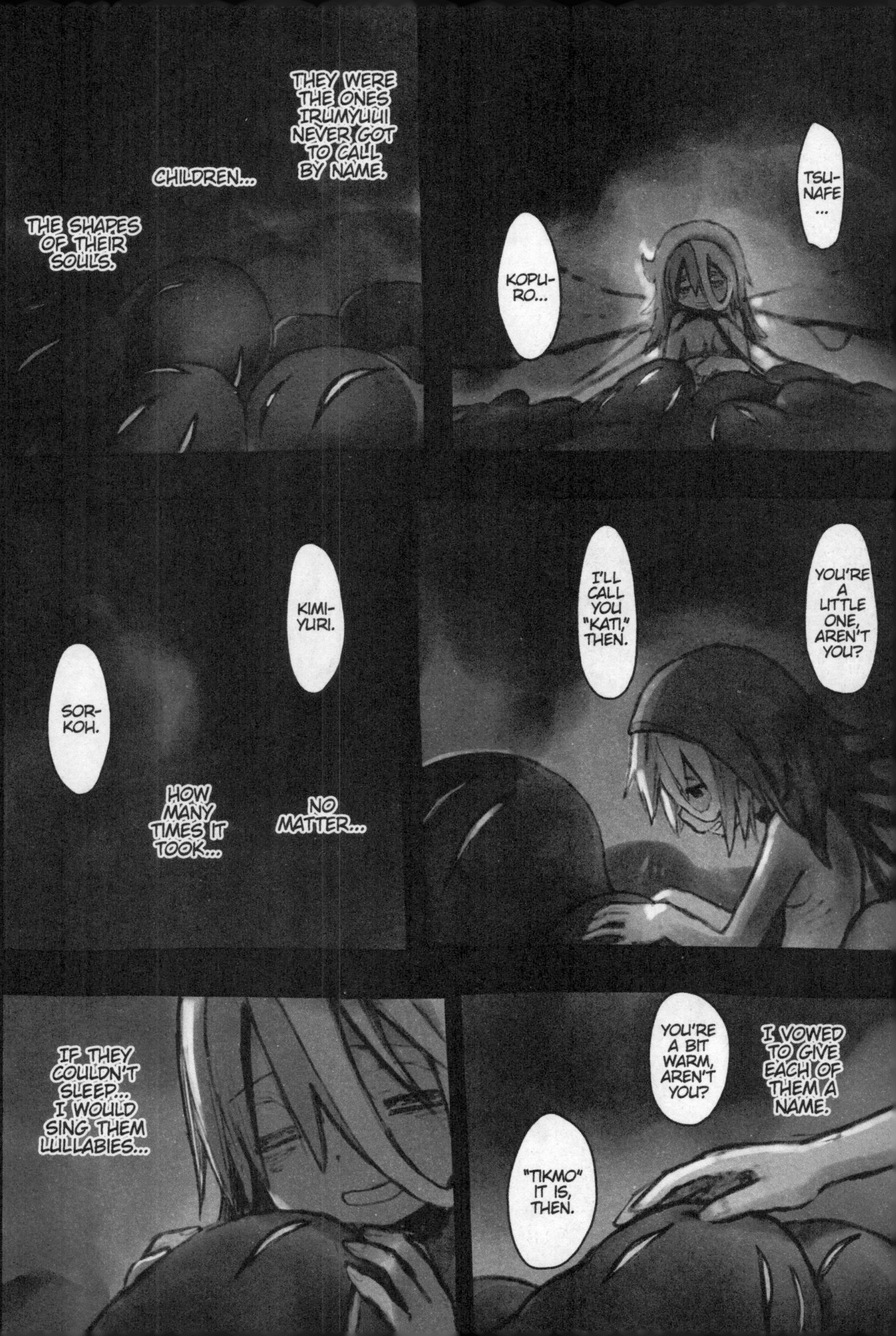
TSU-NAFE...
KOPU-RO...
THEY WERE THE ONES IRUMYUUI NEVER GOT TO CALL BY NAME.
CHILDREN...
THE SHAPES OF THEIR SOULS.
YOU'RE A LITTLE ONE, AREN'T YOU?
I'LL CALL YOU "KATI," THEN.
KIMI-YURI.
SOR-KOH.
NO MATTER...
HOW MANY TIMES IT TOOK...
I VOWED TO GIVE EACH OF THEM A NAME.
YOU'RE A BIT WARM, AREN'T YOU?
"TIKMO" IT IS, THEN.
IF THEY COULDN'T SLEEP... I WOULD SING THEM LULLABIES...

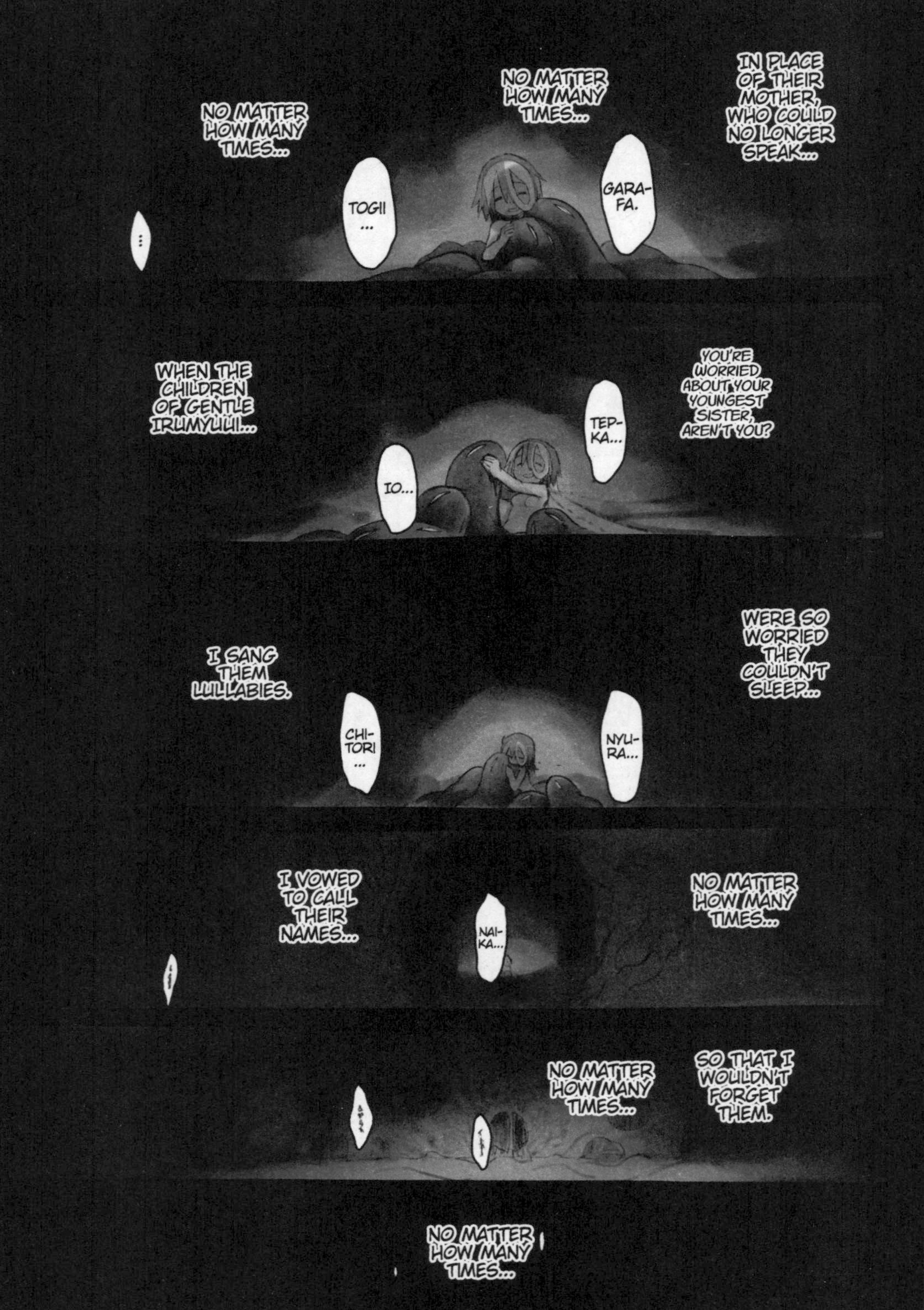
IN PLACE OF THEIR MOTHER, WHO COULD NO LONGER SPEAK...
NO MATTER HOW MANY TIMES...
GARA-FA.
TOGII ...
NO MATTER HOW MANY TIMES...
...
YOU'RE WORRIED ABOUT YOUR YOUNGEST SISTER, AREN'T YOU?
TEP-KA...
WHEN THE CHILDREN OF GENTLE IRUMYUUI...
IO...
WERE SO WORRIED THEY COULDN'T SLEEP...
NYU-RA...
I SANG THEM LULLABIES.
CHI-TORI ...
NO MATTER HOW MANY TIMES...
NAI-KA...
I VOWED TO CALL THEIR NAMES...
SO THAT I WOULDN'T FORGET THEM.
NO MATTER HOW MANY TIMES...
NO MATTER HOW MANY TIMES...

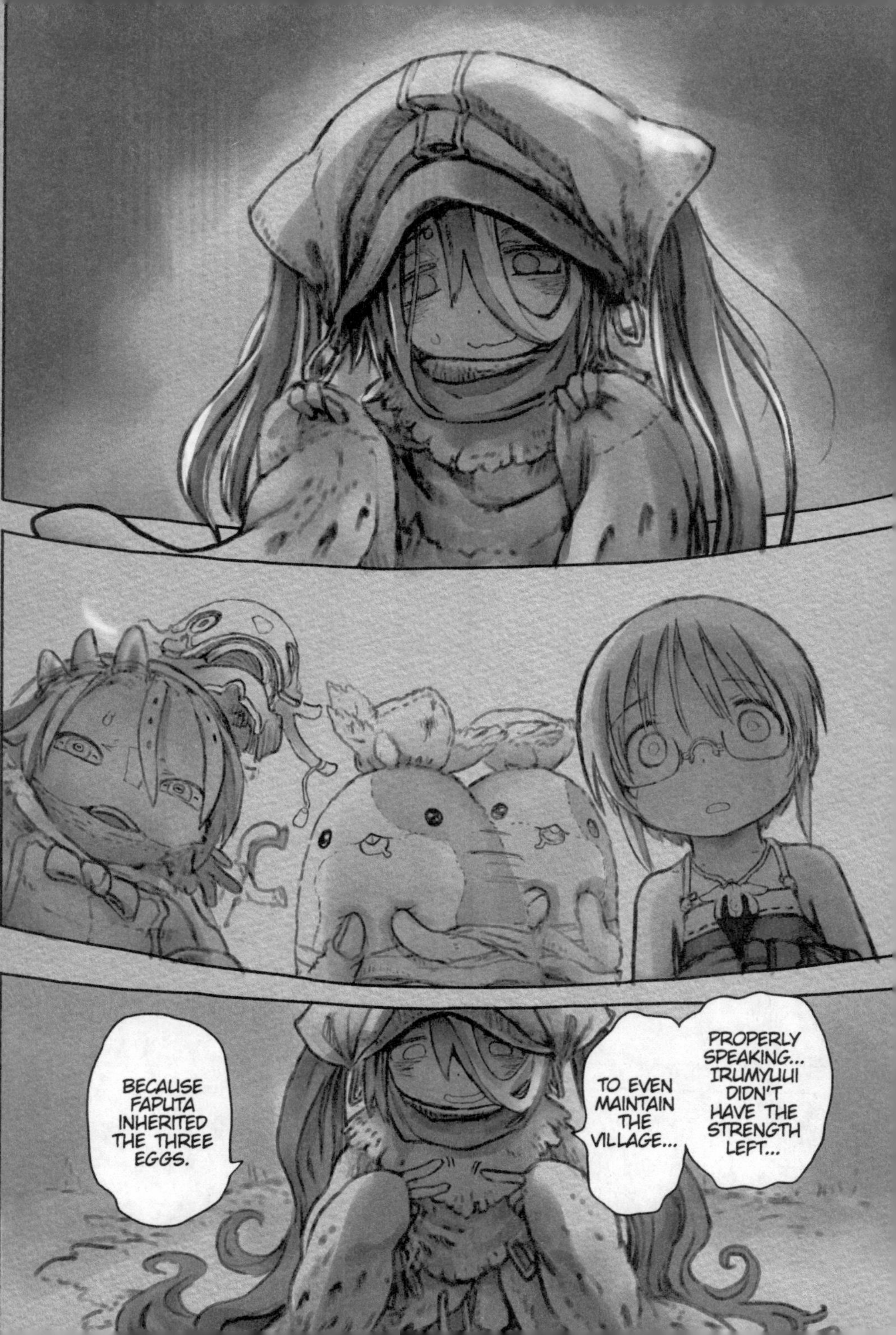
PROPERLY SPEAKING... IRUMYUUI DIDN'T HAVE THE STRENGTH LEFT...
TO EVEN MAINTAIN THE VILLAGE...
BECAUSE FAPUTA INHERITED THE THREE EGGS.

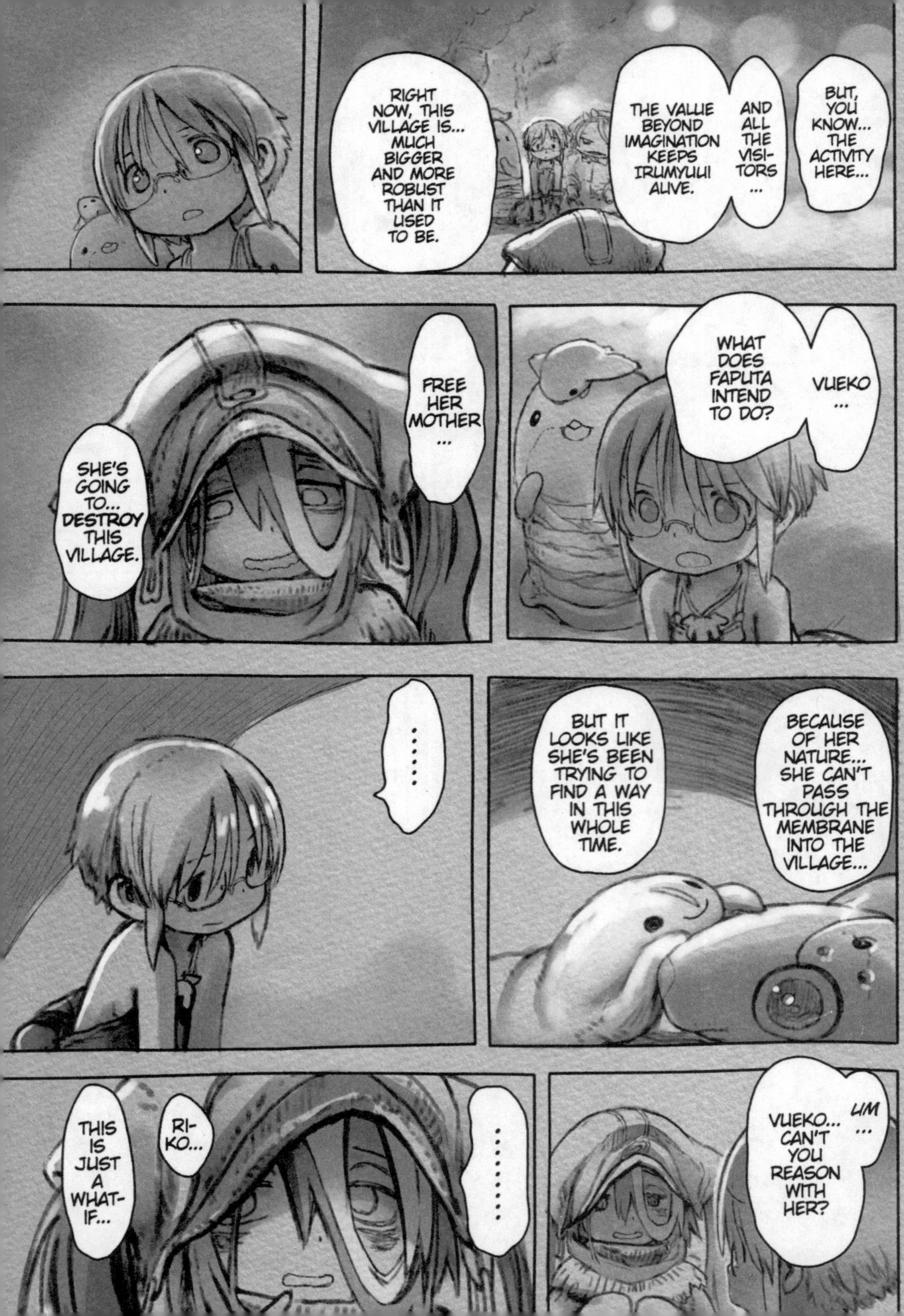
BUT, YOU KNOW... THE ACTIVITY HERE...
AND ALL THE VISITORS ...
THE VALUE BEYOND IMAGINATION KEEPS IRUMYUUI ALIVE.
RIGHT NOW, THIS VILLAGE IS... MUCH BIGGER AND MORE ROBUST THAN IT USED TO BE.
VUEKO ...
WHAT DOES FAPUTA INTEND TO DO?
FREE HER MOTHER ...
SHE'S GOING TO... DESTROY THIS VILLAGE.
BECAUSE OF HER NATURE... SHE CAN'T PASS THROUGH THE MEMBRANE INTO THE VILLAGE...
BUT IT LOOKS LIKE SHE'S BEEN TRYING TO FIND A WAY IN THIS WHOLE TIME.
......
UM ...
VUEKO... CAN'T YOU REASON WITH HER?
....
RI-KO...
THIS IS JUST A WHAT-IF...

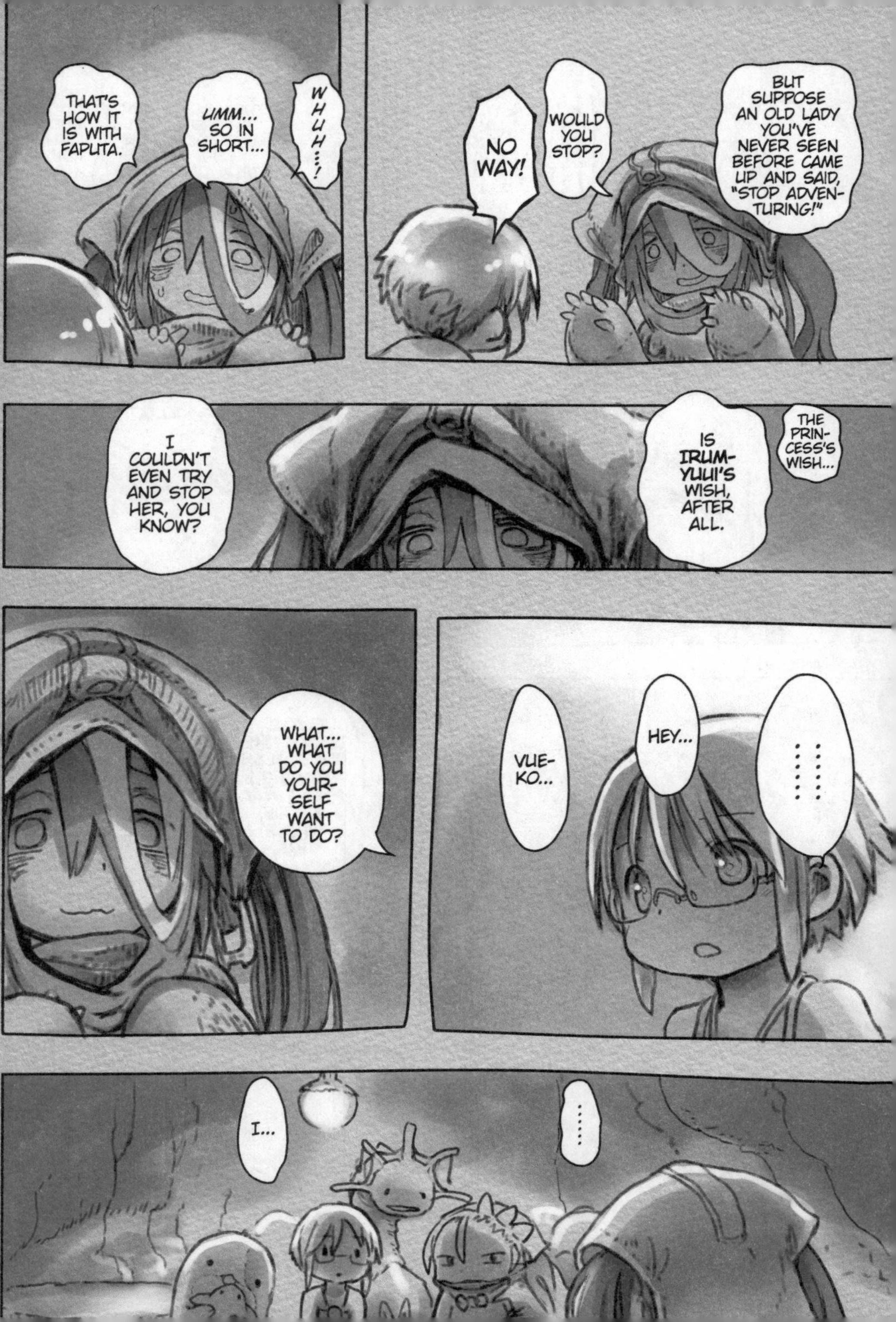
BUT SUPPOSE AN OLD LADY YOU'VE NEVER SEEN BEFORE CAME UP AND SAID, "STOP ADVENTURING!"
WOULD YOU STOP?
NO WAY!
WHUH...!
UMM... SO IN SHORT...
THAT'S HOW IT IS WITH FAPUTA.
THE PRINCESS'S WISH...
IS IRUMYUUI'S WISH, AFTER ALL.
I COULDN'T EVEN TRY AND STOP HER, YOU KNOW?
......
HEY...
VUEKO...
WHAT... WHAT DO YOU YOURSELF WANT TO DO?
......
I...

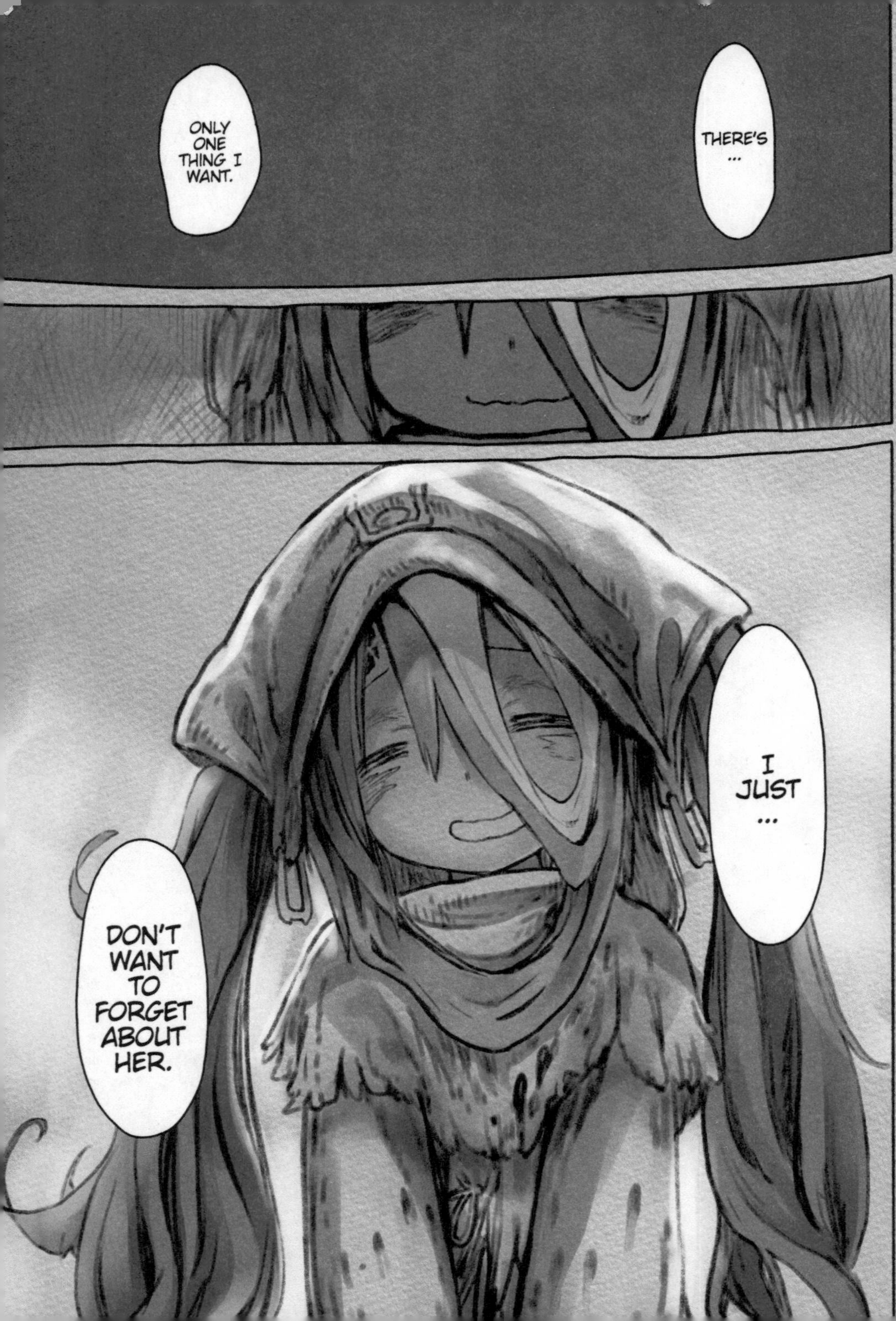
THERE'S ...
ONLY ONE THING I WANT.
I JUST ...
DON'T WANT TO FORGET ABOUT HER.

MADE IN ABYSS

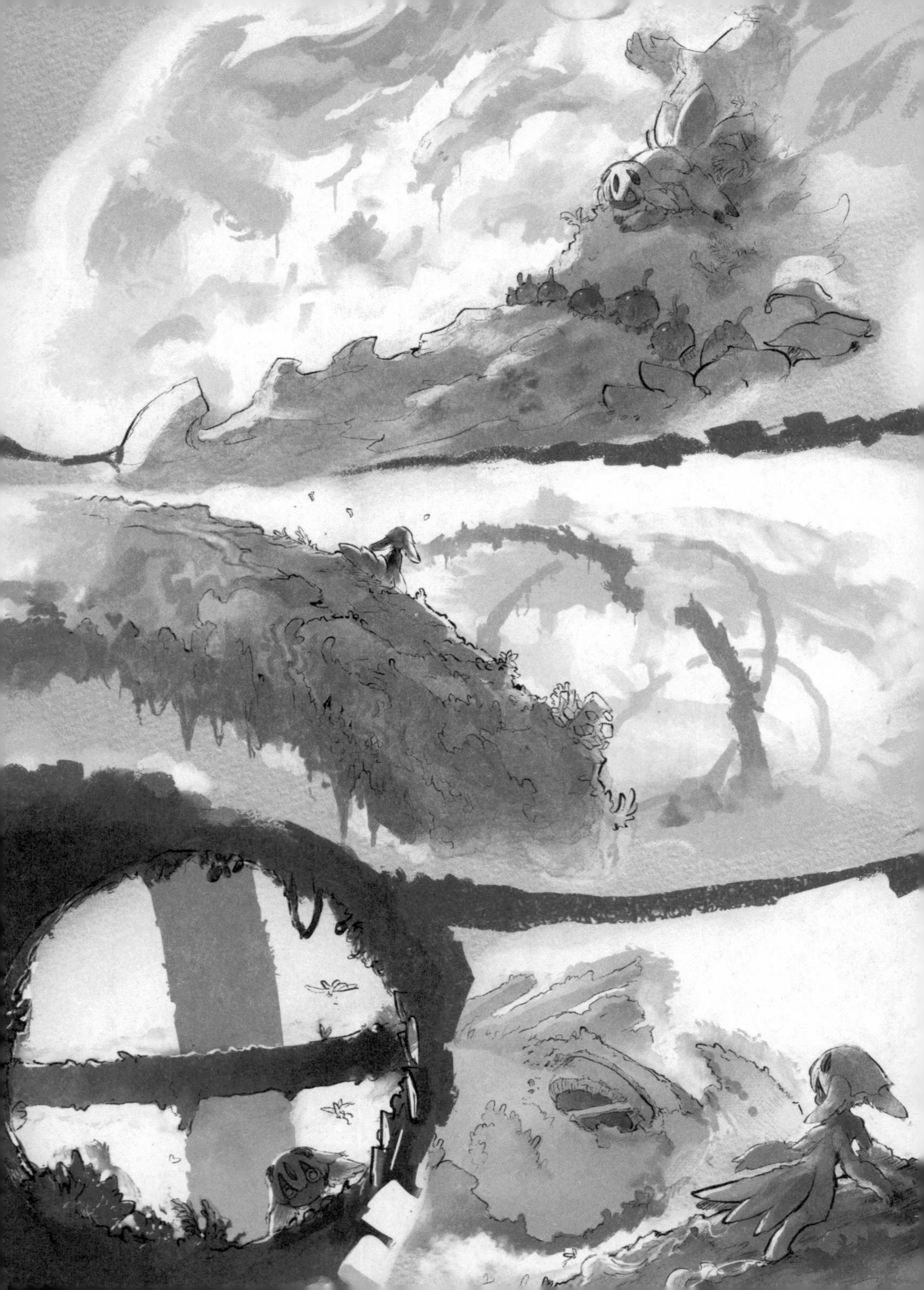

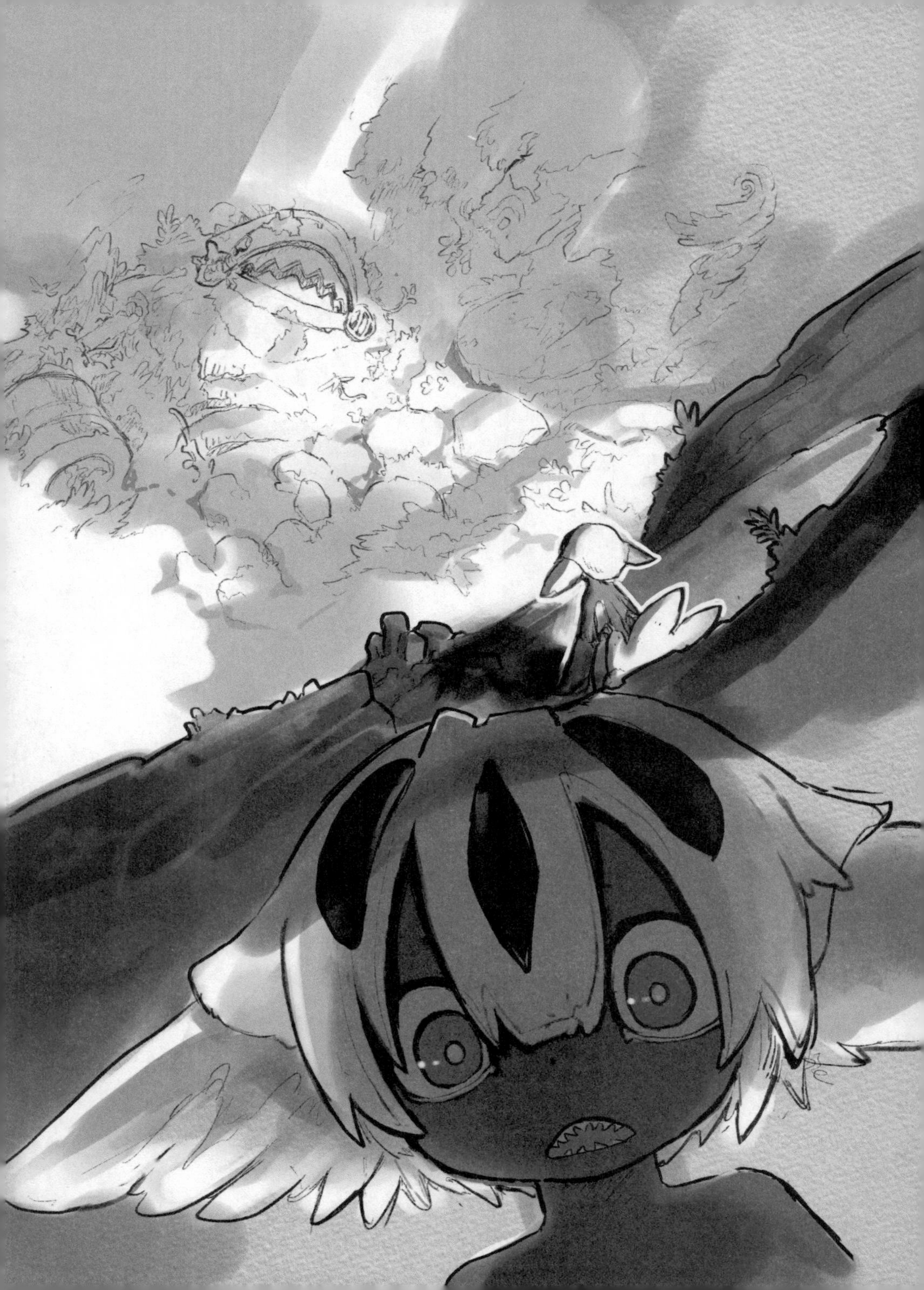

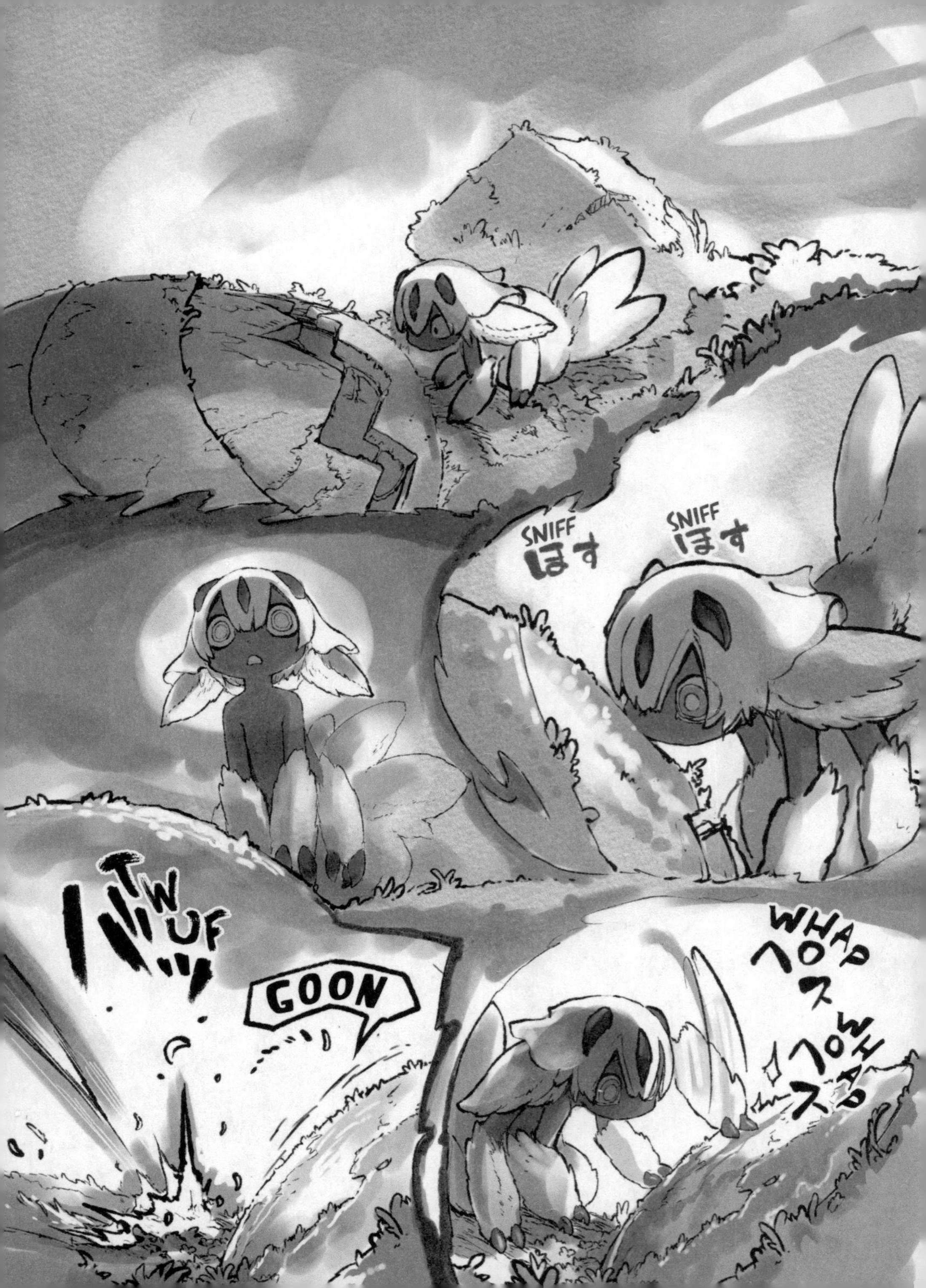
SNIFF ほす
SNIFF ほす
WHAP
WHAP
TWUF
GOON

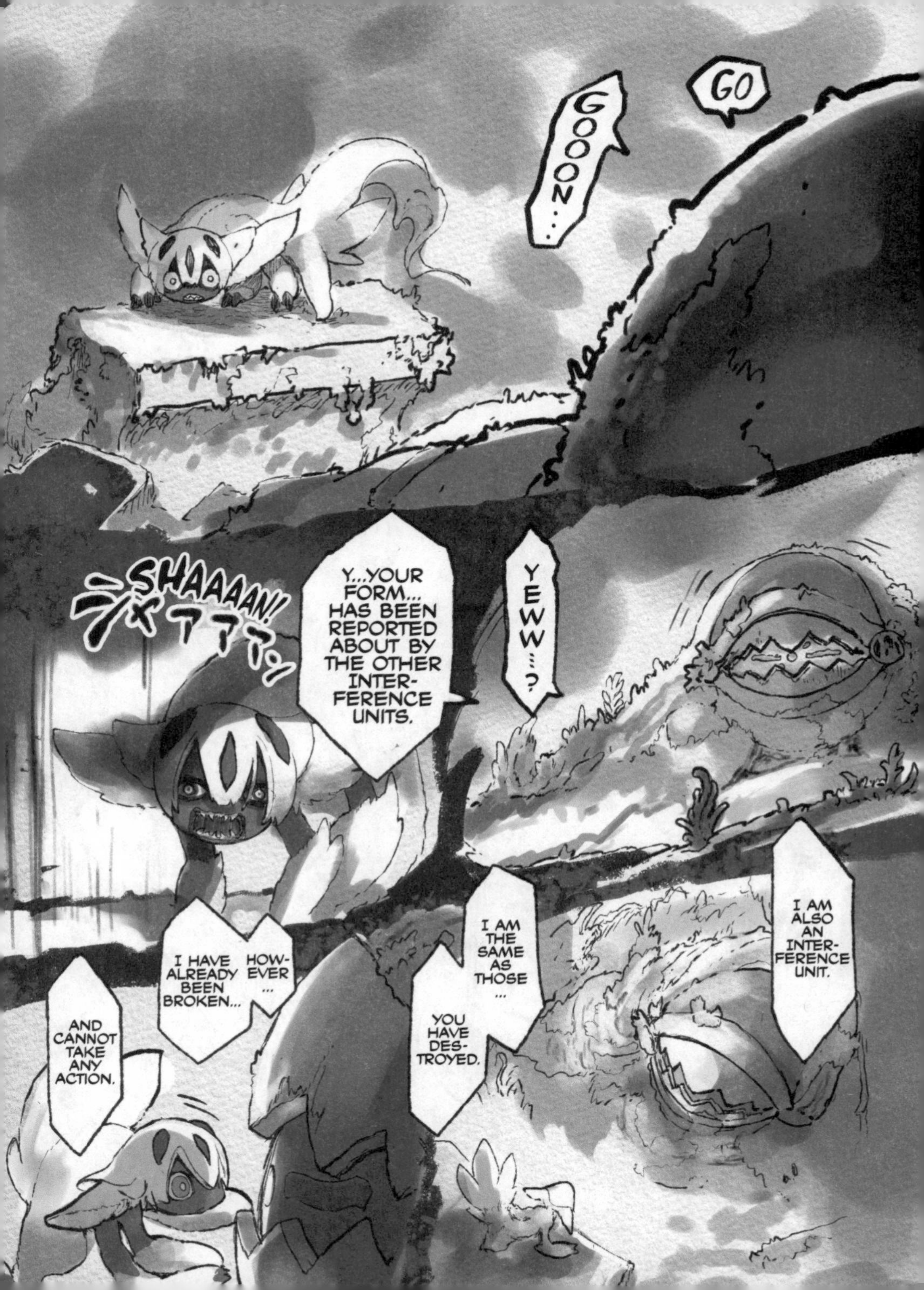
GO
GOOOON...
YEWW...?
Y...YOUR FORM... HAS BEEN REPORTED ABOUT BY THE OTHER INTER-FERENCE UNITS.
SHAAAAN!
I AM ALSO AN INTER-FERENCE UNIT.
I AM THE SAME AS THOSE ...
YOU HAVE DES-TROYED.
HOW-EVER ...
I HAVE ALREADY BEEN BROKEN...
AND CANNOT TAKE ANY ACTION.

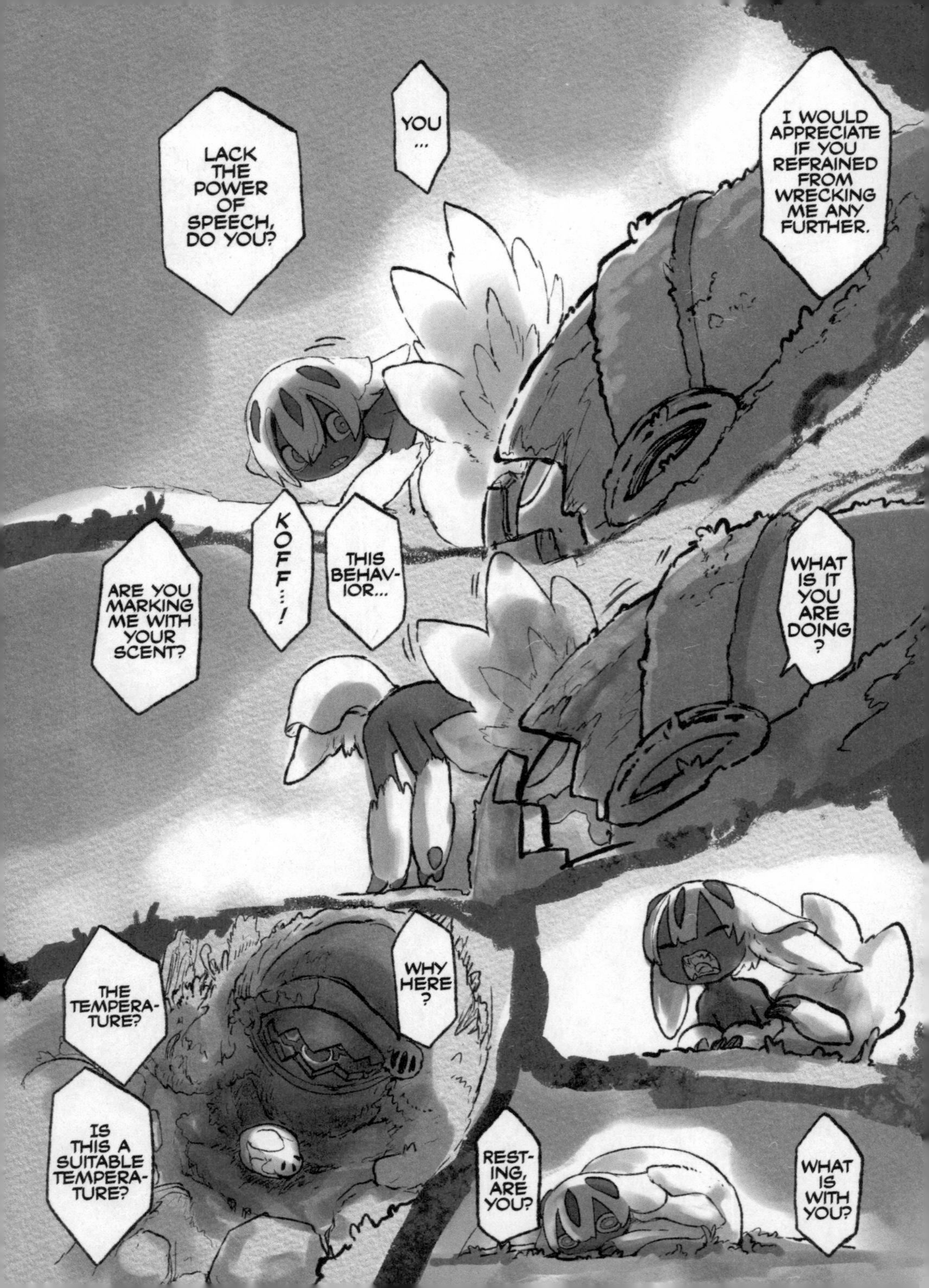
I WOULD APPRECIATE IF YOU REFRAINED FROM WRECKING ME ANY FURTHER.
YOU ...
LACK THE POWER OF SPEECH, DO YOU?
WHAT IS IT YOU ARE DOING?
THIS BEHAV-IOR...
KOFF...!
ARE YOU MARKING ME WITH YOUR SCENT?
WHAT IS WITH YOU?
REST-ING, ARE YOU?
WHY HERE?
THE TEMPERA-TURE?
IS THIS A SUITABLE TEMPERA-TURE?

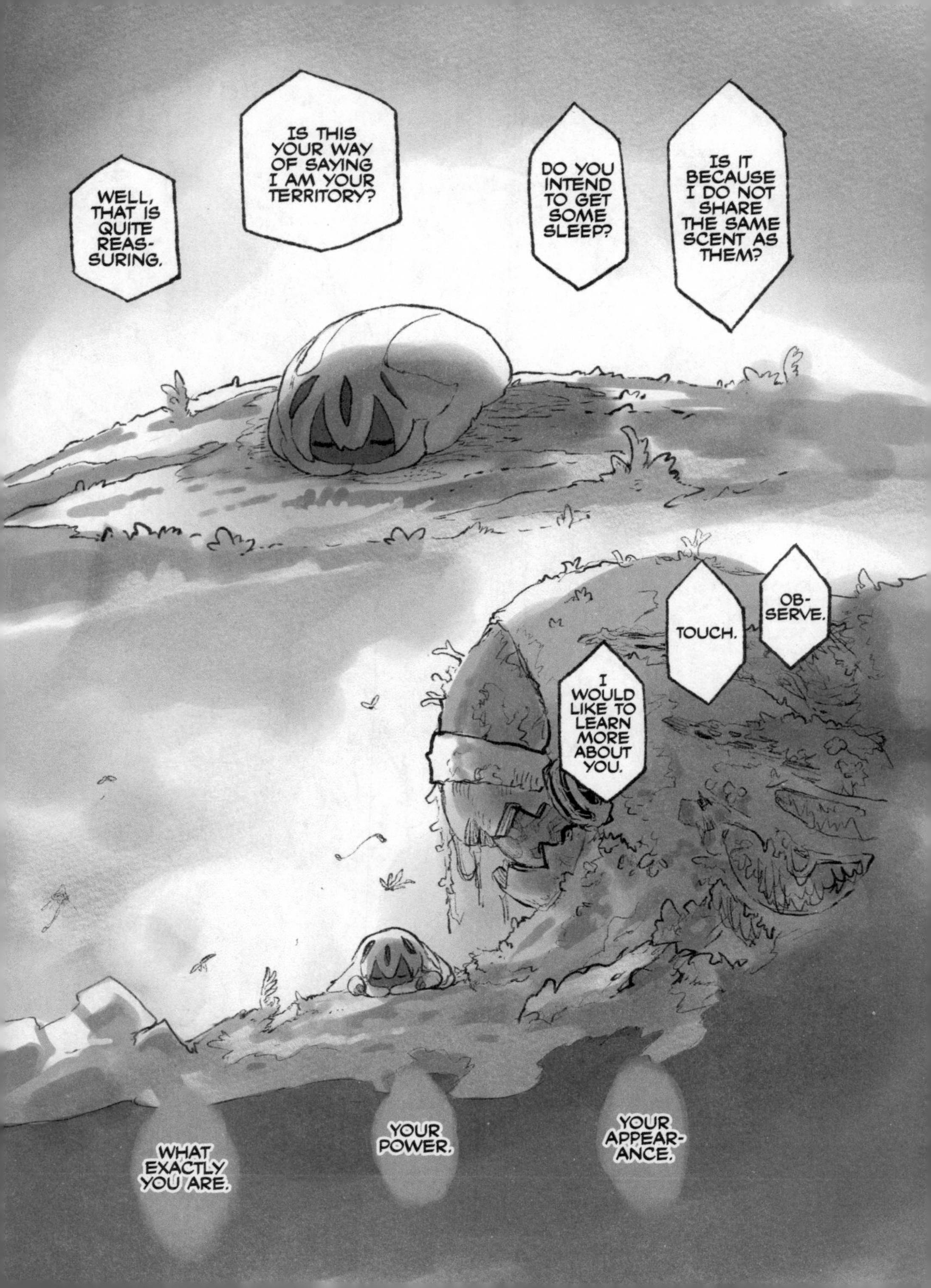
IS IT BECAUSE I DO NOT SHARE THE SAME SCENT AS THEM?
DO YOU INTEND TO GET SOME SLEEP?
IS THIS YOUR WAY OF SAYING I AM YOUR TERRITORY?
WELL, THAT IS QUITE REAS-SURING.
OB-SERVE.
TOUCH.
I WOULD LIKE TO LEARN MORE ABOUT YOU.
YOUR APPEAR-ANCE.
YOUR POWER.
WHAT EXACTLY YOU ARE.

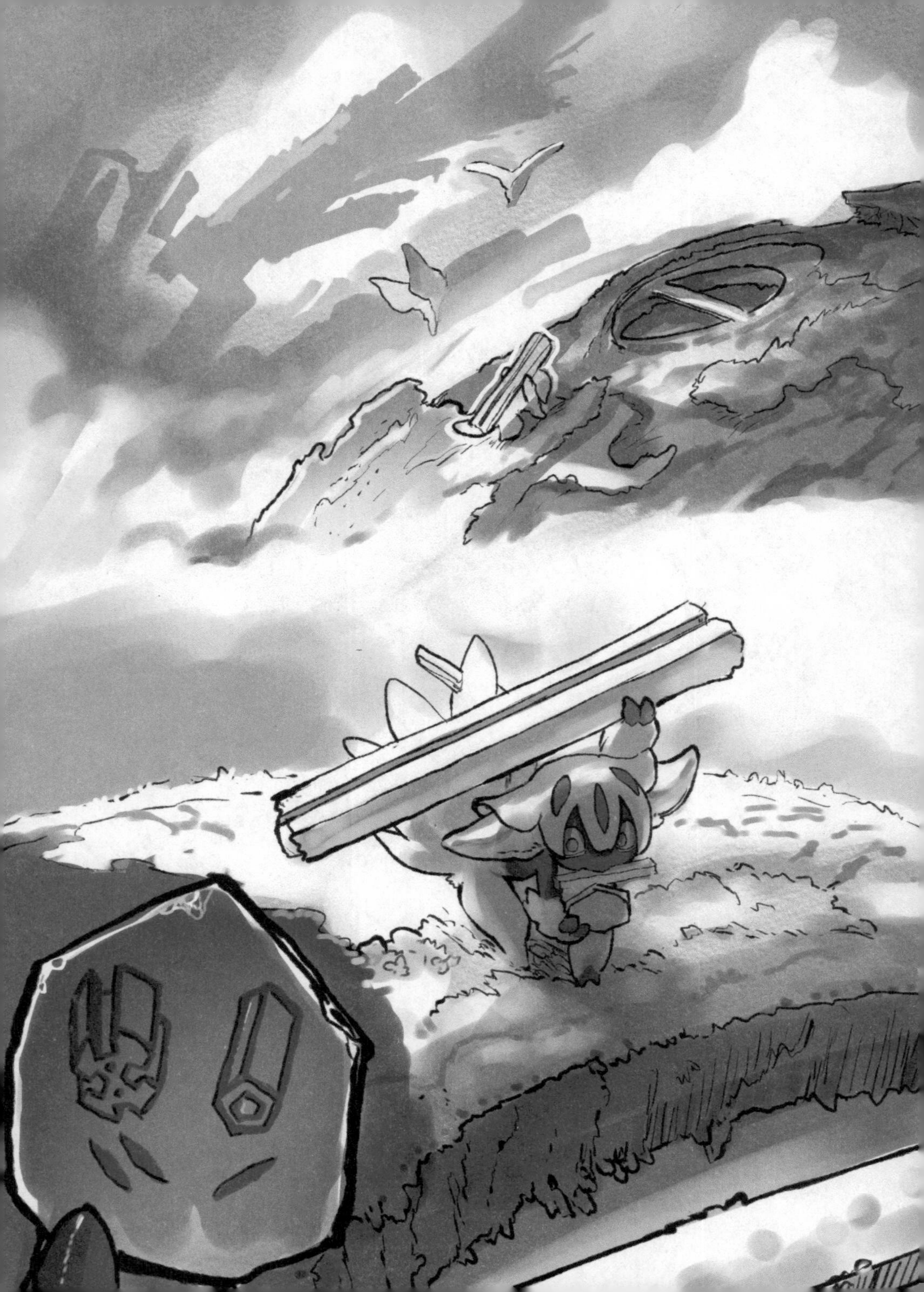

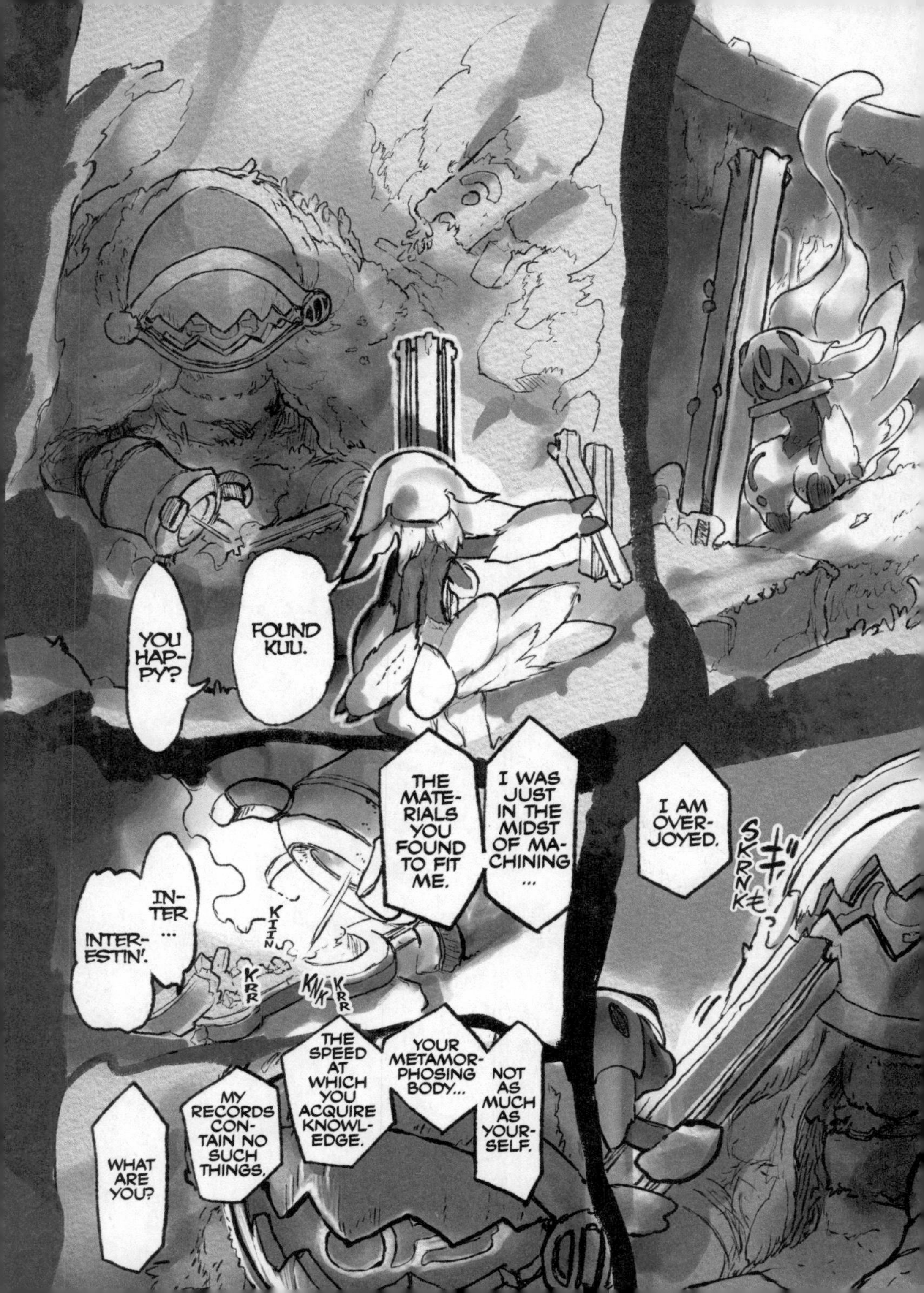

FOUND KUU.
YOU HAPPY?
I AM OVERJOYED.
SKRNK
I WAS JUST IN THE MIDST OF MACHINING...
THE MATERIALS YOU FOUND TO FIT ME.
KIIN
INTER... INTERESTIN'.
KRR
KNK KRR
NOT AS MUCH AS YOURSELF.
YOUR METAMORPHOSING BODY...
THE SPEED AT WHICH YOU ACQUIRE KNOWLEDGE.
MY RECORDS CONTAIN NO SUCH THINGS.
WHAT ARE YOU?

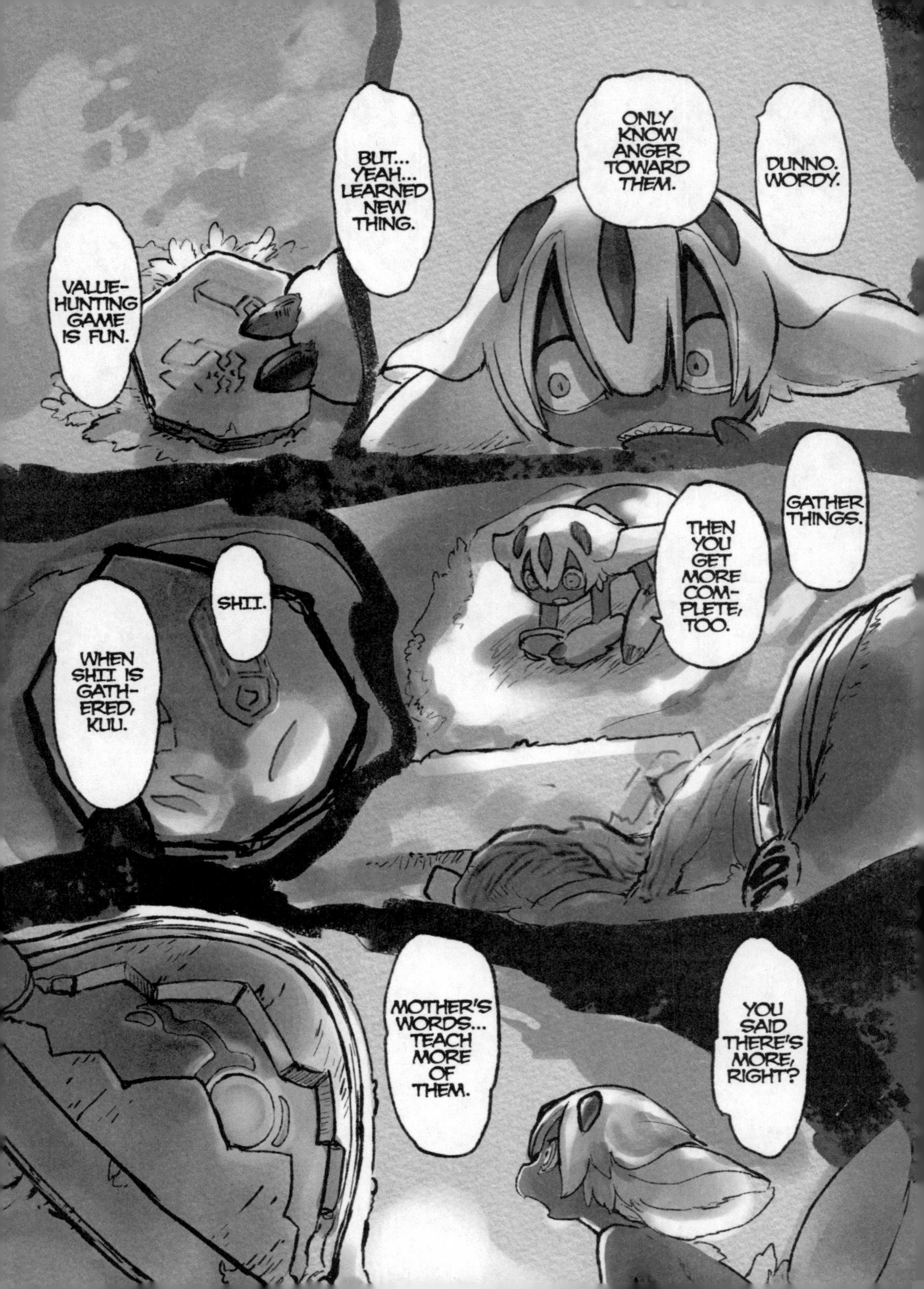
DUNNO. WORDY.
ONLY KNOW ANGER TOWARD THEM.
BUT... YEAH... LEARNED NEW THING.
VALUE-HUNTING GAME IS FUN.
GATHER THINGS.
THEN YOU GET MORE COMPLETE, TOO.
SHII.
WHEN SHII IS GATHERED, KUU.
YOU SAID THERE'S MORE, RIGHT?
MOTHER'S WORDS... TEACH MORE OF THEM.

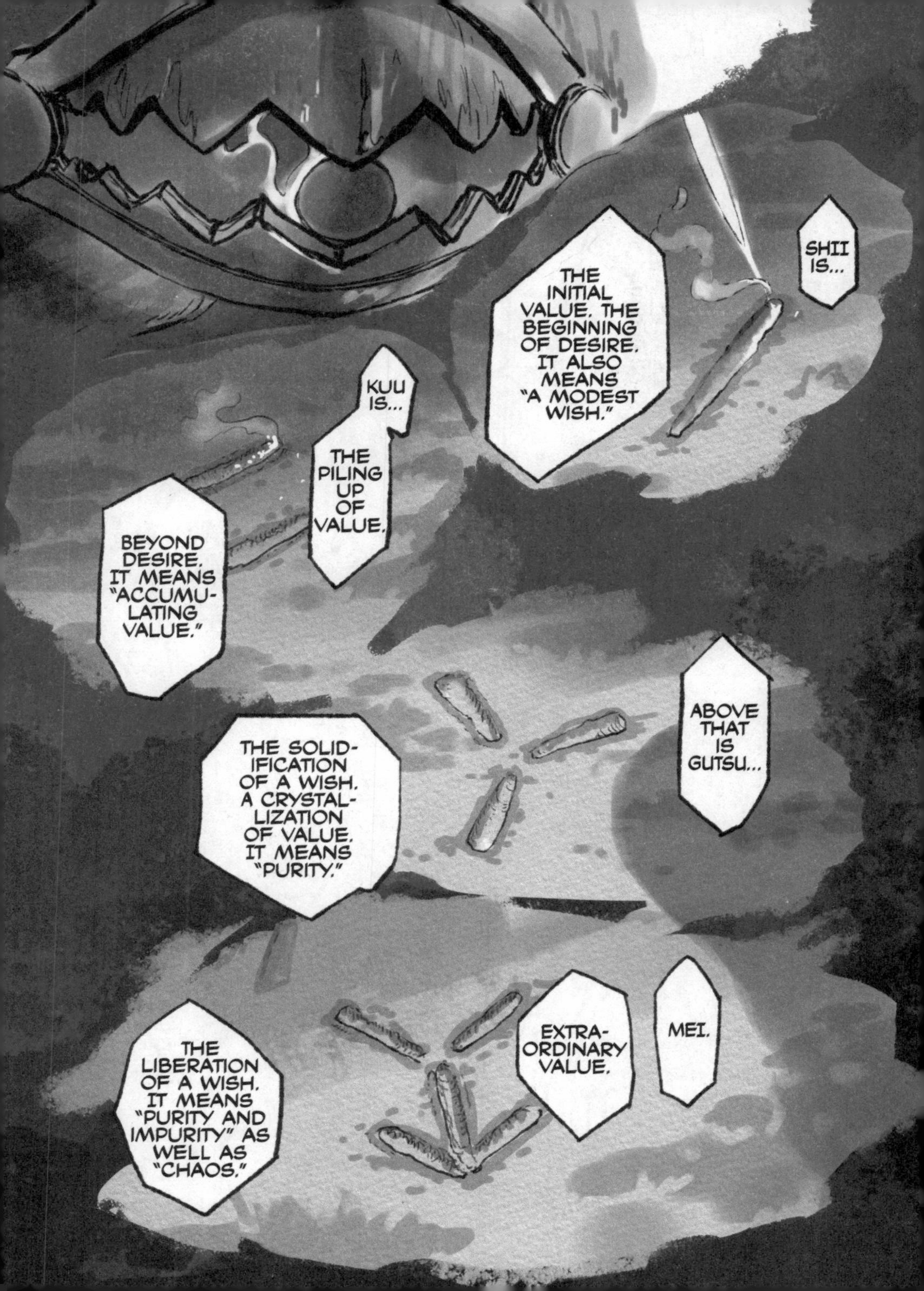
SHII IS...
THE INITIAL VALUE. THE BEGINNING OF DESIRE. IT ALSO MEANS "A MODEST WISH."
KUU IS...
THE PILING UP OF VALUE.
BEYOND DESIRE. IT MEANS "ACCUMULATING VALUE."
ABOVE THAT IS GUTSU...
THE SOLIDIFICATION OF A WISH. A CRYSTALLIZATION OF VALUE. IT MEANS "PURITY."
MEI.
EXTRAORDINARY VALUE.
THE LIBERATION OF A WISH. IT MEANS "PURITY AND IMPURITY" AS WELL AS "CHAOS."

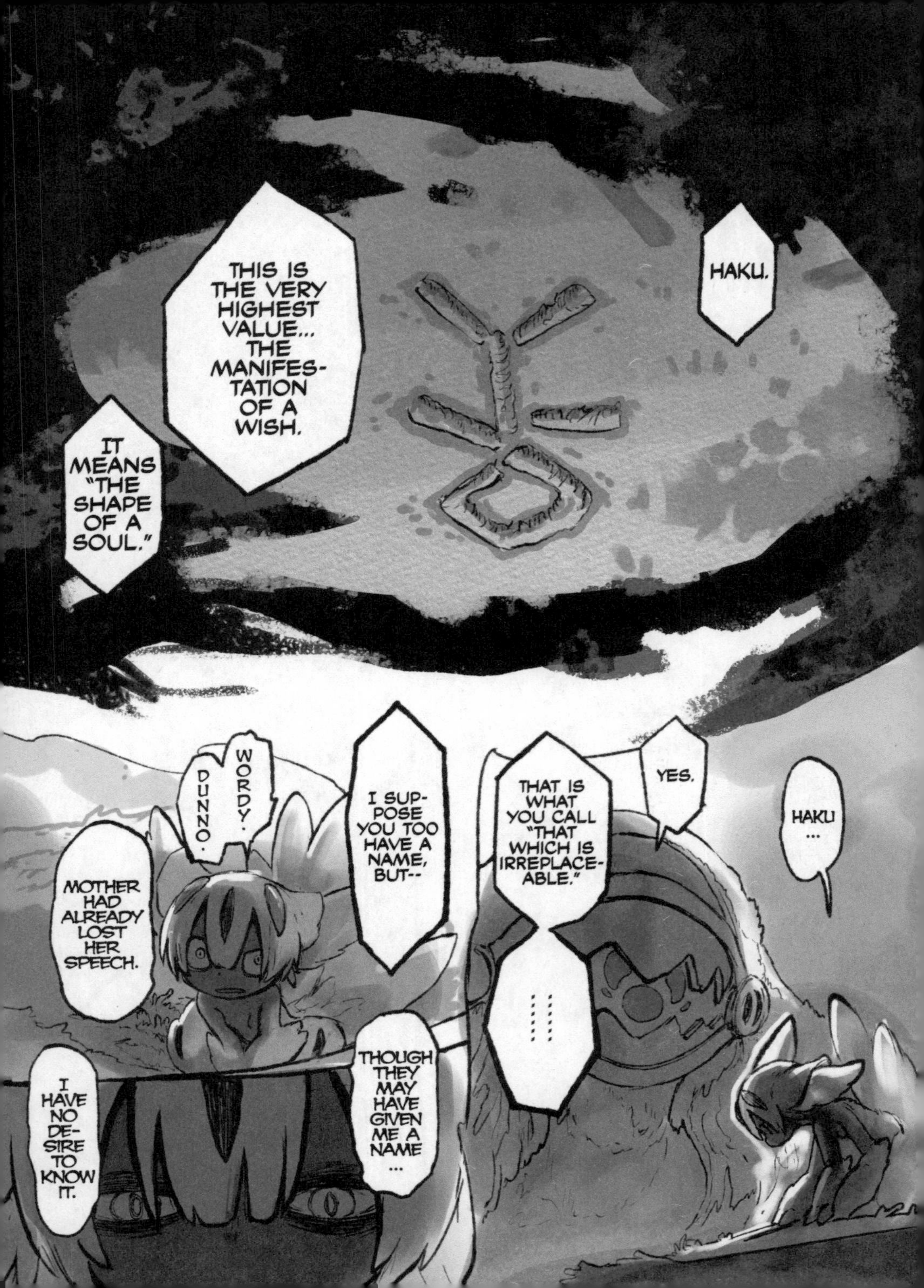
HAKU.
THIS IS THE VERY HIGHEST VALUE... THE MANIFESTATION OF A WISH.
IT MEANS "THE SHAPE OF A SOUL."
HAKU...
YES.
THAT IS WHAT YOU CALL "THAT WHICH IS IRREPLACEABLE."
......
I SUPPOSE YOU TOO HAVE A NAME, BUT--
WORDY.
DUNNO.
MOTHER HAD ALREADY LOST HER SPEECH.
THOUGH THEY MAY HAVE GIVEN ME A NAME...
I HAVE NO DESIRE TO KNOW IT.

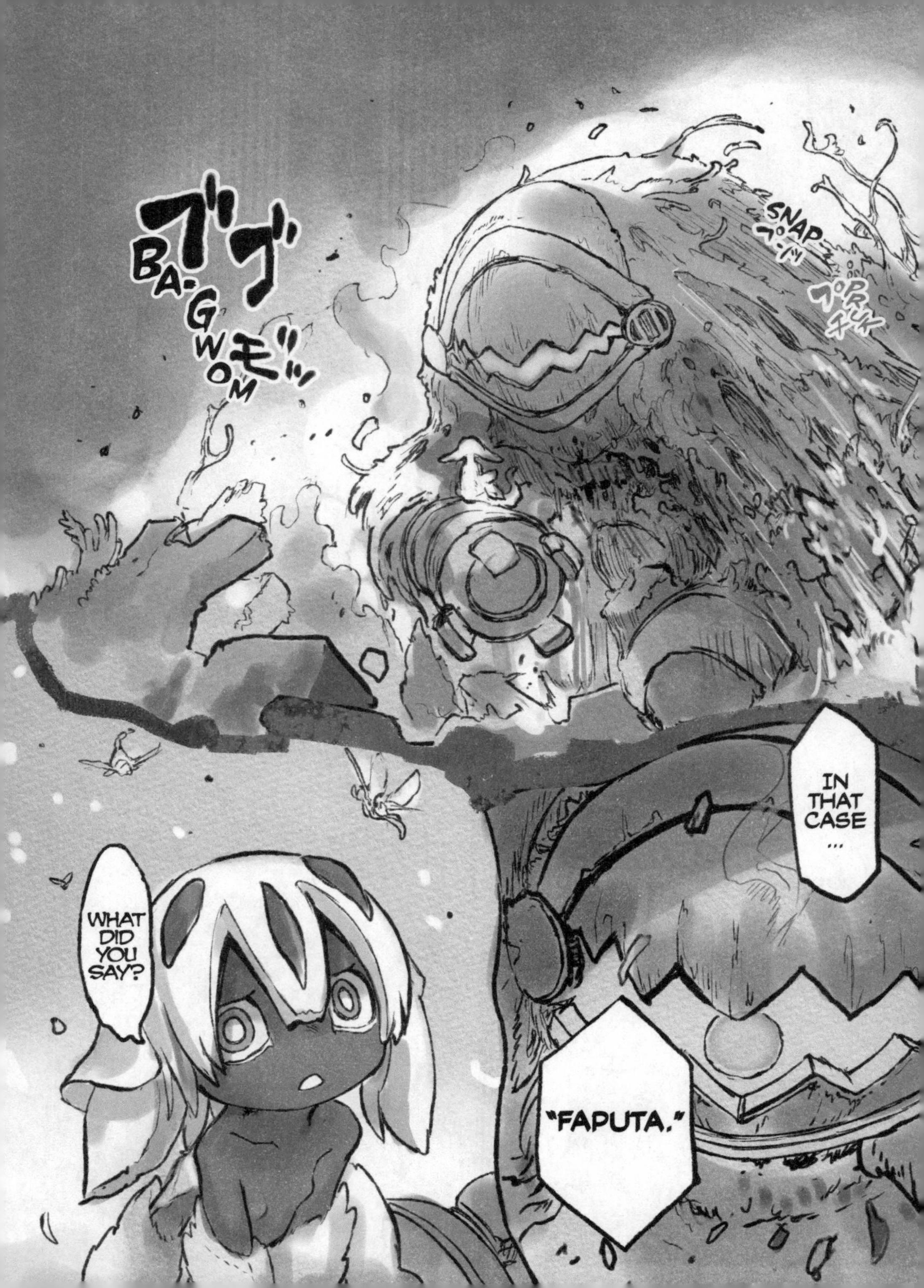

SNAP
PRUK
BA-GWOM
IN THAT CASE...
"FAPUTA."
WHAT DID YOU SAY?

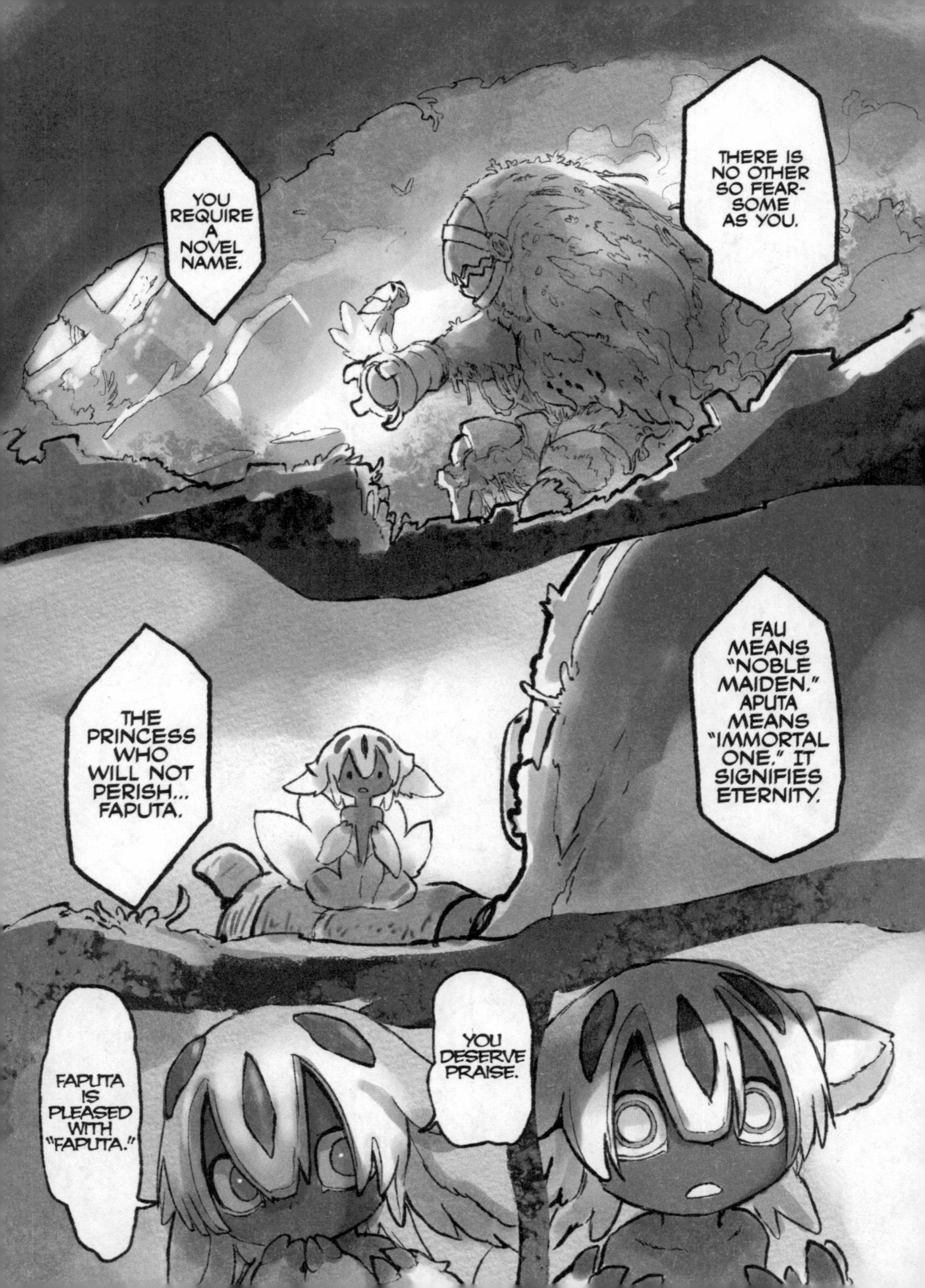
THERE IS NO OTHER SO FEAR-SOME AS YOU.
YOU REQUIRE A NOVEL NAME.
FAU MEANS "NOBLE MAIDEN." APUTA MEANS "IMMORTAL ONE." IT SIGNIFIES ETERNITY.
THE PRINCESS WHO WILL NOT PERISH... FAPUTA.
YOU DESERVE PRAISE.
FAPUTA IS PLEASED WITH "FAPUTA."

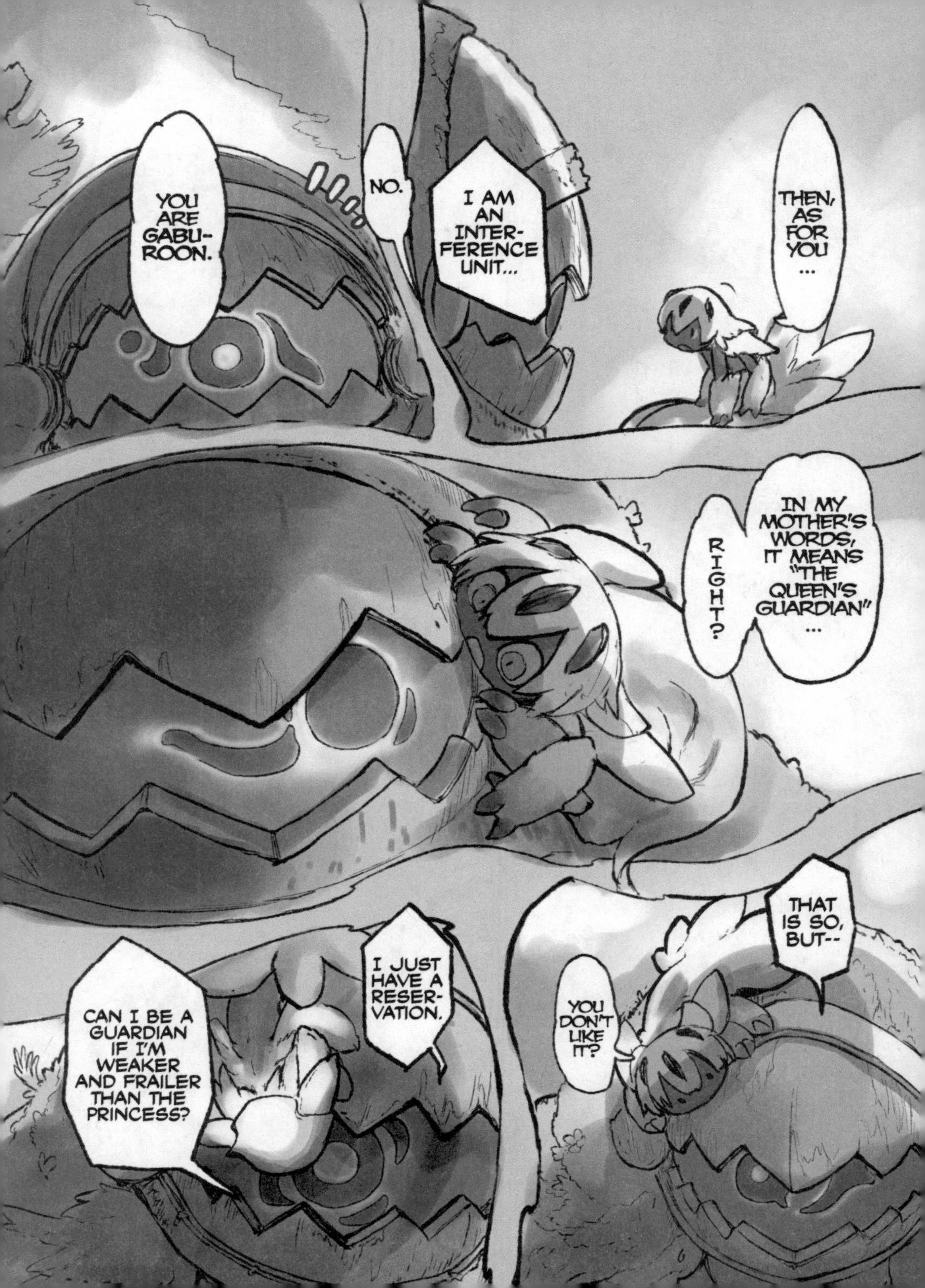
THEN, AS FOR YOU ...
I AM AN INTERFERENCE UNIT...
NO.
YOU ARE GABUROON.
IN MY MOTHER'S WORDS, IT MEANS "THE QUEEN'S GUARDIAN" ...
RIGHT?
THAT IS SO, BUT--
YOU DON'T LIKE IT?
I JUST HAVE A RESERVATION.
CAN I BE A GUARDIAN IF I'M WEAKER AND FRAILER THAN THE PRINCESS?

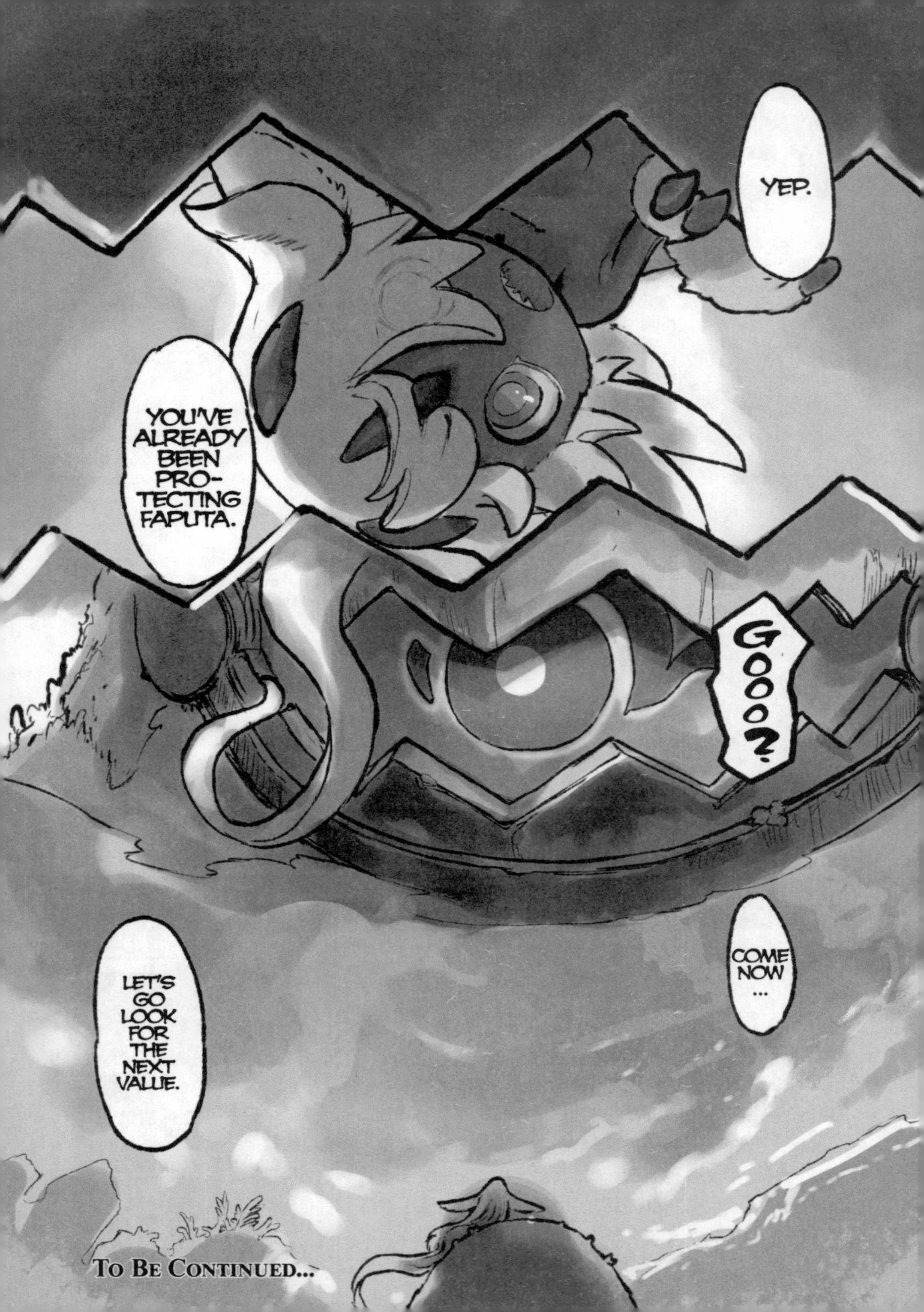
YEP.
YOU'VE ALREADY BEEN PRO-TECTING FAPUTA.
GOOO?
COME NOW ...
LET'S GO LOOK FOR THE NEXT VALUE.
TO BE CONTINUED...

SEVEN SEAS ENTERTAINMENT

MADE IN ABYSS

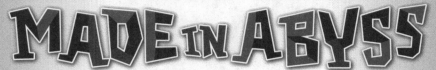

story and art by **AKIHITO TSUKUSHI**

VOLUME 8

TRANSLATION
Beni Axia Conrad

ADAPTATION
Jake Jung

LETTERING AND RETOUCH
James Gaubatz

LOGO DESIGN
Andrea Rodriguez

COVER DESIGN
Nicky Lim

PROOFREADER
Kurestin Armada
Danielle King

EDITOR
Jenn Grunigen

MANAGING EDITOR
Julie Davis

ASSOCIATE PUBLISHER
Adam Arnold

PUBLISHER
Jason DeAngelis

MADE IN ABYSS VOLUME 8

Originally published in Japan in 2019 by Takeshobo Co. LTD., Tokyo.
English translation rights arranged with Takeshobo Co. LTD., Tokyo, through TOHAN CORPORATION, Tokyo.

Seven Seas press and purchase enquiries can be sent to Marketing Manager Lianne Sentar at press@gomanga.com. Information regarding the distribution and purchase of digital editions is available from Digital Manager CK Russell at digital@gomanga.com.

ISBN: 978-1-64505-217-3

Printed in Canada

First Printing: March 2020

10 9 8 7 6 5 4 3 2 1

FOLLOW US ONLINE: ***www.sevenseasentertainment.com***

READING DIRECTIONS

This book reads from ***right to left***, Japanese style. If this is your first time reading manga, you start reading from the top right panel on each page and take it from there. If you get lost, just follow the numbered diagram here. It may seem backwards at first, but you'll get the hang of it! Have fun!!

1
2
3
4
5
6
7
8
9

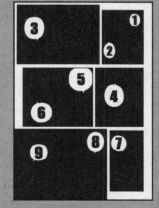